Philosophy, Theology and History of Sport and of Physical Activity

Études philosophiques, théologiques et historiques du sport et de l'activité physique

A collection of the formal papers presented at the *International Congress of Physical Activity Sciences* held in Quebec City, July 11-16, 1976, under the auspices of the CISAP-1976-ICPAS Corporation.

Recueil des communications présentées dans le cadre du *Congrès international des sciences de l'activité physique* qui eut lieu à Québec, du 11 au 16 juillet 1976, sous les auspices de la Corporation du CISAP-1976-ICPAS.

Compiled and edited by

Recueilli et édité par

FERNAND LANDRY, Ph.D.
WILLIAM A. R. ORBAN, Ph.D.

Published by

Symposia Specialists Inc.

Continuing Education in Sports Sciences

Publié par

Released through

SYMPOSIA SPECIALISTS, INC. · 1460 N.E. 129th Street
Miami, Florida 33161, U.S.A.

JOINT PUBLICATION / COPRODUCTION

L'Editeur officiel du Québec

Le Haut-commissariat à la jeunesse,
aux loisirs et aux sports du Québec

Symposia Specialists Incorporated

Associate producers/Producteurs délégués
Michel Marquis
Miriam Hochberg

WORLDWIDE DISTRIBUTION / DISTRIBUTION MONDIALE

Symposia Specialists Incorporated
Miami, Florida 33161 U.S.A.

SOLE DISTRIBUTOR FOR QUEBEC
DISTRIBUTEUR UNIQUE AU QUÉBEC

MIAMI, FLORIDA, 33161

Printed in the U.S.A.

Library of Congress Catalog
Card No. 78-57895

ISBN 0-88372-111-2

Table of Contents / Table des matières

The Scientific Commission/La Commission scientifique ix

Acknowledgments/Remerciements x

Preface/Préface xiv

PHILOSOPHY

Olympics, Olympism and Human Well-Being

Philosophie

Les Jeux olympiques, l'Olympisme et le bien-être de l'homme

Lectures at the Invitation of the Scientific Commission
Conférences présentées à l'invitation de la Commission scientifique

Some Expressed Values Within the Olympic Experience:
A Preliminary Analysis 3
Earle F. Zeigler
The University of Western Ontario,
London, Canada

Signification du phénomène olympique: une analyse 13
Michel A. Bouet
Université de Haute-Bretagne,
Rennes, France

A Political-Philosophic Analysis of Olympism 25
Vladimir S. Roditchenko
Chief, Sports Department, Organizing
Committee of the Olympic Games of 1980,
Moscow, U.S.S.R.

Individual Scientific Contributions
Communications scientifiques individuelles

Limitations of Amateurism as a Meaningful Concept
in Sport 35
Harold J. VanderZwaag
Department of Sport Studies, University of
Massachusetts, Amherst, Mass., U.S.A.

External Determination and Instrumentation of Sport 49
Hajo Bernett
Sportswissenschaftliches Institut der Universität Bonn, Bonn, Federal Republic of Germany

Theoretical Elements for a Diagnosis of Sport 59
José M. Cagigal
National Institute of Physical Education and Sports, Madrid, Spain

The Humanistic Value of Sport 87
V. I. Stoljarov
The State Central Institute of Physical Culture, Moscow, U.S.S.R.

Physical Education: A Prediscipline in Search of a Paradigm 97
Saul Ross
Department of Physical Education, School of Human Kinetics and Leisure Studies, University of Ottawa, Ottawa, Canada

Human Movement as a Field of Study 111
R. Carlisle
Department of Physical Education, Aberdeen College of Education and the University of Aberdeen, Aberdeen, Scotland

On the Elaboration of a General Theory Regarding Sports Activities 119
V. V. Davydov
Institute of General and Pedagogical Psychology, Moscow, U.S.S.R.

Normes du système de la culture physique de l'homme contemporain 125
Zdenek Sprynar
Faculté d'éducation physique et du sport, Université Charles, Prague, Tchecoslovaquie

THEOLOGY

Sport, a Liberating or Alienating Force

Théologie

Le sport, facteur de libération ou d'aliénation

Lectures at the Invitation of the Scientific Commission
Conférences présentées à l'invitation de la Commission scientifique

Le sport, facteur de libération ou d'aliénation 131
Herman de Mulder
Abbaye de Tongerlo,
Westerlo, Belgique

Sport, Religion and Human Well-Being 143
Brian W. W. Aitken
Huntington College, Laurentian University,
Sudbury, Ontario, Canada

Alienation, Liberation and Sport 153
David L. Miller
Department of Religion, Syracuse University,
Syracuse, New York, U.S.A.

Individual Scientific Contributions
Communications scientifiques individuelles

Religious Themes and Structures in the Olympic
Movement and the Olympic Games 161
John J. MacAloon
University of Chicago, Illinois, U.S.A.

La vie et l'existence: Helmuth Plessner
et Martin Heidegger 171
Jean-Claude Petit
Faculté de théologie, Université de
Montréal, Quebec, Canada

Du temps compétitif au temps réalisé:
la fête comme mouvement 179
Maurice Boutin
Faculté de théologie, Université de
Montréal, Québec, Canada

Etude historico-théologique sur la fête
en Israël ancien 187
Jean Martucci
Sciences bibliques, Université de
Montréal, Québec, Canada

The Human Body: Temple, Cage or What? 199
Adrian C. Kanaar
Poughkeepsie, New York, U.S.A.

HISTORY
Histoire

Lectures at the Invitation of the Scientific Commission
Conférences présentées à l'invitation de la Commission scientifique

Historiography of Modern Olympism
Historiographie de l'Olympisme moderne

Historiography of Modern Olympism: Emphasis on the Works of the Socialist States of Europe 211
K. A. Kulinkovich
High Institute of Physical Culture,
Minsk, U.S.S.R.

Historiography of Modern Olympism: Emphasis on Historical Works of Western Europe 217
Horst Ueberhorst
Institute of Sports Sciences,
Ruhr University, Bochum,
Federal Republic of Germany

A Survey of the Historiography of Olympism in North America 229
Jean M. Leiper
Faculty of Physical Education, University of
Calgary, Calgary, Alberta, Canada

The Life and Works of Robert Tait McKenzie
La vie et l'oeuvre de Robert Tait McKenzie

R. Tait McKenzie: The Scientist 237
C. R. Blackstock
Vanier City, Ontario, Canada

Sculptor of Athletes: Tait McKenzie 245
Andrew J. Kozar
Department of Health, Physical Education and
Recreation, The University of Tennessee,
Knoxville, Tenn., U.S.A.

Robert Tait McKenzie: Physical Educator 255
Stewart A. Davidson
School of Human Kinetics,
University of Ottawa,
Ottawa, Ontario, Canada

Individual Scientific Contributions
Communications scientifiques individuelles

The True Course Run by the Marathon Messenger: An Appeal to the International Olympic Committee for a Change 267
Ion P. Ioannides
Ministry of Education, Athens, Greece

The Nemean Festival 273
Dale P. Hart
Department of Physical Education, Brockport State College, Brockport, New York, U.S.A.

The Ancient Greek Pentathlon Jump: A Preliminary Reinterpretive Examination 279
Robert Knight Barney
University of Western Ontario, London, Canada

King Amenophis II: Analysis and Evaluation of His Athletic Ability 289
Zaki I. Habashi
California State College, Stanislaus, Turlock, California, U.S.A.

Women in Sport in the Ancient Western World 301
Reet Howell
Department of Physical Education, San Diego State University, San Diego, California, U.S.A.

History of the Olympic Program and Perspectives for its Future Development 311
Nadejda Lekarska
Bulgarian Olympic Committee, Sofia, Bulgaria

The Olympic Movement Restored: The 1908 Games 317
Maxwell L. Howell and Reet Howell
San Diego State University, San Diego, California, U.S.A.

L'idée olympique de Pierre de Coubertin et Carl Diem et son aboutissement dans l'académie internationale Olympique 327
Norbert Müller
Département d'éducation physique, Université de Mainz, République fédérale d'Allemagne

Les sports face à la politique 333
Louis Burgener
Bern, Suisse

The History of Yabusame (Shooting Arrows From Horseback) 339
Kohsuke Sasajima
Keio University, Japan

The Life of an Early Sportswoman: Eleonora Sears 343
Joanna Davenport
University of Illinois, Urbana, Ill., U.S.A.

Thomas Kirk Cureton, Jr.: A Historical Sketch of His Professional Life and Contributions to Physical Activity and Human Well-Being 349
Walter Cryer
Brigham Young University,
Provo, Utah, U.S.A.

The "Edmonton Grads": The Team and Its Social Significance From 1915 to 1940 357
John Dewar
Laurentian University, Sudbury, Ontario, Canada

Author Index/Auteurs xxi

Subject Index/Sujets xxiii

A Listing of the Complete Series/Titres des ouvrages xxv

LA COMMISSION SCIENTIFIQUE
THE SCIENTIFIC COMMISSION

L'Exécutif – The Executive

Fernand Landry *Québec*
Président – President
William A.R. Orban *Ottawa*
Vice-président – Vice-president
Paul Godbout *Québec*
Secrétaire – Secretary

Membres – Members

Gerald Kenyon *Waterloo*
Arthur Sheedy *Montréal*
Roy J. Shephard *Toronto*
Yves Bélanger *Québec*
Gouvernement du Québec
Quebec Government
Paul S. Woodstock *Ottawa*
Gouvernement du Canada
Government of Canada
Jean Loiselle *Montréal*
COJO
Laurent Bélanger *Montréal*
APAPQ
Gordon R. Cumming *Winnipeg*
CASS – ACSS
Gregg McKelvey *Ottawa*
CAHPER
Gilles Houde *Ville de Laval*

Le Secrétaire exécutif et trésorier
The Executive Secretary and Treasurer

Gilbert Michaud *Québec*

CONSEILLERS INTERNATIONAUX
INTERNATIONAL ADVISERS

Tr Hon. – Rt. Hon.
Philip Noel-Baker *Grande-Bretagne* *Great Britain*
Président – President
CIEPS – ICSPE
Jaudol Ruiz Aguilera *Cuba*
Jean Borotra *France*
Günter Erbach *Rép. démocr. allemande* *German Democratic Republic*
Julien Falize *Belgique–Belgium*
Vladimir Roditchenko *URSS–USSR*
Franz Lotz *Rép. fédér. d'Allemagne* *Federal Republic of Germany*
Tetsuo Meshizuka *Japon–Japan*
Leona Holbrook *EU–USA*
Nadir M. Souelem *Egypte–Egypt*

Le Congrès international des sciences de l'activité physique, 1976
a été placé sous le distingué patronage de L'UNESCO, Organisation des Nations Unies pour l'éducation, la science et la culture.

The International Congress of Physical Activity Sciences, 1976
has been placed under the distinguished sponsorship of UNESCO, United Nations Educational, Scientific and Cultural Organization.

Acknowledgements

The *Scientific Commission* wishes to express its deepest appreciation to the Director General of UNESCO, Mr. AMADOU MAHTAR M'BOW. for having granted the official sponsorship of his organization to the *International Congress of Physical Activity Sciences — 1976.*

The *Scientific Commission* also wishes to express its sincere appreciation and thanks to the governments, as well as to the associations, committees and groups which have provided the financial, scientific and professional assistance necessary for the planning, organization and conduct of the *International Congress of Physical Activity Sciences — 1976.*

FINANCIAL AND ADMINISTRATIVE ASSISTANCE

— THE GOVERNMENT OF CANADA
  - Health and Welfare Canada
    Fitness and Amateur Sport Branch
  - Secretary of State
— THE QUEBEC GOVERNMENT
  - Haut-commissariat à la jeunesse, aux loisirs et aux sports
  - Le ministère des Affaires intergouvernementales
  - Le ministère des Affaires culturelles
  - Le ministère du Tourisme, de la chasse et de la pêche

— THE ORGANIZING COMMITTEE OF THE OLYMPIC GAMES OF MONTREAL

SCIENTIFIC AND PROFESSIONAL COOPERATION AND ASSISTANCE

— International Council for Sport and Physical Education
  - International Committee for Sociology of Sport
  - International Committee of History of Sport and Physical Education
  - International Work Group for the Construction of Sport and Leisure Facilities (IAKS)
  - Research Group on Biochemistry of Exercise
  - Working Group on Sport and Leisure
— International Council for Health, Physical Education and Recreation
— International Society for Sports Psychology
— International Society of Cardiology
— International Sports Press Association
— Association internationale des écoles supérieures d'éducation physique et de sport (AIESEP)
— International Society of Biomechanics
— American Alliance for Health, Physical Education and Recreation (AAHPER)
— American Academy of Physical Education
— American College of Sports Medicine
— National College Physical Education Association for Men (USA)
— Council for National Cooperation in Aquatics (USA)
— Canadian Association for Health, Physical Education and Recreation (CAHPER)

  - History of Sport and Physical Activity Committee
  - Sociology of Sport Committee
  - Philosophy Committee

Remerciements

La *Commission scientifique* exprime sa haute appréciation au Directeur général de l'UNESCO, M. AMADOU MAHTAR M'BOW, pour avoir bien voulu accorder le patronage de son organisme au *Congrès international des sciences de l'activité physique — 1976.*

La Commission scientifique tient aussi à exprimer ses remerciements les plus sincères aux institutions gouvernementales, ainsi qu'aux organismes, associations et comités qui lui ont procuré les appuis financiers, scientifiques et professionnels nécessaires à la planification et au déroulement du congrès.

L'ASSISTANCE ADMINISTRATIVE ET FINANCIERE

— LE GOUVERNEMENT DU CANADA
- Santé et bien-être social Canada
  Direction générale de la santé et du sport amateur
- Secrétariat d'Etat

— LE GOUVERNEMENT DU QUEBEC
- Haut-commissariat à la jeunesse, aux loisirs et aux sports
- Le ministère des Affaires intergouvernementales
- Le ministère des Affaires culturelles
- Le ministère du Tourisme, de la chasse et de la pêche

— LE COMITE ORGANISATEUR DES JEUX OLYMPIQUES DE MONTREAL

COLLABORATION SCIENTIFIQUE ET PROFESSIONNELLE

— Le Conseil international pour l'éducation physique et le sport (CIEPS)
- Le Comité international pour la sociologie du sport
- Le Comité international de l'histoire de l'éducation physique et du sport
- Le Groupe international de travail pour les équipements de sport et de loisir (IAKS)
- Le Groupe de recherche sur la biochimie de l'effort
- Le Groupe de travail Sport et loisirs

— Le Conseil international sur l'hygiène, l'éducation physique et la récréation (ICHPER)
— La Société internationale de psychologie du sport (ISSP)
— La Société internationale de cardiologie
— L'Association internationale de la presse sportive
— L'Association internationale des écoles supérieures d'éducation physique et de sport
— La Société internationale de biomécanique
— American Alliance for Health, Physical Education and Recreation (AAHPER)
— American Academy of Physical Education
— American College of Sports Medicine
— National College Physical Education Association for Men (USA)
— Council for National Cooperation in Aquatics (USA)
— Canadian Association for Health, Physical Education and Recreation (CAHPER)

- History of Sport and Physical Activity Committee
- Sociology of Sport Committee
- Philosophy Committee

ACKNOWLEDGEMENTS

- Exercise Physiology Committee
- Psycho-motor Learning and Sports Psychology Committee
- Biomechanics Committee
- Administrative Theory and Practice Committee

— Canadian Council for Cooperation in Aquatics
— Association des professionnels de l'activité physique du Québec (APAPQ)
— Canadian Association for Sports Sciences (CASS-ACSS)
— La Ville de Québec
— L'Université Laval

The Scientific Commission extends its deepest gratitude to all the individuals who, in the last three years, have worked behind the scenes in a most efficient and generous manner.

By formal resolution of the Scientific Commission at its meeting of April 28, 1977, Messrs. Fernand Landry and William A.R. Orban, respectively President and Vice-President of the Corporation were mandated to carry out the production of the official proceedings of the CISAP-1976-ICPAS (resolution CS 77-01-11).

NOTICE

By decision of the Scientific Commission, *French* and *English* were adopted as the two official languages of the International Congress of Physical Activity Sciences – 1976.

In these Proceedings, the communications appear *in the language in which they were presented* for French and English and *in English* as concerns the papers which were delivered in either German, Russian or Spanish. Abstracts in the two official languages accompany each paper included in Books 1 and 2 and the seminar presentations in the other books of the series.

REMERCIEMENTS

- Exercise Physiology Committee
- Psycho-motor Learning and Sports Psychology Committee
- Biomechanics Committee
- Administrative Theory and Practice Committee

— Le Conseil canadien de coopération en activités aquatiques
— L'Association des professionnels de l'activité physique du Québec
— L'Association canadienne des sciences du sport (CASS-ACSS)
— La Ville de Québec
— L'Université Laval

La gratitude de la Commission scientifique s'étend à toutes les personnes qui, au cours des trois dernières années, et trop souvent dans l'ombre, ont apporté leur efficace et généreuse collaboration.

Par résolution de la Commission scientifique à sa réunion du 28 avril 1977, MM. Fernand Landry et William A.R. Orban, respectivement président et vice-président de la Corporation, ont été mandatés pour effectuer la production des actes du CISAP-1976-ICPAS (résolution CS 77-01-11).

AVERTISSEMENT

Les langues *anglaise* et *française* furent adoptées par la Commission scientifique commes langues officielles du Congrès international des sciences de l'activité physique – 1976. De ce fait, les communications apparaissent au présent rapport officiel *dans la langue où elles ont été présentées* pour ce qui est de l'anglais et du français, et dans la langue *anglaise* pour ce qui est des communications qui furent faites dans les langues allemande, russe et espagnole.

Des résumés dans chacune des deux langues officielles accompagnent chacune des communications qui paraissent aux Volumes 1 et 2 ainsi que les présentations faites par les conférenciers invités dans les autres volumes de la série.

Preface

The staging of international scientific sessions on the occasion of the Olympic Games has become a well-established tradition.

The themes of the congresses held at the times of the Games celebrating the last five olympiads illustrate that the movement has indeed become multidisciplinary and international.

In choosing *Physical activity and human well-being* as the central theme of the Québec Congress, the Scientific Commission endeavored to offer to the eventual delegates from the entire world, on the eve of the Olympic Games of Montreal, a large and democratic platform for the sharing of knowledge and the exchange of viewpoints on the problems now confronting sport internationally. For each one of the *subthemes* retained in the program, four speakers of different disciplines and of international reputation were invited by the Scientific Commission to give their viewpoint or that of their discipline on the proposed subjects. Additionally, the Scientific Commission offered a series of twenty (20) seminars of monodisciplinary character, in which at least three specialists of international reknown were invited to express themselves on selected topics. One hundred and twenty-seven (127) speakers from all corners of the world thus accepted the invitation of the Scientific Commission and were present at the Québec Congress.

Over and above the thematic and disciplinary seminars which constituted the heart of its program, the Scientific Commission also reserved a large portion of the time to the presentation of individual scientific contributions in sixteen (16) different disciplines and in six (6) special events.

The work sessions, numbering more than eighty (80), made it possible for more than three hundred (300) authors from all corners of the world to present the results on their research and scholarly work.

The central objective of the whole Congress was to bring frontier knowledge pertaining to sport and physical activity in general to the attention of the maximum number of persons. To that effect, the invited speakers were urged to present — the results of the latest research or scholarly work on the subjects proposed — the most convincing facts or ideas — the disciplinary practices, questions or issues which were in greater debate or contention — whenever

Préface

La tenue de sessions scientifiques internationales à l'occasion des Jeux olympiques est une tradition maintenant bien établie. Les thèmes des congrès qui ont effectivement eu lieu aux temps de célébration des cinq dernières olympiades confirment certes la multidisciplinarité et l'internationalisme du mouvement.

En choisissant pour thème du Congrès *L'activité physique et le bien-être de l'homme*, la Commission scientifique canadienne souhaitait donner aux délégués éventuels du monde entier, à l'occasion des Jeux olympiques de Montréal, une plate-forme large et démocratique permettant un libre échange des points de vue sur les problèmes qui confrontent le sport partout. Pour chaque *sous-thème* retenu, quatre conférenciers de disciplines différentes et de réputation internationale furent invités par la Commission scientifique canadienne à venir donner leur point de vue ou celui de leur discipline d'appartenance sur le sujet proposé. En plus, la Commission scientifique avait prévu la tenue de séminaires à caractère monodisciplinaire, donnant l'occasion à au moins trois spécialistes, dans chacune des vingt (20) disciplines impliquées, de faire état des connaissances sur des sujets choisis. Un total de cent vingt-sept (127) conférenciers de tous les coins du monde répondirent ainsi à l'invitation de la Commission scientifique canadienne et furent présents à Québec.

Au delà des séminaires thématiques et disciplinaires constituant le coeur du programme, la Commission scientifique a voulu réserver une place importante du programme à la présentation de communications scientifiques individuelles dans l'éventail des disciplines impliquées.

Les sessions de travail, au nombre de plus de quatre-vingt (80), permirent à plus de trois cents (300) auteurs de livrer à leurs pairs de tous les coins du monde les résultats de leurs réflexions et de leurs recherches.

Le rapport scientifique que constitue la présente série de publications se veut donc un bilan général de ce que dit la recherche et de ce que sont les réalités de la pensée et de la pratique courante, à travers le monde, sur des sujets précis touchant l'activité physique en général. Notre Commission scientifique canadienne avait à cet effet incité tous les auteurs à faire ressortir — l'état des connaissances, des

possible, the various implications relative to the education, health, or well-being of the people.

It was judged acceptable at the Québec Congress that speakers addressing themselves to the same topics present complementary, differing or even opposed viewpoints on the subjects, questions or issues at stake. It was in the discussion periods, which were made an essential and integral part of all work sessions, that the data and the viewpoints were exposed to questions, commentaries and criticisms from the audience, in the full respect of democratic principles and of the basic regards due to each person.

The reports which constitute the present series of publications are in reality the responsibility of their authors; consequently, they should not be interpreted as necessarily reflecting the opinion of the editors or those of the members of the Canadian Scientific Commission.

We believe that in actual fact, the body of knowledge relative to the potential contribution of physical activity to human well-being will have progressed significantly at the time and as a result of the Québec session.

The series of volumes constituting the present scientific report illustrates, in our opinion, the fact that the Canadian Scientific Commission has endeavored to build a program which was consistent with the highest contemporary international standards. To that effect, the Scientific Commission had chosen to function on a democratic basis which it believes unprecedented in this type of international effort; both the quality and the representativity of the professional and scientific organizations which were invited to contribute to the total endeavor do indeed illustrate this fact.

The members of the Canadian Scientific Commission believe that they were correct in assuring that there would be place, within the framework of the CISAP-1976-ICPAS program, for contributions stemming from all the branches and sectors of human knowledge which may be interested, from one angle or the other, in physical activity and sports as contemporary phenomena.

The success of the Québec Congress is owed outright to the efforts of the members of the Scientific Commission, the International Advisors, the members of the Executive, the Executive Secretary and Treasurer as well as to those of the numerous collaborators who have in fact consecrated so much energy to the pursuit of the objectives. At the critical stages of our collective endeavor, the professional and scientific contributions of a large

travaux de recherche et des réflexions de pointe sur le sujet, — les faits et/ou les idées les plus convaincants, — les pratiques ou les questions en discussion et en contention, — le cas échéant, les implications diverses qui touchent l'éducation, le bien-être, la santé ou la qualité de vie des citoyens.

Il était bien sûr accepté au Congrès de Québec que des conférenciers différents présentent, sur un même sujet, des vues personnelles, complémentaires, divergentes, ou même carrément opposées. Ce fut à ce sujet dans les périodes de discussions, parties intégrantes de toutes les sessions de travail, que les données et les points de vue ont été exposés aux questions, aux commentaires et aux critiques, dans le plus grand respect cependant des principes démocratiques et des égards dus à la personne.

Les travaux qui paraissent à la présente série n'engagent donc en fait que leurs auteurs; ils ne doivent pas être interprétés comme reflétant nécessairement les opinions des éditeurs ou celles des membres de la Commission scientifique.

Nous croyons cependant que l'ensemble des connaissances relatives à la contribution potentielle de l'activité physique au bien-être de l'homme aura progressé de façon significative, au moment, et comme résultant de notre session de Québec.

Les divers volumes du présent rapport scientifique illustrent bien, croyons-nous, le fait que la Commission scientifique canadienne s'est appliquée à édifier un programme qui soit conforme aux standards les plus élevés de l'heure et a de plus choisi de fonctionner sur des bases démocratiques sans précédent dans ce genre d'effort international. Les qualités et la représentativité des organismes scientifiques et professionnels qui ont été mis à contribution dans l'ensemble du projet témoignent, entre autres, de cet état de choses.

Nous croyons avoir eu raison d'avoir voulu et d'avoir fait qu'il y ait place, dans le cadre des débats du CISAP-1976-ICPAS, pour des apports en provenance de toutes les branches du savoir humain qui s'intéressent à l'activité physique sous l'une ou l'autre de ses formes.

Le succès remporté par le Congrès de Québec ne saurait cependant que revenir de plein droit aux membres de la Commission scientifique, aux Conseillers internationaux, aux membres de l'Exécutif, au Secrétaire exécutif et trésorier, ainsi qu'aux nombreux autres collaborateurs, bref à tous ceux et celles qui, effectivement, ont mis la main à la pâte. Aux moments les plus importants de notre cheminement critique, les apports professionnels et scientifiques en

number of persons, foreigners as well as Canadians, have indeed been generous, efficient and noteworthy.

The co-editors

William A.R. Orban, Ph.D.
Vice-president of the
Scientific Commission

Fernand Landry, Ph.D.
President of the
Scientific Commission

provenance d'un grand nombre de personnes, étrangers et canadiens, ont été en effet on ne peut plus généreux, efficaces et marquants.

Les co-éditeurs

William A.R. Orban, Ph.D.
Vice-président de la
Commission scientifique

Fernand Landry, Ph.D.
Président de la
Commission scientifique

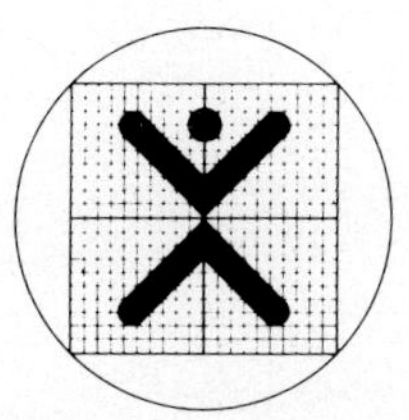

Philosophy

Olympics, Olympism and Human Well-Being

Philosophie

Les Jeux olympiques, l'Olympisme et le bien-être de l'homme

Some Expressed Values Within the Olympic Experience: A Preliminary Analysis

Earle F. Zeigler

The responses and opinions of a stratified sample of Olympic athletes from Canada are analyzed with reference to the social values they associate to their athletic and Olympic experiences. The values expressed are discussed in an historical and philosophical perspective, due consideration being given to contemporary social forces as value determinants.

Introduction

What is "the Olympic experience" all about? For whom is it intended — the athlete, the officials, the country where the Games are held, the actual spectators, those who follow it through the various media, the community of man throughout the world? We could well argue that the Olympic experience is held to provide a fine experience for all of those entities just mentioned. However, my fear is that we talk blithely about it all and have made practically no attempts to analyze the experience in an even reasonably careful manner. In this presentation we will consider some of the attitudes and opinions held by (1) people who have been involved in the Olympic Games in the past; (2) people who will be involved in the 1976 Montreal Games; and (3) people who are training for the Games, but who for some reason may not qualify.

To arrive at certain answers in this preliminary analysis, I employed aspects of historical, philosophical and descriptive methodology and techniques as follows: (1) a review of the "good" and "bad" in historical perspective; (2) some consideration of social forces as value determinants; (3) a glimpse of axiology (the study of values) as a subdivision of the discipline of philosophy; (4) a summary and analysis of the responses from the athletes themselves; and (5) a brief summary including a few conclusions.

Earle F. Zeigler, The University of Western Ontario, London, Canada.

The "Good" and the "Bad" in Historical Perspective

In this respect I am using the term "value" as equivalent to the concepts of "worth" and "goodness," in which case evil would then typically be referred to as "disvalue." Further, I believe it is possible to draw a distinction between two kinds of value, namely, *intrinsic* value and *extrinsic* (or instrumental) value. When a human experience has intrinsic value, therefore, I mean that it is good or valuable in itself — or as an end for its own sake. An experience that has extrinsic value is one that brings about goodness or value also, but such goodness or value serves *as a means to the achievement of something or some gain in life.*

In the English language where even the word "meaning" has eight different meanings, the term "ethics" is employed typically in three different ways (each of which has a relation to the other). First, it is used to classify a general pattern or "way of life" (e.g., Christian or Muslim ethics). Second, it refers to a listing of rules of conduct or a so-called moral code (e.g., professional ethics). Finally, it has come to be used when describing inquiry *about* ways of life or rules of conduct (e.g., that subdivision of philosophy now known as metaethics).

The primary focus here momentarily should be on metaethics and its central questions. What is meant when one searches for the good or the bad? What guarantee is there that any such intent is correct? Can there be right standards for use in judging actions or things to be good or bad? If such value judgments are made, how do they differ, if at all, from judgments that are value-free (or value-neutral) in nature? Further, it is difficult to know whether to proceed from the general to the specific or vice versa (i.e., from the good in general to the good, e.g., right conduct, in particular, or in the opposite direction).

Even a cursory examination of the history of ethics substantiates that it is a description of "irregular progress toward complete clarification of each type of ethical judgement" [2]. It could be argued that the changing political, economic and other social influences since the early development of Greek ethics required the development of a new way of conduct over the centuries just as there is a need for altered standards of conduct today [1, 5, 6]. Socrates began the development of standards for the qualities of goodness, justice and virtue. Plato gave a spiritual orientation to such thought, as he believed that these timeless qualities or ideals had been defined in a world beyond the ken of man. Aristotle, conversely, sought his answers in what now have been designated as the sciences and the social sciences. Plato's approach to goodness was through comparison with so-called universal ideals, while Aristotle's conception of "happiness" resulted from the accomplishment of more natural goals. Individual good was related to social good, but the ideas of moral responsibility and free will were not viewed with the same importance as was to become the case later in Christian thought.

For the next 2000 years ethical thought was oriented much more to practice than to theory. This is why the meanings of the various ethical terms or concepts were not altered to any significant extent, even though moral codes and life purposes were viewed quite differently. So-called modern ethics flourished during the period of marked social change of the 16th and 17th centuries. It was being argued that ethics should indeed be contrasted with science, because the assumption was that the experimental analysis of nature was to be ethically neutral. On and off, thereafter, we can discern a continuing struggle between the two great traditions of utilitarianism and idealism, or the attempt to distinguish between naturalistic ethics and moral law. Later, James and Dewey were able to avoid the almost ageless distinction between value and fact by a type of reinterpretation that blurred the controversial issues for those who were willing to accept ethical judgment as simply a matter of applying human reason to the results of scientific (empirical) investigation by ascribing value to those human acts so designated as valuable.

Social Forces as Value Determinants

A student of the history of ethics, or the history of anything for that matter, soon realizes the importance of the major social forces as determinants of the direction a society may take at any given moment in history. One approach to such analysis is the complex "theory of action" developed by Talcott Parsons and others. Because this theory is typically so firmly grounded in the descriptive and experimental methods of science, it seems logical to employ it as a background or underlying social pattern that can be used to place any theory of individual or social values in perspective. Parsons's general action system may be regarded as a type of empirical system that is composed of four subsystems (culture, the social system, the personality and the behavioral organism). The theory is that these subsystems compose a hierarchy of societal control and conditioning [3].

Culture as the first subsystem of the action theory provides the basic structure and its components "and, in a sense, the 'programming' for the action system as a whole." The structure for the social system has to be more or less harmoniously related to the functional problems of social systems, and the same holds for the structure and functional problems of the personality and the behavioral organism, respectively. Further, the subsystem of culture exercises "control" over the social system and so on up and down the scale. Legitimation is provided to the level below or "pressure to conform" if there is inconsistency. Thus, there is a " 'strain toward consistency' among the system levels, led and controlled from above downward."

What is immediately important to us is to keep in mind the four levels of structure within the social system itself (i.e., Canada as a social system within, say, North American culture). Proceeding from the highest to the lowest level, from the general to the more specific, we find four levels again that are designated as (1) values, (2) norms, (3) the structure of collectivities and (4) the structure of role. Of course, all of these levels are normative in that the social structure is composed of sanctioned cultural limits within which certain types of behavior are mandatory or acceptable. We should keep in mind that values are at the top — the highest level — and that there are many categories of values (scientific, artistic and values for personalities, etc.). As Johnson explains, "Social values are conceptions of the ideal general character of the type of social system in question" [3]. The basic point here for us to remember is that individual values will typically be "conditioned" by the social values prevailing in any given culture and that there will be strong pressure to conform.

Values as a Subdivision of Philosophy

Until philosophy's "age of analysis" became so strongly entrenched in the Western world at least, it was argued typically that the study of values was the end result of philosophizing as a process. It was felt that a person should develop a system of values consistent with his/her beliefs in the subdivisions of metaphysics, epistemology and logic. Some believed that values existed only because of the interest of the valuer (the interest theory). The existence theory, conversely, held that values exist independently. According to this theory a person's task is to discover the "real" values — to give existence to their ideal essence. The experimentalist theory explained value somewhat differently; values that yield results which have "cash value" bring about the possibility of greater happiness through the achievement of still more effective values in the future. One further theory, the part-whole theory, postulated that effective relating of parts to the whole brings about the highest values. Axiology itself does have various domains. First and foremost, of course, is the subdivision known as ethics, which has to do with morality, conduct, good and evil, and ultimate objectives in life. One of the other important subdivisions under axiology deals with the "feeling" aspects of a person's conscious life — esthetics. Esthetics, the philosophy of taste, asks whether there are principles that govern the search for the beautiful in life. Because there has been a need to define still further values in human life, we now have specialized philosophies of education, religion, sport, etc.

Now that we have a brief overview of the question of values (and we must keep in mind that we are considering the question of values within the Olympic experience for the athletes themselves) we are recommending that the athletes — in addition to the question of whether values are intrinsic or extrinsic — ask themselves whether they believe values are objective or subjective. In other words, do values exist whether a person is present to realize them or not? Or is it people who ascribe value to their various relationships with others and their physical environment? If a competitive sport program in which the person strives to earn a place on his/her country's Olympic team fulfills long-range aims and immediate objectives inherently valuable to youth, it is worthwhile whether the rest of us recognizes this value or not. If, on the other hand, it were proved scientifically that high-level sport competition has relatively little value, intrinsic or extrinsic — that the majority of people in the social system sees no need for it — then according to the subjective theory of value, it should be eliminated.

Just prior to the discussion of the responses from the Olympic performers, the question discussed earlier — intrinsic or extrinsic value — will be reviewed very briefly. It ties in with the qualitative aspects of the question of values. Some things in life are desired by the individual, whereas others may be desirable mainly because society has indicated its approval of them. A continuous appraisal of values occurs. As mentioned above, a value existing in and for itself is said to have an intrinsic value. One that serves as a means to an end, however, has become known as an extrinsic or *instrumental* value. When intense emotion and appreciation are involved, this gradation of value is called esthetic. High level Olympic sport competition presumably offers many opportunities to realize such esthetic values. In many of the world's cultures, it is unfortunately true that such high level sporting competition is regarded far too narrowly. Thus, many confine esthetic values to experiences in the established fine arts and literature.

Responses from a Sampling of Olympic Athletes

Earlier it was pointed out that a biased sampling of Olympic athletes (actually two thirds of some 30 athletes from among one university's participants in the Games) responded to an open-ended questionnaire about the values that he/she found within competitive sport at the high level of participation in the Olympic Games and trials. Despite the inherent limitations of this approach, the results obtained were very interesting. The responses have not been tabulated on a percentage basis, nor has the question of statistical significance been considered. Further, it must be kept in mind that the respondents might well give the types of responses that would be expected of Canadians in an evolving democratic society where there would be no opportunities for careers as professional athletes in the particular sports represented within this preliminary survey (i.e., no hockey players were included in the sample).

Basically, then, the *intrinsic* values of the Olympic experience were listed much more frequently and much more importantly by these men and women athletes whose activities ranged over the past 25 years. A number of those responding indicated the importance of "striving for a set goal in life — a really tough one to achieve." They felt that the experience had "made them better persons" by giving them the opportunity to impose the severest kind of "self-discipline" upon themselves. (The words in quotation marks here are actual quotations from the responses.) The Olympic experience had provided them with a chance for "personal fulfillment," an opportunity to "live life most fully." Here was a ready-made "chance to prove yourself," and I "felt the need to do so." Actually, the largest number stated literally as individuals that "I was proud that *I* was involved." It — the experience — gave me an "added sense of personal worth."

Of the some 20 respondents, only a few people mentioned the idea of "developing loyalties to people and institutions" and the opportunity to work "cooperatively" with others in the possible achievement of a common goal (victory). One indicated that he felt there was a "carry-over value" into later life, and that he has experienced a "continued desire for excellence." Three participants mentioned that they felt a keen "awareness of country" because of the actual experience. Only one spoke specifically of the training experience leading up to the competition, although a number of others implied the value of such training with their various comments. Two respondents mentioned that they had "gained knowledge of people from other cultures," and only one mentioned that he felt a "sense of humility" being with the world's greatest athletes.

Insofar as the so-called extrinsic values are concerned, it is a bit unusual that more were not listed. Two respondents said that the extrinsic values were definitely "secondary" to their way of thinking. One stated that they were "important, but were greatly outweighed by the other aspects of the experience." Several mentioned that their Olympic experience gave them "greater status in society," and one stated that in Canadian society the fact that he won a gold medal seemed "more important" to his relatives, friends and colleagues. Three mentioned that the travel itself had been important to them, while one indicated that "the lasting friendships" made would undoubtedly mean much to him in the years ahead.

Interestingly enough, only three or four people mentioned aspects of the experience that could be identified as *disvalues.* One stated that the disvalues were undoubtedly increasing over the years. Another cited examples of individual behavior that were distasteful to him and others. Three people were quite concerned by all of the "politics" evident on the part of officials from their own and other countries. Two mentioned the overemphasis on nationalism and the keeping of team scores and medal counts by representatives of the media. One person went so far as to say that the Olympic experience had actually been a detriment to his career because of the time, money and energy spent.

Conclusions

A preliminary analysis was made of "some expressed values within the Olympic experience" based on the responses from a stratified population of Canadian men and women Olympic athletes over a period of 25 years with an affiliation with one university. After placing the concepts of "good" and "bad" in historical perspective, the importance of social forces as value determinants was discussed. Values, or the study of axiology, was explained briefly as a highly important and (to some) culminating subdivision of the discipline of philosophy.

Responses from the athletes themselves were tabulated in regard to the values or disvalues of "the Olympic experience." The large majority of the respondents directed a preponderance of their statements to what they felt were the intrinsic values resulting from the experience. Extrinsic values were indicated, but they were considered to be largely secondary in nature. The greatest importance of the experience was obviously that which related to the achievement of personal goals, the opportunity to prove oneself and pride along with an added sense of personal worth because of the involvement.

On the assumption that the fundamental values of social systems have a strong influence on the individual values held by most citizens in a country, a preliminary comparison might be made between the value system of Canada and the values mentioned prominently by the Canadians who have been involved in "the Olympic sporting experience." Lipset [4], basing his study on pattern variables established by Parsons as the means for classifying the fundamental values of social systems (e.g., self-orientation — collectivity orientation or how separate needs are perceived in relation to the defined interests of the larger group), stated that there now seems to be consistent movement in Canada toward the twin values of equalitarianism and achievement (values which have been paramount in American life all along). He found further that Canadians were quite achievement-oriented, universalistic, equalitarian, and self-oriented, but were exceeded in these characteristics by Americans to a degree [4]. An important point to consider here is that there has been reluctance on the part "of Canadians to be overoptimistic, assertive, or experimentally inclined" [4].

In this preliminary investigation we are dealing with a select group of athletes, of course, but it is true that they attached the greatest importance of their athletic experience to the achievement of personal goals. It is quite possible, of course, that the attitudes of Canada and Canadians are changing. In the area of national and international sport, we are now witnessing a strong effort on the part of the federal government to become optimistic, assertive and experimentally inclined. Further, many Canadians are now showing an attitudinal change in the direction of regarding the United States as "the leading defender of traditional social forms." It is not possible to make a definitive statement on the basis of this preliminary analysis, of course, but there does seem to be some movement away from an earlier quite consistent "middle ground position" between the United States and England on the part of Canada. This area does seem to offer opportunities for further investigation by sport historians, philosophers and sociologists.

References

1. Brubacher, J.S.: Modern Philosophies of Education, ed. 4. New York: McGraw-Hill, 1969.
2. Edwards, P. (ed.): Encyclopedia of Philosophy. New York:The Macmillan Company and The Free Press, vol. III, 1967, p. 82.
3. Johnson, H.M.: The relevance of the theory of action to historians. Soc. Sci. Q. 46-58, 1969.
4. Lipset, S.: National Character. *In* Koulack, D. and Perlman, D. (eds.): Readings in Social Psychology: Focus on Canada. Toronto:Wiley Publishers of Canada, Ltd., 1973, pp. 6, 9.
5. Zeigler, E.F.: Physical Education and Sport Philosophy. Englewood Cliffs, N.J.:Prentice-Hall, Inc. (In press.)
6. Zeigler, E.F.: Personalizing Physical Education and Sport Philosophy. Champaign, Ill.:Stipes Publishing Co., 1975.

Expérience olympique et valeurs sociales; une analyse des expériences vécues par les athlètes

L'auteur analyse les opinions exprimées par un échantillon d'athlètes canadiens au sujet des valeurs sociales qu'ils associent aux expériences vécues lors de l'entraînement et de la compétition olympique. Les commentaires de l'auteur sont d'ordre historique et philosophique et portent en particulier sur les systèmes de valeurs en tant que déterminants de certains aspects de l'éthique personnelle et sociale.

Signification du phénomène olympique: une analyse

Michel A. Bouet

Significance of the Olympic Phenomenon: An Analysis

The author discusses the Olympic Games and the Olympic Movement from a semiotic standpoint. He uses eight constructs with which various aspects of the Games are considered as specific but interdependent systems: the sports program, the question of national identity, the sports events as such, the sites, the results, the ceremonies, the various symbols. It is postulated that the Olympic Games may indeed serve a specific social purpose in magnifying and glorifying sport, the human body and the consciousness that society has of itself, on a world scale, at least at the time that the Games are staged to celebrate the beginning of a new olympiad.

Introduction

Pour mieux comprendre la signification du phénomène olympique, je crois nécessaire d'analyser les *systèmes sémiques* qui la véhiculent dans les Jeux olympiques. J'aborderai donc ceux-ci sous l'aspect d'une construction sémiotique, plutôt que de m'attacher aux discours sur l'"Olympisme" (toutefois, dans la réalité même des Jeux, nous incluons évidemment le code qui les fonde, c'est-à-dire *Statuts et règles olympiques* [2]). Huit systèmes vont être successivement examinés.

1° Le système des sports

Distincts de ce que seraient des championnats du monde juxtaposés, les Jeux olympiques ont en propre de manifester à la fois la pluralité des sports et l'unité du sport. Ils illustrent le *système* des sports, tout au moins des sports "olympiques" (le code relatif à cette

---

Michel A. Bouet, Université de Haute-Bretagne, Rennes, France.

qualification ne fonctionne pas sans arbitraire ni contingence [4], mais Coubertin avait bien en vue le système total des sports [3]).

La participation des différentes spécialités aux Jeux olympiques fait ressortir les liens d'identité, de complémentarité, d'opposition qui les articulent les unes aux autres dans une configuration d'ensemble où s'établissent entre ces spécialités des rapports de structure et de sens qui sont de nature à justifier les interprétations sémiotiques du système des sports [5-7].

C'est à différents niveaux que le système des sports est signifiant: a) au niveau de l'ensemble du système, chaque sport en correspondance avec les autres, joue en quelque sorte sa partition sur les grands thèmes de signification du sport; b) au niveau de chaque figure du sport, nous avons d'une part le code plus ou moins conventionnel des gestes, des règles, des actions et des accessoires définissant la spécialité, et d'autre part tout son halo de connotations symboliques et expressionnelles qui tiennent au vécu subjectif des groupes et des individus.

L'atmosphère de totale "participation" propre aux Jeux olympiques favorise la libération de toute ces valeurs de signification inhérentes au système des sports et qui sont au-delà de la technicité et de l'objectivité des performances. Mais le système des sports ne relève pas seulement ainsi d'une sémiologie de la signification. Il débouche aussi sur une sémiologie de la communication [12], dont nous allons indiquer deux aspects principaux fort apparents aux Jeux olympiques: le premier est constitué par le fait que chaque sport réalise une forme de communication gestuelle, directement pour les participants et indirectement pour les spectateurs [1]; le second, toujours dans le domaine des communications non-verbales, réside dans la signalisation et d'une façon plus générale encore, dans la mise en images que suscitent les sports: c'est alors comme éléments de leur système général (les uns par rapport aux autres et fonction donc d'un code), qu'ils sont représentés. Comparez à cet égard le progrès de codification en même temps que d'expressivité réalisé entre les deux systèmes de pictogrammes des sports en usage à Mexico et à Münich, l'un restant au fond métonymique et déictique, l'autre constituant plus un véritable système et auquel correspondait, dans un registre plus figuratif, le système des "affiches officielles."

2° Le système des appartenances nationales

Si l'on considère la réalité des Jeux Olympiques (et, aussi bien, certaines "règles olympiques" [2]), on s'aperçoit que le système des appartenances nationales y régit la présence des individus, qu'ils soient concurrents, officiels ou même spectateurs. Il est bien évident que la ville organisatrice représente aussi et incarne un pays. La vocation internationaliste et universaliste des Jeux elle-même rend fatal le souci de marquer la participation de chaque patrie par ses signes d'identification. Par ailleurs, dans le gigantisme olympique, il semble que l'individu ait plus que jamais le besoin de se rallier à un groupe intermédiaire: sa notion le lui fournit d'autant plus inévitablement que le contexte mondial du nationalisme a envahi les Jeux.

Certes la règle 8 s'énonce [2]: "Les Jeux sont des compétitions entre individus et non entre pays." Mais comme ceux-ci prennent leurs champions pour emblèmes, et que le titre et le rôle de champion deviennent des signes plus importants que celui qui les porte fugitivement, la dimension individuelle a vraiment du mal à s'imposer, n'y arrivant peut-être qu'avec des athlètes exceptionnels, tels un Owens. Mais alors c'est une sémantisation par la légende qui les guette.

C'est selon le système des appartenances nationales que sont engagés et présentés les concurrents, c'est le cadre de ce système qui est rappelé lors de la distribution des récompenses. Les spectateurs eux aussi s'en réclament, et c'est en lui qu'ils communiquent. Toute rencontre aux Jeux paraît se vivre plus inter-nationalement qu'inter-individuellement.

En tant que les appartenances à des entités nationales connotent de nombreuses propriétés en rapport avec les attributs géographiques, culturels, raciaux, idéologiques, leur système relève évidemment d'une sémiologie de la signification. Mais, sauf peut-être en ce qui s'agit du pays organisateur, les phénomènes correspondants d'expression demeurent assez limités et réduits à des indications, car il semble que l'appartenance nationale se saisisse et s'affirme plutôt sur les signes qui la dénotent, et comme extérieurement. Ces signes relèvent d'une sémiologie de la communication: drapeaux (hissés aux mâts, arborés en tête des délégations, agités par les spectateurs), hymnes nationaux, tenues distinctives de sport ou de céremonie, écussons, insignes (avec leurs motifs souvent symboliques). Il est à noter que les insignes, mais aussi bien des maillots ou survêtements par exemple, servent fréquemment de "souvenirs" échangés et de marques d'amitié lors de contacts entre participants de différents pays.

3° Le système des rôles

Lorsque l'on porte attention aux différentes catégories de personnes qui se trouvent aux Jeux olympiques et qu'on examine comment elles y prennent fonctionnellement part, on est en face de rôles: athlète, concurrent, entraîneur, accompagnateur, médecin, masseur; "délégué technique," "officiel technique" (arbitre, juge); officiel (membre du CIO, de Comité national olympique, de fédération), représentant de Gouvernement; journaliste, cinéaste; et ne composant certainement pas la moindre des catégories, les spectateurs. Ajoutons encore: interprètes, spécialistes de l'information, hôtesses, personnel de sécurité, etc.

Sans pouvoir détailler ici à quels niveaux et comment tous ces rôles s'articulent entre eux, insistons seulement sur le fait qu'il s'agit bien d'un système: chaque rôle est solidaire des autres, et tous ensemble ils assurent le déroulement des Jeux. Mais à côté de cet aspect fonctionnel de leur système et liés à lui, il y a ses aspects sémiotiques, à savoir: 1° les rôles en interaction sont réglés par des codes; 2° ils interagissent en se servant de systèmes de communication; 3° le rôle tenu confère un sens à la participation de celui qui le tient, et ses actions prennent valeur de signes. D'une façon générale, en s'inspirant de vues lévi-straussiennes, on pourrait dire que ce système des rôles s'entre-répondant "apparaît comme une sorte de langage, c'est-à-dire un ensemble d'opérations destinées à assurer, entre les individus et les groupes, un certain type de communication [10]," et ce qu'il produit, n'est autre chose que les Jeux même, et l'Olympisme qui est leur message. Aussi chacun aux Jeux est-il bien conscient d'être investi d'un rôle en référence à l'Olympisme; au fond, on est convaincu que l'*essentiel est de prendre part*, non tant aux compétitions qui ne sont guère que la matière première des Jeux, mais à la "célébration" qui en est l'élément signifiant.

A la sémiologie de la communication au sens strict, appartiennent les marques de rôle (uniformes, brassards, etc.), et les codes de signaux employés dans l'exercice du rôle, et aussi certains gestes et certaines postures propres au rôle mais moins conventionnels (geste du vainqueur sur le podium, etc.). La façon dont les spectateurs tiennent leur rôle n'est pas sans impliquer l'usage de signes, d'attitudes et d'expressions plus ou moins implicitement codifiés, et dont l'émission en général a pour support le groupe en masse. Cependant, il existe aussi aux Jeux des manifestations d'encouragement et d'ovation dûment organisées par des groupes plus restreints.

Nous n'avons fait jusqu'ici qu'indiquer les implications systémiques et sémiques du fameux slogan "all games, all nations," en le complétant par un troisième volet: "toutes les catégories de personnes concernées par le sport" (dirons-nous: "tous les amateurs de sport"? . . .). Nous passons maintenant à deux systèmes qui composent des Jeux olympiques leur structure spatio-temporelle éminemment concentrée.

4° Le système des évènements

Les Jeux olympiques sont rigoureusement cadrés dans le temps. D'abord, c'est la périodicité avec laquelle, tous les quatre ans, ils consacrent l'inauguration d'une Olympiade. Ensuite, les Jeux sont constitués, en quinze journées, par le déroulement d'un nombre défini d'épreuves sportives qu'encadrent les cérémonies d'ouverture et de clôture. Ce programme, où chaque compétition a son moment assigné, je l'appellerai *le système des évènements.* Synchronique et diachronique à la fois, il y a en lui du successif structuré (éliminatoires, demi-finales, finales . . .) et du simultané organisé, puisque les différentes spécialités ont parallèlement leurs épreuves mais agencées avec certains décalages, de façon à laisser des possibilites de choix au spectateur olympique, nécessairement éclectique, qui se compose ses propres Jeux et qui prise surtout les finales. L'ordre de succession et de simultanéité des épreuves des Jeux (dirons-nous: du jeu des épreuves?) est un système rigoureusement réglé. Chaque évènement au niveau de sa présentation dans le programme est indiqué comme signe de son avènement, et comme élément signifiant de l'ensemble du tableau des épreuves. Puis tour à tour chaque évènement a irrévocablement lieu. De signe, il devient manifestation, témoignage. Suivant les circonstances et la façon dont il s'est déroulé, il prend une figure concrète irrévocable, contribuant ainsi à dessiner peu à peu le contexte d'ensemble des Jeux, lequel se transforme diachroniquement, à la manière de l'Histoire, et réagit sur la signification de tout ce qui s'accomplit. C'est alors que les Jeux se trament effectivement et que le système des évènements devient système expressionnel. Une perturbation dans l'apparition et l'ordre des évènements compromet l'unité des Jeux et bouscule leur sens de totalité temporelle. Enfin, le système des évènements fournit les repères de l'orientation temporelle de tous les participants, tant pendant qu'après les Jeux (temps du récit).

5° Le système des lieux

C'est un des traits fondamentaux des Jeux olympiques que l'unité de lieu suivant laquelle les évènements divers qui les composent sont concentrés dans un même ensemble spatial: "l'enceinte olympique" (Règle 53). Les Jeux de Münich à cet égard étaient plus concentrés que ceux de Mexico; en conséquence, ils ont assuré peut-être plus fortement la fonction des Jeux olympiques d'être "à la fois l'emblème et la démonstration" de la "puissance sportive" (pour reprendre des termes de Coubertin [3]). Les Jeux olympiques impliquent donc *un système des lieux*. Le stade principal est au coeur de ce système; les autres installations doivent être considérées comme ses satellites. Un autre lieu-pivot est le village olympique," aussi près que possible du stade principal" (Règle 37). La proximité dans le système des lieux olympiques est signifiante; elle est de nature proxémique. Un texte de Coubertin [3] témoigne remarquablement du sentiment qu'il avait de cela et combien il comprenait la fonction signifiante de l'architecture et son importance pour le message olympique lui-même.

Pendant la durée des Jeux, ces lieux olympiques se détachent sur le fond de la cité organisatrice, comme la figure même de sa célébration des Jeux. Et leur système joue pour elle comme un principe suivant lequel elle re-distribue ses propres espaces et monuments par rapport aux Jeux; ceux-ci prennent ainsi une signification *olympique* que contribuent à souligner les banderoles et autres décorations disposées dans la ville. En même temps, les valeurs propres de l'architecture locale ne sont pas sans diffuser dans la signification des Jeux tenus en telle ou telle cité. Le design des sites olympiques est l'objet d'une recherche architecturale qui dessine autour de leur appropriation fonctionnelle des formes destinées à évoquer un style et des symboles susceptibles de pénétrer tous les participants, pour les mettre dans les dispositions où ils pourront à la fois mieux *participer* et mieux communiquer.

6° Le système des résultats

Des évènements sortent les résultats, à partir desquels s'établissent les classements et s'attribuent les récompenses. Tout cela relève d'un autre système que celui des évènements. Le nombre qui chiffre la performance vient s'inscrire dans un corpus qui peut-être lu à part, sans voir et vivre les évènements. En dépit de la Règle 44 énonçant que "les Jeux olympiques ne sont pas des compétitions entre nations et les classements par pays n'ont aucune valeur," il s'est établi la coutume de comptabiliser les résultats et les médailles par pays. Je me rappelle avoir vu à Münich des tableaux synoptiques où était tenu à jour le nombre des différentes médailles dont s'enrichissaient les nations participantes au fur et à mesure des compétitions.

Les chiffres donnant la mesure des performances ainsi que les numéros de classement tombent dans la catégorie des "procédés de communications systématiques par l'emploi de chiffres," si importante à notre époque quantitativiste et scientifique; ils sont associés à l'utilisation du système des idéogrammes universels représentant les unités de mesure. Cette emprise sémiotique du nombre sur les Jeux, dans l'émission d'incessants messages découpés en signes stables et constants, et qui contrastent avec la pure hétérogénéité qualitative du devenir évènementiel des Jeux, exprime, dans le seul langage qui soit homogène et le même pour tous, l'idéal olympique d'universalité et de légalité; c'est également ainsi qu'est assurée la seule réduction de tous les sports à un commun dénominateur capable de manifester leur unité de participation. Si l'on admet que les résultats chiffrés et les classements sont comme le texte qui s'écrit des Jeux, la traduction simultanée de ce texte dans le langage des médailles (les "diplômes" semblent avoir moins d'importance) opère le passage du sémiotique au symbolique, en même temps que du résultat à la récompense. Il y aurait à dire sur les figures stylisées et emblématiques qui sont gravées sur les médailles, comme aussi à commenter l'extension du système des médailles à des fonctions purement commémoratives (Règle 43) et à la "monnaie olympique." La symbolique de l'or, de l'argent et du bronze serait également à considérer (remarquons, en passant, que la Règle 43 parle de *vermeil*, et non d'or). Au compte encore du système des résultats: le poids attaché aux victoires olympiques, et même à la simple sélection aux Jeux.

7° Le système des cérémonies

C'est par les cérémonies surtout et par leur solennité que les Jeux olympiques se distinguent d'une simple série de championnats mondiaux. Tel était bien le voeu de Coubertin. Le système des cérémonies se compose principalement de celles qui sont soigneusement réglées par le protocole olympique: ouverture des Jeux, serment-promesse, remises des prix, clôture des Jeux. Mais il faut compter encore toutes les cérémonies et festivités de moindre importance qui sont tenues dans le cadre des Jeux, et les nombreuses réceptions que la présence de l'élite mondiale des sportifs et des officiels suscite. Enfin, la ritualité et la solennité des Jeux s'étendent à tout ce qui s'y déroule, contribuant ainsi à créer l'atmosphere de fête, voulue d'ailleurs par leur rénovateur, qui entendait de cette façon l'héritage grec prestigieux dont il se réclamait.

Les cérémonies constituent bien, (tant toutes ensemble que chacune séparément) des systèmes culturels de signes porteurs de signification, réglés par des codes et dont le but est d'établir la communication entre les participants de les articuler les uns aux autres dans les rôles qui les identifient, et au-delà, de les faire communier dans quelque chose de plus grand qu'eux-mêmes. C'est le groupe qui est émetteur et à la fois récepteur du message olympique que le système des cérémonies assume, et par lequel l'action de *faire* du sport "se sémantise" et devient, au sens de Prieto [13], la *cérémonie de faire* du sport.

Les cérémonies ont certainement une fonction importante dans la création de cette "*eurythmie*", chère à Coubertin (tout autant que "la liberté d'excès") comme aussi aux organisateurs des Jeux de Montréal. Sémiologiquement nous pourrions, dans le système général des Jeux olympiques, attribuer aux cérémonies une sorte de fonction "phatique" [8].

8° Le système des symboles olympiques

Un symbolisme dont les principaux éléments ont été forgés par Coubertin, puis par Carl Diem, et qui aurait pu rester artificiel s'est au contraire fortement imposé. Peut-on imaginer non seulement les Jeux mais aussi l'Olympisme sans l'estampille des Anneaux, sans la Flamme? Il est vrai qu'en choisissant ces symboles, les pères de l'Olympisme avaient su mettre la main sur des formes et des valeurs symboliques particulièrement puissantes et archétypales, telles que le cercle et le feu, au sujet desquels en effet se vérifie à plein ce qu'écrivait de Saussure: "le symbole a pour caractère de n'être jamais tout à fait arbitraire; il n'est pas vide, il y a un rudiment de lien naturel entre le signifiant et le signifié" [14].

De plus, comme Coubertin lui-même l'a avec un sûr à-propos sémiologique remarqué, les cinq couleurs des Anneaux entrelacés et le blanc du drapeau sur le fond duquel ils se détachent, représentent les drapeaux de toutes les nations sans exception, puisque ceux-ci ont tous au moins une de ces six couleurs parmi les leurs. Le symbolisme de la Flamme est plus directement signifiant, plus riche de connotations diverses (le Sacré, la Vie et la Jeunesse, Prométhée). Mais, surtout, Diem en concevant le relai par lequel le flambeau est porté de l'antique Olympie où il est allumé jusqu'au site des Jeux, lui a ajouté une dimension d'*action symbolique* à l'échelle de ce monde. A Mexico, les organisateurs avaient su joindre le symbolisme olympique et néo-hellénique de la Flamme au symbolisme de feu nouveau selon la tradition-précolombienne.

Ces deux symboles majeurs, véritables marques de fabrique des Jeux olympiques s'accompagnent d'une prolifération d'autres figures emblématiques que l'on trouve notamment sur les médailles, les monnaies et les timbres crées à l'occasion de chaque olympiade, et qui constituent donc les emblèmes plus particulièrement liés à chaque célébration singulière des Jeux et à la cité et au pays qui les organisent. Un emblème propre à chaque célébration des Jeux, et même une mascotte (cette année Amik, succédant à Waldi) complètent le système des symboles distinctifs. Le système des symboles olympiques serait à élucider au carrefour même de la sémiologie de la signification et de la sémiologie de la communication. C'est en lui que la double et ambivalente nature sémiotique des Jeux semblerait chercher à atteindre un point de résolution.

Après la présentation, nécessairement successive de ces huit systèmes, trois remarques s'imposent:

1. Ils sont tous des organisations sémiques c'est-à-dire que chacun articule ses éléments, et aussi bien ceux des sous-systèmes qu'on y peut distinguer, comme des éléments interdépendants de sens. On y retrouve, encore qu'à des degrés variés de collusion ou de distinction, les deux pôles du signifiant et du signifié et, corrélativement, une prédominance de l'un ou l'autre des deux types de sémiologie (sémiologie de la signification et sémiologie de la communication).

2. Ces huit systèmes ne fonctionnent pas isolément. Et il est bien évident que le propre des Jeux olympiques est d'être au contraire le lieu de leurs interférences, ou plutôt de leur synergie. Nous n'avons pas le loisir ici d'analyser en détail les modes de leurs combinaisons. Disons qu'il y a des liens d'association, avec conditionnement réciproque comme c'est le cas notamment entre système des sports, système des appartenances et système des rôles. Il y a aussi des systèmes qui, dans une certaine mesure, se prolongent mutuellement ou se téléscopent comme c'est le cas entre système des cérémonies et système des symboles, ou entre système des évènements et système des résultats. Il y a encore des systèmes complémentaires (lieux-éléments). Enfin des relations les plus intéressantes peut-être sont celles qui se développent entre systèmes dont l'un joue à l'égard d'un autre ou de plusieurs autres le rôle de signifiant ou de signifié: le système des symboles olympiques est particulièrement remarquable à cet égard; mais encore le système des évènements est signifiant du système des sports; et le système des résultats est signifiant du système des évènements. A la limite on conçoit donc entre les différents systèmes tout un jeu de correspondances sémiotiques. Les Jeux olympiques se révèleraient donc aussi comme des jeux sémiotiques; et par ce biais peut-être ils rendraient au sport une nature ludique.

3. Les éléments sémiotiques des Jeux sont largement repris par les media et par la publicité; ils sont traités alors selon une véritable

rhétorique. Maintenant, quant à la question générale de la signification ultime des Jeux olympiques, je serais tenté de dire que pour l'instant on est en face de plus de signifiants que de signifiés, et que leur polysémie est flottante, en dépit de leurs structurations serrées et conjointes. Les huit systèmes à caractère sémique que nous avons identifiés me semblent être finalement au croisement de deux courants qui privilégient tous deux les signes. L'un est ancien et même archaïque, c'est celui du signe dans la tradition religieuse, le signe-symbole d'un au-delà, le signe qui contre-signe et sacralise. L'un est moderne, dans la ligne de la consommation de signes et d'images par la société de masse; il marque l'emprise de structures sémiotiques semblant fonctionner pour elles-mêmes. Mais dans les deux cas on trouverait peut-être le même discrédit de l'individu qui n'est plus libre de proférer une véritable parole créatrice, et entre les deux donc le même vide.

En tout état de cause, nous nous sentons réservés devant l'entreprise de certains auteurs qui comme Jeu [9] ou Metheny [11] interprètent d'emblée le symbolisme des Jeux olympiques en travaillant tout de suite au plan du signifié, sans être attentifs aux mécanismes des systèmes sémiques. Peut-être aussi ai-je commis l'erreur inverse? Et tandis que leur discours rejoindrait le généreux arbitraire de celui des fondateurs et des "trustees", mon analyse pécherait par la vaine prudence que j'ai mise à me borner à décortiquer surtout les structures du signifiant. Cependant il serait quand même possible d'aller un peu plus loin, en avançant que la machinerie fondamentalement sémiotique des Jeux opère une cartaine *mise en scène* olympique, se rapprochant d'une *liturgie* (ce qui a fait dire à un linguiste de mes confrères: "au fond, même si les Jeux étaient faits d'avance, ils seraient quand même célébrés"). Cet respect en quelque sorte "religieux" des Jeux, doublé de leur caractère festif, semble largement reconnu; et Coubertin l'avait voulu. Mais sur le problème de savoir quel est en définitive l'objet de la mise en scène et le sens ultime du message, je reste pour ma part à m'interroger. Il semble, à un premier niveau, que cet objet soit le *sport*, et que ce soit lui le glorifié (la haute performance et les champions n'étant en fait que des moyens servant à opérer cette glorification). Mais, à un deuxième niveau, et quelles que soient ici les prétentions de l'olympisme à exalter à travers le sport l'âme et le caractère, je me demande si le *corps humain* n'est pas, dans les ritualisations olympiques, le dieu de la fête, porté au degré le plus élevé de sa puissance: "citius, altius, fortius"; les sports alors ne seraient à nouveau que les moyens employés pour faire apparaître le dieu. Cette interprétation permettrait de rejoindre à la fois les Jeux de l'antiquité et leur version renouvelée en notre temps. En effet, comme ceux-là procédaient d'une culture imbue du culte du corps, les Jeux modernes procèdent d'une culture qui a du corps la nostalgie, et qui est de cette façon tout autant portée à le magnifier.

Toutefois, à un trosième et dernier niveau, le corps à son tour n'est peut-être plus que le support d'une autre mise en scène, celle de l'image que se donne d'elle-même la *société*. L'importance prise par les Jeux viendrait alors de ce qu'ils sont la seule occasion où la société contemporaine de coopération-compétition se fête, à l'échelle de la conscience *mondiale* qu'à maintenant de soi l'Humanité.

Références

1. Bouet, M.A.: Signes et symboles dans l'activité physico-sportive comme lieu de communcations humaines. *In* Trabajos Cientificos, III Congreso Mondial de la Sociedad Internacional de Psicologia del Deporte, Madrid, 1975, tomo I, pp. 113-123.
2. Comité olympique international. Statuts et règles olympiques. Lausanne, C.I.O., 1971.
3. Coubertin, P. de: L'idée olympique, discours et essais. Stuttgart:Carl Diem Institute, 1966, pp. 20-35.
4. Csanadi, A.: Le programme olympique. Revue olympique. 89-90: Mars-avril 1975, pp. 86-89.
5. Franke, E.: Sporting action and its interpretation. *In* Grupe, O. (ed.): Spor in the Modern World. Heidelberg:Springer Verlag, 1973, pp. 530-532.
6. Gebauer, G.: The logic of action and construction of the world, a contribution to the theory of sport. *In* Grupe, O. (ed.): Sport in the Modern World. Heidelberg:Springer Verlag, 1973, pp. 533-535.
7. Gebauer, G.: Leistung als Aktion und Präsentation. Sportwissenschaft, 2:182-203, 1972.
8. Guiraud, P.: La sémiologie. Paris, 1971, p. 12.
9. Jeu, B.: Le sport, la mort, la violence. Paris, 1972.
10. Levi-Strauss, C.: Anthropologie structurale. Paris, 1958, p. 69.
11. Metheny, E.: Symbolic Forms of Movements: The Olympic Games. Dubuque, 1965, pp. 35-42.
12. Mounin, G.: Introduction à la sémiologie. Paris, 1970, pp. 11-15.
13. Prieto, L.J.: Etudes de linguistique et de sémiologie générales. Genève, 1975, pp. 125-141.
14. Saussure, J.: Cours de linguistique générale. Paris, 1966, p. 101.
15. Tyszka, A.: Komunikacja symboliczna jako jedna Z funkcji sportu. *In* Sport W spoleczenstwie wspolczesnym. Warszawa, 1973, pp. 143-168.

L'auteur traite des Jeux olympiques et de l'Olympisme d'un point de vue sémiotique. Il considère que les nombreuses facettes des Jeux olympiques peuvent être mises en perspective sous la forme de huit systèmes spécifiques et interreliés: les spécialités sportives en tant que telles, l'identité nationale, les événements, les sites, les cérémonies et l'ensemble des symboles. L'auteur se dit d'avis que les

Jeux olympiques peuvent certes avoir une fonction et une utilité sociales qui seraient celles de magnifier et de glorifier le sport, le corps humain et la conscience que la société a d'elle-même. Cet état de conscience est de toute évidence particulièrement aigu et universel au moment où les Jeux olympiques marquent la célébration d'une nouvelle olympiade.

A Political-Philosophic Analysis of Olympism

Vladimir S. Roditchenko

The author discusses the significant transformations which have occurred in international sport since de Coubertin's revival of the Olympic Games and shows that the modern Olympic Movement as well as the Olympic Games as such cannot be understood and used for the greater benefit of mankind outside of the consideration and respect of differing ideologies, theories and sociopolitical systems.

On the eve of the Games of the XXIst Olympiad, an outstanding public event of global importance where the world's best athletes are to gather and meet in friendly competition, one feels particularly aware of the importance of the problem our Seminar is to study: "Olympics, Olympism and Human Well-Being." The main reason for this impression lies in the growing importance of sport in all levels of social life — a trend most characteristic of our time.

The fact itself that an international scientific congress is discussing Olympism from the political-philosophic point of view and that scholars representing different philosophic and ideologic directions and different political views are present here is of great significance. It shows that the concept of sport as a strictly "nonpolitical" phenomenon is now out of date and quite anachronistic.

It goes without saying that in a 20-minute address one is unable to present an exhaustive treatment of the problem; therefore, we have set ourselves certain restrictions and will concentrate on the following:

1. Significant transformations in the concept of Olympism since Pierre de Coubertin's times.

2. Political-philosophic aspects not only of Olympism in general but of Olympic sports competitions (a less known aspect of the

---

Vladimir S. Roditchenko, Chief, Sports Department, Organizing Committee of the Olympic Games of 1980, Moscow, U.S.S.R.

problem) as well. The character of these aspects will be revealed on the basis of the relationship between Olympic competitions and the whole system of international sport [14, 15].

3. Preference given to the political rather than the philosophical aspects of the problem. As for now, our knowledge of these aspects is inadequate in comparison to their practical importance at the present stage of historical development of Olympism. In our opinion, this inadequacy is accounted for by a well-known bias relative to the political side of Olympism.

The years 1973 to 1976 saw a further development of the Olympic movement as a worldwide mass phenomenon, a strengthening of democratic and realistic tendencies in the management of this movement, and a number of valuable contributions to the theory of Olympism. These contributions were made not by scholars alone, but also by IOC members, sports leaders, statesmen and politicians of many nations.

The Xth Olympic Congress in Varna, Bulgaria, became a milestone in the development of modern Olympism. The Congress discussed many long-neglected problems of the Olympic movement and stressed its social role as one of today's most important mass movements.

As to theoretical research in the strict sense of the word, it has undergone a shift from the study of the aspect of continuity between ancient and modern Olympics (a trend typical, for example, of the Olympic Academy [16]) toward the analysis of present-day Olympic realities. In our opinion, this shift is a natural consequence of the fact that many Olympic scholars have become aware of the sociopolitical importance of the Olympic Games in today's world.

Two principal realistic trends should be noted in the Olympic studies:

1. Progressive values of the Olympic idea (Olympism) are recognized by virtually everyone.

2. Notwithstanding that, a confrontation of antagonistic class ideologies is taking place in the field of Olympism.

The principle of nondiscrimination on the basis of race, birth, political or religious convictions is a universally recognized humanitarian fundamental principle of the Olympic movement. This principle may be regarded as immanent to sport as such. But certain scholars tend to hyperbolize the principle of "equal opportunities" in sport and seem to forget that the process of sports training — a sine qua non of sporting success — is largely dependent upon socioeconomic factors.

A historical continuity between ancient and modern Olympism is an established fact. But certain scholars tend to hyperbolize the importance of ancient social patterns of Olympism for the modern society. Others try to present the Olympic ethical code as a kind of universal religion. Yet the majority of scholars rightfully stress the continuity of humanitarianism and realistic traditions of Olympism [17].

Although one may still hear that despite tremendous socio-economic changes in the world the core of Olympism remains unchanged since Coubertin's time, hardly an earnest scholar would now treat the Olympic movement as something fully independent of the outer world in the social, political and ethical sense. Only a few people still hold the compromised theory of social autonomy of Olympism and sport in general.

From the point of view of Marxist-Leninist dialectical and historical materialism which constitutes a methodological basis for history, theory and sociology of physical culture, sport is an objective necessity for the development of mankind. The Olympic Games as a social phenomenon lie in the sphere of dialectically complex relations and tendencies of social development and are, therefore, influenced by many different factors (although a reverse process of influence of the Olympic movement upon the social progress can also be observed).

Ideological confrontation is as typical of the modern Olympism as is general recognition of its realistic content. As Mlodzikowski put it [12], the ideological and political dominants are most evident in top-level sport and, therefore, it simply cannot, with its present scope and importance, remain beyond ideology both in practical and theoretical aspects.

All attempts to present Olympism as something uninfluenced by class and state ideologies were historic failures. Moreover, these attempts practically impoverished the Olympic movement, hindered its social efficiency and prevented it from full realization of its humanitarian message.

It is well known that during the last decade some of the bourgeois sociologists have been giving up their long-professed "deideologization" theory and looking for an ideology capable of withstanding the confrontation with the Communist ideology. In the course of this search some of them, like Lenk [10, 11], have put forward a doctrine of sport as a model of the "success society." The presentation of Olympism as a universal classless ideology is also a part of this new development.

There is still another new trend in the bourgeois ideology of sport, namely, pessimistic predictions of the forthcoming decline and fall of the Olympic movement. This trend is typical, for instance, of many French bourgeois sports writers. Their concepts were analyzed by Joliff [6] and summarized by him in the form of the following oppositions: mass vs. elite; neutrality vs. politization; amateurs vs. "state athletes"; "liberal" vs. "totalitarian" states; ethos vs. science; and pleasure vs. success.

An analysis of these and similar concepts reveals their peculiarities:

1. Hyperbolization of drawbacks and negative aspects of the Olympic movement. The reason for this lies in the growing dissatisfaction of bourgeois sports leaders and ideologists with the constantly improving sports prestige of the Socialist countries (thus, at the Games of the XXth Olympiad in Munich 11 Socialist countries whose athletes constituted only one tenth of all the participants won 47% of all medals).

2. Attempts to put top-level sport and "sport for all" in an artificial opposition to the disadvantage of the former. The motives are the same — lack of success in top-level sports for capitalist countries.

3. Extension of vices typical of the Olympic movement in bourgeois countries to the Olympic movement as a whole.

4. Attempts to "cure" actual diseases of the Olympic movement by persuasion alone, while they can be fully eliminated only in the process of radical socioeconomic changes.

Summing up the existing viewpoints on Olympism and stressing their progressive aspects, it would be fully justified to say that at present, the moral and ethical message of Olympism is not the only and not even the principal part of Olympism. Under conditions existing in the modern world, primary importance should be attached to the Olympic movement as (a) a factor of world peace (the international aspect of Olympism) and (b) an instrument of social management, including management of sports development (the national aspect of Olympism).

Proceeding to the evaluation of Olympism in its international aspect, I should like to recall a conceptual statement of Lenin: ". . . all economic, political and spiritual life of mankind is already more and more internationalized under capitalism. Socialism fully internationalizes it" [9]. This trend finds its reflection in the significant quantitative growth of the Olympic movement, the genuine "competition explosion" of the 1960s and 1970s. On the basis of this development, the role of sport in the hierarchy of today's political values is becoming ever more important.

As a consequence of this, advanced political forces of our time come to accept everything valuable and progressive in the Olympic movement.

As Brejnev put it: "The Olympic Charter adopted by the International Olympic Committee expresses the desire of athletes of the whole world to promote the development of confidence and goodwill among nations and the creation of a better and more peaceful world. ... Therefore the appeal of the IOC for the consolidation of peace and international cooperation, like its work to organize major friendly meetings of athletes of all continents — the Olympic Games — enjoys the greatest appreciation and support in the Soviet Union" [3].

Peace in the Marxist-Leninist sense of the word is not only an absence of war (because a nonwar period may be used for the preparation of a new war) but a stable normal situation which enables the progress of mankind. This concept of peace provides a theoretical basis for Olympism, a scientific explanation of its social function [4].

Extending Volkert's recent conclusion [18], one may say that practical realization of the idea of peaceful coexistence between countries with different social systems would lead to a growth in practical importance of Olympism, since Olympism is a reflection in sport of this dominant idea of realism in world politics.

This function of sport was stressed in the Final Act of the European Conference for Security and Cooperation in Helsinki, 1975: "In order to expand existing links and cooperation in the field of sport, the participating States will encourage contacts and exchanges of this kind including sports meetings and competitions of all sorts, on the basis of the established international rules, regulations and practice." Thus top-level sport and its acme, the Olympic Games, have become an integral part of the materialization of detente and an important political factor.

As Pavlov stressed, "The higher the number of sports meetings, the greater is the responsibility of state institutions dealing with sports for the realization of Olympic principles of noble rivalry and friendship among the young people of the world" [13].

In contrast with this constructive position, some persons in the Olympic movement, although advocating in certain instances the necessity of closer interaction with governments, tend at the same time to stress the alleged tendency toward nationalism and chauvinism in the Olympic movement. It must be noted that such a viewpoint finds an approval in the extreme right-wing bourgeois press which evaluates the Olympic Games in the following way: "This sporting vanity fair does not serve the interests of sport but only selfish nationalism. . . . Chauvinism and the boosting of national feelings — that is the mainspring of Olympic hysteria. To speak of importance of the Olympics in international understanding is of no sense."

Lord Killanin, the IOC President, speaking to Guy Lagorge of the *France-soir*, did recognize that "the repercussions of the Games are so wide that sporting actions become political ones." But in connection with the use of the Games as an instrument for the demonstration of national power, he alleged that ". . . an athlete is not regarded as a personality anymore. He is, alas, only a representative of one or another system. This is . . . the principal distortion of modern Olympism" [7].

All these troubled statements concerning the "Olympic nationalism" are nothing else but remnants of the concept of "nonpolitical sport" which springs from the failure to understand the realities of modern class society. The most important thing is that the governments' interest in the Olympic success means, at one and the same time, increased aid to national sports movements and strengthened authority of the Olympic movement.

In our opinion, the evident progress of Olympism in the recent decade is accounted for not so much by its intrinsic ethical values as by the progress in world politics, the growth of the Olympic movement's authority in the political field and, last but not least, by efforts toward the democratization of the Olympic movement constantly exerted by Socialist and developing countries. It is on this basis that the Olympic movement itself is playing an ever-growing part in the democratization of world sports and the elimination of every discrimination, including racial discrimination. The position of the IOC toward the racist regimes in South Africa and Rhodesia is of great significance.

The Olympic movement thus owes its important social position to its increased contacts with states and other political institutes. In this connection, the principle of independence of national Olympic movements proclaimed in the Olympic Charter deserves a most detailed analysis.

Another important reason for the increased social role of the Olympic movement lies in its function as a factor of social management. Here the leading part is played by information about the Olympic Games as a specific form of social information.

An analysis of Olympism reveals the existence of close interdependence between the Games as a sociopolitical phenomenon and the development of mass media. This kind of relationship reveals itself most obviously in the aspect of Olympism relating to the Games and in the whole system of international competitions during the four-year Olympic span as well. The Games are generally understood as only a pinnacle of the modern sports system with its hierarchy of prestige and other values.

The search for the most common property of sports competitions has led us to a conclusion that there exists a qualitatively new feature common to them all: as a result of technological revolution in the field of mass media, it is now possible to regard the whole system of competitions, together with its pinnacle, the Olympic Games, as an efficient tool of social management and of governing the ideological process in particular.

As Afanasiev [1] put it, the production and reproduction of ideas is a result of efforts made by those who create and develop an ideology as well as those who introduce it into mass consciousness.

It is quite rightful, therefore, that the political-educational function of the Olympic movement constitutes under proper social conditions an integral part of the ideological process and that bodies responsible for the development of Olympic sports on the national level take an active part in the management of this process. The Communist Party of the Soviet Union regards sport as an important factor in the upbringing of the new man.

We should like to mention just another aspect of the problem of "Olympism and social management": the whole system of competitions, as well as any given competition, is an efficient instrument of governing the sports movement on all levels, from grass-roots training to the system of world competitions. The Olympic Games possess the greatest managing effect, as they influence both governing bodies responsible for national sports development and masses of youth drawn into sport by the example of Olympic winners.

As Borzov, a twofold Olympic Champion, rightfully stated [2], the influence of Olympic winners upon millions of young athletes is now the most important aspect of Pierre de Coubertin's concept of "pyramid" raising an athlete to the summit of sporting glory.

Here lies the main field of interaction between modern Olympism and the theme of this Congress — human well-being — sports activity inspired by the best constructive elements of Olympism and taking place under proper socioeconomic conditions is a way to health for the young people and for the people at large.

But it would be unscientific to ignore difficulties and problems of the Olympic movement, although they are caused mostly by factors of a subjective nature. To successfully overcome these difficulties, we must consequently fight against the inhuman practice of doping, for the preservation of unity of the Games despite any attempt to dismember them on the plea of opposing the "gigantism," for further improvement of the Olympic program (the work done in this field by the IOC Program Commission deserves our appreciation).

An analysis of Olympism from the political-philosophic point of view reveals a strong tendency toward the consolidation of ties between the Olympic theory and practice of the Olympic movement. We are in agreement with Landry [8] and others who say that Olympism can only be studied in depth by more than one discipline of science. An interdisciplinary approach to sport and Olympism is vital. No less vital is a well-grounded choice of directions for further studies. In our opinion, the best approach to this problem has been formulated by Falize and Erbach in their report prepared for the 1976 UNESCO conference of Ministers of Sport: "It is necessary to preserve and develop elements inherent to competitive sports and corresponding with such Olympic principles as friendship among nations, respect for laws, fair play; these elements can serve as an example for mass-scale sports, stimulate the development of the individual and educate the younger generation. This is the field to which scientific research can contribute most abundantly" [5].

The years 1977 to 1981 will no doubt see new and important developments in the field of Olympic theory as a result of the new interest in the Games brought about by their staging, for the first time in history, in a Socialist state. The XIth Olympic Congress forthcoming in 1981 will also greatly contribute to the theory of Olympism.

References

1. Afanassiev, V.G.: Ideology in the Socialist Society. Kommunist 12:1975.
2. Borzov, V.: Who needs records. Literatowinaja Gaseta, February 1975.
3. Brejnev, L.I.: Speech pronounced on the occasion of the opening of the 59th Session of the I.O.C. Sovetski Sport, June 1962.
4. Eichel, W.: Die olympische Idee und ihre gesellschaftliche Funktion in Kampf um Frieden und Völkerverständigung. Theorie und Praxis der Körperkultur 9:1970.
5. Falize, J. and Erbach, G.: Scientific Research in Sports. CIEPS-ICSPE Publication, 1975.
6. Joliff, G.M.: Les jeux olympiques, pour ou contre? Sport et Plein-Air 194:23, 1976.

7. Lagorge, G.: Les jeux atteints des nationalismes. France-Soir 23:12, 1975.
8. Landry, F.: Quelques réflexions sur l'activité physique, le sport et l'olympisme. Mouvement 10:3, 1975.
9. Lenin, V.I.: Theses on Nationalism. *In* Complete Works, 23:318.
10. Lenk, H.: Ideologie oder Mithos Stuttgart, 1972.
11. Lenk, H.: Werte, Ziele, Wirklichkeit der modernen olympischen Spiele. Schorndorf, 1972.
12. Mlodzikowski, G.: Ideologia, polityka, sport. Kultura Fiziczna Czerwiec, 1974.
13. Pavlov, S.P.: The contribution of sport to the consolidation of international understanding. Theoria i praktika fisitcheskoï koultowry 7:1975.
14. Roditchenko, V.S.: Sportliche Wettkämpfe als soziale Erscheinung. Theorie und Praxis der Körperkultur 7:1973.
15. Roditchenko, V.S.: Competitive sports as objectives and means: Informational aspects. Theoria i praktika fisitcheskoï koultoury 7:1974.
16. Szymiczek, O.: The fundamental principles of the Olympic ideology. *In* Report of the Tenth Session of the International Olympic Academy at Olympia. Athens, 1970.
17. Talaleyev, Y.A.: Socio-historical comprehension of Olympism. Theoria i praktika fisitcheskoï koultoury 2:1975.
18. Volkert, R.: Zur bürgellichen Theorie der "Leistungsgesellschaft" und zu dem dieser Gesellschaftstheorie unterstellten Modellcharakter des Sports. Theorie und Praxis der Körperkultur, 12, 1975.

Une analyse politico-philosophique de l'Olympisme

L'auteur fait état des transformations que le sport international a connues depuis le renouvellement des Jeux olympiques par de Coubertin. Il se dit d'avis que le mouvement olympique et les Jeux olympiques comme tels ne peuvent être compris ni ne peuvent être utilisés pour le plus grand bien de l'humanité que dans une perspective dans laquelle l'on considère et respecte entièrement les différentes idéologies et philosophies contemporaines ainsi que les systèmes socio-politiques qui en découlent.

Limitations of Amateurism as a Meaningful Concept in Sport

Harold J. VanderZwaag

Introduction

In an essay in a recently published book [3], I attempted an analysis of amateurism, both from the standpoint of the ideal concept and the realities of the world today. This led to the conclusion that the disparity between the ideal and the realities may be largely attributed to certain prevalent conditions in sport, which extend far beyond any consideration involving amateurism. Thus, there is reason to believe that amateurism is lacking in meaning as a significant concept in the conduct of sport programs. There may be those who will continue to work for a restoration of the amateur spirit in sport. But significant change in that direction is not likely unless there are, first of all, major departures from the current manifestation of the sporting endeavor. The purpose of this paper is to elaborate on those conditions in sport which seem to work at cross purposes to the implementation of ideas regarding amateurism. Before we proceed with the delineation of those factors which make sport what it is (or isn't), it seems appropriate to summarize that which is known about amateurism as an ideal construct.

Meaning of Amateurism

After one sorts through all the verbiage about amateurism, only a few significant thoughts remain as constants in the apparently endless discussion. The amateur is a person who participates in a given activity for the sheer enjoyment which he derives from that participation. This primary point of identification has several subsidiary implications. Amateurism is not associated with the earning of money or financial gain in any form. The idea of an avocation looms large in the role which is associated with the amateur. With that one finds the related ideas involving play,

Harold J. VanderZwaag, Department of Sport Studies, University of Massachusetts, Amherst, Mass., U.S.A.

recreation, fun, enjoyment and diversion. An amateur in sport participates in a certain game of sport because he enjoys playing that particular game. He is not primarily motivated by external reasons, whatever those reasons might be. His motivation stems from an internal enthusiasm for the game or related activity in sport. Whatever prompts that motivation does not extend beyond the individual and his sport.

These are not new thoughts regarding amateurism. In some form or another, they have been expressed for many years by those who would strive to establish or maintain an amateur sport program. Furthermore, minor variations of these central ideas have been well articulated by several theorists of the topic. The works of de Coubertin [1], Heatherington [4], Keating [6] and Weiss [11] can be consulted for more detailed discussion of amateurism as an ideal construct. Our intent here is not to belabor the discussion. The frame of reference for amateurism is fairly well known. The same cannot be said for the limiting factors of implementing amateurism in sport.

Prime Considerations in Sport

Competition

Sport, in its purest form, is competitive. Although there are many lead-up or peripheral activities in the total realm of sport, competition still lies at the core of the sport endeavor. There are those who would prefer to make sport much less competitive than it is, but that does not change the central thrust of competition in sport.

Observation leads to the conclusion that competition breeds competition. In other words, it is difficult to limit the scope of competition. The mushrooming effect of competition is very evident in the sport realm. In particular there is a strong tendency to extend the competition outside the context of the game. Within the game, competition is embodied in the striving to win. Such striving poses no real problems for proponents of amateurism. There is nothing which suggests that the amateur should not desire to win and try to win. To the contrary, the idea of the "hard fought" contest is consistent with almost any of the classic conceptions of the amateur. However, there is much competition within sport and associated with sport which extends beyond the striving to win within the context of the game.

Even before the whistle blows for the first "official" game, we find athletes competing to "make the team" and then to gain a starting position on the team. There is scarcely any way of avoiding those two modes of competition in sport if there is to be an organization according to teams. In many cases that particular kind of competition does not stop there. External factors, of a social nature, cause some athletes to compete for a team captaincy, a position on an all-star team, or a most valuable player award. In addition, there are other modes of competition in sport of a more abstract nature. Athletes may compete for the praise of the coach, to receive the plaudits of spectators, or to gain peer approval.

So, is there too much competition in sport? There may well be, but significant change is not likely to occur unless there is first of all a major departure from the structure of sport as we know it today. The question might just as well be reworded to ask: Is there too much sport?

It should be quite obvious that the pervasive nature of competition in sport and through sport works counter to the principle of amateurism. It is difficult for athletes to restrict their interest to the sheer enjoyment of playing the game when there is so much in sport which prompts other motivations. In general, it is most difficult to isolate the competitive aspect so that it does not extend beyond the boundaries of the game. Furthermore, whenever we note that extension, we also observe the first dent in the amateur armor.

Records

The world of sport is also known for its records. In fact, from one perspective it might be said that records provide the focus for organized sport. At least, it is the record which serves as the major object of attention in reporting and noting the results of competition in organized sport. Without records there is good reason to believe that the majority of sportswriters and sport commentators will soon be out of business. There are those who would probably hasten to add that such would be the most desirable state of affairs. At the same time there is absolutely no reason to believe that sport promoters, participants and followers are about to ignore records. So, we might as well face up to record keeping in sport and attempt to determine the impact of that activity in relationship to the ideal of amateurism.

Records in sport are essentially of two types. First, there is the kind which makes note of the highest level of achievement in any given activity or aspect of that activity. In turn, this sort of record can be further differentiated according to the individual or personal record and what might be called the group record. Actually, the latter also includes a whole variety of possibilities, including universal, national, conference and team records. The second principal type of sport record is found in the expression of current standing and related notations. Under this general category we find such items as the current won-loss record for a given team, conference or league standings and the notation of the individual athlete's achievement to date. That, too, involves many possibilities. A few examples are batting averages in baseball, total goals scored in hockey and rebounds in basketball. It appears that this kind of record is usually either a percentage notation or a cumulative index of some facet of performance. All of these possibilities merely point to the fact that the realm of sport offers abundant opportunity for the keeping of records.

We now turn from quantitative considerations to a look at records as a qualitative factor in the sport endeavor. There is a question as to the significance of records in motivating the athlete and assessing the merits of his participation. Although he does not place an ultimate value on records, Weiss indicates that records do have considerable importance in the conduct of sport. "Records tell us something about what a man has done. They do not tell us what he is. To know what he is, we must know what he would be. And to know this we must know what he now does" [11]. Both Schacht [8] and Fraleigh [2] are inclined to suggest that Weiss attributes too much significance to records in sport. They apparently are concerned about the extent to which records detract from the pleasure of participating for the sake of the activity without regard to any external motivation. The debate seems to be largely one involving means versus ends. On the other hand, Weiss is not really suggesting that the real importance of records is to be found in the end result. He sees records as the motivating factor in the athlete's pursuit of excellence. In his conception, an athlete is (as an athlete) whatever he demonstrates himself to be in the course of the game. This demonstration is motivated by that which he would be, namely, to be excellent in sport. That is where records come into the picture. For Weiss, and others who share his perspective, records serve as a symbol of relative excellence and prompt the continuous striving for improvement.

Even though everyone may not agree with Weiss' stance regarding records in sport, his postulation brings to light another difficulty in attempting to preserve a code of amateurism.

Those involved with sport are bent on giving attention to records. Furthermore, records serve to promote those interests which are, at best, less than those associated with amateurism. Why is that true? Records point to a result which was established within the game but which also can be used outside the game context. Many people may deplore the secondary usage of the record, but that does not change the fact that the record is there for those who would use it to serve their purposes. Use of Olympic results by the media can be cited as a classic case in points. For years advocates of the Olympic amateur ideal have been asserting that the major thrust of the Games is individual participation for the pure satisfaction of competing with and against others on an international basis. However, the media and all those who support that enterprise have never been content to let it stop there. Olympic records are used for a variety of purposes, hardly any of which could be associated with amateurism. Reporters feel quite free to report the standings of competing nations throughout the course of the Olympics. There is almost constant referral to previous Olympic results. Furthermore, individual records in the Olympics serve as a major springboard for the signing of full-fledged professional contracts. Who is to prevent all of this from occurring even if that is the desire? As long as there is recordkeeping, the records will be used as seen fit by those who have access to the records. It just so happens that sport offers abundant opportunity for the notation of records.

Equipment and Facilities

One often hears reference to the idea that sport is too commercial. It may indeed be *too* commercial; that depends upon the value judgment of the person who is assessing the nature of sport. What is more clear is that sport does have a commercial base. Any indication of excessive commercialism can only be attributed to neglect or failure to limit the scope of the commercial dimension in sport.

Why is sport tied in with commercialism? One reason can be found in the relatively strong dependence upon facilities and equipment. There are relatively few contemporary sports which do not require something special in the way of equipment and/or facilities. Furthermore, the sport facilities usually involve considerable capital outlay. Equipment expenditures can also be a significant factor in the sport endeavor. Among many other sports, skiing is a good example of the relatively large extent of investments in both equipment and facilities. In brief, it often requires money to get involved with sport. Likewise, the availability of funds is a most important factor in the maintenance of sport programs.

What has all this to do with amateurism? Cannot an organization expend funds for equipment and facilities and still offer an amateur sport program? The simple answer is "yes," but it is also an answer which is fraught with numerous uncertainties. The situation is not too different from that which was noted in regard to competition. Just as it is difficult to restrict the scope of competition, it is also a severe challenge to curtail the proliferation of commercialism in sport. When it is not restricted, we find another deterrent to the implementation of the amateur idea.

A few examples might help to illustrate the thought that facilities and equipment also represent a limiting consideration in making the case for amateurism as a meaningful concept in sport. Although the examples represent particular cases, it is hoped that they will demonstrate the explosive nature of facilities and equipment in triggering the commercial impact in sport.

In the United States, during the past 50 years, billions of dollars have been spent in constructing football stadiums and field houses, primarily for basketball. It is quite obvious that the majority of these structures were built with the spectator as a prime consideration. Collectively, these facilities symbolize much which is not amateur in American intercollegiate sport. Of course, it could again be argued that they should not exist, but the point is that they do exist. We have seen no widespread evidence that boards of trustees have made decisions to tear down such structures. Rather, they stand there as symbols of collegiate sport in the United States. Whether that is good or bad is beside the point; such facilities do not begin to epitomize the notion of amateurism. The chain reaction in the other direction is so well known that it hardly needs mention. The stadium should be used if its continued existence is to be justified. Fuller usage is considered more desirable than limited usage. This leads to efforts to advertise and other forms of marketing. Spectator appeal is, at least in part, related to winning teams. To produce winning teams requires competition with other schools to obtain the better athletes. These athletes soon recognize that they are participating for reasons other than their enjoyment of competing in a well-played game of football or basketball. We can stop there. Why does it make any sense to speak of amateurism in the context of such a chain reaction?

A similar situation exists in regard to the Olympics. It is now a well-known fact that the construction of facilities represents a major crisis for some large city every four years. The recent problems in preparation for the Montreal Games stand as a dramatic case in point. But even without any special problems the mere provision of elaborate Olympic facilities points to the inherent limitations in conducting the activities in what some people would choose to call an amateur spirit. The facilities represent all that is commercial with regard to the Olympics. That is to say nothing about the equipment expenditure for the teams of each competing country. Again we would ask: Is it realistic to expect that Olympic competitors will approach their participation in an amateur mood amidst such an outlay of funds?

One more example will be cited in an effort to demonstrate the link between sport equipment and that which is, at best, less than amateur in sport. It didn't take sporting goods manufacturers long to recognize that their sales could be stimulated through endorsements by appropriate athletes. Today, such endorsements are a widespread practice. Furthermore, in securing such endorsements, there is often no distinction between the so-called amateur and the obvious professional. Again, someone will hasten to add that this is only because the amateur code is not followed. But is it realistic to expect that any accomplished athlete will not be lured into the commercial web associated with the sporting goods industry?

Training

There is not a successful athlete or coach who does not recognize the importance of training in highly competitive sport. What is probably more frequently overlooked is the extent to which the training also affects the ability of the athlete to be amateur-like in his sport participation. Somehow or another, training and amateurism just don't go hand-in-hand. Why is that true? Also, why do we witness the incessant drive toward more and better training throughout the realm of sport?

As used here, training refers to the total preparation of the athlete for competition in some form of sport. In other words, training is more than just physical conditioning. It includes all the various components of the practice sessions. Within that context, a golfer might be said to be in training when he spends several hours a day hitting various shots on the practice fairway. The physical dimension is always foremost in training for sport, but the physical encompasses several aspects and cannot be divorced from the idea of total preparation. Weiss offers a philosophical description of training which is at least a subconscious recognition of every athlete and coach:

> Training — of which therapy is a special instance — is the art of correcting a disequilibrium between mind and body

> either by altering the vector, or, more usually, by adjusting the way in which the body functions until the body follows the route that the vector provides [11].

Within that frame of reference it is almost impossible to avoid training if sport is to be anything more than a completely informal activity, having the essential characteristics of play. However, as soon as sport is organized, it begins to take on other characteristics. That is where training comes into the picture. Organization breeds competition, and competition breeds training. Likewise, as with competition and commercialism, there is virtually no way to control the extent of training. Competitors soon realize that they must increase their efforts at training in order to "stay in the ball game" with opponents who took the initial step in augmenting their training. Furthermore, who is to prevent one from taking that initial step? That is why we today find many collegiate athletes in the United States who are in training for their sport during most of the year. The NCAA may legislate the dates for starting the formal practice sessions. But there is no apparent way to control the training efforts of a given athlete.

When athletes train extensively there are several factors which tend to draw them away from the amateur idea in sport. For one thing, there is the pure investment in time which is involved in extensive training. Almost any Olympic athlete can attest to the fantastic amount of training time which is required in order to have a good chance at qualifying for his national team. Such an investment in time almost has to have the effect of diverting the athlete away from what would normally be considered his principal concern, be that as a student or in some other occupation. Under those circumstances, is it reasonable to view the participation within the realm of an avocation? Along with the pure time factor, there is also a commitment and dedication for an athlete who is really in training. In general, these ideas are also not compatible with the notion of amateurism. Then, too, a rigorous training program is identified with the thought of hard work. Even though play might be conceived as an attitude of the mind, it is difficult to imagine that very many athletes find much fun in their training programs. Supposedly, to play is to have fun. Likewise, it would be stretching a point to imagine that a nonplay attitude in a training program will result in the sheer enjoyment of playing the game when the competition begins. In other words, it is not likely that most athletes will train merely for gaining later satisfaction in a well-played game.

The Coach

The evolution of the role of the coach has been another concomitance in the development of organized sport. Today, many people accept that role without giving much thought to other possibilities. What is that role? Basically, it is one in which the coach exerts a strong influence on the conduct of sport. Although this influence is primarily felt in the pregame preparations, or what could be called the training period, it does not stop there. It is well known that coaches, in varying degrees, also extend their role to that which takes place during the actual contest. This occurs in a number of different ways which need not be cited here. However, the coach's influence does not even stop with the termination of the game. Many of the postgame results can be attributed to the fact that the coach is a central figure in the sport endeavor. As one example, it has become common practice to identify the success of the team with the success of the coach.

In several regards, that role also limits the maintenance of an amateur standing in sport. To begin with, the mere presence of a coach causes the athlete to focus some of his attention beyond the context of "just playing" the game. There is a natural tendency for the athlete to be somewhat concerned about the reactions of the coach. This is particularly true when the coach makes the selections for the positions on the team and in the starting line-up. Furthermore, in the contemporary world of sport, this almost always seems to be the situation. Change in players' attitudes resulting from the presence of a coach can already be seen in various sport programs for youth when they make the transition from informal, pick-up games to some kind of organized sport, they at the same time become what might be called "coach conscious."

From a general perspective, it appears that coaching contributes to a shifting from internal to external considerations. That factor is heightened whenever coaches are paid for their involvement in the conduct of sport. Ideally, there is no reason why paid coaches cannot guide the efforts of amateur athletes. However, there are several factors which stand as constant road blocks in efforts to achieve that ideal.

In most cases, to be paid is also to be held accountable for services rendered. This leads to efforts to evaluate the contribution of those who are to receive the remuneration. When coaches are paid for their coaching, they, too, are subject to accountability and evaluation. Unfortunately, or fortunately (again, dependent upon one's value judgment), there is one yardstick for evaluation which is omnipresent in the realm of sport. That, of course, is the won-lost record. Sport contests produce a number of concrete therefores which primarily yield a series of wins and losses. Sport critics may spend the rest of their lives deploring the focus on such results, but that will not change the ready availability of the record as a criterion for success; it is there for those who wish to use it. Within school settings, there is frequent reference to the idea that coaches should be evaluated as teachers. However, amid efforts in that direction, the coaching record stands as one element of substantiation amid a whole range of variables and uncertainties. The truth of the matter is that many of those who are required to evaluate teachers also yearn for something more definite in the way of a yardstick.

Even when the coach is not evaluated on his won-lost record, he also faces a special problem of accountability. He is usually then evaluated on his efforts to attain that record. Kaelin probably said it all in regard to the modern attitude regarding the coach and his performance. "Give us more coaches who are willing to put their jobs and reputations on the line by going for the well-played game. Let us at least try to go out and win one for the Gipper, who has become in spite of the legend a symbol of the aesthetically dissatisfied sports fan" [5]. It is important to add that Kaelin's "well-played game" is one in which the desire to win is of prime importance. He deplores the efforts of certain football coaches to play for ties in order to avoid losing.

There is nothing in Kaelin's remarks which suggests that he is obsessed with the importance of won-lost records. To the contrary, he seems definitely intent on shifting the focus to the striving to win within the context of the game. Yet, there is a paradox in his position which points to the dilemma which faces all coaches and athletes who would prefer to be amateur-like in their involvement with organized sport. Kaelin says, "Give us more coaches who are willing to put their jobs and reputations on the line . . ." One need go no further than that statement to realize the limitation involving coaching and amateurism. Can an athlete truly pursue a sport as an avocation when his performance is directed by a coach who is pursuing his tasks as a vocation? The answer may be a reserved "yes," but there is good reason to be a skeptic, particularly when that coach is forced to put his job and reputation on the line.

Spectators

Kaelin's remarks also bring to the foreground another limiting factor in defending amateurism as a realizable goal in much of contemporary sport. We are referring to the presence and influence of spectators. This is not to infer that spectators are an essential component in sport. It is to suggest that any discussion of amateurism in sport is incomplete without noting the effects of the spectator.

Both Martens [7] and Singer [9] discuss the effect of the spectator on the athlete's performance. In turn, both refer to the work of Zajonc [12] within the framework of the "social facilitation theory." The consensus seems to be that top level performance is stimulated by the presence of spectators whereas those participants in the earlier stages of learning will be adversely affected by spectators. In either case, there appears to be a relationship between spectators and athletic performance. There has also been some conjecture that athletes are relatively unconscious of the crowd. However, most conclusions in that regard are based on statements of athletes who claim that the crowd did not affect their behavior. At the same time, one can find ample testimony in the other direction.

Regardless of any evidence in social psychology, there is good reason to believe that spectator sport is quite a different human activity than is sport in the exclusive form of participation. Furthermore, any problems associated with amateurism in sport really only relate to spectator sport. There may be those who would argue that the only true sport is spectator sport, but examination of that contention is outside the major thrust of our inquiry here.

It seems important to recognize that the influence of the spectator is not restricted to any possible effects on athletic performance. There is also the important matter of motivation for the athlete. Performance is obviously related to motivation, but it is the latter which provides the key to understanding the inherent tension between spectator sport and pure amateurism.

The spectator represents a large potential in shifting the interests of the athlete from internal satisfaction in playing the game to external rewards associated with the game. The addition of spectators does not dictate an attitude of professionalism, but it is clearly a step in that direction. Once that step is taken it is only a matter of the degree to which the professionalism will be promoted.

Weiss' description of the professional clearly points out the disparity between spectator sport and the antithesis of professionalism, namely, amateurism:

> A professional, strictly speaking, is one who takes some end other than the playing of the game to be his primary objective. His aim may be to win, no matter how, to

> entertain the spectators, to give encouragement to his government, to get publicity, or to make money. It makes no difference which of these it is. He is a professional if his play is governed by considerations which do not follow from the nature of a contest or a game [11].

Careful examination of the various possibilities, as listed by Weiss, all point essentially in the same direction — spectators. Winning, entertainment, government support, publicity and money making all have some kind of tie-in with the attraction of spectators.

An interesting question arises when one considers the possibilities for shifting the tide in the other direction — away from spectator sport. Who is to legislate that people should not enjoy being spectators of sport? Furthermore, as long as the interest is there, we will always find sport promoters who strive to capitalize on that interest.

Summary and Conclusions

Are there amateurs in sport? Yes there are, but the number is not nearly as great as many promoters of sport would lead us to believe. The primary reason for this is that most of organized sport leads the participant in the other directions. In addition, sport seems to be conducive to increased efforts toward organization. There are certain prime considerations which more or less characterize contemporary sport, with its organizational flavor. These are competition, records, equipment and facilities, training, the coach and spectators. The latter may provide the real key in understanding the limitations of amateurism because it appears that the first five are outgrowths of the spectator appeal in sport.

The importance of recognizing these limitations is to be found in the wave of publicity which is designed to dupe the public in believing that the realm of amateur sport is much larger than really is the case. Why are certain sport promoters interested in such deception? Amateurism has traditionally been associated with that which is good and pure.

It appears that only two courses of action await those who would still endeavor to change the current situation. The first is to remove those conditions which characterize modern sport. That option is far from being a realistic one because there has been so much momentum in the other direction; at this point, it is virtually like trying to "roll back Niagara Falls." The second is to work toward the elimination of the extensive hypocrisy which seems to be part of everyday existence in much of organized sport.

References

1. de Coubertin, P.: The meeting of the Olympic Games. N. Am. Rev. 170:809, 1900.
2. Fraleigh, W.: On Weiss on records and on the significance of athletic records. *In* Osterhoudt, R. (ed.): The Philosophy of Sport. Springfield, Ill.:Charles C Thomas, 1973.
3. Graham, P. and Ueberhorst, H. (eds.): The Modern Olympics. Cornwall, New York:Leisure Press, 1976.
4. Heatherington, C.: The Foundation of Amateurism. *In* Weston, A. (ed.): The Making of American Physical Education. New York:Appleton-Crofts, 1962.
5. Kaelin, E.F.: The well-played game: Notes toward an anesthetics of sport. Quest X:16-28, 1968.
6. Keating, J.: The heart of the problem of amateur athletics. J. Gen. Educ. 16:271, 1965.
7. Martens, R.: Social Psychology and Physical Activity. New York:Harper & Row, 1975.
8. Schacht, R.: On Weiss on records, athletic activity and the athlete. *In* Osterhoudt, R. (ed.): The Philosophy of Sport. Springfield, Ill.:Charles C Thomas, 1973.
9. Singer, R.: Myths and Truths in Sports Psychology. New York:Harper & Row, 1975.
10. Weiss, P.: Records and the men. *In* Osterhoudt, R. (ed.): The Philosophy of Sport. Springfield, Ill.:Charles C Thomas, 1973.
11. Weiss, P.: Sport: A Philosophic Inquiry. Carbondale, Ill.:Southern Illinois University Press, 1969.
12. Zajonc, R.: Social Facilitation. Science 149:269-274, 1965.

External Determination and Instrumentation of Sport

Hajo Bernett

Introduction

There is a pervading international opinion to interpret the critical function of historic reflection as a criticism of ideology. This view needs philosophical rationalization, since the notion of ideology can be interpreted in many ways. I support the non-Marxist notion of ideology.

It is from the point of view of the "open" society and pedagogic concern that I want to adopt the motto of the congress. Most of the speakers may consider it — as is the international custom — a noncommittal theme, but I want to take it seriously and set up two theses: First pertaining to open societies, which are constituted pluralistically, and know no binding dogmatics, in which freedom is the primary condition of "human well-being." Second the externally influenced, exploited athlete cannot learn from experience the profound meaning of well-being, namely, happiness.

My ideologically critical examination is concentrated on historical constellations of sports and systems of physical education, which have submitted the athlete to ideological impositions. In this connection five typical phenomena of instrumentalization will be presented in which references are made to the totalitarian systems which integrate sport and the athlete in their alleged "higher" aims.

It is ultimately a philosophical problem to determine the independence of sports and physical education and this will be discussed in this paper.

The Nationalist Ideology of the Gymnasts

The German gymnastics of the early 19th century, a creation of Friedrich Ludwig Jahn, devoted physical exercises to the service of national education, to the task of mobilizing the people to fight for

---

Hajo Bernett, Sportwissenschaftliches Institut der Universität Bonn, Bonn, Federal Republic of Germany.

liberty against Napoleon and to unite splintered Germany politically. This political and national setting made the gymnastic movement a patriotic movement. "Yes, to a higher aim leads our game," as it says in the song of the gymnasts.

We can historically understand such a movement, perhaps we can even defend its historic spirit, but one may criticize this irrational belief of the gymnasts as a German national characteristic related to the uniqueness and perfection of German nature. This shows a dangerous mark of ideology: the criterion of exclusivity, the delusion of national and racial superiority. During the 19th century, as long as the gymnasts followed republican and liberal ideas, the racist element of the ideology in the national character was latent.

The ideological obsession of national and racial exclusivity became of historical interest when, at the end of the 19th century, Austrian fanatics purged their association of Jews and demanded from the whole German Gymnasts Federation to adopt the discriminating "Aryan Paragraph." When the German Reich's gymnasts refused for liberal reasons, the German-Austrians resigned their membership in 1904. This action marked a further ideological prepossession: fanaticism.

Let's take a step back in our analysis. Nationalism and chauvinism are consequences of the French Revolution of 1789. This laid the groundwork for an expansion of the German nationalist ideology in Central Europe. The gymnastics of Jahn became firmly established in 1843 in Prague, but provoked an unexpected counteraction: in 1862 Czechs founded a gymnastic association of their own, the "Sokol" ("falcons"), a political movement which opposed the German national movement in Bohemia. The idea of physical and moral strengthening of a nation by physical exercises seized Croatians, Serbians, Bulgarians and Poles. The Sokol movement finally inflamed the ideology of Pan-Slavism, the racial-conscious association of all Slavic peoples. This federation of Slavic Sokol ideas in 1908 had a leading motive: its Germanophobia, hatred of the Germans. Thus the nationalist mania of German gymnastics finds on Slavic territory a highly undesirable parallel, where intolerance and fanaticism dominate. The national and racial consciousness of power, strengthened by gymnastics, incites the militant elements of a nation.

A parallel event in the West completes the setting: the gymnastics introduced in France at Jahn's time corresponds with the nationalist aims of the Sokol. After the defeat of 1871 close contacts were established based on the agreed upon hatred of the Germans. The French gymnastic clubs were dedicated to retaliation and chauvinism

— to the great annoyance of Pierre de Coubertin, the founder of the modern Olympic Games.

Criticism of an ideology demands identification of its consequences. The recent historic events make this evident: the monomania fixation on national behavior combined with the radical anti-Semitism claimed many victims. The nationalist monomania also incited chauvinism in Central Europe, which during the two world wars led to the worst excesses.

Play and Sport as a Means of Preliminary Training

A typical case of permanent degradation of sport to a usable and compliant instrument for self styled "higher" aims is the premilitary training, practiced all over the globe. A historic model up to the recent past was the martial education of the Spartan ephebes. However, in this ancient world agonistics, cult and warfare were still closely entangled. Only the gymnastics of the Athenians, the "Model of Athens," stated Coubertin, were freed from the militant purpose, and took an educational function. Nevertheless, following generations — beginning with the Romans — were to glorify and copy the model of Sparta.

Let us now put aside ancient history and look at the orientation of school gymnastics in the 19th century in Germany. After the ban of gymnastics in 1820, it was readmitted as "physical exercises" in 1842 by the Prussian King, but in Prussia's military and authoritarian state these lessons soon assumed spurious military characteristics. The disciplining methods of school gymnastics became a convenient means to train law-abiding subjects. The Prussian Minister of Education claimed "to combine gymnastics fruitfully with the military training of the nation."

This alleged "fruitful connection" is our problem: the instrumentalization by political powers, the willingness of the advocates of physical education, who have taken advantage of a professional gain in prestige at a time when their teaching had been recognized by the highest ranking authorities.

A further example from German sports history: At the end of the 19th century the creditable German "Play movement," originally a pedagogic reform movement for the regeneration of the rigid school gymnastics, drifted toward militaristic characteristics. With the ultimate favor of His Imperial Majesty, the leaders of the "Play movement" worked out training schedules, which transformed the sports and physical exercise programs of the youth to military education. With the loss of the First World War and the treaty of

Versailles (1919), which abolished universal conscription; prohibited every kind of premilitary training; and prohibited the misuse of school sports programs. Not so in public sports: the officials of the German sports clubs claimed the necessity of a sports "School of The Nation" as an indispensable "substitute" for universal conscription. In complete accordance with the Reich's Minister of Defense the sport officials even demanded a compulsory sports law for the German youth to preserve fitness for military service of the nation. These leaders were passionate sportsmen who were nationalists, who politically tended toward the Right and could not free themselves from the obsession that sports had to serve the reestablishment of national power and greatness.

A "leitmotif" of the sports education program formed the education for fitness to compete in the "political physical education" of National Socialism. Without reflecting the problem of transfer, they were convinced that the sportsman trained for courage, determination, toughness, and the will to fight also made a capable soldier. German sports was highly regarded in terms of these objectives. Due to its credence in the ancient Sparta model, it lost every aspect of sport's intrinsic value; the totalitarian system was so preoccupied with its own ideas and values of sport that it integrated them into the Nazi ideology.

On the basis of my specific field of research I could deal in greater detail with this analysis, but I prefer to draw attention to parallel phenomena in Europe. In Switzerland still today they hold the firm opinion of the necessity of a general "elementary education," which prepares those who leave school with sport skills required by military service. Here sport fulfills a military propaedeutic function, which in its universal acceptance rested unchallenged until 1947, when a Federal law introduced the principle of voluntarism. Only recently have they rejected the traditional union of sport and national defense and separated sports competition from the Military Department.

In France the officers always acknowledged the contribution of sports. In 1919 Coubertin received a letter of thanks from a French marshal, which apostrophized him to be one of the "fathers of victory." Sports in and out of school have been supported by the French Ministry of War since 1928. When military service had to be reduced to one year for economic reasons, the Ministry of War ordered a systematic "préparation militaire" (military preparation) with sports content, even at the universities.

In the 1920s in England a premilitary education at school was pursued, too, but these organizations for the advancement of future officers interfered with sports programs. Where sport exists for its own sake to such a great extent as in the "Motherland of Sport," it can't be easily misused or even used for indoctrination.

The example of Italian fascism is of interest only in passing, because the "Lex Mussolini" of 1934 worked toward a "militarized nation" not through sports programs, but merely by military means.

In the so-called socialist countries of Eastern Europe they followed the Soviet example. "Ready for work and defense," this motto of the sports badge is symbolic expression for ideological submission. Work — in Marxist doctrine — is the central value of man's life. Man is defined as a "productive resource." Will to fight is necessary to defend the workers' and peasants' state, which is the development into the perfect social system of communism, against the professed threatening aggression of imperialism. Therefore, military application of sports belongs to the standard program of education of young people. The relevance of premilitary training in the Warsaw Pact states varies with the changes of the world political situation, the indoctrination of the political system through sports prevails. Since the political system is a totalitarian one, this ideologically substantiated function has an absolute strong and binding character.

When will sport and sports education finally and universally be freed from this influence? Does sport at all have the strength and substance to emancipate itself from the directives of ruling powers and ideologies? We will now try to formulate a provisional answer to these questions.

Economic External Determination of Sport

In the 20th century the economic dependency of sports in the so-called capitalist systems is an actual fact. Here we don't talk about the direct commercial interest (e.g., the sport equipment industry), not of the market, but of the fundamental relationship between the economy and the human productive resource (physical as well as mental) which can be increased by sports. Human resources in terms of its practical value and efficiency, however, finds little support in research of contemporary history. The available documents indicate that economy primarily expects an educational contribution from sports, and not a massive "exploitation," as the marxists believe. Ignorant of the learning-transfer problems German industrialists of the 1920s financed sports, expecting that competitive sports and games would stimulate diligence, efficiency and readiness to be used by the state. Thus sports again was caught up in the whirlpool for an ulterior purpose: it was less a pretraining for defense of their country, than a catalyzer for economic recovery of the nation.

While the private economy, previously considered legitimate, fell into public disrepute in the so-called socialist states, they didn't shy at using sports and physical culture for the increase of productivity. Even in this sphere the Soviet Union became the model for its sister nations. Their experiments with the so-called sport-break in firms and factories led to the result, confirmed by physiologists, of an increase in productivity of 8% to 12%. Consequently, it was considered acceptable to define the sports rest period as a "part of production process," a definition corresponding with the ideologically claimed primacy of work.

In the "socialist" countries, for example in the German Democratic Republic, the effective relation between "productivity and sports" has been scientifically investigated since 1954. True to Lenin's words, that the "increase of work-productivity" was the vehicle for the victory of socialism, a "gymnastic break" was introduced in the state-owned firms to help to achieve the goals of the public sector of the economy.

The demands of planned economy, and the impulses of rationalization also affected the education process, and the principle of "polytechnic education" fundamentally changed sports programs. A "Seven Year Plan" (1959-1965), obligatory for all economic and cultural levels, also contributed to adjust the whole education process to the character of a work and production process.

Under the pressure of the economic situation, and due to the model of the "politechnical education" — deduced from Karl Marx — the following changes became evident in school sports programs.

1. The physical basic training concentrated on the systematic training of movement efficiency, economic functional capacity, and technically oriented skills. The qualitative attributes of motoricity of work and sports were declared identical.

2. In sharp contrast to the idea of "freedom from purpose," which was attacked as a "bourgeois lie," the principle of applicability prevailed. To put the attribution of work into practice, preference had been given to applicable sports skills. Handling gymnastic equipment and motor abilities for work were tested.

3. A strict collective education in physical education was intended for the consolidation of the foundation of the socialist working morale, which means above all a kind collective discipline.

4. In test models, which have been acknowledged as pioneer achievements, they tried to introduce effective methods of industrial

work process into sports programs. Due to the model of the Soviet Stachanow system, standards of performance were raised, "time of loss" eliminated. The principle of "intensification" tended toward a total rationalization of education.

Thus we realize that in different economic and social systems sports can suffer the same fate, if there is a lack of critical resistance.

Physical Culture and Sport as a Weapon in Class Struggle

When in the 19th century with the international workers movement workers sports was constituted, its officials adopted the end-and-means thinking of the political opponents. They separated from the existing federations to contribute to the formation of the working class by the motivating and disciplining influence of sport.

To clarify the sides a violent ideological campaign was debated. The "bourgeois" sports was assumed to be abused by the ruling class to divert the oppressed proletariat from political thinking and action, to offer an escape from economic misery and get him a harmless, compensatory satisfaction. The sports for the working class was advocated from the ideological view as: a "counter-weapon" of oppression; a proletarian physical culture program for a biological strengthening for the inevitable class struggle; a proletarian team sport for a medium of solidarity and of collective spirit at the service of social liberation. The worker-sportsmen saw themselves as a militant advance party of the proletarian revolution.

The example of the Federal Republic of Germany shows that within a democratic political system it is possible to integrate social strata and remove historic conflicts. When the German Sports Federation (1950) was founded, former officials did this without putting forward sports as a "weapon" of class struggle again. But when at the end of the 1960s the social conflicts were aggravated, stimulated by the students movement, the hatchet "sport" was revived. Sport critics of the "New Left" once more came to the conclusion that state and monopolistic dominated sports had to harmonize socially the dangerous masses with this approved means. They studied the model of revolutionary workers' sports from the times of the Weimar Republic and postulated once more the foundation of a class-specific combat organization to advance the social emancipation of the oppressed. Without any reservation against an instrumentalization of sports, the materialist faction attacked the "idealistic" idea of a "free time" sports.

Although this revival of class sport remained a digression, it reveals the constant temptation to use sports as a political means to power.

Sport as a Medium of Political and Ideological Representation

The current public function of sports is the tendency to make it a means of collective expression and subvert it to political interests. The first to recognize this use of sports was the national-socialist state.

With the organization of the Olympic Games, when the opportunity of a "propagandist effect" occurred, Hitler exceeded the moderate requirements of the organizing committee with the order to set up an oversized "Reich-sports field," and with it the first monumental structure of the Third Reich. The organizing committee admitted that all publicity and reportage were entirely financed and controlled by the Reich's Minister of Propaganda. The resultant prestige, which the Nazis hoped for, didn't fail to come — the memoirs of the ambassadors accredited in Berlin bear witness of this.

If I use a second example from the sphere of the socialist states, this is not meant to discriminate a political system, or even to put up the thesis of affinity in substance of the political Right with the Left.

In 1948 the Central Committee of the Communist Party of the Soviet Union claimed world records in the most important sports events to prove the superiority of the socialist system. Following their Soviet example, the leaders of sport in the German Democratic Republic made it their "patriotic duty" to demonstrate vividly the superiority of the entire "socialist culture" with the highest degree of sports achievement. In the GDR, too, the state party repeatedly demands by resolutions of the Central Committee to reach the world levels of performance in competitive sports and excel all political opponents in a worldwide competition between socialism and capitalism. Because of the triumphant success of this sports policy, in the GDR one is convinced of having contributed considerably to the international recognition of the state by the increasing prestige of elite sports.

With the demand for a proof of superiority the hegemonic aspirations in sport, practiced since 1900, have entered a new stage. The competitive athlete is not only a citizen of a state, but also an exponent of a political system and obliged to attest to the sociocultural quality of the system.

The Question of Independence of Sport

The result of this investigation confronts us with the alternative either to let the trend toward instrumentalization in sport take its course or to plead for the adherence to a relative independence. My political and pedagogic partiality implies the second step. So in conclusion I will try to elaborate briefly the idea of independence and self-destination.

1. The emancipatory development of the independence of sport is first of all a genetic fact. It can be proved historically that the field of play, dancing and gymnastic activities during the millennia broke away from the original cult of war and work to build structures of their own. It would make no sense genetically if current high level of sports development would return again to the ancient political instrumentation.

2. With its rapid expansion all over the world, modern sports has taken its own shape, which can be analyzed by means of philosophical phenomenology. Its essential patterns can be ascertained from historical sources, and the statements of competent representatives of the sports movement can be interpreted (Bernett). One can search for the self-experience of the participants, investigate their specific time and space experience and describe the world of experience of sports as a structure of its own, its symbolic meaning (Bouet), and thus understand the "character of a world of its own" of this sports reality (Lenk). In consideration of the special situations, models of activity and rites one has even talked of a "world exclusion" of sports (Krockow). If the phenomenon is appreciated pedagogically, the "immanent sense of sport" seems to be an educational quality of our culture, founded anthropologically (Klafki). Thus we realize how sports appears to be an original reality from the various human-scientific points of view.

3. Understanding sports in the industrial era increasingly as a complementary phenomenon, a special importance was attached to its independence. From this legitimate point of view notions have been formed in German usage like "complementary time," "countertime" and "free time." Although these notions fell into discredit due to the Left social criticism, one should not give them up. After having passed through a phase of total sociologism, sport may interpret itself again a "free time" and identify its own world with the "dimension of spare time." So sports can help to plan leisure time as a "time of liberation."

4. The skeptical talk of the total political dependence of sports should give way to the idea that the great sports organizations all over the world have a considerable political weight. They can even represent a concrete political power factor, which — like in the Federal Republic of Germany — is accepted as a "partner" of government. Despite some tendencies in an opposite direction (in-

creasing external determination of the International Olympic Committee) in democratic societies the emancipation from political reglementation can be successful. The approved principle of state subsidization, which complements self-responsibility, must not clash with this goal.

Summary

I have shown which ideological pressures led sports to dependency and have shown where the basis of its freedom and independence may be realized. Finally I turned my reflection to pedagogics: to the extent that sports may be submitted to arbitrary use as a medium and instrument, the sportsman likewise may be alienated of his personal primary motivation by "higher aims." The words of the philosopher Immanuel Kant is appropriate for sports politics. "Man never is to be regarded as a means to an end, but rather as an end in himself." In this sense, also sports can help man to achieve an autonomous personality.

Theoretical Elements for a Diagnosis of Sport

José M. Cagigal

Introduction

In this last quarter of the 20th century, sport has become one of the most remarkable human phenomena. If we were to judge its social importance or its personal interest by the space it occupies in the news media, we should have to place it in the first rank in world activities. To illustrate this, I take the following figures concerning the volume of sports news from a Spanish news agency (EFE):

From 25 to 30,000 words a day! "On Sundays," says the agency's report, "it's like the Tower of Babel. Quite apart from the usual sports news (in itself quite abundant), we have broadcast this season 3,200 special reports of 2,000 words each, on the average, which makes a total of 6,400,000 words in specially commissioned reports." It may be calculated that in the 12-month sports season, "Alfil" (EFE sports section) broadcasts nowadays a total of 14,200,000 words, including normal services and specially commissioned ones. As a basis of comparison, suffice it to say that the total volume of nonsports news broadcast by EFE each year amounts to about 50,000,000 words.

Certainly, it is not the news media that give a proper evaluation of human events; they do not even serve as an objective measurement of social behavior and interests. But they are symptomatic. The mass media are a feature of our time, and for this reason, they must be accorded special significance in our diagnosis. Indeed, if we wish to analyze the prototypes of the behavior of man today, the trends, interests, motivations, ruling habits and, consequently, the human experiences of the time we live in, we cannot scorn what the news agencies offer us in a quantitative fashion. Sport, after politics, has pride of place. Should this be interpreted as meaning that sport is the most important thing, after politics? Does sport today mean more for man than science, or economics, agriculture, medicine, industry?

José M. Cagigal, National Institute of Physical Education and Sports, Madrid, Spain.

Of course, this is not the correct interpretation. But the fact is there in all its eloquence, with its particular value, detected through a distinctive channel of our time.

People who study sport, as well as those who are involved in it (leaders, trainers, participants, etc.) are not surprised by these facts. People are also well aware of the fact that sport is a large-scale activity that inundates society: it interests all people, it is quite simply an important contemporary phenomenon. Consequently, society is under the obligation to reflect upon it; its properly qualified agencies, scientific, cultural and technical institutions, must broach the subject in all seriousness and rigor.

This, in fact, has begun to happen over the last few years, although without any serious strategy behind it. The occasional isolated efforts to deal with sport which originated at the beginning of the 20th century in different fields of knowledge (as a classic example we may mention those of the French educator, de Coubertin) were followed by more systematic efforts carried out by a variety of institutions; from the 1940s onwards, and later, particularly from the 1960s, attempts were made to plan and make research at an international level. Several international congresses of an interdisciplinary nature for the study of sport led experts in different fields and specialized institutions to revise their work programs; thus we may cite the scientific and cultural gatherings, of an increasingly specific kind, promoted by organizations such as the International Federation of Physical Education (FIEP), the International Council of Health, Physical Education and Recreation (ICHPER), the International Association of Physical Education and Sport for Women and Girls (IAPESGW), the International Association of Higher Schools of Physical Education (AIESEP), etc. It was above all after the Congress of Sports Sciences held at Munich in 1972 under the auspices of the International Council of Physical Education and Sports (CIEPS-ICSPE) that people became generally aware at a world level of the existence of the vast number of studies and research on sport.* The attention of those responsible for science in general was drawn to this and, at the same time, to the need to rethink as rigorously as possible that enormous and necessary effort. The World Congress of Sports Sciences held at Moscow

*Research from an overall scientific viewpoint had already achieved a remarkable degree of development in the 1960s, through the encouragement and guidance of specific associations such as the International Association for the Sociology of Sport, the International Society of Biomechanics, the International Society of Sports Psychology, etc.

(1974) and this International Congress of Physical Activity Sciences of Quebec City follow this line of international development.

These three congresses have been criticized for being too large and crowded and especially for trying to deal at one and the same time with too many subjects. To try to study such a complex phenomenon as sport from so many different scientific viewpoints is viewed by some as an enterprise foredoomed to failure. I shall not discuss this specific reproach. In general, those who criticize congresses do not appreciate that their main value lies not so much in the classified and often simultaneous exposition of subjects but rather — in the new efforts of discussion study and research which they promote; — in the documented "Proceedings" which are published afterwards, and in which, alongside many more or less routine papers, there always appear new and really valuable contributions; — in the personal contacts during the congress days between colleagues of similar scientific interests; — and, above all, in the opportunity to sound out the general state of research at the present time.

A look at the contributions to the Munich, Moscow and Quebec congresses leads to two conclusions of an increasingly obvious nature: science and the field of culture have discovered sport once and for all, and sport has recognized the pressing need for science. But, at the same time, each scientific field clearly applies its own methodology; the many problems of sport are thus tackled without clear definitions of the aims pursued or of the courses of action to be followed. There is a lack of interdisciplinary agreement. This astonishing and so varied phenomenon that we might call "contemporary sport" first made on science technical demands applicable to its practical needs. It is only recently that people have become aware that it is even more urgent to resort to philosophy as a necessary point of departure for interdisciplinary viewpoints without which the particular routes of progress may remain puzzling.

I

The programs for sports research which are now beginning to take shape generally take as their starting point either the best possible arrangement of a number of papers or studies undertaken and carried out in response to the particular demands of a given situation, or, at the most, a general classification of the areas of sport, of a more or less a priori or propaedeutic nature. Such classifications, meritorious, necessary and in a sense illuminating as they are, are not necessarily based on a fundamental theory or concept of sport.

As a recent example we may take the publication of a policy of sports research launched by a body that plans and does the study of sport with genuine seriousness and concern for coordination: *Priorities for Research in the Sciences of Sport* ("Schwerpunktprogramm der sportwissenschaftlichen Forschung") drawn up by the Federal Institute for Sports Sciences (Bundesinstitut für Sportwissenschaft) in the Federal Republic of Germany. It is not my intention to write a single line of criticism of this program. I use the publication of this research plan, which came out in March 1976, precisely because it is representative of one of the most serious interdisciplinary scientific movements which have emerged recently in sport.

The list of priorities in each specialty is expressed as follows:

I. Performance and improvement of performance
- Specific training theories for different sports
- Bases and system of improvement of performance
- The medicine of performance
- Structure of clubs and associations
- Aspects of the personality peculiar to sport
- Simultaneous, immediate and rapid information in training and teaching
- Routine diagnosis of motor performance
- Sports injuries and lesions
- Cooperation between school and club
- Sport as a part of the curriculum in primary education

II. Regeneration through training

III. Sport as a therapeutic measure (e.g., diabetes, high blood pressure, patients after a heart infarct or with coronary conditions)

IV. Role of the sports teacher and trainer

V. Play and sport in nursery schools

VI. Sport in old age

VII. Sport for the disabled

VIII. Preparation of a thesaurus in sports medicine

IX. Initiation of a Management Information System

X. Problems of improving investments

XI. Planning facilities and equipment
- Standardization problems
- Sports facilities for schools and institutions of higher learning
- Sports facilities for leisure time activities

XII. Working out of an information system in the field of sports and leisure facilities

The basic technical scientific topics are classified under the following general areas:

1. *Sports medicine*
2. *Science of education*
3. *Psychology*
4. *Sociology*
5. *Theory of movement and training*

The authors of the document criticize their own approach as such: "Since the division of subjects at the Federal Institute for Sports Sciences makes a classification of certain research topics difficult, such topics are classified *pragmatically* within the existing disciplines. For example, the Philosophy of Sport, the History of Sport and also Sports and Politics are classified as part of the discipline of sports pedagogy, while Economics and Sports Law are classified under Sports Sociology."

This explanation makes the situation quite clear. The *Bundesinstitut für Sportwissenschaft* realistically adopts the pragmatic position of classifying the scientific matters in whatever way the practical requirements demand.

The organizers of the International Congress of Physical Activity Sciences of Quebec City have also made a considerable effort in order to achieve a proper arrangement of the sciences, and finally, have chosen a practical, propaedeutic classification which aims to be in agreement with most currently valid scientific views.

It may be that efforts to review the currently valid stereotypes are just beginning. This shows that we urgently need a theory of sport, a theory of physical activity in general, worked out with the help of all the facts that the different areas of knowledge can provide. Logically, however, such a theory is prior to these areas of knowledge, for it is the presupposition of the scientific paths that are to be followed.

In a preparatory document for the conference of sports ministers held in Paris in April 1976, Falize and Erbach [2] suggested a "conventional" division of research into the following areas:

1. *Technical* (learning processes, training, in accordance with efficiency principles).

2. *Fundamental* (taking as a starting point the reality of the human being, his growth, development and personality).

3. *Applied* (to physical activity, play, sports in general).

4. *Operational* (with practical verification and possible correction of the knowledge).

Research is to take as its starting point the special status of *man in movement* and the interrelated sequence of human behavior patterns and social realities derived from this state.

Without going into the practical problems that this and other classifications raise, such as for example the demarcation lines between *applied* and *technical* research, with their mutual dependence and interferences, it is clear that this is merely a "conventional" classification, as the authors themselves state.

These divisions of research should be indifferently applied to the three main areas of which sport is composed: "elite sport," "school sport" and "sport for all."

The authors obviously sketch a theoretical framework which may be systematically applied. However, they do not seek to justify their theoretical classification; this is by no means absurd, it only corresponds to a series of self-evident realities. But, for example, is not school sport to a certain extent part of major sport-for-all classifications? Does not the practice of sport in school find in sport for all one of its most powerful educational values? Is it not the case that the separation of school sport from other kinds of sport corresponds to an elementary sociological reality which regards the school as a social unit, rather than as a structure in which sport is only somehow qualitatively different (a quality resulting from a distinct, clearly defined human attitude)?

Despite their shortcomings, classifications of this type are useful, we might almost say necessary. I do not know if it will ever be possible to start from basic principles and not from "pragmatic" frameworks of a "conventional" or stereotyped nature. But it is by no means useless that we should realize and acknowledge that such an approach is provisional.

Moreover, the same type of applied research may present different characters and lead to different results, according to the aim pursued, especially in the field of the sciences of behavior.

The personality conflicts resulting from a prolonged and demanding agonistic situation may be approached with a view to readjusting personality, finding a return to equilibrium so that an athlete can continue competing and achieving maximum performance. The same conflicts may be studied in order to eliminate the sportsman's state of anguish, but also in thinking of his life outside sport.

A study of a boxer's or wrestler's motivation before a contest may be conducted with a view of winning, of acquiring the habit of bettering himself for important fights. The type of psychology which studies this sportsman's behavior at the time of an all-important competition is psychology geared toward championship performance. The champion interests the society (club, federation) or Society. On the other hand, if psychology studies the motivation of a boxer/wrestler with a view of forming in him generally responsible habits, of getting him used to wanting to better himself, both in important and unimportant fights, of arousing and adjusting in him motivated mechanisms which may be used on any occasion in life, then it is becoming a science applied to man in sport, but in service to man himself.

The feasibility of different approaches in certain areas of research does not imply that they stand in opposite directions. The rationalization of this standpoint must not be taken to the extremes. In most cases, the two approaches complement each other. "A sportsman who is trained so that when competing he is in full control of his emotions and is capable of giving his best performance ('man in service of sport') comes to learn a form of self-control that may be of advantage to him in other situations in life ('sport in service of man')" [1].

A responsible policy in the scientific planning of sport should take into account not only the specific goals of each particular study, but also what it is intended to obtain in general with the development of the science of sport and what in the long run man himself may be led to achieve as a result of research findings.

But if science applied to sport may be adversely affected by a lack of theory, the effects on sports action and organizational policies are even more marked. At least a piece of applied research has its results and its data which are there available for use at any time. Any work in science that is carried out with scientific integrity is valid. However, this is not necessarily the case with all policies. A sports organization properly applied to the requirements of society and to the human needs of its time usually proves to be highly beneficial. But an organization based on old-fashioned objectives and lacking in theoretical verification may have catastrophic effects on the society of its time.

There are still, for example, many national sports organizations which, apart from owing their success to historical and social conditions which no longer have any validity for the present, justify their sports policy plans with the old platitude that you get more champions from a large mass of players. They are stuck fast in the romantic concept of Coubertin's pyramid. They even sometimes seek out apparently modern ideas based on the quest for a balanced development of sport to be achieved by insuring that "elite" sport does not grow out of proportion with sport for the masses or "sport for all." They are not really set for a serious intrinsic analysis of what is really meant in today's world by "elite sport," "sport for all," "educational sport" and other concepts which are constantly and loosely used. The consequences of this lack of rigor — in the last analysis, this lack of responsibility — means constant blind fumblings, disoriented planning and crises in the structures of sport.

To this must be added the need that the governments of nations — politics in its specific sense — justify their propaganda activities with humanistic and educational slogans. The claim that first-class competitive sport is nowadays the natural result of the development of sport at grassroots level undertaken for the sake of education and human progress sounds like blarney, even when it is wrapped up in solemn rationalizations. Top-class competitive sport today is just one more political propaganda weapon to be wielded in national dialectic; it is artificially encouraged and is quite alien to the task of sports education, although not incompatible with it.

II

One legitimate starting point for a theoretical consideration of a social phenomenon is to leave aside its operative structures and analyze the way a man behaves toward that social phenomenon. In the case that concerns us, sport, we shall have to place at the center of our analysis, not the abstraction termed sport, but the real protagonist, the *sportsman*, or, more strictly expressed (in order not to fall into stereotyped conceptions as a result of the linguistic phenomenon of specification), *the man who experiences sport.*

Today, sport may be experienced in widely differing ways; as entertainment, as a health-producing activity, as a form of release, as mere self-expression, as confrontation with the self, as a profession, as a social activity to be promoted, as a labor activity, etc. Moreover, the word "sport" or "sportsman" has many different meanings. A resident from any of our city districts may think of himself as a sports enthusiast because he attends his club's football matches every Sunday. But this same citizen also calls the man who goes skiing in the mountains every weekend a "sports enthusiast."

Here we have two very different forms of human behavior: sitting on the terraces to watch a spectacle and making an intense physical effort; and yet the same concept describes them both — "sports enthusiast."

It is plain that sport is not a term with a single meaning; it refers to different human behavior patterns and to disparate social realities. But there is something common to all the meanings, something which, if it does not lie in the individual way of experiencing sport, does point to a social area and a unifying dynamism which the man in the street accurately intuits and retains as a single reality.

Participants and Spectators

In the first place, there are two different ways of experiencing sport: as an active participant or as a spectator. The former uses his body, or rather he *is*, when in action, *his own body expressing his entire personality*.

The word sport has been defined in many different ways. In traditional definitions, the first predicate was usually the concept of play. In the second place were its competitive nature and physical exercise. Nowadays, the play attribute is more controversial. I shall not discuss the subject here. The fact is that the primary attribute of sport is now *activity* or exercise. This is why chess and bridge are less and less commonly regarded as sporting activities. Sport is action, praxis; it is man in movement, making active use of his locomotor apparatus (wholly or partially).

The active sportsman (strictly speaking, this expression would be a tautology) may have through his praxis different aims and appetencies (play, health, self-expression, work, etc.), but basically he is a man whose behavior gets its specific character from one kind of action — sporting action.

But, leaving the personal, individual aspect, sport is, socially considered, made up mainly of people who are *not active*. It is through them and for them that so much is spoken nowadays about sport, that the pages of the newspapers are filled with sports news and that sports broadcasts are made. This majority to whom the sports messages are addressed cannot be considered not to belong to sport, because it consists of people who participate in and support sport in our time; it experiences sport, and sport also belongs to it. It is an integral part of sport.

It would be a utopian idea foredoomed to failure to try and invent a new concept alien to that of sport in the activity sense in order to include in it the spectator, who, from the standpoint of locomotor sporting action, is passive — i.e., he does not participate in such activity, he does not experience sport through it.

Nevertheless, the man in the street nowadays uses the word sport to refer almost indifferently to both participants and spectators, and in matters of linguistic rightness, ordinary people are not to be corrected.

There is no alternative other than to accept that both participants and spectators form part of that wide-ranging, many-sided surprising phenomenon we call sport and to divide those involved merely for the sake of analysis and clarity into two main groups: *active participants* (players) and *spectators.*

In studies and theoretical investigations about sport of a more or less traditional nature, the qualities or characteristics which define sport refer only to the former — the protagonists. So, for example, when Coubertin attributed to sport the qualities of "initiative, perseverance, intensity, a quest for improvement and contempt for danger"; or when Carl Diem defined sport as "a form of play that bears within it value and dignity, practised with dedication, subject to rules, integrating and uplifting, and desirous of achieving the best possible results"; when Melchiorri said that "sport is a discipline which is first applied to the soul and then, by means of the appropriate technique, is transferred by man to his body in order to free himself from mechanical submission to the physical world" . . . "an activity of the spirit whereby man rids himself of a primary incarnation anguish through a rigorous procedure that renders it analogous and of similar dignity to other pure spiritual activities, such as science, art and morality"; or at a more recent date, Slusher, when he describes sport as an opportunity to obtain "authentic being, a genuine existence, through spontaneous, free activity, with progressive self-control and improvement." All these and other qualities more or less traditionally applied to sport refer directly to the active sportsman, to the man who *plays*, not the man who *watches.*

From this identification or configuration of sport as a definite kind of human behavior arose the tendency to reject as sport everything other than this activity, such as the behavior of the spectator. "That is not sport; it is something else," people said; and it was not worthwhile saying anything more. In this way, for a certain period of time, a few authors thought they had found an easy way of settling the matter. But this purist, romantic, somewhat a priori attitude involved turning one's back on a vast phenomenon which, as the 20th century advanced, continued to grow as a sports entity or structure. The problem, instead of seeming clearer, had become more complicated.

Amateurs and Professionals

This is another traditional dichotomy in the treatment of sport. If we wished to deal with this subject in depth, we would have to fill many pages which would not be directly relevant to the essence of the issue at stake in this paper. Nevertheless, it is a topic which has been the object of sports controversies throughout the 20th century.

Between two sports enthusiasts who play basketball, and whose behavior on the court may show no practical difference, it is nevertheless possible to make distinctions based on the aims of their behavior patterns which may be different in terms of human attitudes, i.e., as a personal outlook and position in their respective sporting behavior: one may play to earn money, the other, to enjoy himself.

This picture is too simplistic; many professionals indeed do enjoy themselves as they perform. For his part, the amateur may enjoy himself, also act and better himself in order to assert his personality, for the sake of prestige, or to obtain some psychological gratification; perhaps, deep down, unconsciously, to become a professional (where professionalism is accepted, or otherwise its equivalent in social stability or prestige).

A complex piece of human behavior, such as participation in a reasonably high-level competitive match, may thus be moved by many different motivations, such as the impulse to enjoy onself, the desire to be socially accepted, the wish to improve one's health, obtaining the admiration of a certain person or persons, or occasionally, a compensatory response to a humiliation which has given rise to feelings of inferiority, or a search for social relations. At a deeper level, the motivations may be a series of impulses to action produced by complex childhood learning processes, unconscious responses to old Oedipian provocations, to diffuse identifications and introjections, to the breakdown of various frustrating mechanisms and, in more ordinary language, an urge for success and glory, for self-assertion, or merely an impulse to action. There are usually multiple causal factors involved in a complex, culturized piece of behavior, such as the participation in a football match, a basketball game, etc.

If a football player is offered the additional incentive of earning money, this will become another motivation that will come into operation with the others, giving rise to certain partial changes in his behavior when he competes; but it does not necessarily eliminate the other motivations; it completes them and makes them usable from a new standpoint. Financial benefit may make an athlete change his life and cause him to take up sport as his profession. Then, from a social point of view he will become a professional footballer; but his specific activity on the field is not moved exclusively by the desire to earn money or provide his life with economic security. His original enthusiasm, his desire to be admired, and in the deepest patterns of his behavior, his childhood behavioral links, may indeed subsist and continue to operate. The professional footballer is not radically different from the amateur. The main difference lies in his social status and in the role accepted by the professional. They are sociological rather than personal differences.

The attaching of excessive importance to the amateur vs. professional conflict comes originally from the difficulty that romantic writers about sport found in ridding themselves of the a priori platitudes inherited mainly from Arnold and taken up wittily by Coubertin, according to which sport is something highly noble, replete with moral values, chivalry and idealism — the very ultimate in human behavior. Coubertin even went so far as to speak of the "religio atletae." This trend was furthered by an excessive idealization of the ancient Greek competitors, which began to contrast with the vulgar interests that gradually began to contaminate the desire to play the game of 20th century sportsman, even Olympic competitors.

An excessively elementary, Cartesian conception of Olympic purity was the second, practical determining factor behind the conversion of the amateur vs. professional conflict into a key issue in 20th century sport. The history of the praises of "amateurism" — a concept which, given the socialization of sport, can only be defended on class grounds — the "Olympic oath" (later the Olympic "promise"), the famous rule 26 and its rhetorical development of long and unintelligible explanations, etc., all serves to show to what extent a relatively peripheral aspect of sport itself has managed to become a sacred dogma linked to its very survival.

It seems as if a whole ancient and diffuse tradition of a dualistic, Arian nature, deeply rooted in Western civilization and especially in its ideas on education, came to bear on 20th century sport in order to divide it into good and bad. It was good, pure, unsullied and heavenly if there was no money involved. When money made its appearance, however, sport immediately became evil, faithless, corrupt and infernal. Those in charge of international Olympics are still struggling to shake off this phantom. The Olympic leaders are entrusted with two responsibilities of a quite different order which, at the present time, are associated with different attitudes; hence the conflict. On the one hand, they are the official defenders of the Olympic ideological heritage, that series of human, educational values incarnated in the disinterested practice of sport: nobility, chivalry, fair play, the Olympic truce, the urge to better oneself, the improvement of the race, etc. On the other hand, they are the official organizers and controllers of the Olympic Games which take place twice (summer and winter) every four years. These Olympic Games or Olympiads are the most important sporting spectacle in the world today. This means that they are the very summit of sport as spectacle. Consequently, all the accretions and byproducts which have gradually become attached to sport as a result of its spectacular nature — among these, we may mention political propaganda and financial benefit — exert their full effect on the Olympic competition, too. In their dilemma of which position to choose, the Olympic leaders decided to defend the slogan of Olympic purity, and in so doing, quickly found themselves in a blind alley. The interests attached to the Games as a tremendous spectacle do not disappear, for they cannot; quite the contrary — they are increased and, therefore, simply camouflaged. The result of all this is the diatribes, the sacred rhetoric which is heard when someone is disqualified as a professional, or for having accepted financial rewards. Participants are required to promise that they will never participate in sport for the sake of money, and injustices are committed. But, what is worse, the image of official sport, instead of being enhanced through such attitudes, is discredited. People begin to speak of the hypocrisy and deceit of the Olympics.

It is quite inexplicable that persons of an undoubtedly high cultural level should not realize that they are looking at a mirage. Whatever values we may find in playing sport, be they educational, hygienic, social or others, will continue to exist as long as sport is still indulged in for its own sake. Nowadays there is a real mushrooming of movements that follow this trend of stressing the spontaneous development of sport played for its own sake, such as "the other kind of sport," "sport-for-all," "sport for the masses," "leisure sport," "sport as education," etc. The spectacular nature of the Olympic competitions has no longer anything to do with this spontaneous, active reality of sport, which, far from being in decline, is constantly expanding as a movement quite separate from top sports competitions.

It is time that the problem of amateur and professional status, which undoubtedly exists and causes disputes, be put in its proper, secondary place. It is not the center of sport. It is not the key to its salvation or its disappearance. It is one more problem, an important one, that requires clear thinking and resolute action. But it is not the cornerstone of sport.

The distinction between the active sportsman who acts and the passive one who watches and, as a subdivision of the active type, the distinction of the sportsman who plays as a means of earning his living — the professional — and the sportsman who plays for other reasons — the amateur — all show a certain degree of analytic or classification fad. Especially in the second classification, the limits are indeed not clearly drawn. When does a footballer who receives bonuses for each match join the professional category? Officially, from an association standpoint, there is a stage or category in which he is termed a "professional." But even then, at certain competitive levels, is this really the case? Can it always be said that this is his real profession? And of those who swell the ranks of the amateurs, just how many are there who spend all their time playing sport? How many are there who would give it up if they did not hope to become professionals?

A sportsman who plays sport with professional status, or rather, who experiences sport *as* professional, adds something to the way he used to play it, but does not substantially change his attitude just because he is earning money or because sport is now his job. There are other elements in his professional situation, other realities which, in that world of professionalism, will involve him in a much more profound change of attitude.

The Theory of Sport as Individual Praxis as Opposed to Sport as Spectacle

A professional footballer (or an American basketball player, a Japanese baseball player, or a professional cyclist, whether he be Belgian, Dutch, French, Italian, Spanish or Portuguese) plays his sport subject to new factors that did not exist when he was an amateur. He has a contract to honor; he is subject to labor legislation and may also be penalized. His performance must exceed a certain basic required minimum, if he does not want to risk his contract being annulled. He is subject to criticism and pitiless demands from his employers and his fans and finds himself involved in top-level propaganda. His contract obliges him to play even when he does not feel like doing so and to train vigorously and at regular intervals. His performance has gradually become serious and has lost its play character. He is said to be a "professional player," a curiously paradoxical expression. If he lives up to what was expected of him, he will get new contracts; if he goes beyond these expectations, he will become a champion, an idol, and his price will rise. The Dutch footballer Cruyff managed to earn, between contracts, bonuses and commercial fees, valued at more than 30,000,000 pesetas ($500,000 U.S.) between 1975 and 1976, according to figures published in the newspapers. The Valencia Football Club has paid 200 million pesetas in new contracts to footballers for the 1976/77 season. The American Boston Celtic basketball players earn over $200,000 a year. In 1974, American football produced over $4 million in television rights. The gate money at the heavyweight championship fight between Muhammad Ali (Cassius Clay) and Frazier in 1975 amounted to over $6 million.

Regardless of the greater or lesser accuracy of some of these figures, it is obvious that at top levels of professional sport, fabulous quantities of money are at stake. This means that at such levels, the sportsman's attitude toward sport and his personal frame of mind are determined by new and powerful motivational variables.

Where does the success of top competitive sport come from? Occasionally, it has been claimed that it is all a question of artificial social structures built up by major economic and political interests. There is a great deal of truth in this; but these artificial structures would not remain standing if they were not founded upon realities inherent in the phenomenon of sport itself.

The professional sportsman does not experience a substantial change of attitude merely because of the money. What engulfs him in a new world of interests, choices and decisions is a much more complex reality. What is it in sporting behavior that gives rise to such gigantic multinational structures, such manifestations of loyalty to international leaders — of which there is not the slightest sign in the world of politics — and such veneration for the idols?

As a starting point in the search for a reply, may I be allowed to include at this juncture a brief metaphysical excursus taken from my book *Sport in Contemporary Society:*

> Sport is a typical, specific human activity; it is an anthropological event. The protagonist or centre of this event is the sportsman: a human being who behaves in a characteristic way, specified by a certain kind of "praxis" — liberating exercise, of a play type, and a coming to grips with his own personal capacities, oriented towards competition. Any being, apart from being in itself, is in an outwards direction; it may be "denominated" (in the

terminology of Scholastic philosophy) or "illuminated" (Heidegger). It ceases to be an "ontic" reality and becomes an "ontological" one (id.). This "illumination" or mental categorization which proceeds from man, does not penetrate the whole reality of being; it touches being in a partial, tangential, peripheral manner, and generally, as a result of this tangential contact, being is "denominated" and described. Modern psychology has brought to a high stage of development the ego-environmental binomial — the environment which influences and partially transforms the ego, the ego which gives itself to and communicated with the environment; and a third relation, when the environment is another man: the ego is mentally categorized, described, denominated, and in some way classified.

These thoughts could be expressed in the "ego-circumstances" terminology of Ortega. The circumstances condition and partially transform the ego. The ego in turn influences and transforms the circumstances; and finally, the circumstance man describes, mentally categorizes, situates and circumscribes the ego. On this third dynamic, which relates exclusively to the human circumstance, rests the whole existential philosophical basis of the human sociological relation, which was later to give rise to all the theory of roles, status, stereotypes, etc.

The way in which being — specifically man, and in our case, the sportsman (man with this particular "praxis") — is touched, shaped, illuminated and "circumstantiated" by the other-circumstance, is conditioned by some primarily visible, or rather manifest, self-evident factor in being itself. The point of contact of the illumination that comes from the milieu is not just any point or aspect; it is something primarily apprehensible, some original manifestation. This primary manifest factor or category of the sportsman is his status as a spectacle, i.e., his spectacular potential or capacity. Sports "praxis" is plainly a visible, sensorial one, in the same sense that human theatrical activity is. Sport is a genuine, fundamental dramatic phenomenon. For this reason, the first description it receives from the outside is spectacle. It is not that the sportsman aims at making his performance spectacular. He is moved by a different motive. But what he does is immediately spectacular in nature. The first searching gaze that alights upon him from the outside and goes in for no abstraction or intellectualization, views him as spectacle. That is why he is so classified. The theatre, especially in the case of plays that are conceptually not very complicated, is also a spectacle from the first external viewpoint. But the difference is that the theatre is in its very origin essentially spectacle. Sport is not. Sport is spectacle as a result of a description from the outside. The theatre is a concrete species of the genus spectacle. It is *spectacle* as theatre. Sport is only spectacle as a first description. Its origin is found, not in spectacle as sport, but in *sport* as spectacle. The sportsman, with the "praxis" associated with him, bears, whether he likes it or not, a spectacle within him; he is a spectacle-bearer, he displays it. Many consequences are to be deduced from this first predicate of spectacularity.

The man in the street, in spite of the enormous development undergone by sport, has not invented a different word to describe spectacular sport; he continues to call it simply "sport." Without intellectualization or abstractions, the man in the street with his direct form of expression respects the primary display phenomenon which emerges from sports "praxis" itself.

Where does sport obtain this astonishing capacity to gain respect and admiration, to be sought, argued over and even paid for? Undoubtedly from the spectacular nature of the "praxis" itself. Man trying to better himself through his physical abilities, and thus competing with himself or an opponent, exerting himself to achieve ever-new triumphs, is a spectacle; what is more, since this spectacle is a dynamic of elementary forces — for such is man's physical strength — it is intelligible for every mentality, for the learned and the ignorant alike. Sport has then a universal spectacular attraction.

Consequently, the first basic classification we must make, on the basis of the very nature of the sports phenomenon is: *sport as "praxis"* and *sport as spectacle.* Essentially, sport is "praxis"; from an extrinsic description, it is above all spectacle; from this, performance sport is derived, in response to the needs of society. This may in turn lead to sport as a profession, as an exhibition or display, as an instrument, etc.*

The key to the great importance that sport has taken on lies in its spectacular nature. This is why there are idols and money. And this spectacular quality has been discovered by modern states and is exploited by them for political purposes. The Olympic Games are perhaps the most important *peaceful battlefield* of our time. Top performance sport has developed, above all, in response to a need that is certainly artificial, but nevertheless genuinely urgent: a need to find top champions and achieve striking results which will serve as easily understandable propaganda for the masses. International dialogue through sport is a source of prestige. But since it is not possible to carry on a sports dialogue in a decorous manner without great champions, there arises an urgent need to cultivate them. This is how the champion-producing "factories" arise, with their paid or "subsidized" or "militarized" or "nationalized" sportsmen. In the top-level competitive world sport, champion "breeding" has become established, with sportsmen segregated from the mass of ordinary practitioners in a more or less artificial sort of life, with all its consequences. Are these champions a natural product of ordinary people who play sport? To maintain such a thesis would be tantamount to assuming that those who study sport were childishly credulous.

However, precisely because of the vitality and the biological and human significance that lies in sport in its original state, in the very decade in which *sport as spectacle*, *elite sport*, *sport as achievement* has expanded so much, movements in support of spontaneous sport have also developed. Witness the success of "sport-for-all," "the second kind of sport," "sport as leisure," etc., already mentioned previously.

---

*In the Spanish original, the author includes at this point a note in which he points out that the translation of the word "espectáculo" into other languages, particularly English and German, may offer some difficulty since the word "spectacle" is not an entirely satisfactory equivalent. While this may be so, it is questionable whether other substitutes such as "show," "display" are generally any better, though they have been used in specific instances in the text. In general the meaning should be plain from the general sense of the argument, and from the following explanation, with which the author completes the footnote: "When I speak here of *sport as spectacle*, I refer to sport in so far as it is spectacular and bears within itself spectacular properties. What we call here sport as spectacle is sports activity, aims, methods and structures from the viewpoint of this spectacular nature of sport." (*Translator's note.*)

This coincidence confirms the thesis that at the beginning of the last quarter of the 20th century, the concept of sport refers to two major diverging tendencies which, as they develop and become structured, gradually become quite dissimilar entities, each driven by quite different requirements. *Sport as "praxis,"* on the one hand, based on the human need for competitive play movement in the form of a particular manner of expression, which may include spontaneous and organized sports alike, but presupposes a deliberate piece of behavior aware of the human and social values of sport, such as health, relaxation, entertainment, social integration, etc. And on the other hand, in a different direction, *sport as spectacle*, satisfying different requirements than the former kind of sport, motivated by major political propaganda and by economic and commercial interests. In this dichotomy of sport as "praxis" and sport as spectacle, which is much more essential than the amateurism vs. professionalism one, we may include other types of not specifically professional spectacular performance, such as top competitors in countries that do not permit professionalism but where fundamentally, sports performance in top competition is motivated by similar claims as in countries with structures that allow professionalism.

These two main aspects are not entirely independent; they condition and influence one another, and sometimes even interfere with one another. But they follow different paths and fulfill different functions. There is no need to set one against the other; rather, they should be encouraged to thrive together in society. Their conceptual convergence — both are called "sport" — will continue nonetheless to cause problems and confusion.

III

The effect of so-called *sport as spectacle*, and the gigantic, overpowering structures it supports, on personal behavior is so great that the difference between the spectator's experience and the protagonist's (between the public and the players) is vastly reduced and almost eliminated in practice by the powerful dichotomy of *sport as praxis* and *sport as spectacle.*

The main protagonist, the player, is on the field or the court, running and sweating. The spectator sits on the terraces. However, he identifies himself with the protagonist in such a way that he projects upon him a part of his own experiences, longings and expectations. The player-protagonist and the spectator may be quite a distance apart physically, but they are closely linked as people. The vicissitudes of their experience coincide: both of them exult in the scoring of a goal, feel frustrated when they make a mistake, protest against an unjust decision and take courage when the game gets tough. After a win, the spectator uses the first person plural: "we've won." In defeat, owing to a well-known defense mechanism, this grammatical form is sometimes replaced by the third person plural: "they've lost." But this is an unimportant exception to the general link of experience which brings the spectator and the active participant to share the same sports adventure.

In the places where sport as spectacle occurs on a large scale, the spectator thinks about his team's victory all through the week; he contributes personally to maintaining the organization of sport with his daily offering when he buys his sports newspaper, when he pays his club membership fees and with his constant presence, encouragement and expectations.

It is necessary to investigate more closely, and if possible measure, to what extent this powerful social force of sport as spectacle, vigorous and dominating, like a colossus feeding on its own needs, obligations, interests, functions and structures, affects and conditions all those who participate in it, i.e., all those who *experience* sport from the standpoint of *sport as spectacle*, moved by it in such a way that they become distinct from those who live their sports experience as players, in a different environment and with other motivations, needs and purposes. That is, we should have to see to what extent the active sportsman who takes part in sport as spectacle — the professional player, for example, is closer in his experience to the spectator than to the active sportsman who has nothing to do with the sporting spectacle.

Apparently, from a physical viewpoint, all active sportsmen — the participant in sport as spectacle and the mere amateur player — perform the same piece of behavior. But from a human viewpoint, the top competition sportsman experiences a quite different world.

The player of *sport as spectacle* (whether professional, Olympic, subsidized, holding a scholarship, etc.) in his competitions, training, refusal to indulge in bad habits, etc., is characterized by one fundamental attitude: he seeks maximum performance. But it is no longer a mere personal urge to improve, to better himself, that he felt when he took up sport and which was an incentive to excel in his performance and be discovered and selected. Now, apart from the traces that remain of that initial desire for self-improvement, he feels a need of maximum performance imposed upon him by his club, his association, his trainers and his fans. If he fails, he risks losing his economic support or his contract. But not only this: a new series of social demands have joined the reasons for his behavior, and so there comes a time when he has no choice other than to go on training, exerting himself, trying to beat records and better himself. His fans, his club companions, his fellow countrymen and his relatives all become one of the habitual motives of his behavior. In his practical ethical code, motivations such as "not to disappoint such a lot of people," "I can't fail now," play an increasingly decisive part. It is the force of the social role that through its performance, its necessity and its routine, gradually takes up more room in his personality; he cannot fail in this role without risking a social and also personal breakdown.

The sportsman who competes in spectacular sport has changed the pleasure of sports play into a job, with all the ingredients of psychological transformation that compulsory work implies. There will be days and weeks when training will bore him, when family problems will make it difficult for him to play. However, he will have to overcome them, because of his obligations toward society or toward his club or association, because of his personal principles of accepted responsibility; in just the same way as an office worker, a manual worker or an executive cannot simply not turn up for work. He owes himself now to this world of sport as spectacle. His sporting actions, his shot at the basket or at the goal, his high jumps over the bar have a human aspect, a vital attitude quite different from that of those who play sport for pleasure, spontaneously and without compulsion, even if formally there may seem to be a similarity. They are quite distinct behavior patterns.

Just as the spectator identifies himself with the protagonist and needs him for his weekly psychological nourishment and thus gets rid of part of the trivial and sordid aspects of compulsory everyday life with his hopes for victory, the active player also extracts the nourishment for his sporting existence from the spectator and comes to need his encouragement and admiration more and more. He relies on the news reporter's praise and pays the closest attention to forecasts of victory or defeat. He is immersed in a social dialectic from which he cannot free himself; he serves a powerful, solid structure which he can only shake off by giving up playing sport. We might almost say that he is a prisoner of his condition as a sportsman, of his public, of propaganda and its pitiless rules, of his own acceptance of a social role and, underlying all this, of certain social infrastructures dependent upon economic and political forces.

This talented sportsman one day took a train called sport as spectacle and, while carrying out the same exercises and apparently behaving in the same way as before, after a time found himself in a strange place, with different surroundings, where he will now be obliged to live. He is now much closer to his public, his managers and superiors than to his former sports companions who did not take the train.

In this kind of classification, there is always a danger of radical interpretations. Despite the plainly different nature of the two kinds of activity, it is very difficult to establish definite limits. For example, what kind of sport does a regional footballer play? It is not possible to give a straight reply to this. He is a youth who undoubtedly plays for the fun of it, but he is paid bonuses and traveling expenses; he brings a few hundred fans to the football field at his home town, who pay money to watch the matches; he is obliged to go through regular training sessions, even if he does not want to. Is this spontaneous football or spectacle-football? Social currents do not usually have clearly defined limits; they are impulses and tendencies, sometimes ephemeral, sometimes more lasting; they have representative subjects that are perfectly identifiable, more questionable borderline areas, often impossible to classify; but this does not mean that the social trend is not plain to see.

We might compare these two major kinds of sport with sea currents. Sea currents are not completely separate from one another. It is impossible to know with certainty if a given molecule of water belongs to the current or is outside it. Thousands of millions of molecules at the edge of the current cannot be classified inside or outside it. But the current, though it has no clearly marked bed, exists and flows along; there are central nuclei, enormous masses of water which receive its effect and flow, for example, from the warm waters of Mexico to the western coasts of Europe; and these coasts are warmer than those at an equivalent latitude in North America.

It is in this way, and not as hermetic, static structures, but as dynamic entities, as operative trends, that these two great social dynamics into which sport divides should be understood. Indeed, it is impossible to say of a regional class footballer at a given moment which area he belongs to, or in which direction he is moving. The motivations of his sports behavior at any given time are complex. He enjoys playing football, and that is why he plays. But it would not displease him if he were to earn a lot of money playing football, and become a celebrity or idol. At that particular time, it is not clear whether he belongs to sport as spectacle or sport as praxis. Perhaps in time his behavior will be less ambiguous.

But even if the limits are not clearly defined, even if on many occasions the two kinds of sport that exist in our time become mixed, or occur together in a single individual or situation, even if they interfere with each other, they nevertheless continue relentlessly on their way, constantly drifting further apart because of the different needs they satisfy — on the one hand, sport as spectacle, sought by sensationalism, political exhibitionism, financial gain, and rocked on the carousel of advertising; on the other, sport as "praxis," sought more and more because of the need for exercise felt by "homo sedentarius," and because of a pure impulse toward physical activity, a trend toward simple entertainment and pleasure and a search for strength-replenishing leisure. Sport as spectacle does not destroy the other kind of sport; it simply has less and less to do with it. People who mix them, or set one against another, are either incompetent sports organizers or out-of-date sports educators.

IV

I now offer a few brief suggestions concerning the first practical consequences that may be inferred from this consideration of sport today.

The contribution that this classification may make to sports sciences is less important for the natural sciences than for the social or educational sciences, or the sciences of behavior in general. For example, the finding of a new functional recovery curve under certain working conditions is suitable for maximum performance and spontaneous sport alike. The discovery in biomechanics of a new kinetic implication in the performance of a sports movement is valid for all the situations in which such a sports movement is required. However, from an educational point of view, the acquisition of a technical-sporting skill must be approached in one way if the intention is to produce a champion and in a different way if it is intended simply to provide an enjoyable personal experience by means of this technical-sporting performance. The fact is that many of the mistakes that are made in practical sports education are the result of applying to school teaching the knowledge that has arisen around the great sporting achievements. A biomechanically perfect technique for a jump may always be a useful piece of learning. But it may well be a pedagogic error to subordinate a subject's contact with sport, his personal improvement through it, his sport experience, to getting him to perform the movement with taxonomic perfection, for while this is most important for performance sport, it is secondary from the sports educational standpoint. Such errors, which are very common, are the result of a one-sided consideration of sport.

Physical sports education (or sports instruction, or physical education for schoolchildren, according to the terminology in fashion), which falls entirely within the area of sport as praxis, or rather uses sport as praxis for its educational purposes, may be classified on any of the following levels of objectives: (1) knowledge of the body through individual experience; awareness of its capacities and possibilities of action, experience of the self through physical exercise; (2) acquisition of certain basic patterns of movement, certain forms of coordination broadly valid for a large number of tasks, and of certain generic responses suitable for solving the most varied problems of psychomotor performance; (3) learning of certain specific movements, suitable for definite tasks which will turn up frequently in life; (4) acquisition of certain sports learning patterns which will capacitate the subject to meet social sports demands in the society in which he lives; learning to play a sport well, owing to the requisites of a specific society; (5) acquisition of habits of sports behavior as a result of enjoyable experiences of physical sporting exercise. This requires the subject to have enjoyed his sports lessons; his sports experiences should be happy ones. As a result of enjoyable experiences, sport-playing habits will have been set up, or in other words, the learning processes for sports behavior for the rest of life will have been carried out; and (6) intellectual conviction that such learning processes, physical sports movements and skills, the playing of sport in general, are right, useful and healthy. The subject should know the reasons why certain learning processes are positive and for what specific tasks.

The first two objectives refer to basic psychomotor learning processes. No. 3 refers to psychomotor learning processes adapted to specific tasks frequent in life. No. 4 refers to social learning. No. 5, to psycho-affective learning or linking, and No. 6, to intellectual knowledge and conviction. In this way, the whole person is involved in his own participation in sports education.

It is possible to classify on these six levels the many specific objectives which constitute the highly complex task of physical sports education, or education through physical sporting activity, or education by movement. However, what happened was that the findings of technical perfection taken from top-class sport were added to an old-fashioned conception of physical sporting education, which consisted of acquiring stereotyped skills, no attention being paid to other levels of the personality involved. This meant that the significance of levels 3 and 4 of the previous list of objectives was stressed, i.e., it was attempted to achieve the most perfect possible performances. Such performances are useful, providing they do not replace general learning, such as 1 and 2 and do not interfere with affective and intellectual link-ups, 5 and 6.

This conception of sport as a social subsystem, free from the obsession for maximum performance, a model execution and stereotyped perfection of movement, would help and enrich to an enormous extent modern tendencies such as motor learning schools, natural gymnastics, etc.

Leaving the field of sports pedagogics to which this brief note has referred, the application of the sport as praxis/sport as spectacle dichotomy brings immediate results in any other area of the behavioral or social sciences. It is not the same thing to seek the recovery of a sportsman so that he will integrate once more into the sports group he broke out of, with a view to getting back a champion of decisive importance in the team's importance, as to seek his recovery from his maladaptation to the group with a view to overcoming a neurotic or psychopathic conflict and achieving a definitive personal reeducation, regardless of his competitive activity. The quest for peak performance timed to coincide with periods of all-important competitions does not involve the same scientific objectives or the same procedures as the attempt to get an individual to improve his personal condition by reaching a certain level of performance. Sometimes the two tasks coincide, but often they do not. In any case, the aim of the scientific work is different, and the results may well turn out to be different, too.

Today, a very high percentage of the behavioral sciences applied to sport concentrate on competitive sport, stimulated by the demands of performance sport. Clubs, associations, countries and states all are involved in the dialectics of sports triumphs. Their present levels of success can no longer be achieved without the use of rigorous science. This has given rise to a great development of research applied to sports performance and to sport in general. From this scientific progress, many other advances will be derived, applicable to other levels of sports praxis, even physical sports education. But we must avoid confused thinking and disputes and clarify the different objectives we are seeking. In the first place, it must be recognized that most of the science applied to sport is in service of top sports performance. This would allow scientific policy to be reformulated. It is not a question of opposing the efforts directed toward sports performance, but of recognizing clearly that the other kind of sport is really rather more starved of science than what is generally believed.

There are fields of the human and social sciences applicable to sport as praxis which are still untouched, or rather that are conditioned by the requirements of top performance sport. The broad horizons of sport as a modern leisure activity, as a form of liberation from the technological ethos, as a dynamic of group living adaptable to everyday life, etc., have been very little studied if the comparison is made with direct applications to maximum performance. First-class competitive sport (as a result, I repeat, of the spectacular nature of sport) has become such a large and powerful phenomenon that nowadays it almost constitutes an original, closed social system (Lüschen). Science gradually adapts its lines of approach to this system, and thus a science of sport almost takes shape; a science created in response to the originality of human behavior in search of optimum performance and the structures that have been set up as a consequence of this behavior. Except for a few areas of education, there is an almost complete lack of a science that seeks to use sport for life, so that man, from childhood on, may derive profit from that sports behavior for his individual and social learning processes, his habits, his self-knowledge and his convictions.

In contrast to the great advances achieved in the field of performance sport, in sport as praxis we are still virtually in the period of common-sense statements, a priori convictions and moralizing platitudes. And yet sport for all, sport as play, enjoyment, health, etc., is needed and sought by people more and more; and though it can serve all these functions, it is almost forgotten by science.

Another field in which the application of the two kinds of sport would have immediate and wide-ranging consequences is the managing of sports policy in general.

Since I have already gone far beyond the limits assigned to this paper, I shall confine myself to mere assertion, leaving the development of the subject for another occasion.

The top administration of sport in general is structured in almost every country on the basis of the concept of so-called modern sport (the product of the movements for the drawing up of rules and codes and for the internationalization of sport, originating in 19th century England, the educational-sporting ideas received by Coubertin and redeveloped by him, and certain platitudes and outbreaks of a more or less racialist character, to the effect that the sports champion is a symbol of the health of a whole people). The new, major impacts to which sport has been subjected, and which have given rise to a profound change in its contemporary reality (political exhibitionism, a cult of the immediate and the sensational for publicity purposes, sport as a highly desirable consumer product, etc.) have not been included in the consideration of the political levels of sport.

Sport is still considered as a more or less homogeneous, unified entity. The familiar commonplaces, such as "the great champions come from a large mass of ordinary players," or "champions are a symbol of a good development of sport at the base," etc., are still frequent among sports authorities, especially in their rhetorical dialectic.

A real consideration of present-day sport might result, among other things, in the following: separation — at least a functional one — between the bodies responsible for the two kinds of sport and separation of budgets, which would avoid permanent squabbling and suspicions about the justice of sports investments.

The responsibilities incumbent upon the authorities in the two kinds of sport are quite different: the first would have a political prestige function, which is very important nowadays. Champions are necessary in a modern state; their dialectical and political function is not to be scored, nor should funds for producing them be given sparingly. The other function would be, by means of sports spectacle, to channel, facilitate and control the major elementary entertainments of the people. The other authorities would be entrusted with an educative task of organizing and providing leisure occupation and promoting social development.

In the time we live in, the last quarter of the 20th century, it is anachronistic to maintain opposition or rivalry between the two kinds of sport.

References

1. Cagigal, J.M.: Sport in Contemporary Society. Madrid, 1975.
2. Falize, J. and Erbach, G.: Scientific Research in Sports. CIEPS-ICSPE Publication, 1975.

The Humanistic Value of Sport

V. I. Stoljarov

The question of the humanistic value of sport is one of its role and importance to man and, more generally, to the whole of mankind. To put this problem in greater perspective, it is a number of specific questions as to the influence of sport on man's organism, his structure of ethical norms, value orientations and esthetical ideals, on social relations (socialization, group formation and dynamics) and forming of an individual's, social groups' and the whole society's needs and their meeting; development of specific cultural values within the sphere of sports and their relationship with social values pertaining to material and spiritual cultures; sport's contribution to social progress, protection of a person's freedom and dignity; forming an all-around harmonized individual and establishment of truly humane relations among persons, nations and so on.

All these questions have been posed and discussed on many occasions in recent years. Numerous reports and speeches were dedicated to them during the Olympic Scientific Congress held in Munich in 1972 [5] and the World Scientific Congress on "Sport in Modern Society" sponsored in Moscow in 1974 [13]. They were touched upon in many magazine articles, books and monographs [2, 3, 10, 14, 16-18, 21-23].

What commands such an unprecedented interest in problems concerning the humanistic value of sport?

First, it is necessary to take into account the fact that the problems of humanism and a humanistic value of various social phenomena become especially acute in the present-day era of great sociohistoric changes, scientific and technical revolution and the relentless ideological struggle of the two opposite social systems.

These questions concern not only scientists and politicians but also society at large. This process is particularly reflected in the formation of numerous "humanistic" societies and unions, such as "The League of Belgium Humanists," "The American Association of Humanists," "humanistic" societies in France, the Federal Republic of Germany, Norway and other countries. There are various

---

V. I. Stoljarov, The State Central Institute of Physical Culture, Moscow, U.S.S.R.

widespread conceptions under the banner of humanism. We mean here the American psychologist Fromm's "humanistic psycho-analysis," Elluele's "Christian personalistic humanism," existentialist "freedom philosophy" of man, Aron's "psychosomatic humanism," the American economist Galbraith's "harmonic humanism" and the extremist humanism of the so-called new left. All these conceptions are confronted by the theory of true humanism, consistently developed in the works of Marx, Lenin and modern marxist philosophers [8, 9, 12, 20], and they are being put into practice in the Soviet Union and countries of the socialist community. The representatives of different conceptions of humanism run into controversies over a wide range of problems which the practice of social development raises. Among all these problems, that of the humanistic value of sports is of interest to us and plays an important role.

Since a relatively short period of time sport became a major phenomenon of the social life while until the end of the 19th century it was a privilege of the elite few who practiced it for pleasure. At present millions of people practice sport. Sport takes first place regarding press coverage, number of spectators (for example, the Maracana sports stadium in Rio de Janeiro can absorb up to 200,000 people) and those watching sports on TV. (Experts believe that about 1.5 billion people watched the XXth Olympic Games of Munich on TV.)

It is important to indicate that a trend to more and more intensive development of sport, particularly in Socialist countries, can be clearly observed. For example, in the Soviet Union the total number of those engaging in sports increased by more than one thousand times in less than 60 years. It is crucial that the physical culture movement require rationally organized forms and be organically involved in the system of social relations. In our country a stabilized state system of physical education was created which is supplemented by a developed and actively functioning amateur physical culture movement. At the present stage it is one of the most massive social movements rapidly becoming an all-people one. There are now 217,873 physical culture and sports organizations in our country uniting 50 million persons. It serves more than one quarter of the population in age ranging from 10 to 59. About 15 million persons are in groups of general physical training, recreation, tourism and fishing. The ranks of those practicing physical culture and sports increased by 7 million persons only in the period from 1971 to 1975.

The sociological investigations of the place of physical culture and sport in the structure of our country carried out in different years provide evidence that there is an increase both in the overall amount of sport practice and its share in the structure of leisure time.

Studies carried out by Strumilin in working families of the cities of the central part of the country in 1922 to 1924 showed that working men had spent 1.5 to 2.9 hours on sports practice a month or 20 to 40 minutes a week (about 1.0% to 1.7% of his total leisure time [19]). Women did not practice sports at all. Physically active leisure meant for them only dances and walking. Those who practiced sports and physical culture constituted only 6% to 8% of all questioned.

According to the studies of 1929, male workers in Moscow spent 6.9 hours on sports practice and female workers 0.9 hours a month. These figures meant 3.8% and 1.3% of their total leisure time [11]. One third of the working men and 6% to 7% of the women spent their time on physical culture and sport [11].

Studies made by Artemov in 1963 in Krasnojarsk (Siberia) showed that men had spent an average of 2.66 hours on sports and physical culture practice a week and women, 0.7 hour a week. The workers in Krasnojarsk spent the following time on physical culture and sport: men — 5.8% during six working days and 9.5% of the total leisure time on holiday; women — 1.3% and 5.6%, correspondingly. (Percent is given according to the total leisure time.) In total, about 60% of men and over 20% of women at least once a week practice physical culture and sports [1].

The facts show that today sport is taking a more and more important place in daily life, particularly in the structure of leisure time. But to what extent is all this justified from the point of view of humanistic ideals and principles? Must sport, from this point of view, take so important a place in the system of various forms of human life activity, including the structure of leisure time? What must be the optimum time spent on sports in the leisure time of various groups of the population and what balance should there be with other forms of human activities? Which is the ideal correlation between sports activity and education in the structure of time which different groups of population have at their disposal, or which is the ideal correlation between time spent on sport spectacles and that on sports practice?

It is difficult to answer these questions without preliminary consideration of the humanistic value of sport, of its role and importance for man and the whole of mankind.

Different points of view on the problem of the humanistic value of sport are expressed by sport researchers. Some recognize the humanistic value of sport while others reject it. But in doing so, both the first and the second refer to certain facts.

Those who concede an important humanistic significance to sport in a modern society refer to the fact that sport is one of the major means of consolidating an individual's health, his physical development, without which he cannot be a full-fledged member of society. Sport essentially and positively affects not only an individual's physical development but also his spiritual sphere, that is, emotions, esthetic views, ethical and world outlook. Sport provides great opportunities to form highly ethical consciousness and behavior. It is acknowledged that sporting activity is heuristic and creative. During this activity and as a result of it an individual's abilities, cultural ideals and norms of behavior of permanent human value are revealed and fully developed. Sport affords every person great possibilities for self-perfection, self-expression and self-assertion. Sport satisfies people's joy in contacts, emotional co-experience and co-participation, joy of victory and pride of man and of his inexhaustible abilities. Modern sport has an important meaning for developing human contacts and interrelations not only within one country but also among all nations. It plays a considerable part in consolidating peace, mutual understanding and friendship of different nations. The development of sport is one of the important aspects of democratization of society because it helps people to take an active part in social life.

Those who reject the humanistic value of sport refer to other groups of facts. In particular they say that some athletes trying to achieve the highest results take drugs which menace their health. In a number of cases sport is employed as a means of diverting masses from pressing sociopolitical problems and of manipulating public opinion. These researchers also say that sport may even provide grounds for international conflicts. As an example they cite the bitter fighting which arose between two states of Central America and was called a "soccer war." There are noted incidents of violence, hooliganism and vandalism which occurred during sporting contests. According to the Italian newspaper *Gazzetta dello sport*, fans invaded football fields three times in the end of 1974; one youth was nabbed while being at a stadium in Blackpool; many British towns were seriously damaged as a result of rampaging enraged fans armed with bicycle chains, stones and iron rods [4]. Data of the same sort are provided by the French newspaper *L'Equipe* [7].

To show the inhumane character of sport, some researchers, as for example the French observer Meyer, refer to the complexity of rules and an increasing number of sporting contests which happened during the last years in all kinds of sport [6]. These researchers also point out the highly intensive training, commercialization of sport and increasing dependence on scientific and technical achievements. All this forms the basis for attacks on sport and for describing it as a manifestation of "an individual's aggressive instincts," "an individual's pathology," as well as for conclusions on a person's alienation in sport and its inhumane character [15].

Thus, controversial points of view are being presented on the problem of the humanistic value of sport. Before giving our own view of the question and joining one of the points of view mentioned above, we should like to discuss *an approach* to the problem itself. We are inclined to do that, first of all, because research of the two trends mentioned above gives certain facts and arguments. In trying to comprehend and appreciate the approaches of the different researchers on the problem of the humanistic value of sport, we should point out cases of oversimplification and one-sidedness. Sometimes it is believed sufficient to analyze only the influence of sport on the human organism. Recognizing a certain humanistic value of sport some researchers mean only its significance as an important means of physical education and perfection of a person, a means of restoring and consolidating his health. In such an approach to the problem, the sport is contrasted to the cinema, the theater and other elements of culture affecting human personality.

In describing the social significance of sport, some researchers often concentrate all their attention on the "benefit" which an individual or a social group can derive from it, the benefit being interpreted as an amount of material things, as success or "prosperity" which can be achieved by means of sport.

The one-sided approach to the problem of the humanistic value of sport is revealed by the fact that only the impact of sport on sportsmen is considered while sport's deep influence on spectators, fans and all those involved in it is in some way ignored.

Apart from this, those trying to solve the problem of the humanistic value of sport sometimes reduce the latter to one of its forms, to mass sport or to high performance sport without clear distinction and without taking into account historic trends in the development of sport.

It is necessary to appreciate sport's impact on the individual and on mankind in an inclusive way in order to provide the correct solution of the problem of the humanistic value of sport.

In the first place an estimation of sport's influence on the human organism health and efficiency should be given. Furthermore, it is necessary to reveal the specific cultural values which are being formed in the sphere of sport and then compare them with other social values pertaining to material and spiritual cultures. It is also crucial to discern the mechanism by means of which sport has an impact on a person, his structure of ethical traits, value orientations and esthetic ideals. Sport's influence upon forming and meeting various individual needs, position in society, living conditions, prestige, rights, freedom, life as a whole, etc., cannot be ignored either.

It is also important to estimate sport's role and importance for a person, and to determine its impact on social relations, group formation and dynamics, and interrelations of various countries, nations and peoples. At the same time sport's influence must be taken into account not only on sportsmen themselves but also on all those connected with sport in some way, including coaches, spectators and fans.

The difficulty in solving the aforementioned problems consists also in the necessity for compiling a full list of forms of sport, sporting practice and activities in order to obtain a perspective of the humanistic value of sport in an all-inclusive way. (There is need to differentiate mass sport, physical culture, high performance sport, professional sport, different kinds of sport, organized and unorganized sport and so on.) One must also take into account trends of further development of sport and a possibility of new forms arising. It is necessary to consider the problem of the humanistic value of all forms of sport, sporting practice and activities in a differentiated manner.

This is thus the first important prerequisite for a correct solution of the problem of the humanistic value of sport.

Secondly, it is impossible in our mind to give a correct solution to this problem without taking into account the fact that the contents, character and trends in sport, its positive or negative impact on a person and social relations, depend essentially upon managers and organizers, coaches, physicians, mass media representatives, sport researchers, leaders of national and international sporting organizations and so on.

The humanistic character of sport mostly depends upon the creative and hard activity of all these persons, on their knowledge, skills, honesty, decency, persistence and diligence. These traits determine whether sport is a benefit for a person, a humanistic value or if it is a clearcut inhumane phenomenon. It is known that sport can promote consolidation of people's health if strict medical control over athletes and sport practice itself is based on scientifically sound recommendations. On the contrary, sport can be harmful to a person's health if sport practice and contests are arranged without proper medical control, in defiance of physicians' and coaches' recommendations or if scientifically sound recommendations and prescriptions are deliberately ignored. Sport gives widest opportunities to form highly ethical consciousness and behavior in people, but at the same time it can deform a personality.

In acknowledging the importance of the conscious activity of man for realization of the humanistic value of sport we must, however, take into consideration that this activity itself decisively depends upon the concrete social conditions, laws, aspirations and aims fostered by the society within which they live and work.

These concrete historic conditions and laws determine an approach to sport in a given society, and the aims for which it is used, as well as all organizational structure of sport by means of which these aims and hence a social significance of sport are being put into practice.

When sport is essentially influenced by receiving maximum profits, when a person tries to achieve only a high sporting result with a view of experiencing a success exploited in commercial interests, as it is all under capitalism first of all in the sphere of professional, commercial sport, then a healthy, educational and cultural, that is, humanistic character of sport is overshadowed and cast away into the background.

Only the social system the main purpose of which is an individual himself, his all-around and harmonious development, and not aims alien to him (for example, receiving a profit) is able to create conditions favorable to a full and adequate realization of the humanistic value of sport. As the real practice of social development shows, such a system is socialism and communism.

The approach to sport in a socialist society, resulting from the main regularities of its functioning, differs from that in a capitalist society in that it is always taken into account under socialism first of all the healthy, educational and cultural tasks, mostly effectively solved by sporting means, putting into practice humanistic principles and ideals: an ideal of an all-round and harmoniously developed individual, the principle of peaceful coexistence of states with different social systems, consolidation of peace and mutual understanding of peoples. All these things form the basis in a socialist society for solving various organizational problems of sport and determining trends and perspectives of its development. To achieve just these aims by sporting means the Communist Party and the Soviet Government direct the work of all organizations, leading figures, coaches responsible for development of physical culture and sport, as well as of the press, radio and television officials. For the same purposes has been created in our country the stable state system of physical education supplemented by a highly developed and actively functioning system of spontaneous physical culture movement of the people. Just to these ends measures were taken in the last years to promote the mass physical culture movement to become an all-people one; to insure a harmonious and proportional development of mass sport and high performance sport; to raise the effectiveness of the educational work with sportsmen, spectators and so on.

All this does not mean, of course, that under socialism there are no difficulties in solving humanistic problems by means of sport. But in a socialist society there are created real conditions to overcome these difficulties, to form in a most effective way a humanistic trend of sport and display it.

Now let's make final conclusions on the problem of the humanistic value of sport.

We tried to show that it is impossible to consider in an abstract way the humanistic value of sport or its inhumane character, as well as other social phenomena, such as science, technology and so on. Sport acquires this or that content, character, trend or value depending upon concrete historical conditions, a social structure within which it develops, and upon conscious activities of persons who arrange the sport and use it for certain purposes.

Therefore, it is possible to provide a correct solution of the controversy between those who acknowledge the humanistic value of sport and those who deny it, only from the viewpoint of the Marxist real humanism which is hostile to a mere "moralizing," that is, to take only an abstract ethical ideal of a universal nature of man without seeing its connection with concrete historical circumstances and objective regularities of social development. The Marxist humanism not only puts forward the idea of an inclusive and harmonious development of an individual as an alternative to his dichotomy and one-sidedness, but in addition Marxism shows those objective historical regularities and processes which create real conditions for his formation and those social forces which by their actions give rise to these conditions.

The Marxist view of the humanistic value of sport differs from its abstract-humanistic understanding in that it clearly realizes the necessity and indicates the ways of creating corresponding material and sociopolitical conditions which allow passage from the sphere of abstract and philanthropic considerations of a humanistic value of sport into the sphere of a practical use of sport as one of the important means of an all-around and harmonious development of an individual as it is under socialism and communism.

References

1. Artenov, V.A.: Budget-Time studies — Physical Culture and Sport among Workers and Students. Moscow:V.N.I.I.F.K., 1972.
2. Baitsch, H. et al: The Scientific View of Sport. Berlin:Springer Verlag, 1972.
3. Bernard, J.: Le sport, la mort, la violence. Editions universitaires, 1972.
4. Gazetta dello Sport. (Italy) 14.02.1975.
5. Grupe, O. (ed.): Sport in the Modern World, Chances and Problems. Berlin:Springer Verlag, 1973.
6. Journal l'Equipe. (France) 26.01.1976.
7. Journal l'Equipe. (France)26.10. 1975.
8. Kechelava, V.V.: Real and imaginary humanism. Moscow: Mysl, 1975.
9. Kovaliev, S.M.: Real humanism and its adversaries. Moscow:Politizdat, 1973.
10. Lenk, H.: Leistungsport: Ideologie oder Mythos? Stuttgart, 1972.
11. Mikheev, V.: Budget-Time study of the workers and other employees of Moscow and surroundings. Moscow, 1932.
12. Pechenev, V.: Humanitarian Socialism versus True Socialism. Moscow: Milodaja Guardia, 1974.
13. Philosophy, History and Sociology. Abstracts from the International Scientific Congress — Sport in the Contemporary Society, Moscow, 1974.
14. Ponomariev, I.I.: The Social Role of Physical Culture and Sport. Moscow: F.I.S., 1974.
15. Rösch, H.E.: Ist das noch Sport? Kritische Anmerkungen zum Sport und zu den Olympischen Spielen. Freiburg:Herder, 1972.
16. Sport and Individualism. Various articles. Moscow:F.I.S., 1975.
17. Sport w spoleczénstwie wspólczesnym. pod. red. Z. Krawczyka. Warszawa, 1973.
18. Slusher, H.S.: Man, Sport and Existence, a Critical Analysis. Philadelphia: Lea and Febiger, 1967.
19. Stroumiline, S.G.: Economic Questions Concerning Work. Moscow, 1957.
20. The Problem of Humanism in the Marxist-Leninist Philosophy, History and the Present. *In* Myslwtchenko, A.G. and Souvarova, L.I. Moscow:Politizdat, 1975.
21. Van der Zwaag, H.T.: Toward a Philosophy of Sport. Reading:Addison-Wesley, 1972.
22. Weiss, P.: Sport, a Philosophic Inquiry. Carbondale, 1969.
23. Zeigler, E.F.: Problems in the History and Philosophy of Physical Education and Sport. Englewood-Cliffs, N.J.:Prentice-Hall, 1968.

Physical Education: A Prediscipline in Search of a Paradigm

Saul Ross

The broad field called physical education has undergone a change in aspirations, a change in status, a change in structure and a change of focus in the very recent past. The magnitude of these changes, coming about in such a short period of time, and continuing at present, calls for serious examination and philosophical analysis. With specific pertinence to this conference, an understanding of the broad field called physical education through an examination of the substantive and cognitive structures of this new, complex entity should bring to light its relation to human well-being, both in terms of the whole structure and in terms of its component parts.

A major turning point [41] in the evolvement of physical education in contemporary times occurred in 1964 with the appearance of Henry's paper [15]. The previous concern with justifying physical education as a profession was supplanted in the thinking of a number of scholars by the problem of defining, describing or delineating a discipline.

While the literature on the topic, physical education as a discipline, covers a wide range of subtopics and contains many different views, four important themes can be discerned. Each will be treated briefly.

The first theme centers on the attempt to distinguish between the professional aspects and the disciplinary endeavor. In doing so a distinction has been made between physical education as a program conducted in schools or as a teacher preparation program on the one hand, and human movement [10, 12, 32, 38, 39] as the object of study of the discipline on the other hand. Human movement has received broad, but not unanimous support as the object of the discipline; man moving [2, 13] is preferred by some of our colleagues.

Acceptance of human movement as the object of study poses a problem. Curl [11], representing the British view, sees the study of

Saul Ross, Department of Physical Education, School of Human Kinetics and Leisure Studies, University of Ottawa, Ottawa, Canada.

human movement as a complex, many layered entity that involves many disciplines. He selects the Hirstian concept, field of study, as a more appropriate organization for knowledge rather than a discipline.

A second theme comes from the opposition to human movement as the object of the discipline. This objection is voiced by the scholars with an expressed interest in sport as a unique, special phenomenon worthy of study. Sheehan [37] and Loy [25] are spokesmen for this position. It has been argued that sport consists of movements by human beings and thus the study of sport could be subsumed under the rubric of human movement.

The third theme involves the approach taken by Sheedy [35, 36] who focused on the nature and type of theory appropriate to the disciplines and discussed the conditions required for the realization of theory in physical education. In addition, he surveyed the entire field and offered his views on the relationship between the discipline and the profession, and the role of research and university teaching. He regards physical education as an anthropological discipline which should have as a first priority the development of a new methodology which is appropriate for the uniqueness of the subject matter to be studied.

The fourth theme, the subdiscipline approach, has received the most attention and is prevalent in our field today. This approach was launched with Henry's statement that the scholarly field of knowledge basic to physical education consists of such diverse fields as anatomy, physics, physiology, cultural anthropology, history, sociology and psychology [15]. Kenyon moved beyond Henry when he delineated sociology of sport as a subdiscipline [18], and, using that as the model then called for a "consortium of discipline-like subfields, each focusing attention upon one or more aspects of human movement" [19] to form the discipline entitled human movement studies. Somehow the various subdisciplines or subfields in the consortium are supposed to combine to form the discipline of physical education.

This approach was endorsed by The Big Ten Body-of-Knowledge Project in Physical Education [45]; they identified six specific subfields of specialization: (1) Exercise Physiology; (2) Biomechanics; (3) Motor Learning and Sports Psychology; (4) Sociology of Sport Education; (5) History, Philosophy and Comparative Physical Education and Sport; and (6) Administrative Theory. Other lists of subdisciplines which comprise the discipline of physical education can be found in the literature.

A short time later the most extensive list appeared. The Physical Education Discipline Group of the Committee of Deans and Directors of Schools and Faculties of Physical Education in Ontario identified nine discipline subdivisions: (1) History of Sport and Physical Activity; (2) Philosophy of Sport and Physical Activity; (3) Sociology of Physical Activity and Sport; (4) Social Psychology of Physical Activity and Sport; (5) Psychology and Psychomotor Learning; (6) Administrative Theory; (7) Exercise Physiology; (8) Growth and Development; and (9) Biomechanics.*

Appreciation is expressed here for the work being undertaken in each of the subdisciplines. Higher levels of scholarship, development of new and more sophisticated research tools and measuring devices, increased rigor and expansion of horizons can be found in all the subdisciplines; important intellectual advances are being made. However, what must be made very clear is that as presently constituted, the subdisciplines, each on an individual basis or as a consortium, cannot be the discipline of physical education [34]. The clearest criticism of the belief that the subdisciplines constitute the discipline of physical education comes from Kleinman, who points out

> that whatever these people do in the sciences, be they the behavioral or physical, they are not doing physical education. If they study muscle fatigue, they are doing physiology. If they study mechanics of movement they are doing physics. If they study behavior, they are doing psychology. If they study games and sports they are doing sociology. But these fields are disciplines in their own right. They are certainly not the discipline of physical education [21].

A discipline must have its own practitioners [44], scholars committed to that discipline [1] and not to another field, however closely allied it may be to the original discipline. We cannot expect, nor should we expect, one discipline, or subdiscipline, to do the work of another [16].

Three comments arise from this short historical sketch and brief descriptive analysis. First, and most importantly, is to point out that although there are differences in the various approaches taken to attempt to solve the problem, the difference in the approaches is transcended by the common agreement, explicit or implicit, for the need to delineate or define a discipline for physical education.

---

*Physical Education Discipline Group — Survey Form 2.

Second, the subdisciplines, as presently constituted, cannot comprise the discipline of physical education, but they have the potential for becoming the basis of a new discipline, an autonomous discipline with its own endogenous subject matter. This proposition leads directly into the third comment, the importance and function of a paradigm in the development of a discipline. The concept of a paradigm has not received attention, to date, in the physical education literature.

Prior to exploring the concept of a paradigm it is necessary to explain that the position taken here is that a discipline, entitled physical education, does not appear to exist. What exists at present is a number of disciplines, or subdisciplines, with a direct interest in studying human movement, or man moving, or physical activity, or sport, or some combination thereof. Taken together this entity fits more aptly under the heading of the Hirstian concept, field of study, rather than a discipline.

Attempts to label the consortium of subdisciplines as a discipline fall short when examined in light of some of the more comprehensive statements regarding what comprises a discipline. At this point one casts an envious eye at the physical sciences where it appears definitions are more precise and concrete, lending themselves to measurements that can produce clear yes or no answers. A discipline, which appears to be an amorphous, abstract entity, defies such clear-cut definition. Instead, what is found are lists of characteristics or criteria, with much commonality but some divergence.

A simplistic listing of criteria — domain, conceptual structure, syntactical structure — is an inadequate measuring device. More extensive lists, which represent more profound understanding and thereby provide better measuring devices, exist in the literature. Nixon reviewed the writings of some of the scholars, pointed out the lack of overall agreement and then summarized seven main criteria:

A discipline

1. has an identifiable domain
2. is characterized by a substantial history
3. is rooted in appropriate structure
4. possesses a unique integrity
5. is recognized by the procedures and methods it employs
6. is recognized as a process as well as noted for its products
7. relies on accurate language [26]

King and Brownell view a discipline as a community of discourse. As a result of their detailed study they identified ten isomorphic features as the characteristics of disciplines.

A discipline is

1. a community of persons
2. an expression of human imagination
3. a domain
4. a tradition
5. a syntactical structure — a mode of inquiry
6. a conceptual structure — a substance
7. a specialized language or other system of symbols
8. a heritage of literature and artifacts and a network of communications
9. a valuative and affective stance
10. an instructive community [20]

A similar list has been developed by Heckhausen [14], and Adler's five conditions for philosophy [1] can also be regarded as an appropriate extensive set of criteria.

If one takes the consortium of subdisciplines as the discipline of physical education and analyzes that entity within the context of the lists presented, it will show the lack of unity, the absence of integration and the incohesiveness.

The apparent cohesiveness, or integrity, of a discipline comes about as the result of the enunciation or articulation of what Kuhn in his book [22] has labeled a paradigm. Paradigms are taken "to be universally recognized scientific achievements that for a time provide model problems and solutions to a community of practitioners" [22]. The emergence of a paradigm can be regarded as a manifestation of a scientific revolution.

Kuhn [22] suggests that when an anomaly appears, caused at times by either the failure or breakdown of some equipment, or when unanticipated results occur in an experiment, or when something entirely unexpected transpires, extraordinary investigations are conducted to explain the phenomenon. Ordinarily, work in a discipline advances by small increments as knowledge is advanced based on accepted postulates, axioms, principles and generally accepted laws. When this process is disrupted and the extraordinary investigations lead to the formulation of an entirely new theory that can be called a paradigm, then a scientific revolution has occurred.

The most obvious examples of scientific revolutions are those famous episodes in scientific development that have often been labeled revolutions before. Names associated with these events include Copernicus (astronomy), Newton (physics), Lavoisier (chemistry) and Einstein (physics). These new theories, considered as paradigms, had great impact on their respective communities. "Each of them necessitated the community's rejection of one time-honored scientific theory in favor of another incompatible with it. Each produced a consequent shift in the problems available for scientific scrutiny and in the standards by which the profession determined what should count as an admissible problem or as a legitimate problem-solution" [22].

For an on-going discipline a new theory implies a change in the rules governing the prior practice of normal science. Inevitably, it reflects upon much scientific work already successfully completed by that community of practitioners. That is why a new theory, however special its range of application, is seldom or never just an increment to what is already known. Its assimilation requires the reconstruction of prior theory and the reevaluation of prior fact, an intrinsically revolutionary process [22].

In a mature science when a new theory emerges, for it to become a paradigm, it "must seem better than its competitors, but it need not, and in fact never does, explain all the facts with which it is confronted" [22]. Paradigms define the scope of inquiry, provide a unifying concept for a community of practitioners and point the difection for much scientific work.

A paradigm, when it represents a scientific revolution in mature science, possesses two characteristics — it is an achievement sufficiently unprecedented so as to attract an enduring group of adherents away from competing modes of scientific activity and, second, at the same time it is sufficiently open-ended so as to leave a multitude of problems for the redefined group of practitioners to resolve. An example of an open-ended problem can be found in the work done by our colleagues in physiology of exercise in relation to the concept of physical fitness which is subdivided into two categories, maximum work capacity and isometric-isotonic contractions. In both cases an immense number of research reports exist in the literature based on a seemingly infinite number of methods, conditions and categories of subjects tested for MVO_2 and the effects of isometric, isotonic and isometric-isotonic contractions on various subjects at various levels of fitness under an infinite number of varying conditions for a myriad number of applications in a multitude of sports and rehabilitative situations.

For a prediscipline, such as physical education, a paradigm obviously would not compete with other, pre-existing theories. Rather, it would provide the base from which a new generation of scientific work would evolve. The presence of a paradigm "determines the framework within which 'normal science' works. It sets the pattern of puzzle solving . . . the important thing being that it confidently indicates that however complicated or whatever clues may be missing, the puzzle is capable of solution. This leaves plenty of scope for the ingenuity of the solvers and for the invention of new ideas for solving" [9].

The enunciation of a paradigm brings to the fore aspects which previously were not perceived nor discussed. The paradigm may state the problem in a different way and thereby generate a shift in the subproblems noticed and investigated. Two concomitant activities arise: (1) focus on the rules of scientific practice with its inherent discussion and development of new methods and (2) philosophical analysis, or philosophy of science, increases its attention to the presuppositions and to the articulated extensions of the paradigm.

First efforts to produce a paradigm for the prediscipline, physical education, may result in the enunciation of a number of tentative theories, each competing for prominence. "The early versions of a paradigm are mostly crude, solve few problems, and solutions given for individual problems are far from perfect" [42]. However, new paradigms explore new problems, and eventually one emerges as offering the better explanation and provides the wider scope for continued scientific activity. The early muddling must not be regarded as a deterrent; correct practice grows out of incorrect practice rather than from a void or from chaos.

A paradigm is a statement of a powerful theory which contains infinitely many facts; intricate analysis is required to bring these out [17]. Deduction is employed in this process, but as new facts are revealed they become data for induction and thus the refinement and/or reformulation of theory continues. New problems are stated, both induction and deduction are used, and the science advances.

Formulation of a paradigm should receive highest priority in physical education because of its powerful force in attracting scholars who would be committed to that discipline and not to other disciplines or subdisciplines. The paradigm would then become the source of the first postulates, axioms and basic premises for the discipline. In one sense it can be regarded as the start of the discipline. Since the formulation of a paradigm is such an important matter, attention is now turned to the problem of where to start the search for a paradigm.

Since the premise in this paper is that the discipline of physical education does not yet exist as an autonomous entity and since sustained efforts are being made to bring about a discipline, it is advantageous to know how new disciplines emerge. Boulding [8] states that there are three ways in which new disciplines develop. One way is akin to cell division in that a new discipline evolves from an established one, i.e., psychology from philosophy. A second way is through the union, real union, of two disciplines, such as biochemistry. The third way stems from Boulding's view of contemporary developments. "We now seem to be entering a period in which the development of new disciplines is taking a new turn. Instead of a new discipline developing quietly within the confines of an old one, or even instead of it developing in the interstitial areas between the two old ones, we find new disciplines developing now which are many-parented and which originate in a great many different fields. . . . There is something abroad which might be called an interdisciplinary movement" [8]. The third way is the result of interdisciplinarity [4, 7].

Juxtaposing Boulding's observation with the development of the subdiscipline approach in the field of physical education indicates the possibility of an autonomous discipline of physical education emerging or evolving through interdisciplinarity. Each subdiscipline would continue to focus on its particular aspect or part of man, generating new knowledge, even though each segment is insufficient to account for man's wholeness. The emergence of the new discipline of physical education with its concern for the whole man [31], focusing on a study of man moving, is a development shared with many sciences.

> We may state as characteristic of modern science that this scheme of isolable units acting in one-way causality has proved to be insufficient. Hence the appearance, in all fields of science, of notions like wholeness, holistic, organismic, gestalt, etc., which all signify that, in the last resort, we must think in terms of systems of elements in mutual interaction [42].

The importance of studying man as a whole would seem to be obvious, aside from the brute fact that man exists as a whole and moves as a whole. Indeed, "Man does not exist to be subdivided, for to sub-divide him is to execute him. Man is an organism, a whole in which segregation of any sort is artificial and in which every phenomenon is a manifestation of the whole" [3]. However powerful the argument in favor of wholeness, it is not to be construed as a statement against parts, for both parts and wholes [24] are real and both aspects need to be studied. Parts will be studied by the various subdisciplines with the discipline of physical education focusing on the study of the whole man — more precisely, man moving [40].

This relation can be seen schematically in the proposed map of knowledge (Fig. 1). In addition, the discipline of physical education would be concerned with what "more than one philosopher has pointed out, what we need most at present is a new integration of the knowledge we already possess" [23]. An identical view was expressed by an eminent scientist [33] in relation to the knowledge explosion in the field of immunology.

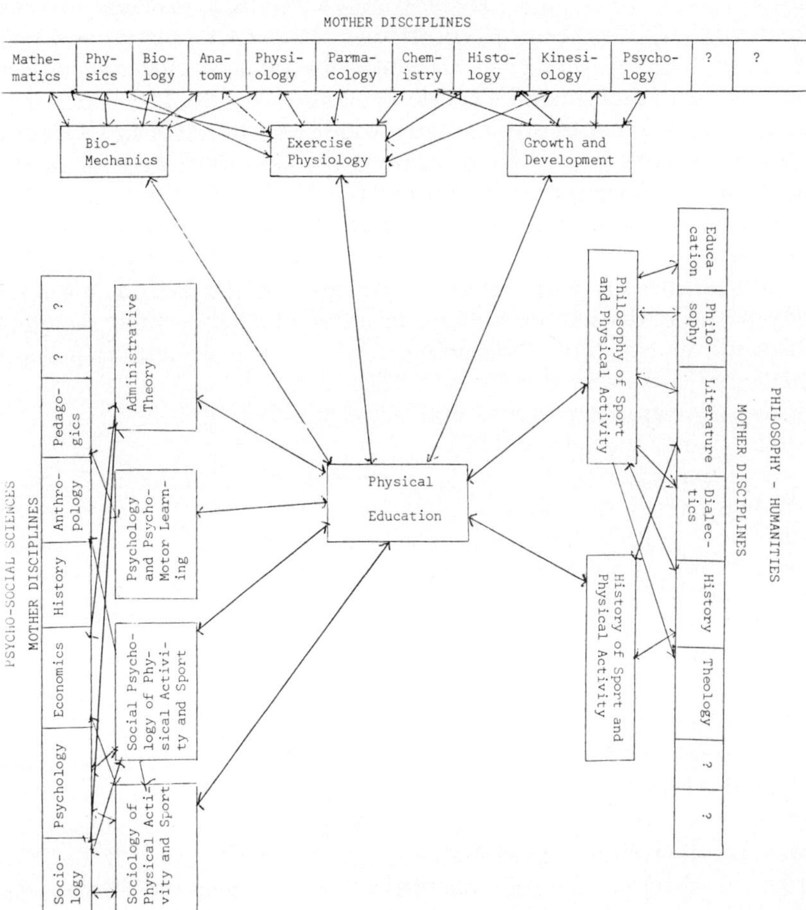

FIGURE 1.

Kuhn maintains that "only very occasionally, as in the case of ancient statics, dynamics, and general optics, do facts collected with so little guidance from pre-established theory speak with sufficient clarity to permit the emergence of a first paradigm" [22]. Physical education faces the same problem, the absence of pre-established theory. Two factors counterbalance this difficulty. The first refers to the actual existence of a number of subdisciplines, each possessing some theories which can be examined for potential contribution to a paradigm for physical education.

Second, recent advances made in epistemology enable us to tackle the problem with better intellectual tools. A number of philosophical conceptual frameworks exist that provide for the possibility of integration of knowledge: Bahm's Organicism as a Way of Integrating Knowledge [5, 6] states the rationale for integration; Piaget's Structuralism and Genetic Epistemology [28, 29] offers new insights into the structure of knowledge; Von Bertalanffy's General Systems Theory [42, 43] provides possible forms for the newly integrated knowledge; and Northrop's Epistemic Correlates [27] shows where similarities are to be found in the various branches of knowledge.

Much difficult work needs to be done in this regard; we have only begun to discuss the topic of interdisciplinarity. There are many obstacles ahead but overcoming them is a real, and important challenge. Success in this venture will reap a rich harvest. "Wisdom is by its very nature an interdisciplinary quality and not the product of a collection of specialists" [30].

For physical education in particular, the development of a paradigm based on interdisciplinarity would mean the start of an autonomous discipline. The additional harvest is stated by Kuhn: "Acquisition of a paradigm and of the more esoteric type of research it permits is a sign of maturity in the development of any given scientific field" [22].

The contributions made to human well-being by the subdisciplines such as physiology of exercise and psychomotor learning are well known and continued contributions are expected. This paper has attempted to clarify the structure of the broad field called physical education and to point out the potential source of an emerging endogenous discipline of physical education based on interdisciplinarity. A considerable amount of work must be done in order to develop the first paradigm for the discipline of physical education. Once established, the discipline of physical education and the subdisciplines that comprise the field should interact to their mutual enrichment. Continued contributions to human well-being should be the net result.

References

1. Adler, M.J.: The Conditions of Philosophy: Its Checkered Past, Its Present Disorder, and Its Future Promise. New York:Atheneum, 1965, pp. 21-42.
2. Alley, L.E.: Reaction to theoretical propositions for curriculum design in health education and implications for the curriculum in physical education. Academy Papers, The American Academy of Physical Education, No. 2, October 1968, p. 20.
3. Anshen, R.N.: Perspectives in Humanism: The future of tradition. *In* Hoyle, F.: The New Face of Science. New York and Cleveland:An NAL Book, The World Publishing Company, 1971, p. ix.
4. Apostel, L.: Conceptual tools for interdisciplinarity: An operational approach. *In* CERI: Interdisciplinarity: Problems of Teaching and Research in Universities. OECD, 1972, p. 151.
5. Bahm, A.J.: Organicism As a Way of Integrating Knowledge. Proceedings of the XIVth International Congress of Philosophy, Vienna, 1968. Vienna: Herder and Co., 1968, Vol. 11, pp. 321-327.
6. Bahm, A.J.: Organicism: The philosophy of interdependence. Int. Philos. Q. III (2):251-284, 1967.
7. Berger, G.: Opinions and facts. *In* CERI: Interdisciplinarity: Problems of Teaching and Research in Universities. OECD, 1972, p. 44.
8. Boulding, K.E.: The Image: Knowledge in Life and Society. Ann Arbor: University of Michigan Press, 1956, pp. 160-162.
9. Calder, R.: Man and The Cosmos: The Nature of Science Today. New York:Frederick A. Prager, Publishers, 1968, p. 23.
10. Crunden, C.: The uncomfortable relation of physical education and human movement. Br. J. Phys. Educ. 3 (1):6-7, 1972.
11. Curl, G.F.: An attempt to justify human movement as a field of study. *In* Brooke, J.D. and Whiting, H.T.A. (eds.): Human Movement — A Field of Study. London:Henry Kimpton Publishers, 1973.
12. Fraleigh, W.P.: The perplexed professor. Quest VII:1-13, 1966.
13. Harper, W.: Movement measurement: The case of the incompatible marriage. Quest XX:93-95, 1973.
14. Heckhausen, H.: Disciplines and interdisciplinarity. *In* CERI: Interdisciplinarity: Problems of Teaching and Research in Universities. OECD, 1972, pp. 83-86.
15. Henry, F.: Physical education: An academic discipline. JOHPER 37(7):32-33, 69, 1964.
16. Kaiser, C.H.: An Essay On Method. Port Washington, N.Y.:Kennikat Press, Inc. 1969, 1952, p. 139.
17. Kemeny, J.G.: A Philosopher Looks at Science. N.Y.:Van Nostrand Reinhold Company, 1958, p. 97.
18. Kenyon, G.S.: A sociology of sport: On becoming a subdiscipline. *In* Brown, R.C. and Cratty, B.J. (eds.): New Perspectives of Man in Action. Englewood Cliffs,N.J.:Prentice-Hall Inc., 1969.
19. Kenyon, G.S.: On the conceptualization of sub-disciplines within an academic discipline dealing with human movement. Proceedings, NCPEAM, 1968, pp. 34-45.

20. King, A.R. Jr. and Brownell, J.A.: The Curriculum and the Disciplines of Knowledge: A Theory of Curriculum Practice. New York:John Wiley and Sons, Inc., 1966, p. 95.
21. Kleinman, S.: The significance of human movement: A phenomenological approach. *In* Bucher, C.A. and Goldman, M. (eds.): Dimensions of Physical Education. St. Louis:The C.V. Mosby Company, 1969, p. 152.
22. Kuhn, T.S.: The Structure of Scientific Revolutions, ed. 2. Enlarged, Vol. 2, No. 2, International Encyclopedia of Unified Science. Chicago:University of Chicago Press, 1962, 1970, pp. viii, 6, 7, 11, 16, 17.
23. Langridge, D. (ed.): The Universe of Knowledge. University of Maryland, 1969, p. 5.
24. Lerner, D. (ed.): Parts and Wholes. New York:The Free Press of Glencoe, London:MacMillan New York, 1963.
25. Loy, J.W.: Sociology and physical education. *In* Singer, R.N. et al: Physical Education: An Interdisciplinary Approach. New York:The MacMillan Company, 1972.
26. Nixon, J.: The Criteria of a Discipline. Quest VII:47, 1967.
27. Northrop, F.S.C.: The Logic of the Sciences and the Humanities. New York:A. Meridian Book, World Publishing, 1971 (c) 1947.
28. Piaget, J.: Structuralism. Maschler, C. (trans.-ed.) New York:Basic Books, Inc., 1970.
29. Piaget, J.: The Place of the Sciences of Man in the System of Sciences. New York:Harper Torchbooks, Harper & Row, Publishers, 1970.
30. Rabi, I.I.: Science. The Center of Culture. New York and Cleveland:An NAL Book, The World Publishing Company, 1970, p. 34.
31. Ramunas, A.P.: The Development of the Whole Man Through Physical Education: An Interdisciplinary Comparative Exploration and Appraisal. Ottawa:University of Ottawa Press, 1968.
32. Renshaw, P.: The nature of human movement studies and it's relationship with physical education. Quest XX:79-86, 1973.
33. Richter, M.: Private communications.
34. Ross, S.: Disciplines, sub-disciplines, and the discipline of physical education. *In* Simri, U. (ed.): Concepts of Physical Education and Sport Sciences: Proceedings of an International Seminar. Jerusalem, the Wingate Institute for Physical Education and Sport in Cooperation with the Sport and Physical Education Authority in the Ministry of Education and Culture, 1974, p. 92.
35. Sheedy, A.: Towards a Theory of Physical Education. 1. Possibility and Conditions of Realization. *In* Simri, U. (ed.): Concepts of Physical Education and Sport Sciences: Proceedings of an International Seminar, Jerusalem, The Wingate Institute for Physical Education and Sport in cooperation with the Sport and Physical Education Authority in the Ministry of Education and Culture, 1974.
36. Sheedy, A.: Towards a Theory of Physical Education. 2. Are the Approaches Based on Formalization and Axiology Compatible? *In* Simri, U. (ed.): Concepts of Physical Education and Sport Sciences: Proceedings of an International Seminar, Jerusalem, The Wingate Institute for Physical Education and Sport in cooperation with the Sport and Physical Education Authority in the Ministry of Education and Culture, 1974.
37. Sheehan, T.J.: Sport: The focal point of physical education. Quest X, May 1968.

38. Sloan, M.R.: Human movement. Gymnasion, Vol. IX, Issue 2, Summer Edition, 1972, pp. 15-18.
39. Smith, N.W.: Movement as an academic discipline. JOHPER 35 (9):63-65, 1964.
40. Struder, G.: From Man Moving to Moving Man. Quest XX:104-107, 1973.
41. Vanderzwaag, H.J.: Sport studies and exercise science: Philosophical accommodations. Quest XX, June 1973, p. 75.
42. Von Bertalanffy, L.: General System Theory: Foundations, Development, Application. London:Allen Lane The Penguin Press, 1971 (c) 1868, pp. 15, 44.
43. Von Bertalanffy, L. and Rapoport, A. (eds.): General Systems. Bedfort, Mass.:The Society for General Systems Research, 12 volumes, 1956.
44. Zaft, S.J.: Alternate conceptions of a discipline of education. A critique and proposal. Unpublished Ph.D. Dissertation, Wayne State University, 1970, p. 113.
45. Zeigler, E.F. and McCristal, K.J.: A history of the Big Ten Body-of-Knowledge Project in physical education. Quest IX, December 1967.

Human Movement as a Field of Study

R. Carlisle

The discipline or field of knowledge which is referred to by the title "Human Movement Studies" is rapidly gaining ground and acceptance in the United Kingdom at the present time. The acceptance and spread of this new study is indicated by the incidence of first degree courses with this new title in colleges of education*; an expanding literature as represented by the Human Movement Series [1]; the appearance of a specialist journal [11]; and the publication of papers which attempt to argue persuasively the case for this new study [3, 5, 10]. While there is a sense in which this trend simply marks a change of title and emphasizes something which already exists within the study of physical education, there is another sense in which a radical development is taking place which is hostile to the concept and practice of physical education. Furthermore, it is clear that the proponents of this development have formed a powerful and effective lobby within higher education. It can be anticipated that Human Movement Studies will expand in schools — it has already appeared as a subject in C.S.E. courses — and that the schools will be forced by an examination system, for which pressure is mounting, to prepare students for courses of a like but advanced nature at college.†

So much for the educational politics of what will be read by some as just the latest version of a movement — the "movement movement" — which has a fairly long, complicated and emotional history in the United Kingdom [7]. However, in this latest formulation academics have sought to unite with "movement theorists" and to make use of certain attitudes and views which are currently fashionable in philosophy of education in Great Britain. This connection or fusion of elements makes a powerful ideology. It is my belief that this conjunction of movement with academic approaches

---

R. Carlisle, Department of Physical Education, Aberdeen College of Education and the University of Aberdeen, Aberdeen, Scotland.

*For example, within the University of London Institute of Education colleges since 1970.

†There are strong indications that these moves are afoot in Scotland.

and a certain kind of philosophy contains some questionable features and will prove to be a retrograde step in the study of human movement. The danger exists that academic studies will develop at the expense of the phenomenon which is alleged to be their subject matter. In general terms, then, I am concerned about a number of issues: (1) the process whereby movement is to be understood via activity, experiential and practical approaches in relation to or as against academic approaches; (2) the core of Human Movement Studies and the place of movement as a performing art as against the relevance and utility of academic approaches; (3) the place of physical education and, in particular, two of its constituents — dance education and sports education — vis-à-vis Human Movement Studies (dance education and sport education are both in a very unsatisfactory condition in our schools: I am fearful lest the rise of Human Movement Studies will make these two vital branches of physical education even less effective than they are at present); and (4) the place to be accorded in education and scholarship to movement or physical or bodily activity given the establishment of Human Movement Studies. Clearly, there is a wide-ranging cluster of concerns here. In this paper I should like to keep these concerns in mind while criticizing some of what I take to be the fundamental tenets of Human Movement Studies as expressed by Curl in what is the major statement in justification of the subject in the United Kingdom.

The first area of criticism is Curl's discussion of the concept of "human movement" itself. The fundamental features of his line of discussion can be summarized as follows. First, the simple definition of "human movement" in physical terms as "the change of position of the human body or its parts" [3] is rejected on the grounds that a physical or mechanical account of human movement is unable to pick out the distinctive human qualities in human movement. Quite simply, body movements can, after Ayer, be variously interpreted in terms drawn from the context of the movement in question [3]. Second, a behaviorist interpretation of human movement is rejected because of the need to recognize, after Peters, those aspects of the inner life of man concerned with imagination, memory, motivation, emotion, perception and intention [3]. It is interesting to note that Curl's justification is here at odds with Brooke and Whiting who in the introduction to the source book under discussion suggest, without foundation, that a primarily behavioral analysis had been adopted "and with reference to British culture" [1]. Third, Curl concludes that given the need to understand movement in the various contexts or forms of life of which it is a part, "any comprehensive account of human movement will admit of interpretations which depend upon human perception and take their meanings from forms of human culture of which they are an essential part" [3].

On the strict question of Curl's explication of the concept of human movement he recognizes that we are faced with a fairly simple physical concept as indicated by "change of position of the human body or its parts," but a concept which requires a difficult and wide-ranging "comprehensive account." In providing an account which necessarily entails analysis of what it is to be a human being moving, or a person, Curl greatly improves on previous attempts to define movement. (Some unhelpful cases selected at random are, I suggest, "the interaction of man and his environment" [2], "the interaction of man and his movements" [9] and "It is life as we know it" [6].

To be categorical and brief, I want to suggest that talk of analyzing the concept is otiose. What is interesting is that Curl has offered an account of what is involved when human beings move (this is hardly an analysis of the concept) which is in substance also an account of the phenomenon "physical activity." It is also in substance an account of the phenomenon "bodily activity." There are two important points to be made. The first is that "human movement" and "physical activity" have very similar connotations, with the exception that "human movement" has an association with dance in the United Kingdom while "physical activity" has contrasting sporting connotations. It should be stressed that these connections are historically given and do not derive from the concepts themselves. But these connotations do affect the "accounts" given of associated studies.* This is unfortunate both historically and conceptually. The second point is that neither concept is fundamental in the field under consideration because the fundamental concept is the concept of "the body." This is on the grounds that movement is an aspect of bodily activity with which it is not synonymous. This is a simple but fundamental point which has clear implications for "Movement Education" or "Physical Education," call it what you will, and for Human Movement Studies. The implication is that intimately related as mind and body are, an education of the body can be contrasted with the general notion of

---

*Cf. Kleinman, S.: The Significance of Human Movement: A Phenomenological Approach. NAPECW Report. Washington, D.C., 1964, and Sheehan, T.J.: Sport: The focal point of physical education. *Quest* Vol. X, 1968.

education as the development of the mind, of which it is an essential part. Thus we have the contrast between a bodily (or physical or movement) education and intellectual education; or bodily and academic education. This is a contrast which holds no matter what intellectual or academic content a bodily education may include (a content which must be present). This highlights the essential practical nature of this area of education.

A further point to be made is that bodily activity (and bodily education) can be further delineated in terms of whether activity incorporates bodily action merely as a necessarily present element, or whether the activity in question is a member of the class of bodily oriented activities. Traditionally, physical education as a school subject has concerned itself with the practice of distinctively bodily oriented activity. This is to say that the physical element in the traditional activities of the curriculum is a distinctive component. For example, although all the performing arts have a physical component, in dance and mime the primary focus is on the human body; whereas in singing it is on the musical sound produced not the movement of the lips; and in acting it is primarily on character or language. This is not to deny that other arts have physical components, or that dance has other components. Sport and "educational gymnastics" are likewise bodily in this sense. Body work and expression through the body are part of the intrinsic motivation which underlies all play, sport and dance. To fail to recognize this feature and to talk as if these distinctively bodily activities can be satisfactorily lumped together and studied with every other human activity which has a physical or bodily or movement component is to imagine that it would be wise to devise a practical "movement education" which could systematically develop for someone the skills, technical knowledge and understanding of, for example, surgery and typewriting and the manual trades and dance and sport and the expressive movement skills of everyday life, all of which entail movement and are in principle encompassed by its study. The same applies to a theoretical study of the same general and schematic type.

If we now return to Curl's exposition we find that "human movement is not a uniform phenomenon . . . we recognise many forms whose functions range from the most basic organic functions to the most sophisticated functions. Each form has its own particular functions — albeit with much interaction and interdependence" [3]. It is important to establish why such disparate "forms" should be integrated and made the subject matter of a common study. This brings us to a second fundamental consideration, the nature of the discipline or field of knowledge which Human Movement Studies is alleged to be.

Curl is again admirably clear. Human movement is not a uniform phenomenon because movement takes many forms. The many forms must "be analysable and describable in the distinct language which characterises quite different forms of knowledge" [3]. In order to study movement then we must proceed within the forms of knowledge which provide the conceptual schemes, methodology and criteria for establishing validity. This is of crucial importance because as Curl alleges that human movement has no distinctive concepts of its own [3]. Furthermore, a unifying framework is required and we are referred to Hirst's description of "fields of knowledge." Human movement is therefore construed as a "lively centre of interest round which a number of forms of knowledge 'collect.'" As a center of interest human movement has a natural "organic unity." As Curl says, "It might be claimed that human movement is a field of knowledge in which the various 'forms' converge and cohere in an organic fashion, in a mode analogous to the organism itself" [3].

To say that human movement is a center of interest appears to deny the range and complexity of human movement and the differentiated forms which it can take. Rather, movement seems to throw up a great variety of centers of interest. To say that although not uniform, human movement is unitary and has "organic unity" is obscure. The wide-ranging and disparate forms which human movement can take seem to lack organic unity in the sense of lacking either a common function overall, or necessary interdependence between form and form, a condition which only seems to hold between certain basic organic functions and more sophisticated forms. At this point an ambiguity arises because Curl slides from talking about the organic unity of movement itself, the raw data or subject matter for study, to talking about the organic unity of the converging and cohering forms. Clearly, the distinct forms of knowledge, like the movement forms themselves, do not enter into organic relationships. Thus a particular center of interest, say dance, can be picked out as a focus and studied by means of selected forms which develop appropriate insights, knowledge and understanding. Indeed, I go so far as to say that this is the way the study of sport and of dance, for example, should be organized.

This raises doubts regarding the possibility of scholarship which requires mastery of so many disciplines in an extensive field; doubts about the relevance of combining so many possible centers of interest under one heading, when so many centers of interest, particularly sport and dance, require quite separate study; and doubts about the utility of bringing so many disciplines (scientific, esthetic, social and philosophical) to bear on such a wide-ranging phenomenon in an institutional setting. Perhaps the model of a small research team comprised of scholars from different disciplines working usefully together is being taken as the yardstick for the study of human movement at all levels in education. But this is quite misleading.

Another ambiguity concerns the use of the word "study." It seems that Curl's statement applies to the academic study of human movement by means of the disciplines or forms of knowledge. Yet there is also the practical study of human movement, and this need not proceed within the context of academic study. Furthermore, the practical study of certain forms of human movement does employ concepts, and technical knowledge which is not derived from the forms of knowledge as specified by Curl. Against Curl it can be posited that movement does have its own concepts which arise within the form of movement in question and from everyday language and common understanding. A thoroughgoing academic account of the kind elaborated by Curl undermines, on spurious epistemological grounds, the validity of the basic terms, techniques and common understanding which are the primary terms in which we conceive of these activities [4]. Therefore, I suggest that the study of movement, in a full and proper sense, requires a primary commitment to bodily experience followed by appropriately selected academic studies which provide a deepening of understanding. This is the correct model [8]. This is in line with the view that Human Movement Studies should be primarily a practical-esthetic subject, in which bodily experience, intelligence and vitality are central within the distinctive expressive medium which is the human body in operation. This raises the possibility that Human Movement Studies could be established as a distinct discipline with its own core, concepts and modes of awareness derived from bodily experience and expression.

Finally, I should like to take up certain points which Curl makes regarding Human Movement Studies and Physical Education. The basic view expressed by Curl is that although the study of human movement developed within the field of physical education, the two subjects are of different logical categories. Theory of physical education, like educational theory, has a practical function, whereas human movement as a study is not tied to any practical function, and "it is free to develop its own standards of relevance which are intrinsic to it" [3]. As an academic study human movement is free to pursue a "universal object" according to its own intrinsic standards. Physical Education, on the other hand, as a practical study is enslaved by the need to pursue extrinsic aims and objectives. Physical Education is therefore stretched beyond its limits by the growth within it of a field of knowledge concerned with human movement.

The nature of education, and consequently of physical education, is here misconstrued by Curl. This depends upon a failure to appreciate that in one sense education encompasses human knowledge and understanding, that the development of knowledge and understanding serve the ends of education and not vice versa. The forms of knowledge are therefore properly conceived as educational activities because they are concerned with the development of knowledge and the exercise of mental powers. On the other hand, there is a sense of education, more properly Educational Theory, in which there is reference to the processes whereby persons develop knowledge and understanding particularly when they are young. In this sense, Educational Theory is the body of knowledge and practical theories which govern these processes. It therefore seems more appropriate to say that in the first sense, Human Movement Studies is subsumed by education and that the free study, intrinsic standards and pursuit of a "universal object" derive from the nature of education.* In so far as the study of human movement has practical dimensions it is subsumed by physical education. In this sense physical education is a mode of education and not a subject. Like other modes of education, for example moral education and social education, physical education is difficult to define because of its manifold connections with the life of man, its multivalued nature and the range of ways it can manifest itself. Like the study of human movement, physical education can be thought of in two ways: first as having a general connotation, as being education through all or any physical activity; second, as being a restricted concept, and here, I suggest, the notion of bodily oriented activity is one appropriate demarcating criterion. The trouble has been that in practice, physical education has operated in schools in the second sense, yet it has been thought of in terms of the first sense.

I therefore suggest that the true state of affairs is much more complex than Curl would have us believe. Physical education can be

---

*Cf. Peters, R.S.: *Ethics and Education.* London:Allen & Unwin, 1966.

thought of as a mode of education, or as a subject with academic content, or as a purely practical study, each in the general and restricted senses outlined above. It can also operate in a vocational setting, but this is a special case, with its extrinsic ends, which seems to confuse Curl. In the other cases the standards, like those of education in general, are intrinsic, as are the aims and objectives pursued. A difficulty is that Human Movement Studies as interpreted by Curl has become a thoroughly academic study.* As such, I suggest that the purely academic study be left in the main distributed around the various theoretical disciplines concerned. There, specialist and systematic study can be combined with research and proper resources and directed to all and every aspect of human movement. Any organization of studies under a heading like "Human Movement Studies" should, in the light of the foregoing discussions and considerations, I submit, be confined to more restricted ends and purposes.

References

1. Brooke, J.D. and Whiting, H.T.A. (eds.): Human Movement — A Field of Study. London:Henry Kimpton, 1973.
2. Brown, C. and Cassidy, R.: Theory in Physical Education — A Guide to Program Change. Philadelphia:Lea & Febiger, 1963.
3. Curl, G.F.: An attempt to justify human movement as a field of study. *In* Brooke, J.D. and Whiting, H.T.A. (eds.): Human Movement — a Field of Study. London:Henry Kimpton, 1973.
4. Elliott, R.K.: Education and human being. I. *In* Brown, S.C. (ed.): Philosophers Discuss Education. London:Macmillan Press, 1975.
5. Hinks, E.M., Archbutt, S.E. and Curl, G.F.: "Movement Studies": A new standing conference. Univ. London Inst. Educ. Bull., Vol. 23, 1971.
6. Laban, R.: The Mastery of Movement. London:Macdonald & Evans, 1960.
7. McIntosh, P.C.: The curriculum of physical education — An historical perspective. *In* Kane, J. (ed.): Curriculum Development in Physical Education. London:Crosby Lockwood Staples, 1976.
8. North, M.: But where is the movement? A critique. Univ. London Inst. Educ. Bull., Vol. 23, 1971.
9. Paddick, R.J.: The Nature and Place of a Field of Knowledge in Physical Education. Unpublished M.A. thesis, University of Alberta, 1967.
10. Renshaw, P.: Physical education: The need for philosophical clarification. Educ. Teaching, Vol. 87, 1972.
11. Whiting, H.T.A. and Whiting, M.G. (eds.): Journal of Human Movement Studies. London:Lepus Books.

*Cf. Hinks et al [5].

On the Elaboration of a General Theory Regarding Sports Activities

V. V. Davydov

Modern athletic achievements are due in some measure to the work of people in sociology, pedagogy, psychology, medicine and other fields of knowledge. Data submitted to the International Congress on Sports in Modern Society, held in Moscow in 1974, show that joint studies conducted by specialists in many fields of knowledge have contributed to new achievements in sports.

Research projects and the elaboration of the practical recommendations ensuing from them require a certain identity of views on the part of the various specialists involved as concerns the goals set for high athletic achievements and how these may be attained. Researchers must understand the essence of the vital activities performed by the athletes before, during and after contests. Identity of views has been lacking in some cases; there are several reasons for this. One is the fact that no all-embracing theory yet exists about the concept of sports as a special social phenomenon. However, with international sports at its present level, the prerequisites already exist for elaborating an all-embracing theory.

At present it is ascertained that sport is a complex and polyfunctional phenomenon. It influences many aspects of social life such as production, health services, education and ideology. A general sport theory should establish the causes and mechanisms of such an influence, for it is insufficient to reduce a general sport theory to the mere statement of its connections with other aspects of life. Such theory must explain the nature and essence of sport as an independent social institution, with its own special intents and purposes in the life of people.

A general sport theory can be constructed only if one uses (1) the concepts concerning the social life and consciousness of people and (2) the psychological concepts relative to the processes of transformation of these social forms into activity and consciousness of a separate individual nature in sport. This theory synthesizes

---

V. V. Davydov, Institute of General and Pedagogical Psychology, Moscow, U.S.S.R.

sociological and psychological concepts and may serve as a basis for a common approach by specialists from different fields to the problems of sport development.

The Soviet sociologists consider the motor activity of human beings as one of the basic forms of social-historical experience. In such an activity the different social relations are formed and revealed. Motor activity has a long history of development, closely related to the history of labor and armed forces with its disjunction into separate vocations and with its subsequent recombinations. It is obviously necessary to maintain the experience of motor activity, transfer it to new generations and develop it.

It is important to note that in the early stages of industrial production, when physical labor was predominant, the motor activity experience was rather fixed and transferred as narrow partially professional abilities and skills. But with the development of labor (especially when — with the machine era — it became in the 18th and 19th centuries necessary and possible to change the vocations) the *general* content of the vocational motor experiences became more clearly defined. This content meant many types of separate professions, ensured high enough a level of body training and vigour, and served as a basis for health. A general motor experience acquired features of such motor qualities and properties which were necessary for the individual to accomplish different things in labor as well as in social life. The acquisition of a general motor experience is an essential condition of the formation of a human being; it allowed, over and above his professional abilities and skills, to overcome the defects of his body and to resist occupational diseases.

The development of labor demands of a person to be *poly*technically educated; similarly, in the motor-organic field, one needs to be *poly*motorily trained. This specific social task is served by the form of social activity which began gradually to be called *sport*. Its sources are rooted in historically formed industrial and civic demands on the general motor-organic skills of a person. The appearance of sport as a special social institution (the history of this process presumes social research) settles contradictions between partially professional demands to man as a worker and the necessity to have a general motor experience, which embraces all kinds of labor and civic activities. Therefore, from the very beginning, as at present, the formation of sport is itself related to many socioeconomic, ideological and political aspects of life.

Thus born as a social institution, sport acquires its own content, its own specific means of discovering, shaping and transferring of man's motor-organic abilities. These abilities actually should be general and separated from partially professional demands to man's motor experience. Sport is becoming a field of *universalization* of this experience, a means of covering its narrow professional limitations. Such universalization of motion coincides with a wider process of universalization of man's activity in the development of social production. Such is the world-historically importance of sport, its high humanistic content. At the same time, sharp social contradictions appear in this process, including class contradictions, which inevitably are found in sport. A real universalization of activity, particularly of a motor activity, cannot appear within bourgeois productive relations. Realization of all forms of man's universalization implies the transition to a socialist and communist society, where sport acquires its own most developed form and deals with the idea of a real physical perfection of man.

If sport is a means of universalization of motor experience, then it is clear that it has its own *organization* for the achievement of this specific goal. In sport there should be standards and samples of universalization of motor-organic abilities, of which the *athletes* are living carriers. These standards are historically established thanks to the comparison between the movements in the process of making maximum demands to the validity of their competence. Thus, sport needs the contest and matches at condition of maximum loading, which reveal "pure" motor-organic features and abilities of man.

Such an understanding of sport allows us to explain a number of essential moments. First, the public mode and entertainment of sport are becoming clear. We can't imagine matches without spectators who *assess* sport standards and accept them as possible norms for their own motor-organic abilities. In this process the *identification* between the athlete and the spectator takes place (details of this process are described in special publications). Second, the necessity of *big* sport becomes clear, especially that of world competitions in which the criteria of universality of motor experience are being formed, and as "pure" forms of movement and motor abilities are discovered, shaped and perfected (under conditions of social-historical division of labor the professionalization in sport is inevitable, but its future needs a special analysis). Third, the necessity of mass amateur sport is revealed as an actual realization by certain individuals of their identification with the sample-athlete, as a realization of the accepted norms of general motor-organic experience. Due to engagement in sport, one of the conditions of which are the attending and sharp sensations at sport shows, the individuals acquire a need for the universalization of their own movements, for overcoming their own partially occupational motor experience, and, finally, for the betterment of the organic foundations of their own general occupational mastery. Fourth, the necessity is revealed for an organic physical education as a special transfer of foundation of motor experience to the new generations.

The revealing of the social essence of sport leads the researcher to the problem of the transformation of its social necessity into forms of individual activity. At present, for an analysis of this process it is possible to use the theory of activity developed by Soviet psychologists. In any kind of activity it is possible to select the following components: its needs and motives, its special purposes and tasks, as well as actions, operations and means, which are adequate for its solvings. These components are in a definite relation to each other. Thus, the all-embracing theory corresponds to the concepts of need and motives, separate actions — to the concept of goals, a number of operations — to the concept of task condition and so on. Separate activity components might change functions during the process of their development (for example, a goal could become a motive, the action — an operation and vice versa). There are definite stages of analysis of any kind of activity (including sport activity). In the first stage the normative structure of a certain form of activity is established (for example, the needs and motives, which make a person indulge in sport). In the second stage psychological processes are discovered which regulate this structure (for example, the processes according to which man outlines the goals and tasks of his sport activity). The third stage of analysis permits to discover sets of separate psychological abilities included in the indicated processes (for example, the ability to make a program of their own sport actions). In the fourth stage it is necessary to study specifically the development of a certain activity in relation to its functional and age aspects (for example, to study the dynamics of changing of the functions of separate components of sport activity).

To elaborate a general social-psychological theory of sport it is necessary to obtain sets of data which are typical for all stages of its analysis. Although there are many different kinds of data in sports sciences, there are still few data dealing with the notion of the essence of sport described above. Especially, there is little information concerning the conditions in which motivation for sport activities arise; there is also little information pertaining to the understanding of motive dynamics, purposes and tasks that drive separate individuals (in different age stages and different social belonging) into sport. Particularly, there are few actually verified data, which characterize how the identification of an individual is formed as he is drawn into sport with an athlete. We have a few data to clarify the psychological mechanism by which a definite level of identification becomes a real foundation for an active individual participation in mass (or professional) sport. It is most important to reveal these mechanisms to establish the psychological validity of the organization of physical education and for the development of stable and deep sport needs in children and youth. It is impossible to provide effective physical education and draw the youth into sport without educating for such a need, without emotional sensations of belonging to remarkable, beautiful motor features and abilities.

It is worthy to note that on the basis of a general sport theory a number of more partial theories of sport might successfully be developed. Particularly, it is very important to study the history of concrete means of universalization of man's motor-organic experience and to clarify which means of standardization of general motor features are typical for contemporary levels of sport. It is also important to establish particular methods of transformation of standards of general motor features into one that it is possible to achieve in mass sport and in the organization of physical education in the schools.

In the sport sciences, biomechanics and physiology take a special place. Data in these fields may be correctly interpreted within a general sport theory, especially in such partial theories which explain the origin of means of universalization of movements. At the same time, it is well known now that a number of purely physiological processes depend to a great extent upon psychological functions of corresponding organs, within an all-embracing activity of man. Thus, research shows that fatigue in some organ may very much depend upon the functions of other organs involved in the total activity.

The approach presented above for the development of a general sport theory must be detailed in the aspects of its principles and of its actual foundations. It will thus be necessary to make a number of aimed researches in different scientific fields that concentrate on the perspectives of development of contemporary sport.

Normes du système de la culture physique de l'Homme contemporain

Zdenek Sprynar

L'homme contemporain appartient à une société hautement évoluée, qui fait entrer de plus en plus la science dans le rôle de la force productrice au processus de l'appropriation de la nature. Ce processus — la révolution scientifique et technique — se déroule à une vitesse de plus en plus grande et fait entrer dans la sphère des changements révolutionnaires successivement toute l'Humanité; il devient au vrai sens du mot une affaire globale.

Si on considère les normes du système de la culture physique en ce moment de l'histoire de l'Homme où, dans la vie d'une génération, se déroulent des changements beaucoup plus importants que ceux qui ont eu lieu auparavant au cours d'époques entières, il apparaît nécessaire de chercher les relations importantes.

Nous comprenons la culture physique comme une composante de la culture de l'homme dont la spécificité consiste en la formation de valeurs dans le domaine du perfectionnement physique de l'homme et dont les normes générales visent la cultivation des forces créatrices à tous égards et dirigées vers le développement universel et libre de tous les membres de la société.

Cet idéal peut devenir l'objectif historique réel d'une société qui atteindra un niveau du développement des forces productrices indispensables à satisfaire aux besoins culturels de tous les membres de la société, laquelle aura en même temps des rapports de production correspondant à cet objectif.

L'Homme contemporain a besoin et en même temps a droit à une culture physique qui l'enrichit physiquement et psychiquement, qui constitue une partie du combat pour le progrès social et l'arrangement équitable de la société. Aux normes de l'homme contemporain ne correspond point un tel système de la culture physique dans lequel, par exemple, le sport ou l'arène sportive revêt l'aspect de l'opium social. Le sport, l'éducation physique et la récréation, bref tout le domaine de la culture physique, est un phénomène politique.

Zdenek Sprynar, Faculté d'éducation physique et du sport, Université Charles, Prague, Tchécoslovaquie.

Il faut que le système de la culture physique de l'homme contemporain serve au progrès et non à l'analphabétisme social, que le sport international développe l'idée de coexistence pacifique et ne serve pas à encourager le nationalisme et l'agression.

L'orientation vers le progrès social représente la norme fondamentale selon laquelle il faut évaluer le système de la culture physique sous l'aspect des besoins de l'homme contemporain. Le système de la culture physique progressiste est caractérisé par la conception scientifique et systématique d'après laquelle sont mutuellement respectées les lois objectives de la nature et celles de la société, c'est-à-dire les lois du développement de l'homme à tous égards et la satisfaction de ses besoins.

Dans les relations des mécanismes biologiques et sociaux de la culture physique, la signification décisive appartient aux lois sociales. La qualité du système de la culture physique est déterminée par le système social. L'histoire contemporaine offre un tas de preuves concrètes montrant comment la liaison de la révolution scientifique et technique avec les avantages du socialisme crée les prémisses qualitativement neuves et plus élevées permettant la satisfaction des besoins toujours croissants de tous les membres de la société, même dans le domaine de la culture physique.

Quels sont les problèmes de premier plan relatifs aux dimensions biologiques de la culture physique? Il ne fait pas de doute que l'activité motrice consciencieusement menée devient un moyen décisif permettant de combattre les méfaits de l'hypodynamie.

Les exercices physiques apportent un effet de compensation contre les charges psychiques de la vie moderne en faisant appel aux mécanismes si nécessaires de détente et du repos actif.

Les moyens de la culture physique nous aident à combattre l'obésité, à prévenir les maladies de civilisation. Ces aspects ne représentent dans l'ensemble que les premières aides, c'est-à-dire une intervention rapide contre les conflicts que subit l'homme contemporain à cause des changements radicaux des conditions de vie.

Le sens objectif et historique du progrès scientifique et technique se trouve dans la création des conditions servant non seulement à satisfaire les besoins fondamentaux de l'homme, mais aussi le développement universel de ces besoins, incluant la satisfaction du besoin suprême, celui du développement maximal des forces créatrices humaines.

Dans ce sens, l'apport spécifique de la culture physique apparaît sous une lumière nouvelle. A part la direction visée jusqu'à présent, i.e. le développement de l'aptitude et de l'adresse motrices, on retrouve aujourd'hui au premier plan l'objectif du développement d'un fonctionnement harmonieux de l'organisme, le maintien d'une bonne condition physique et des capacités d'adaptation jusqu'à l'âge avancé.

Cela conduit à des changements remarquables dans les processus de l'éducation physique. Au sein de tous ces rapports, les mécanismes d'adaptation apparaissent comme déterminants. Il s'agit de l'utilization programmée, pendant toute la vie, de la richesse (préformée phylogénétiquement) des possibilités d'adaptation de l'organisme humain, et de l'utilisation de l'effet non spécifique de l'adaptation.

En ce qui concerne ces mécanismes, les deux périodes extrèmes de la vie humaine acquièrent, dans la structure ontogénétique du système de la culture physique, une grande importance; l'enfance, surtout les premiers mois et les premières années de vie, est la plus importante pour le développement de l'adaptabilité; à la période des processus d'involution la stimulation des mécanismes d'adaptation maintient pour sa part sur une bonne base les fonctions élémentaires de l'organisme humain.

La structure dynamique de l'activité physique devient ainsi une condition indispensable du régime optimal de vie de l'homme contemporain et en même temps un élément marquant du mode de vie.

L'homme doit être formé à la dynamique de l'activité physique. Plus sa formation à ce besoin élémentaire et biologique sera adéquate, meilleures seront ses dispositions individuelles à satisfaire ce besoin et à incorporer avec dextérité les éléments de son propre système de culture physique dans un programme créateur, dans la vie de famille et dans la structure des rapports sociaux.

Pour permettre ces conditions préalables, la société doit naturellement disposer d'une structure convenable et des cadres qualifiés en tant qu'ingénieurs du système individuel et social de la culture physique.

La société doit aussi disposer d'une structure ramifiée et bien coordonnée des institutions de la culture physique et d'une importante base matérielle et technique. Les installations pour la culture physique se développeront dans l'avenir en meilleur rapport avec la nature et deviendront un facteur important de la formation d'un milieu optimal de vie.

Nous entendons l'homme contemporain dans le sens de tous les membres de la société et non dans celui de l'homme privilégié. De ce point de vue, il apparaît que faire valoir les normes objectives du système de la culture physique ne peut se faire que dans une société sans rapports antagonistes, c'est-à-dire dans une société avec une économie dirigée scientifiquement, développée, et capable de concentrer et d'utiliser les fonds nécessaires à un système effectif de la culture physique correspondant au besoins de l'homme contemporain.

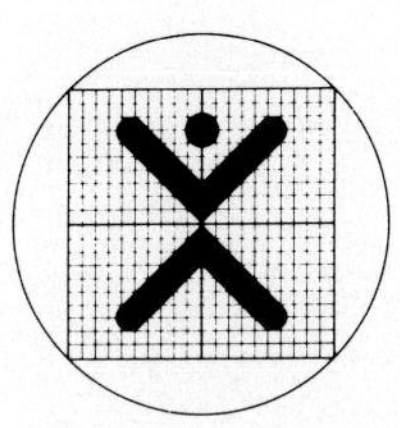

Theology

Sport, a Liberating or Alienating Force

Théologie

Le sport, facteur de libération ou d'aliénation

Le sport, facteur de libération ou d'alienation

Herman de Mulder

Sport, a Liberating or Alienating Force

The author contends that sport should be considered as a phenomenon closely related to the social activity which it requires and mobilizes. He comments on the various forms of sport which are said to present alienating facets, such as, amongst others, high performance sport and professional sport. He discusses various concepts of freedom and liberation and the characteristics of human tasks that have liberating values. It is shown that in the wide spectrum of contemporary sports activities, recreational sport offers excellent opportunities for the learning and practice of human liberty and happiness.

Le sport, facteur de libération ou d'aliénation

Dans un monde en pleine mutation industrielle, économique et politique, les progrès de la science et les développements de la technique créent de nouvelles conditions de vie tant individuelles que collectives. Il y a beacoup de gens qui mènent une vie quelque peu déréglée par suite des agressions de plus en plus violentes de notre monde actuel, un monde mécanisé, énervant, bruyant, pollué . . .

Sous prétexte de faciliter la vie, notre société de consommation engendre une recherche qui a tendance à supprimer tout effort et ainsi à nous condamner à la molesse, la paresse et l'inactivité. Tout cela peut amener à un certain nivellement de vie pouvant conduire aussi à un certain état d'*aliénation de l'homme.* Ce terme a des significations diverses, qui varient en fonction des orientations doctrinales et, à l'intérieur de celles-ci, en fonction des problèmes examinés. Nous le prenons ici dans son sens le plus large: l'état où l'homme est dans l'impossibilité de se réaliser comme homme, pour des raisons structurelles, culturelles et personnelles, l'état où il est

---

Herman de Mulder, Abbaye de Tongerlo, Westerlo, Belgique.

presque impossible pour l'homme d'épanouir ses aspirations profondes d'amour et de liberté.

L'aliénation est le noyau du mal dans le monde, et donc du problème qu'il soulève. Mais l'aliénation se réfère avant tout à ces maux qui, étant provoqués par l'homme lui-même, pourraient aussi être supprimés par l'homme.

Aussi dans le sport l'homme a provoqué du mal. Le sport, comme facteur de la culture humaine, est une création de l'homme. Le sport ne peut se concevoir en dehors de l'activité sociale qu'il requiert, qu'il mobilise et qu'il déclenche. Toutes les institutions, toutes les structures, qu'il s'agisse du droit, de la politique, de la législation, du commerce, du tourisme ou de l'éducation, sont touchées par le sport. Tous les secteurs de la technique sont au service du sport: l'urbanisme, l'électronique, la chimie, la météorologie, etc. Les valeurs esthétiques, la mode, l'éthique, la morale sont mises en question par la pratique et le spectacle sportif. Nous sommes parfois loin du sport que le dictionnaire nous apprend: le sport (mot anglais) vient du vieux français "desport" qui signifiait amusement, délassement, distraction, divertissement, récréation. Et le dictionnaire ajoute en guise de définition: sport = ensemble des exercices physiques se présentant sous forme de jeux individuels ou collectifs, pratiqués en observant certaines règles précises, et sans but utilitaire immédiat!

Dans la pratique sociale le sport n'est pas seulement activité physique mais activité humaine, avec pour corollaire la complexité et les difficultés de lecture qu'entraîne aujourd'hui, en dehors de tout dogmatisme et de toute idéologie prégnante, l'étude de toute activité humaine.

Que constatons-nous aujourd'hui?

Dans la pratique sportive, il existe une grande diversification. Empiriquement nous pouvons déceler quatre niveaux dans cette pratique:

1. le secteur du sport de haute compétition
2. le secteur du sport de profession
3. le secteur du sport de récréation
4. le secteur de la récréation sportive.

C'est surtout au sport de profession en de haute compétition qu'on fait des reproches. Ce sont surtout ces deux types de sport qui sont parfois facteur d'aliénation.

Il y a dans le sport de haute compétition des gens pour qui ne compte que la victoire, des gens qui cherchent à gagner par tous les moyens, qui s'abandonnent corps et âme à la tutelle de l'entraîneur.

Leur vie privée et familiale pâtit forcément de leur activité sportive. Il existe des esclaves d'une profession sportive! Le sport peut aussi être facteur d'aliénation dans des situatious où le sport est l'objet d'utilisations malhonnêtes.

Doper un homme, modifier artificiellement son métabolisme en vue d'un rendement musculaire accru, c'est attenter à la dignité de cet homme, c'est commettre un crime contre l'espèce humaine. Et il y a encore d'autres reproches d'aliénation par le sport: un Etat qui cherche surtout des champions représentatifs, qui ne s'intéresse au sport que parce qu'il y voit un moyen de dériver l'énergie des masses ou parce qu'il y voit un moyen de récupération de la force de travail ou parce qu'il y voit un moyen pour la sauvegarde de l'espèce. La publicité faite autour du sport et des spectacles sportifs, la naissance de toute un industrie d'articles sportifs sont encore à l'origine de plusieurs utilisations malhonnêtes du sport.

Les sportifs, d'ailleurs, dans la recherche de plus en plus poussée de leur rendement, se trouvent lancés dans un mouvement croissant de spécialisation, identique à celui que l'on constate dans le monde du travail. Les critères d'efficacité, de profit, d'utilité et de consommation de la société contemporaine tendraient à amener le sport à une subordination à ces soi-disant valeurs, en le récupérant dans une industrie de loisir. Le sport risquerait alors de n'être qu'une émanation, soit d'un capitalisme industriel, soit d'un système totalitaire ou étatique. Dans le sport en général, on pourrait craindre que la société contemporaine utilise le sport comme moyen de dérivation de l'énergie des masses ou de défoulement des tendances agressives de l'individu. Elle utiliserait le sport au lieu de lui laisser sa valeur humaine de jeu et de liberté. Heureusement nous constatons dans notre temps et comme signe de ce temps, chez les hommes et dans la société, une aspiration et un besoin profond de sociabilité, de participation, d'unité, d'équilibre, de respect de la dignité, de fraternité, de libération.

La signification de la liberté est définie non seulement par ce qu'elle nie, notamment les multiples formes d'aliénation, mais par ce qu'elle affirme, c.à.d. la participation de l'homme à la création culturelle, à la construction d'une communauté fondée sur l'amour et l'amitié. Il reste nécessaire de créer les conditions de la liberté. Il s'agit donc d'une nouvelle culture, mais aussi de nouvelles structures. L'homme libéré est celui qui est individuellement et collectivement en recherche d'une option fondamentale, justifiant à ses yeux ses choix de vie personnelle et collective devenant pour lui motivation profonde. L'homme doit être capable, avec les autres, non pas de s'intégrer simplement dans quelque système que ce soit, mais de transformer et de renouveler tous les domaines de la vie et donc aussi le domaine du sport. Dans la mesure où il n'est pas facteur de rupture mais créateur d'harmonie et d'équilibre dans tous les milieux où l'homme vit et est appelé à se réaliser comme personne et être social, le sport, étant une activité humaine, est facteur de libération.

La libération se présente d'abord comme une tâche humaine, quotidienne, dans tous les domaines de l'existence, du travail comme du loisir, comme de la vie morale, personnelle, conjugale ou familiale. C'est une exigence de notre condition d'homme: affronter un combat avec l'univers, un combat avec l'homme en essayant avec les autres de maîtriser peu à peu l'univers, de se libérer de ses contraintes. Le résultat c'est le bonheur! Le bonheur est quelque qui se gagne, quelque chose pour quoi il faut lutter et se battre.

Le sport est l'un des chemins de la liberté,
l'une des voies du bonheur.

Nous assistons à présent au refus de tout effort, de toute ascèse, de toute compétition au nom d'une civilisation de la jouissance et du plaisir. C'est bien contre ce manque d'enthousiasme et de ferveur, contre cette façon de mal vivre que le sport offre un antidote. Le sport aide à mieux vivre et surtout à vivre plus jeune! Le sport devient un des éléments constitutifs du bonheur humain.

Les sociétés industrielles, à quelque type qu'elles appartiennent, secrètent un certain nombre de maladies du comportement dont les moindres ne sont pas: la dégénérescence physique, la passivité intellectuelle, le suivisme et l'affaiblissement du sens moral, la perte du besoin de communication et du sens communautaire, le manque de joie et l'oubli de la notion de fête. L'égoïsme joue un rôle très important dans la vie de beaucoup d'habitants de nos cités industrielles.

Dans plusieurs pays, les hommes politiques, les syndicalistes, les éducateurs, en quête d'une humanité plus juste et plus heureuse, ont découvert le sport comme moyen pour porter remède au mal. On avance en effet aujourd'hui, dans les milieux les plus divers, que la renaissance à la vie de l'esprit, que la prise de responsabilité sociale et politique, que la régénération du sens moral, peuvent passer par le médium de l'activité sportive.

Le sport de haute compétition et de profession a fait oublier par trop que si le sport est une lutte, il est fondamentalement un jeu et une fête. Et si le jeu c'est la joie, la joie n'est-elle pas une composante nécessaire du bonheur?

Et jouer, c'est se créer, ou plutôt se recréer pour l'homme malade des grandes villes. C'est exprimer la vie, ou plutôt sa vie d'une façon globale et totale, dans les cadres d'une liberté clairement définie et acceptée. Ainsi, en permettant à l'homme brimé par les contraintes sociales de s'extravertir, de s'exprimer librement, et donc d'avoir confiance en soi, le sport ouvre à l'homme la voie de la créativité.

Le problème primordial reste: l'homme, son éducation, sa formation, son épanouissement pour qu'il obtienne et parvienne à sa plénitude, à sa libération totale!

Pratiquement la libération de l'homme par le sport peut s'effectuer aussi bien dans le sport de haute compétition et de profession que dans le sport de récréation et dans la récréation sportive.

Nous sommes persuadé que, dans le sport de haute compétition et dans le sport de profession, c'est surtout cette attitude morale qui constitue le fair-play qui peut apporter sa précieuse contribution à la libération de l'homme. Le fair-play est une *façon d'être*! Le fair-play comprend à la fois le respect de soi-même et le respect de l'adversaire.

C'est le respect de soi-même qui se manifeste par l'esprit de justice et de loyauté; par le respect de l'adversaire, qu'il soit vainqueur ou vaincu; par le respect de l'arbitre et l'esprit de collaboration constante avec lui; par une attitude digne et ferme de modestie dans la victoire et de sérénité dans la défaite. Le fair-play c'est la générosité envers l'adversaire qui avant tout est un partenaire de jeu. Et dans le jeu sportif il y a des règles, écrites et non écrites, qui doivent être respectées.

Le sens du jeu sportif risque d'être dénaturé quand les intérêts commerciaux, le nationalisme, le chauvinisme ou le racisme y jouent le rôle principal. Quand le sport ou la compétition deviennent combat sans merci où les questions de prestige, de popularité, d'argent prennent le pas sur toutes autres considérations, la brutalité et la déloyauté s'installent alors sur le terrain avec la participation de la foule, avec la complicité active ou silencieuse de dirigeants et d'entraîneurs, qui ne voient plus de justifications de leur rôle que dans la victoire à tout prix.

Contre ces déviations du sport il faut à tout prix proclamer le fair-play comme unique loi morale du sport. En Europe et surtout en Belgique, en Hollande et en France, des actions de fair-play sont en cours.

En Belgique c'est l'association *SPORTA* (l'Apostolat du Sport) qui a pris l'initiative de sensibiliser la population pour le fair-play.

Chaque jeune et chaque adulte doit être persuadé, par tous les moyens, que la préservation de l'esprit sportif est la plus impérieuse des exigences. Sans quoi le sport, qui devrait être pour l'homme une source de joie et de bonheur, risque d'être entraîné dans le mortel courant de l'égoïsme et de la violence.

Dans cette action la "Sporta" a demandé la collaboration des éducateurs, des dirigeants, des parents, des arbitres, des pratiquants sportifs, des spectateurs et supporters, de la presse, la radio et la télévision, des fédérations sportives et des pouvoirs publics. Tous ont une responsabilité dans cette action, qui se concrétise dans le "Fair Play Club," dont chacun peut devenir membre. Le seul but du "Fair Play Club" est d'entreprendre des efforts de formation et d'information au sujet de l'esprit sportif avec la coopération bénévole et gratuite de tous ses membres.

Dans le secteur du sport de profession et de haute compétition il y a encore un question des plus aigue qui demande une solution: *le statut social de l'athlète de profession.* Parfois le professionel ou le champion a du mal à se retirer à temps de l'arène. Ce n'est sans doute pas seulement parce qu'il aime ce qu'il fait, mais parce que sa reconversion par exemple, lui pose de nombreux problèmes. De plus, très souvant se posent aussi des problèmes de contrat, de paiement, d'assurance, de pension, de maladie et d'invalidité.

En Belgique il existe auprès du Syndicat chrétien une Centrale de service syndical — Sporta, qui s'occupe de tous les problèmes des professionels en sport. Nous pouvons dire ici que ce Service contribue tres fort à la libération de l'homme dans ce secteur de la vie sportive. Nous ne pouvons qu'espérer que dans beaucoup d'autres pays on s'occupe d'une façon analogue du statut social de l'athlète de profession.

Le sport de récréation, qui est le sport de tant de fédérations, d'associations sportives, de clubs, d'écoles et même d'entreprises, peut être d'une grande importance dans la sécurité des valeurs humaines et donc dans la libération de l'homme.

Le sport de récréation, étant essentiellement aussi jeu, compétition et organisation, étant une activité humaine, dans quelle mesure peut-il être libérateur de l'homme? C'est dans la mesure où le sport est créateur d'harmonie et d'équilibre dans tous les milieux où l'homme vit en développant sa personne, sa personalité, et dans cette dernière tout ce que l'on peut imaginer comme possibilité d'intérêt. Il y a nombre de choses intéressantes que l'on peut cultiver selon sa personalité, mais un élément d'équilibre fondamental, c'est le sport.

Le sport, au moins dans la société industrielle, doit être désormais considéré par tous comme une nécessité vitale au même titre que les disciplines intellectuelles à l'école, comme le travail aussi.

Le sport doit devenir partie intégrante de la vie. C'est un droit civique dont peuvent se réclamer tous les citoyens auxquels doivent être dispensés tous les moyens leur permettant d'exercer une activité physique, tant pour leur santé que pour leur loisir.

Mais tout cela suppose que l'on a une conception saine du sport! Rien n'est sans doute plus merveilleux en l'homme que son pouvoir de garder "l'esprit d'enfance," la fraîcheur des sentiments, les grandes joies des moments profondément heureux que donne *le jeu sportif!*

Une conception saine du sport accorde encore une vraie valeur à la liberté du jeu!

Le jeu en tant que jeu est un phénomène culturel spécifique, où le moment ludique est exprimé pour lui-même, dans sa forme propre. L'approche ludique de la réalité pose l'homme comme un être vivant qui peut transcender sans cesse toutes choses donnés et fixées. Jouer, c'est travailler avec des possibilités sans s'arrêter à leur réalisation, toujours disposé à accueillir la surprise de possibilités nouvelles. Grâce à son pouvoir ludique, l'homme affirme la puissance de sa liberté!

Qu'il suffise de rappeler ici les mots de Jésus-Christ: "Si vous ne devenez pas comme les petits enfants . . .". L'enfant jouant n'est-il pas le symbole de celui qui se libère par le jeu?

Dans un souci de créativité libératrice nous voudrions demander de repenser peut-être le rôle de *l'éducation sportive.*

Le sport offre à l'éducateur des moyens de socialisation à nul autre pareil. Pour l'éducateur le sport est l'un des rares terrains privilégiés qui permettent une coopération volontaire désintéressée au seuil d'une association volontaire de type communautaire, où l'on pratique le sport de récréation. C'est par un tel type de coopération que passe la socialisation de l'enfant et de l'adolescent.

Le rôle de l'éducation est d'apprendre l'homme à se valoriser à travers le jeu et le vrai sport.

Le vrai sport signifie détachement: il faut savoir se priver pour être un vrai sportif. Vis à vis de soi-même il faut savoir dire non à pas mal de désirs. Et dans le contact avec les autres, dans le jeu d'équipe il y a place pour pas mal de renoncement. Le vrai sport signifie émulation et fair-play. Cela suppose que l'on rencontre l'adversaire comme quelqu'un qui peut nous égaler ou même nous dépasser. L'émulation signifie que l'on engage la compétition en voulant gagner, mais en acceptant que l'on peut perdre.

Le vrai sport demande de l'effort. L'entraînement coûte pas mal de sueur, et accepter une défaite et reprendre après celle-ci forme à la persévérance. Les efforts demandés par le sport, tant au plan individuel que dans une équipe, jouent un rôle irremplaçable dans la formation du caractère et de la volonté de l'homme, désirant atteindre son plein épanouissement et donc sa libération totale.

Bien que le sport est pour beaucoup de gens vraiment un facteur de libération, bien que la majorité de la population de l'Europe occidentale — d'après les statistiques — reconnaît que le sport est utile, voire nécessaire à un bon équilibre de vie, les sportifs pratiquants sont toujours en minorité. Cette situation a donné naissance à l'action *Sport pour tous*. Le Sport pour tous, c'est la pratique d'activités physiques, adaptées à tous les âges, que chacun ou chacune exécute à son rythme, suivant ses propres possibilités, dans le cadre de sa vie personnelle ou familiale, ou dans celui de la vie collective, au sein d'une association sportive, d'un club d'entreprise, d'un groupement de plein air ou de tout autre structure. C'est le sport de récréation et c'est aussi la récréation sportive.

Le Sport pour tous n'est pas inconciliable avec le sport de haute compétition ni avec le sport de profession; mais c'est le sport pris par un autre bout, celui de l'activité vitale pour l'homme. C'est faire partager la joie des activités physiques et sportives à tous ceux et à toutes celles, quel que soit leur âge, qui n'ont jamais eu la chance de courir, de sauter, de s'ébattre, de s'exprimer corporellement.

Le Sport pour tous c'est faire comprendre que se donner du mouvement est une condition primordiale dans la société industrielle pour vivre sainement, pour être mieux, à même d'apprécier la vie.

Le Sport pour tous n'est pas le fait de tel ou tel groupe, l'apanage de telle ou telle association, *c'est l'affaire de tous* et c'est une tâche à laquelle chacun devrait collaborer dans le milieu où il se trouve.

En Belgique, cette collaboration est peut-être exemplaire. A côté des fédérations et associations privées, il y a le gouvernement de l'état, des provinces et des communes qui ont pris des initiatives concertées dans le cadre de Sport pour tous. Même dans l'église catholique en Belgique l'on peut constater une sympathie active pour le sport, ce qui se manifeste entre autres dans l'approbation officielle des activités de l'association Sporta.

A côté de l'apostolat sportif dans le secteur du sport de haute compétition et de profession, il y a également les initiatives de vacances sportives pour les jeunes, les adolescents, les familles, les étudiants, les handicapés et le troisième âge. Sporta organise aussi des jours, des weekends et des semaines sous le titre d'Exercices spirituels et sportifs.

Après des expériences très positives avec des jeunes et des adolescents, aussi des prêtres, des religieux et religieuses peuvent profiter de cette initiative. C'est un autre moyen de collaborer à l'épanouissement de l'homme et de sa libération totale.

Est-ce aux Galates ou à notre société industrielle que l'apôtre Paul écrivait: "Le Christ nous a libérés, pour vivre dans la liberté, combattez et n'acceptez pas d'esclavage . . . Frères, vous êtes appelés à la liberté. Que cette liberté ne serve pas de paravent à votre égoïsme. Au contraire soyez au service de tous dans l'amour."

Le plein épanouissement physique de l'homme suppose des valeurs spirituelles sûres.

Ce n'est pas l'homme qui est fait pour le sport mais le sport qui doit permettre aussi à l'homme de vivre sa vie . . . en liberté!

Bibliographie

AAPHER, Values in Sports, Washington, American Association for Health, Physical Education and Recreation, 1963, 130p.

Allmer, H.: Zur Diagnostik der Leistungsmotivation, Konstruktion eines sportspezifischen Motivationsfragebogens, Schriftenreihe für Sportwissenschaft und Sportpraxis, Band 16, Ahrensburg bei Hamburg, Ingrid Czwalina, 1973, 203 p.

Arnold, P.J.: Education, Physical Education and Personality Development. London:Heinemann, 1970, (1968), 172 p.

Auschusz Deutscher Leibeserzieher (ADL), Speil und Wetteifer, Beiträge von den Kongressen für Leibeserziehung 1958 in Osnabrück und 1961 in Göttingen, Schorndorf bei Stuttgart, Karl Hofmann, 1970, 326 p.

Ausschusz Deutscher Leibeserzieher (ADL), Motivation im Sport, V. Kongress für Leibeserziehung 7.-10; Oktober 1970 im Münster, Schorndorf bei Stuttgart, Karl Hofmann, 1971, 394 p.

Bouchard, C. et al: La préparation d'un champion — Un essai sur la préparation à la performance sportive, Québec (Canada), du Pélican, 1973, 563 p.

Bouchard, C., Landry, F., Brunelle, J. et Godbout, P.: La condition physique et le bien-être, Québec, du Pélican, 1974, 317 p.

Bouet, M.: Les motivations des sportifs. Paris, Ed. Universitaires, 1969, 239 p.

Bouet, M.: Signification du sport. Paris, Ed. Universitaires, 1968, 671 p.

Brooke, J.D. et Whiting, H.T.H.: Human Movement — A Field of Study. The Human Movement Series. London:Henry Publishers, 1973, 307 p.

Buehrle, M.: Die sozialerzieherische Funktion des Sports, Schriftenreihe für Sportwissenschaft und Sportpraxis, Band 7, Ahrensburg bei Hamburg, Ingrid Czwalina, 1971, 152 p.

Bundesinstitut für Sportwissenschaft, Auswahlbibliographie zum wissenschaftlichen Kongress "Der Sport in unserer Zeit, Chancen und Probleme," anläszlich der Spiele der XX. Olympiade in München, München, Mintzel-Druck Hof, 1972 (pro manuscripto), 377 p.

Colloque international F.S.G.T., Sport et développement social au XXe siècle, Paris:Ed. Universitaires, 1969, 235 p.

Cratty, B.J.: Social Dimensions of Physical Activity. Englewood Cliffs, New Jersey:Prentice Hall, 1967, 139 p.

Crum, B.J. et De Leeuw, F., Keerpunt in sport — Publicatie van de Wiardi Beckman Stichting, Deventer, Kluwer, 1974, 60 p.

Emmanuel, P. et al: Les loisirs dans la société industrielle, Congrès International de la Fondation van Clé, Antwerpen, 1974, 213 p.

Garaudy, R.: Parole d'homme, Paris:Laffont, 1975, 265 p.

Gerdes, O.: Bezinning op de lichamelijke opvoeding, Een pedagogisch psychologisch-didactische oriëntatie, Groningen, Wolters-Noordhoff, 1975, 3e druk, 158 p.

Ghoos, J. et al: Kerk en Sport, Sportacahier nr. 1, Antwerpen, Sporta, s.d. (1971), 52 p.

Girardi, J.: Christianisme, Libération humaine, Lutte des classes, Paris:Cerf, 1972, 231 p.

Grossing, Speiser, Altenberger: Sportmotivation, Salzburg, Arbeitskreis für Soziologie des Sports und der Leiberserziehung, s.d. (1974), 202 p.

Grupe, O., Kurz, D. et Teipel, J.M.: The Scientific View of Sport, Perspectives, Aspects, Issues. (Organizing Committee for the Games of the XXth Olympiad Munich 1972), Berlin:Springer Verlag, 1972, 288 p.

Grupe, O. (Ed.): Sport in the Modern World — Chances and Problems. Berlin:Springer Verlag, 1973, 615 p.

Herzfeld, G.: Freizeit — Problem und Aufgabe, Stuttgart:Karl Hofmann, 1963, 162 p.

Idenburg, P.A.: Recreatie als maatschappelijk verschijnsel, VNG-Groene Reeks nr. 18, 's Gravenhage, Vereniging van Nederlands Gemeenten (VNG), 1975, 48 p.

Jeu, B.: Le sport, la mort, la violence. Paris:Ed. Universitaires, 1972, 206 p.

Landers, D.M. (uitgever): Social problems in athletics, Essays in the sociology of sport, London:Univ. of Illinois Press, 1976, 251 p.

Landry, F., Robillard, E. et Volant, E.: Jeux Olympiques et jeu des hommes, Collection Terre Nouvelle, Montréal:Fides, 1976, 112 p.

Le Boulch, J.: Vers une science du movement humain, Introduction à la psychocinétique. Paris:les Editions ESF, 1971, 266 p.

Lenk, H.: Philosophie des Sports, Schorndorf:Karl Hofmann, 1973, 251 p.

Moltmann, J.: Het spel van de vrijheid — Gedachten over de vreugde om de vrijheid en het plezier in het spel, Bilthoven, Ambo, 1971, 78 p.

Moosburger, S.: Ideologie und Leiberserziehung im 19. und 20. Jahrhundert, Schriftenreihe für Sportwissenschaft und Sportpraxis, Band 9, Ahrensburg bei Hamburg, Ingrid Czwalina, 1972, 285 p.

Nederlandse Katholieke Sportfederatie, Sportcahier 2, Sport en menselijk welzijn, 's Hertogenbos, N.K.S., s.d. (1966), 43 p.

Nederlandse Katholieke Sportfederatie, Sportcahier, Bisschoppelijke brief over de sport, 's Hertogenbos, N.K.S., s; d., 1967, 64 p.

Nelissen, N.J.M. et Foppen, W.J.: Topsport in het geding, Leiden, n.v. Uitgeverij Meander, 1972, 203 p.

Nelissen, N.J.M. et Foppen, W.J.: Cijfermateriaal behorend bij de publicatie "Topsport in het geding."

Ogilvie, B. et Tutko, T.: Problem Athletes and how to handle them. London:Pelham Books, 1966, 195 p.

Peets, H.: Sport die wichtigste Nebensache der Welt, Bremen:Carl Schünenmann, 1960, 156 p.

Prescher, H.: Sport, Segen oder Fluch unsere Epoche, Frankfurt am Main: Wilhelm Limpert, 1961, 180 p.

Rat Der Evangelischen Kirsche in Deutschland: Sport, Mensch und Gesellschaft — Eine Sozialetische Studie der Kammer für soziale Ordnung der Evangelische Kirche in Deutschland, Gütersloh:Gerd Mohn, 1972, 40 p.

Sack, H.-G.: Sporliche Betätigung und Persönlichkeit, Sportwissenschaftliche Dissertations: Sportpsychologie Band 1, 2070 Ahrensburg, Ingrid Czwalina, 1975, 241 p.

Steuer, W.: Reife, Umwelt und Leistung der Jugend, Stuttgart:Ferd. Enke Verlag, 1965, 118 p.

Thielcke, H.: Sport und Humanität, Tübingen:Rainer Wunderlich, 1967, 43 p.

Vinnai, G.: Fussballsport als Ideologie, Frankfurt a/Main:Europäische Verlaganstalt, 1970, 112 p.

Von Dürckheim, Karlfried (Graf), Sportsprestaties en innerlijke groei, (Oorspr.: Sportliche Leistung-Menschliche Reife, Referat vor der Bundestagung der Deutschen Ol. Ges. in Oberhausen, November 1963, Wilhelm Limpert, Frankfurt a/Main, 1964, vertaald door L. Hoorweg Gunning), Deventer, Uitg. N. Kluwer n.v., 1968, 73 p.

Wagner, H.: Humanismus, Militarismus, Liebeserziehung, München:J. A. Barth, 1959, 196 p.

Wischmann, B.: Leistungssport — ein Mittel zur Selbsterziehung, Beitrage zur sportlichen Leistungsförderung, Band 5, Berlin:Verlag Bartels & Wernitz K.G., 1971, 88 p.

Zeigler, E.F.: Philosophical Foundations for Physical, Health and Recreation Education, Englewood Cliffs, New Jersey:Prentice Hall, 1964, 356 p.

L'auteur soumet que le sport ne peut se concevoir en dehors de l'activité sociale qu'il requiert, qu'il mobilise et qu'il déclenche. Il fait la critique des différentes formes du sport contemporain auxquelles l'on fait des reproches, en particulier le sport de haute compétition et le sport de profession. Il discute de la signification de la liberté et des formes sous lesquelles peuvent se présenter, dans la société contemporaine, diverse tâches humaines et de libération. L'auteur se dit d'avis que le sport bien compris, entre autres le sport de récréation, constitue un excellent chemin d'apprentissage et de pratique de la liberté et du bonheur.

Sport, Religion and Human Well-Being

Brian W. W. Aitken

Sport in North America is presented as a phenomenon which encompasses definite dehumanization factors. In a culture dominated by the *homo faber* image, many human activities, particularly sport with its overemphasis on winning, oftentimes becomes a source of alienation. The case is made for the *homo tempestivus* model of man which combines the virtues of two modes of being first articulated by the classical Greeks: the Appolonian and Dionysian These two ways combined in *homo tempestivus* provide a liberating image of man, can liberate sport from many of its vicissitudes and, in doing so, permit man to find a balance between doing too much and not achieving enough in life.

"Man is something but he is not everything."
Blaise Pascal

Introduction

North Americans have entered upon a love affair with sports. Given the time, money and emotion that we invest on a plethora of sports, one might go further and suggest that sport is rapidly becoming a new cultural religion in North America. Many factors have contributed to this apotheosis of sport. The most obvious of these is a combination of rising personal affluence and mushrooming free time. In an age of leisure sport has replaced work as a central life interest. Another factor is the disappearance of the Puritan detestation of games and amusements. In a sports-crazy society few of us feel that an involvement in sports is a "fearfull Ingratitude and Provocation unto the Glorious God" [2]. But perhaps the most powerful stimulus to the enthronement of sport atop the hierarchy of American activities has been the widespread belief that sport functions as a primary reinforcer of social values and goals. Sport in our culture gives support and sanctification to the North American belief that achievement, success, hard work and discipline are the

---

Brian W. W. Aitken, Huntington College, Laurentian University, Sudbury, Ontario, Canada.

chief ways to godliness. To put this somewhat differently, sport helps to define our personal identity by supplying us with an appropriate image of what it means to be human. Of course, in a pluralistic society there are many images which shape our behavior. And as writers like David Riesman (*The Lonely Crowd*) and Charles Reich (*The Greening of America*) have shown, images of man are always in a state of change. Nevertheless, it is my belief that there is one image which has come to dominate and to shape the behavior of industrial man, namely, that of *homo faber*, man the fabricator. As Keen puts it, "The image of homo faber is the key to the contemporary identity . . . the central organizational image of modern man" [6]. According to this image, man must pursue the *vita activa*, and the goal of all his activity is the fabrication of a world and the fabrication of himself. To put this in religious language, *homo faber* in the absence of religious belief attempts to save himself. Sport in North America not only reflects these promethean aspirations of modern man, but it also tends to support and give credence to the view that "man is the measure of all things."

The Folly of *Homo Faber*

The *homo faber* image of man has had both a positive and a negative effect on the quality of human life in modern industrial society. It was the birth of the *homo faber* image that freed Western man from religious and political tutelage and permitted him to take charge of his own destiny. And certainly man's view of himself as a maker or fabricator has been the major dynamic in the development of a technological society which in turn has bestowed upon man so many indisputable blessings. Mesthene lists some of the fruits of man's "tool making":

> What is new about our age . . . (is that) our technical prowess literally bursts with the promise of new freedom, enhanced human dignity and unfettered aspiration [9].

Yet at the same time the *homo faber* image of a man has created in industrial man a profound sense of alienation. It seems that the more industrial man has assumed control over his exterior world, over his body and his own behavior, the more he has lost touch with his own interior. This despiritualization of industrial man has been extensively documented and analyzed by a great variety of writers for over a century. Marx, for example, writing in the 19th century, warned that industrial-capitalistic society had made man into an economic commodity and Emile Durkheim spoke of the experience of *anomie* or the lack of inner values and norms. In this century the nature of man's alienation has been further dissected from many different perspectives. Fromm suggests that modern man experiences himself "as an impoverished thing, dependent on powers outside himself" [3]. Arthur Koestler calls modern man "the ghost in the machine." Albert Camus has vividly portrayed modern man as a "stranger," and theologian Harvey Cox claims that technological society has perpetrated "a seduction of the spirit." But perhaps the writer who has most poignantly explained the nature and origins of modern man's alienation is Horney, who suggests that alienation results from a deeply imbedded and unresolved neurosis. The neurotic individual is one who devotes all his energy and imagination toward the creation of an "idealized image" of self rather than toward the realization of the actual potential of the self. The neurotic person is driven by a constant search for glory and this search manifests itself outwardly in an inordinate striving for perfection, an insatiable need to excel at everything and by a desire to gain a vindictive triumph over others in every human relationship. The result of this drive for self-glory is self-hatred and self-contempt because of the neurotic individual's failure to live up to the idealized image of himself. What the neurotic personality lacks, argues Horney, is an appropriate sense of his own limitations.

> Every neurotic is loath to recognize limitations to what he expects of himself and believes is possible to attain [4].

This analysis of the neurotic personality gives us a lucid picture of the inner side of alienation. Furthermore, it exposes the folly of *homo faber.* Underlying the *homo faber* image of man is an unwillingness to accept the real self with its limited potential, combined with a neurotic desire to achieve the ideal of the perfect. The tragedy of *homo faber* is that in attempting to be godlike, *homo faber* loses contact with his finite but unique humaneness.

In a culture dominated by the *homo faber* image of man all human activity becomes a source of alienation. But sport in particular seems to be an alienating force. And the element in sport which most acerbates alienation is winning. Of course, winning is an essential component of sport. No matter what the level of sport there is always present a desire to achieve a good or better outcome. Yet in contemporary sport we are confronted with a perverted or alienated form of winning. Today winning does not involve just the desire to demonstrate a superiority of skills which is a normal goal of any game; rather, it involves an inordinate desire to win in an absolute sense, a desire to dominate, to obliterate, to wipe out the opponent.

Winning in our contemporary sports reflects a desire to achieve a vindictive triumph over the opposition.

This alienated form of winning is particularly manifested in professional or highly organized and competitive amateur sport, or in what physical educators and sports' sociologists term "athletics." "Athletics," according to Keating, "is essentially a competitive activity, which has for its end, victory in the contest, and which is characterized by a spirit of dedication, sacrifice and intensity" (unpublished data). In athletics at all levels there is much evidence for believing that Vince Lombardi's often quoted proclamation — "Winning isn't everything — it's the only thing" — has become a statement of faith. And it is my opinion that most of the other vices connected with contemporary athletics, which have been extensively catalogued by writers like Paul Hoch, Leonard Schecter, Bob Lipsyte, Dave Meggyesy, Bruce Kidd and John MacFarlane, all have been accentuated by the inordinate desire to win, to achieve a vindictive triumph over the opposition. Drug abuse; the taking of bennies before and tranquilizers after the game; excessive commercialization, the buying and selling of players in a fashion reminiscent of a cattle auction; the specter of violence, the brutal intimidation of an often superiorly skilled opponent — all have been prompted by the increased pressure to win an ultimate victory. Even the increased technologicalization of sport can be interpreted in the same light. Today athletes more than willingly submit themselves to new sports techniques: the time study of performance, power skating, isometric exercise programs, or use the latest scientifically refined equipment. (Who can forget the science fiction costumes designed by Messerschmidt of the German bobsledders at last winter's Olympics!) Why? The answer is obvious: to enhance their chances of winning. Unfortunately, not everyone can be a winner. Even perennial winners suffer an occasional defeat. Muhammad Ali has blown a fight or two, Secretariat suffered at least one loss in his career and the Montreal Canadians do manage to lose at least a handful of games each season. The tragedy of the modern athlete is that he is not prepared to accept and live with defeat. Defeat or failure evokes feelings of frustration, doubt, anxiety and self-contempt, and these feelings in turn only tend to further aggravate the basic drive toward self-glorification. But in the process the game is destroyed. The modern athlete, obsessed by the desire to achieve his idealized image, has no qualms about circumventing the rules of the game. Cheating is condoned and violence is tolerated, if the goal is victory.

But winning in this perverted or alienated form characterizes not only athletics but sport in general. According to Keating, sport is a broader reality than athletics. Sport "is a kind of diversion which has for its direct and immediate end, fun, pleasure and delight, and which is dominated by a spirit of moderation and generosity" (unpublished data). In a society of rapid change which makes personal identity extremely tenuous, in a society where high-powered advertising pushes an idealized image of self in order to sell more goods and services, even the Saturday sportsman is driven to seek an ultimate triumph. In playing our games we all nourish fantasies of playing pick-up hockey like Bobby Orr, making a curling take-out like Hec Gervais or putting like Jack Nicklaus. But our own limited skills waken us rudely from our pipe dreams resulting in feelings of frustration and self-contempt which manifest themselves outwardly in a great variety of unsportsmanlike conduct, i.e., the breaking of curling brooms, the hurling of golf clubs or arguing with the umpire or referee.

It must be noted that this perverted or alienated form of winning characterizes not only the participants in sports but the spectators as well. The average fan (the term fan is, after all, an abbreviation for fanatic) seeks not just entertainment but a satisfaction of his inner drive for perfection, success and absolute victory. This perhaps explains the inordinate identification we make with sports heroes in our culture. Through our favorite sports stars and teams we vicariously achieve the self-glory we never experience in everyday life. As a New York sports reporter put it in a moment of self-reflection:

> For 27 years I have designated certain athletic teams as extensions of myself, their defeats and victories are my own and at age 34 there is little I can do about it [10].

No area of sport today then is exempt from this perverted or alienated sense of winning. All sport consequently acerbates modern man's alienation from his real self. What John McMurtry says of pro football can be applied to all sport: "Pro football is a sick society's projection of itself into public spectacle" [8].

The Case for *Homo Tempestivus*

Sport, however, need not be a primary agent of alienation in human life. On the contrary, sport can liberate men to experience human wholeness. Maheu eloquently lists the possibilities for human well-being implicit in sport.

> Sport is an order of chivalry, a code of ethics and aesthetics, recruiting its members from all classes and all peoples. Sport is a truce; in an era of antagonisms and conflicts, it is the respite of the gods in which fair competition ends in respect and friendship. Sport is education . . . that of character. Sport is culture because it creates beauty and above all, for those who usually have the least opportunity to feed upon it [7].

Sport can create human well-being or wholeness in a great variety of ways. But for sport to have this liberating impact on human life, what is required a priori is for modern man to adopt a new image of man or a new understanding of what it means to be human. As I have mentioned, it is the *homo faber* image of man which is at the root of modern man's alienation. But this does not mean that this image of man should be discarded completely. The *homo faber* image of man does point to something essential in human life. We are born to create, to fabricate and to do, but not exclusively. It seems to me that the *homo faber* image presents us with too limited a view of man. Man has other needs to be satisfied if he is to be authentically human. It is my belief that we need to develop in our culture a more holistic view of man, if he is to experience a measure of well-being.

In theological circles the writer who provides us with the most comprehensive analysis of authentic humaneness is Keen, who states that authentic man is best understood as *homo tempestivus*, the timely, seasonable or opportune man [6]. *Homo tempestivus* combines the virtues of two modes of being in the world which were first articulated by the classical Greeks. One is the Apollonian way, which incarnates all those virtues which were associated with the god Apollo. The Apollonian way is characterized by the ego, reasonableness, order, discipline and balance. The Apollonian man is driven to create order and meaning out of the chaos of experience. He needs to know and to control in order to gain security. The Apollonian way is the dominant thrust in the *homo faber* mentality; they share the same desire to fabricate a meaningful world. But the Apollonian mode of being contains a virtue which is totally lacking in the *homo faber* mentality, namely, balance. Writes Keen, "Wisdom or authentic life in the Apollonian tradition consists of learning the rules and boundaries, and distinguishing with clarity between that which belongs to mortality and that which is immortal, between the knowable and the unknowable, the possible and the impossible, man and God" [6]. In short, the Apollonian way always strives toward the mean. The Socratic admonition "nothing in excess" is the categorical imperative.

The second mode of being in the world is the Dionysian way. In the pantheon of Greek gods Dionysus was a wild and mysterious god associated with wine, feasting, fertility and change in general. The Dionysian way espouses those virtues avoided by the Apollonian way: ecstasy, license, revelry, feeling and wonder. Wisdom in the Dionysian tradition involved an openness to novelty and to a diversity of experiences and, most importantly, an unwillingness to accept any limitations. Where the Apollonian mode of being fears and attempts to order chaos, the Dionysian mode of being affirms and celebrates chaos.

Both of these modes of being in the world, according to Keen, have serious defects and, if followed exclusively, can lead to pathological behavior. The Apollonian model can create in an individual feelings of captivity, limitedness and impotence. In seeking order and security, the Apollonian man forfeits freedom and spontaneity. The Dionysian model, on the other hand, can lead to feelings of anomie, grandiosity, limitlessness and omnipotence. The Dionysian man lacks an internal order and a healthy sense of limits.

These two models of human life are of course perennial, and they often conflict. The current conflict between the so-called counter-culture — espousing feeling, "doing your own thing," being open to new experiences — and the mainstream of contemporary society — advocating order, security and conformity — is an example of the perennial conflict between these two modes of being. Keen's point is that authentic human life can be experienced only if a delicate balance is struck between the two models of behavior. But the question is how? "How is it possible to combine the virtues of Apollo and Dionysus within a single model of man" [6]? The answer, according to Keen, is that we must see time and not space as the primary organizing principle in human experience. Time, he argues, is the primary context in which we live out our lives. And it is because time is the stage of human life that Keen believes the image of man as *homo tempestivus* is so evocative. *Homo tempestivus* is the timely or opportune man. He has the sense to do the fitting or timely thing at each moment. The fitting thing might involve ordering, fabricating or limiting oneself, but it also might mean enjoying, celebrating or letting things happen. *Homo tempestivus* can act in either an Apollonian or Dionysian way; the determining factor is what the present moment demands. The writer of Ecclesiastes (3:1-4) has captured well the wisdom of *homo tempestivus*.

> For everything there is a season, and a time for everything under heaven . . . a time to break down and a time to build up, a time to mourn and a time to laugh.

Homo Tempestivus and Liberation

Keen's notion of *homo tempestivus* offers us a profound insight into the nature of man. It offers a model for behavior which can help men to achieve a measure of wholeness. With respect to sport I believe that this image of man as *homo tempestivus* can liberate sport to be sport. As I have stressed, sport in itself is not alienating; sport has become a major dehumanizing factor because of the kind of culture we live in. In North American society we impose on sport the values and ideals implicit in the workaday world. This is not to suggest that sport can ever function exclusive of society. I hold to an integrationalist view of society and human life. Each component of any society is to some extent a microcosm of the whole. Nevertheless, in our society, the dominant forces, captured in the *homo faber* image of man, tend to destroy the reality and essence of sport. *Homo tempestivus* is a liberating image of man because the timely or opportune man is free to participate in sport for its own sake. Sport, after all, is a form of play and what Huizinga suggests of play is also true of sport. "Play . . . is a free activity standing quite consciously outside 'ordinary' life as being 'not serious.' . . . It is an activity connected with no material interest, and no profit can be gained by it. It proceeds within its own proper boundaries of time and space according to fixed rules and in an orderly manner" [5].

Homo tempestivus has the sensitivity to know when to play, when to drop the cares of the everyday world and to enter into another realm and accept its specific rules and realities. But this is not to say that in playing sports *homo tempestivus* rejects one of the two modes of being that shape his identity. Playing should not be identified exclusively, as it so often is, with the Dionysian mode of being in the world. Every human activity, sport included, requires a balance between these two modes of being if it is to provide a sense of well-being. Sport does involve a discharge of emotion, spontaneity, exuberance and letting go (of rationality), but it also can involve a creation of and a willingness to accept order. It involves an acceptance of limits, but at the same time an openness to new experiences. In other words, both the Apollonian and Dionysian modes of being should function in sport and this applies to both the athlete and to the casual sportsman. The athlete needs to balance his discipline, regimentation and drive for victory with spontaneous and exuberant play, and the sportsman needs to balance his spontaneous and nonserious play with some acceptance of rules, meaningful competition and some desire to improve his skills. Without this balance sport can become a dull and perhaps dehumanizing experience for both.

Homo tempestivus always seeks the mean between extremes and this has some interesting ramifications for winning. As I have argued, winning is an essential part of sport. As Weiss has pointed out, from the beginning of time men have involved themselves in sport and been absorbed by it because it is one of the few areas of life which gives every man an equal chance of attaining a limited degree of excellence [11]. Winning in contemporary sport, however, has as its goal not just the achievement of a limited degree of excellence, but the achievement of an absolute, unlimited victory. It seems to me that the *homo tempestivus* image of man can liberate us from this perverted and alienated sense of winning. *Homo tempestivus*, the timely man, seeks a balance between doing too much and not achieving enough. Once again, whether *homo tempestivus* is involved in athletics or casual sport he strikes this balance. The athlete by definition attempts to excel, to win the contest, but he does not attempt to win an ultimate, cosmic victory because he knows he cannot be God. The casual sportsman, on the other hand, is not satisfied with spontaneous or undirected play. He does compete in the game in a less skillful and more relaxed way than the athlete, but he plays with the knowledge that in playing the game to the best of his ability he can experience a measure of victory. The *homo tempestivus* image of man then can liberate sport to be sport and, in so doing, it permits sport to convey on human life a measure of wholeness.

But the *homo tempestivus* image of man has one last ramification. I believe that it can not only liberate sport to be sport, but that it also can liberate men for religion. *Homo tempestivus* does not impose the reality of the workaday world on the game; he is free to experience the game as another world, as an extraordinary happening. Berger has perceptively captured this extraordinary or religious dimension of play. He writes:

> When one is playing, one is on a different time, no longer measured by the standard units of the larger society, but rather by the peculiar ones of the game in question. In the 'serious' world it may be 11 am, on such and such a day, month and year. But in the universe in which one is

> playing it may be the third round, the fourth act, the allegro movement, or the second kiss. In playing one steps out of one time into another. . . . In other words, in joyful play it appears as if one were stepping not only from one chronology into another but from time into eternity [1].

In other words, in playing, suffering and our movement toward death seem to be bracketed and suspended for the moment. And the joy one experiences in this situation is apprehended "in a barely inconceivable way, as being a joy forever" [1]. Because authentic sport gives to us this experience of an extraordinary time, it can act as a "signal of transcendence"; it can give to us a ground for believing that there is a mysterious reality at the foundation of human experience and that this reality is trustable.

References

1. Berger, P.: A Rumour of Angels. Pelican, 1969, pp. 76-77.
2. Dulles, F.R.: A History of Recreation: America Learns to Play. Appleton, Century, Crofts, 1965, p. 18.
3. Fromm, E.: The Sane Society. Fawcett, 1955, p. 114.
4. Horney, K.: Neurosis and Human Growth. Norton, 1950, p. 50.
5. Huizinga, J.: Homo Ludens. Beacon Press, 1950, p. 13.
6. Keen, S.: An Apology for Wonder. New York:Harper and Row, 1969, pp. 117, 153, 196, chap. 6.
7. Maheu, R., cited by McMurtry, W.: Report on the Investigation and Inquiry into Violence in Amateur Hockey, August 1974.
8. McMurtry, J., quoted by Hoch, P.: Rip Off the Big Game. Doubleday-Anchor Book, 1972, p. 8.
9. Mesthene, E.: What Modern Science Offers the Church. Saturday Review, Nov. 19, 1966, p. 30.
10. Schwartz, J.: Harper's Magazine, May 1973.
11. Weiss, P.: Sport: A Philosophical Enquiry. Southern Illinois University Press, 1969.

Le sport, la religion et le bien-être de l'homme

L'auteur se dit d'avis que le sport en Amérique du nord présente des traits déshumanisants. Dans une culture où l'*homo faber* domine, beaucoup des activités de l'homme, en particulier le sport avec son emphase exagérée sur la victoire, deviennent des sources d'aliénation. L'auteur propose comme modèle l'*homo tempestivus* que les Grecs de l'antiquité ont été les premiers à évoquer et dans lequel se fondaient deux modes d'existence, l'*apollinien* et le *dionysiaque*. Selon l'auteur le modèle de l'*homo tempestivus* peut libérer le sport de beaucoup de ses vicissitudes et permettre à l'homme de mieux équilibrer dans sa vie ses intérêts et les sollicitations et obligations qui en découlent.

Alienation, Liberation and Sport

David L. Miller

Theological aspects of play, games and sport are examined in a sociological and anthropological perspective. The author contends that sport is a religion whose theology is "playfulness-in-games" and/or "gameness-in-all-play." The seemingly paradoxical connection between liberation and alienation in sport is impossible to handle in an "either/or" connotation in theology. Sport is said to open a way into an imaginal theology of depth. A depth theology of sport is best viewed as polytheistic; this concept proves useful in the understanding of the multiple forms that man's reality and existence take in play, in sport and in life.

"There is a game called Cops and Robbers, but none called Saints and Sinners."

W. H. Auden

Either/Or: A Rejected Perspective

The poet's epigram dissociates games and theology. It reflects a typical sentiment which feels that play is one thing and religion is quite another. If a theologian is to have a place in these pre-Olympic discussions concerning sports, then Auden's position must be faced and resisted.

Theological resistance to the poet is somewhat awkward since his notion is precisely a theological one. Hence, there is an irony: it is necessary to reject theology in order to practice theology!

The particular theology that accompanies Auden's sentiment is that of Kierkegaard. Specifically, it is the Danish existentialist's "either/or" with regard to faith and life that is at stake. Auden distinguishes not only the frivolity of games and the seriousness of life, but also art and polytheism, on the one hand, and Christian monotheism, on the other. In an essay called "The Shield of Perseus," Auden bases the polar oppositions explicitly and self-consciously on Kierkegaard's distinction between the comic and the

---

David L. Miller, Department of Religion, Syracuse University, Syracuse, New York, U.S.A.

tragic ways. Crucial to the theologian's argument is an idea that he takes to be obvious. It is the idea of the transcending distance between finite and infinite, between man and God. There is separating them an "infinite qualitative distinction," Kierkegaard argues. Hence, faith is a relation to the infinite which has no connection to Cops and Robbers and other finite sporting [2].

There may be a similar presupposition lurking with apparent innocence in the title of this disciplinary seminar: "Sport, A Liberating or Alienating Force?" It goes without saying that the terminology of this title — "liberation," "alienation" — is as typically existentialist as Auden's use of Kierkegaard. But further, the phrasing of the title is in terms of an "either/or," and it poses a question whose options place transcendence over against finitude.

Thus, there is an additional irony. Ours is a seminar the implicit perspective of whose topic suggests an end precisely to the theological discussion of that topic. In the terminology of the epigram: if sport has to do with Saints and Sinners, then sport cannot be sport, because there is no game Saints and Sinners, as there is one called Cops and Robbers.

From Egypt to America: Theologies of Play, Games, and Sport

There has been considerable argument during the last 20 years to suggest that religion has more to do with Cops and Robbers and that there is more play among the Saints than Auden's epigram would lead us to believe. In 1947 Henderson connected all games played with a bat and ball to the Temple of Osiris at Papremis, the second millennium tomb of Beni Hasan, and the Shrine of Hathor for Thothmos the Third, each of which depicts a ball game in relation to ancient Egyptian religious rituals of cosmic conflict [5]. Novak, like Henderson, links secular games to a religious function. "Sports is, somehow, a religion," Novak writes. In fact, he argues that "sports are best understood as a religion." But, contrary to Henderson, Novak connects sports to contemporary American Civil Religion, not to ancient Egyptian ritual [18].

Between the anthropology of Henderson's theology of sport and the sociology of Novak's, and especially in the late 1960s and early 1970s, there was an important burgeoning of theology and play studies [4, 7, 8, 10, 11, 16, 17, 19, 20]. I also contributed a work to this outpouring [13].

There is a crucial difference between Novak's and Henderson's theology of games, on the one hand, and the theology and play studies, on the other. The sociology and anthropology of religion in the former leads to a stress of the game-element in sport, whereas the latter's theology often emphasizes an ideal play-aspect of a life beyond game [15]. (Note the attempt to balance this in Miller [14].) When play forgets the gameness of existence it views the world through innocent eyes, like the child or the Romantic, at the beginning, or from the point of view of some end-time, a Kingdom or Utopia. On the other hand, when games are stressed to the exclusion of the play-element, the vision is classic, heroically and Olympianly so. The view is adult, from the midst of the sport of finitude. It is not incidental that Novak writes, "In my fortieth year . . ." [18].

Of course we all know better. We know that in sports there is no play without game, nor game without play, no childlike romance without adulterated realisms, no freedom apart from discipline, no kingdom of winners without a simultaneous apocalypse of losers, no innocent starts or victorious finishes without agonizing middles. The thrill of victory and the agony of defeat is also agony in victory and even thrilling defeats. There is no either/or on the field of sport. Sport is religion, indeed; but it is a religion whose theology is both/and — playfulness-in-game and gameness-in-all play.

Thus, there is something amiss when Moltmann retains a traditional theological either/or, using the terms of our seminar title and attempting precisely to relink a play *mythos* (theology) with a game *ethos* (ethics). He writes: "It is possible that in playing we can anticipate our liberation and with laughing rid ourselves of the bonds which alienate us from real life" [16].

The Liberation of the Other: A Sporting Alternative for Contemporary Theology

Novak says that sports "belong to the world of imagination" [18]. Perhaps the imagination of sports, its figures and metaphors, can provide an alternative to theology's perspective of "either/or," alienation or liberation, playfulness or gameness.

But not only theology needs the imaginal touch of sport. "Liberation" is a political as well as a theological metaphor, and a literal "either/or" in politics continually makes ideological division between liberation and every alien. "Liberation" is a term that in our time implies a world of Viet Cong and Palestinian guerilla armies, Women's Movements and Patty Hearst. The term also suggests a whole self-improvement and growth enterprise connected to Esalen's psychology. We want to be liberated, politically and psychologically, and in the popular imagination the liberation we hope for is as distantly separated from alienation as is infinite from finite in traditional theology.

The terms "alienation" and "liberation" themselves have imaginal histories that cannot sustain such an "either/or" vision. "Liberation" means "freedom," and the term invokes the name of the Roman god, Liber, deity of growth, a new god, not Greek, an invention of Roman religion. The word "alienation" is related to "alias," and to the Latin *alius*, which means "other." When alienated, one is an alien. "I am not myself; I am someone else; I have another name, an alias, an other's name; I am a 'stranger in a strange land.' " These last words refer to Abraham — to his liberation, not to his alienation. To be alienated is to liberate the other. To free the other is to discover the alias, to be stranger to oneself, to find a new name.

This seemingly paradoxical connection between liberation and alienation is impossible to handle in an "either/or" world of theological imagination. But it is precisely in simultaneity that the world of sport dwells. *Simul justus et pecatur* (Luther): at once Saints and Sinners and Cops and Robbers.

Who is the "other" for the athlete? For the runner or swimmer it is a clock. For the discus thrower or pole vaulter it is the tape measure or the distance mark. For the dash men and women it is hurdles and a finish line. It is slalom poles for the skier, an antagonist for the boxer, and other teams for those polo players in deep water and those hockey players skating on sheets of glaring ice. But more: the clock, the tape, the mark, the hurdle, the finish, the course, the antagonist, the team — both our team and theirs, all these are within. The athlete trains to liberate the other, the *alius*, the alien, the alias. These others must be participated, watched, cared for, leaned upon, anticipated, felt, respected, joined, fought. Alienation ("making other") is the name of the training game of liberation in sport.

Thus, so-called heroes of sports are in one sense precisely not heroic. The athlete says, "Not, I, but the pace of the race carried me." "I became one with the contest." "The game played itself in its final moments." "The rhythm of my legs took over; they ran by themselves."

When the athlete or spectator senses these depths, no longer is it a matter of games, *ethos*, heroic behavior "out there." Nor is it any longer a matter of the element of play, *mythos*, a subjective feeling "in here." Rather, such sporting insight leads toward a new theology, no longer an "either/or," but now an alchemy of sports, an opus of athletics, games being deepened toward death in life and play being amplified toward life not without dying. To liberate alienation does not mean to overcome something, transcending it once and for all. Rather, it means a con-fusion of life and death, play and game. These moments of experience are sensed synchronously. They are a complex, a curious holiness, not without suffering. They are attended by the triumphant agony of the other in the victorious defeat of heroic egoism. Sport opens a way into an imaginal theology of depth.

Remythologizing the Olympics: From Play to Polytheism in Theology

A depth theology of sport locates the action of contest not in the opposition between athlete and other, between God and man, between win and loss. Rather, it discovers athlete and other, divine and human, win and loss, playfulness and gameness, liberation and alienation all to be simultaneous moments within the soul of sport itself, within the sportive nature of soul. Such a theology is not "either/or," not dualistic, not dialectical, not even monotheistic. Its God is not wholly Good, wholly Other, or wholly any One thing at all. Rather, a depth theology of sport is "both/and," polytheistic. Its gods and goddesses carry opposition and contest within. Apollo is impulsive and moderate; Aphrodite, loving and jealous; Athene, graceful and warring; Hermes, kind and treacherous. In polytheism there are not only many gods, many Others, but the otherness of each is itself a complex, a contest, a variety. It is no accident that the culture that gave birth to the Olympic Games was polytheistic in its theology and that it celebrated its sports as religious festivals. Seeing this connection between polytheistic theologizing and sports helps to account for an interesting aftermath to studies in theology and play.

Cox followed his work on play with a book which ends by calling for a "pluriform future," for "radical pluralism" in theology [3]. Similarly, Keen has written two works since *To a Dancing God*, each of which invites theological polytheism. Keen writes about the necessity of "multiple stories," many myths, the tales of many gods and goddesses, to understand the human situation [9]. And in Keen's most recent work, the author speaks against the ability of theoretical monisms of all sorts to express adequately "the multiplicity that is deeply within each of us" [6]. Novak, too, writes about play as "pagan" and hints at a polytheism at work in, say, Notre Dame/Alabama football games by referring to Apollo and Dionysus. Novak also observes that sport is, as he puts it, "in some as yet unexplored way a ritual conducted under the sight and power of the gods" [18]. My own work was an attempt precisely to explore this as yet unexplored terrain [12].

The point here is that only a polytheistic theology is sufficiently multiplex in its many deities and in each god and goddess, sufficiently "both/and" in its *mythos* and *logos*, sufficiently full of the word made image, to account for the interaction of game and play, alienation and liberation, in sport.

However, not every polytheistic theology will suffice. Some are too literalist or one-dimensional, focusing on the multifacted nature of behavior, missing the multiplex of every single act. For example, the *Odes* of Pindar, though they be the best remembered of ancient sports writings, are not a proper model of a polytheistic theology of sport. They celebrate too much Olympus in every Olympiad. Pindar constantly relates sports to the victorious heroism and to the manipulative control signaled by Heracles, Zeus and Apollo. In Pindar's olympian polytheism, winning transcends losing, liberation overcomes alienation. Victorious death and the alias of the many others are ignored. Pindar's polytheism is finally one sided because it does not include chthonic modes of athleticism as part of the game. Pindar has no deities to agonize the *agon* (struggle, strife), the *alea* (chance, Fate), and the *ilinx* (vertigo, thrill, breakdown). Until we can imagine the dedication of sports, not only to Zeus, Apollo and Heracles, but also as celebrating Hermes, Hades and the Furies, there is not yet the liberation of the Others required by the experience of the fields of sport.

The sports arena is a Trojan War, to be sure (Pindar's heroic olympianism). But, more deeply, all the gods and goddesses, not only the bright and shining ones, people the soul of sport. Their presences, too, are experienced by the athlete, however dimly, however silent, however hidden.

Traditional theology, then, can teach sports that it has a historical religious origin and a present secular religious function. It can even teach sports something about the metaphysical nature of its play. But perhaps more importantly, sports teaches religion something about its self-understanding, something about its salvific monotheism, its heroic theology. Sports teaches a new theological perspective that is in fact very old. It is a perspective that does not isolate its ultimate concern in play (a romantic, pietistic *mythos*), nor in game (a sociopolitical *ethos*), nor in alienation (an existentialist philosophy), nor in liberation (a behavioral literalism). The theological vision of sports, rather, is multiplex in imagination. It sees through play, game, liberation and alienation to the agonizing liberation of the many Others. It sees polytheistically. It sees, with the French writer Alain, that "the gods are moments of man," and that

> out of its [the image's] silence we form the hidden and lurking presence, the mysterious other side of reality which make us believe that everything is full of souls, or, as Thales said, that everything is full of Gods [1].

References

1. Alain, E.-A. C. The Gods. New York, 1974, pp. 13, 125.
2. Auden, W.H.: The Dyer's Hand and Other Essays. New York, 1968, pp. 371, 429, 432, 456.
3. Cox, H.: The Seduction of the Spirit. New York, 1973, pp. 321, 324, 325.
4. Cox, H.: The Feast of Fools. Cambridge, Mass., 1969.
5. Henderson, R.: Ball, Bat, and Bishop. New York, 1947, pp. 8, 9, 19, 20, 22 ff., 36 ff.
6. Keen, S.: Beginnings Without End. New York, 1975, pp. 15, 37ff.
7. Keen, S.: To a Dancing God. New York, 1970.
8. Keen, S.: Apology for Wonder. New York, 1969.
9. Keen, S. (with Anne Valley Fox): Telling Your Own Story. Garden City, N.Y., 1973, pp. 2, 3, 42, 140.
10. Martin, G.: Fest und Alltag. Stuttgart, 1973.
11. Martin, G.: Wir wollen hier auf Erde schon . . . Das Recht auf Glück. Stuttgart, 1970.
12. Miller, D.: The New Polytheism. New York, 1974.
13. Miller, D.: Gods and Games. New York, 1970, 1973, pp. xv-xxx.
14. Miller, D.: Playing the game to lose. *In* Moltmann, J.: Theology of Play. New York, 1972.
15. Miller, D.: The kingdom of play. Union Sem. Q. Rev. 25:3, Spring, 1970.
16. Moltmann, J.: Theology of Play. New York, 1972, p. 3.
17. Neale, R.: In Praise of Play. New York, 1969.
18. Novak, M.: The Joy of Sports. New York, 1976, pp. x, xi, 47, 209, 218, 225ff.
19. Pieper, J.: Leisure: The Basis of Culture. New York, 1963.
20. Rahner, H.: Man at Play. New York, 1967.

Le sport, facteur de libération ou d'aliénation de l'homme

L'auteur examine divers aspects théologiques du jeu et du sport dans une perspective sociologique et anthropologique. Il montre que le sport peut être considéré comme une sorte de religion dont la théologie touche les aspects ludiques du sport autant que les aspects sportifs du jeu. Le paradoxe apparent entre les facteurs d'aliénation et de libération que l'on retrouve dans le sport ne peut être résolu dans une perspective du tout-ou-rien. L'auteur considère que le sport a des liens étroits avec le monde de l'imaginaire. Ses formes et ses métaphores offrent de riches éléments pour la considération du polythéisme en tant que concept pouvant expliquer en profondeur les formes multiples de la réalité de l'homme et de son existence.

Religious Themes and Structures in the Olympic Movement and the Olympic Games

John J. MacAloon

Introduction

From its earliest years, the lexicon of the modern Olympic Movement has been filled with religious terminology. Pierre de Coubertin (1863-1937), the founder of modern Olympism, consciously and unambiguously regarded it as a religious phenomenon. Its ideology he described as a "philosophico-religious doctrine," containing an ethics, world-view, metaphysics and mythology [3]. Olympism is based, he wrote, on "the idea of a religion of sport, the *religio athletae*" [3]. "Like the athletics of antiquity," Coubertin claimed, "modern athletics is a religion, a cult, an impassioned soaring, capable of going from 'play to heroism' " [3]. The Olympic Games were described as a sacred "festival of human unity," a "factory of life-force," "a cult," "a series of rites and ceremonies," an "apotheosis," "a pilgrimage to the past and a gesture of faith in the future" [3]. Of all the ancient commentators, he was fondest of quoting Pindar: "The Gods are friends to the Games" [3]. Coubertin cherished what Bowra has called Pindar's interest in "the part of experience in which human beings are exalted or illumined by a divine force . . . a marvelously enhanced consciousness . . . [which for Pindar and for Coubertin] was the end and justification of life." Like Pindar, Coubertin "saw victory in the Games as raising questions of mystical and metaphysical importance" [2]. "I therefore think I was right," Coubertin wrote, "to recreate from the outset, around the renewed Olympism, a religious sentiment transformed and widened by Internationalism and Democracy which distinguish the present age, but still the same as led the young Greeks to the foot of the altars of Zeus" [3]. Thus, to Coubertin, the Olympic Movement was a religious revitalization movement [21], the International Olympic Committee "a college of disinterested

John J. MacAloon, University of Chicago, Illinois, U.S.A.

priests," Olympic competitors "new adepts of the religion" and spectators and coaches "the laity of sport" [21]. Thus, if we accept for the moment the definition of religion provided by his contemporary Emile Durkheim — a system of beliefs and practices relative to sacred things which unite into a moral community those who adhere to them — we can see how systematic were Coubertin's claims for the religious nature of Olympism [9].

But what are we, as professional students of religion, to make of these claims? Does this religious language have any substantial basis, or is it merely metaphorical? Does it project simply the personal fancies of a romantic Frenchman? Or does it accurately reflect a dimension of Olympism and the Olympic Games which we are not accustomed to thinking about? To answer these questions we must first specify more closely what "sacred things" were to Coubertin, what religious tradition his thought belonged to and exactly how the Olympic Games were to function as a vehicle for these religious strivings.

Coubertin and Humanistic Religion

Coubertin's aristocratic family was devoutly Catholic, though there were freemasons on his father's side. His mother had thoughts of the priesthood for her son, but young Pierre rebelled against such proddings. The Christ story fascinated him, but in a universal way. The boy found Christic parallels in the myth of Laocoon, whose famous statuary an ancestor had unearthed in Rome. By the time he emerged from the Jesuit college to which he was sent, he was equally fascinated by the Yahweh of the Old Testament and the pantheon of the ancient Greeks.

His mature religious stance was the product of three elements. The first was a loose deism which manifested itself solely in life crises. It emphasized ritual and had a Platonic cast to it. (A typical, French male pattern which he discussed in his writings [5, 6].) The second was what he called his "Hellenism," a fascination with the religious ethos of ancient Greece. He wrote:

> Hellenism is above all the cult of humanity in its present life and its state of balance. And let us make no mistake about it, this was a great novelty in the outlook of all peoples and times. Everywhere else cults are based on the aspiration for a better life, the idea of recompense and happiness beyond the tomb, and the fear of punishment for the man who has offended the gods. But here it is the

> present existence which is happiness. Beyond the tomb there is only regret at the loss of it; it is a diminished survival [3].

As his own end approached, his Christian faith in an afterlife reemerged. He wrote, "My soul, poor little parcel detached from a universal intelligence, aspires to return to its mysterious source" [10]. But even his last rites had a decidedly "pagan" cast to them. In accordance with his wish, his heart was severed from his body and interred beneath the stele which bore his name in the grove of Zeus at ancient Olympia.

This emphasis on a cult of humanity in its "present life" is the third element in his personal religious quest and the one most decisive for Olympism. On the one hand, there is a rejection of Christian metaphysical dualism. Coubertin writes:

> There is a paganism — the true form — which humanity will never shake off, and from which — I risk this seeming blasphemy — it would not be well for it to free itself from completely; and that is the cult of the human being, of the human body, mind and flesh, feeling and will, instinct and conscience [10].

On the other hand, there is an aspiration for a religion of collective humanity, focused upon the "earthly city" of man, rather than the heavenly city of God.

This religious quest has, of course, a long pedigree in French social thought. It took on renewed intensity in the troubled, early years of the Third Republic, the social milieu in which Coubertin came of age and which decisively influenced his thought in this matter and several others, as I have elsewhere argued [13]. Coubertin analyzed and favored French attempts to separate Church and State and increase religious tolerance, at the same time decrying all excesses of anti-clericalism [6]. Like de Tocqueville before him, he admired and celebrated the American example [6, 7]. He also applauded the way the new French Republic had served as "the operating cause" by which the Catholic Church had been "turned towards a new world" of industrialized democracy [6, 7].

At the same time, he was wary of certain more extreme claims in French thought. He sympathized with Auguste Comte's search for a "religion of humanity," but questioned its positivist, materialist bases in a way which anticipated modern critiques [5, 6, 8]. He rejected radical "secularism" and "rationalism," understanding that any truly religious system, including Comteian atheism, necessarily included "non-rational" dimensions of faith and metaphysical encounter.

> The thought of professing a *rational* religion, compatible with their exact knowledge, charms them and elevates them in their own eyes. In reality, there is no such thing as a rational religion. A really rational religion would exclude all idea of worship, and would consist only in a set of rules for upright living [6].

Science and religion, he argued, are perfectly compatible and cannot and do not replace one another in the modern world.

> Reason, which the Frenchman so readily obeys, has finally established the necessity of the religious sentiment. Science has shown that it is powerless to take its place. If one glances about him, he perceives how profound is the religious sentiment in our epoch. Never has the moral sense been so developed, never have moral principles been more fully admitted and practiced [6].

Compare the recent anthropological formulations of Geertz [11].

What about the second important religious theme in French thought and history, the notion that it is the State itself which is the proper object of humanistic religious striving? In order to characterize Coubertin's thought, we need some crucial distinctions made most clearly by his contemporary Marcel Mauss [15]. Mauss distinguishes the concept of "nation" in the strict sense from the "state." The former consists of the ensemble of all citizens and their shared traditions, their language, aesthetic, morality, will, customs, form of progress, character and mentality . . . "in sum the Idea which leads it" [15]. (Or, what we should today call its "culture.") The "state," on the other hand, refers in more limited fashion to the doings of its government. Coubertin applauded attempts to revitalize and maintain religious sentiments surrounding the former, but was deeply suspicious of any cult of the State itself. True and laudatory patriotism always owed, for him, to *la patrie*, not — at least not necessarily — to *le gouvernement.* The limiting condition of this cult of the nation was that it remained compatible with internationalism and did not degenerate into "nationalism," in the negative sense of the term as we use it today.

Mauss distinguishes between "cosmopolitanism" and true "internationalism." The first denies the significance of nationality and discreet cultural traditions and argues for a "world citizenry" in which all such differences should be overcome and left behind (certain streams of Marxist thought, for example). By contrast, "true internationalism" argues that cultural differences are an enduring and marvelous feature of the human landscape and that, therefore, world peace and understanding must be sought in the recognition and celebration of human diversity, not in the destruction of it. In other words, *mankind* exists, not *in spite of*, but *because of* cultural differences.

This was Coubertin's position. National patriotism and internationalism not only need not contradict one another, but were fundamentally interdependent.* Coubertin's notion of a "religion of humanity" centered around this philosophical anthropology.

But, as we heard Coubertin himself state above, more than a set of philosophical statements and "rules for upright living" is required of anything which would call itself a religion. We have now seen something of the world-view and ideology which Coubertin poured into Olympism, as well as some relationships it has had with traditions of religious thought. We must now attempt to specify more closely what conditions would make Olympism *itself* a *religious* ideology and would make the religious language with which Coubertin described the Games something more than metaphorical aspirations.

The Olympic Games as a Cult of Humanity

The anthropological study of religion has lately focused on the nature of sacred symbols, as evidenced in the work of Victor Turner [16-19] and Clifford Geertz [11]. Geertz writes:

> Sacred symbols function to synthesize a people's ethos — the tone, character, and quality of their life, its moral and aesthetic style and mood — and their world-view — the picture they have of the way things in sheer actuality are, their most comprehensive ideas of order [16].

This synthesis of ethos and world-view

> . . . objectivizes moral and aesthetic preferences *by depicting them as the imposed conditions of life implicit in a world with a particular structure*, as mere common sense given the unalterable shape of reality. On the other hand, it supports these received beliefs about the world's body *by invoking deeply felt moral and aesthetic sentiments as experiential evidence for their truth* [16]. (Emphasis added.)

---

*Cf. Bellah [1], pp. 168-186, especially pp. 185-186.

Coubertin had a strong, native insight into the power of sacred symbols, reaffirmed by his own religious visions in the chapel of Rugby School in 1883 and at ancient Olympia during his founder's pilgrimage of 1894 [3, 4, 10]. The resurrected Olympic Games, already imbued with the sacred aura of the Greek heritage, would provide, he thought, just the set of symbols and symbolic events needed to serve as vehicles for the "comprehensive ideas of order" discussed above. Moreover, he understood that Olympic symbolism, to be effective, had to bring these metaphysical and metasocial ideals into "fit" with the "particular structure" of "real" life.

> To ask the peoples of the world to love one another is merely a form of childishness. To ask them to respect one another is not in the least utopian. But in order to respect one another, it is first necessary to know one another. To celebrate the Olympic Games is to appeal to History [3].

By "history" he meant not only the dead past, but the living history of persons and peoples as it continuously unfolded. The dramatism and emotional interest in the Games would provide "the deeply felt moral and aesthetic sentiments" necessary as "experiential evidence" for the truth of Olympism's propositions about the unity of mankind, the respect for cultural differences and the cult of the individual human being.

But how is this "faith in the future" to be achieved? How is it that the tenets of Olympism were to command religious belief instead of simple philosophical interest? Geertz and Turner, speaking generally of all religious systems, emphasize ritual. Geertz writes:

> It is in ritual — that is, consecrated behavior — that this conviction that religious conceptions are veridical and that religious directives are sound is somehow generated. . . . In a ritual, the world as lived and the world as imagined, fused under the agency of a single set of symbolic forms, turn out to be the same world [11].

Coubertin understood this well.

> The question of the ceremonies is one of the most important to settle. It is primarily through the ceremonies that the Olympiad must distinguish itself from a mere series of world championships. The Olympiad calls for a solemnity and ceremonial which would be quite out of keeping were it not for the prestige which accrues to it from its titles of nobility [3].

In his appreciation of the need to ritualize not only the athletic contests, but the opening and closing of the Games, the prize giving, the IOC meetings, etc., Coubertin shared with his contemporary Durkheim a recognition of the power of ritual and festival. Durkheim had argued that a ritual attitude of sacred respect was at the root of all moral commitments [12].

> This means moral remaking cannot be achieved except by means of periodic reunions, assemblies, meetings where the individuals, being closely united to one another, reaffirm in common their common sentiments: hence come ceremonies which do not differ from regular religious ceremonies, either in their object, the results which they produce, or the processes employed to gain these results. . . . If we find a little difficulty today in imagining what these feasts and ceremonies of the future could consist in, it is because we are going through a stage of moral mediocrity and transition [9].

As "festivals of human unity," the early Olympic Games had to work against what Coubertin called "recalcitrant public opinion" predisposed to see in public rituals "only theatrical displays incompatible with the seriousness of international muscular competitions" [13]. He took consuming interest in every ritual detail, for, like Durkheim, he believed that rituals "with true nobility and eurythmy" [13] were a "factory of life-force," producing what we should today call "altered states of consciousness." (The source of his fellowship with Pindar, noted above). This "life-force" was to Coubertin a sacred "mana" qualitatively different from any simple emotional "intensity" generated regularly by games. As Geertz writes: "A man can indeed be said to be 'religious' about golf, but not merely if he pursues it with passion and plays it on Sunday: he must also see it as symbolic of some transcendent truths" [11]. For Coubertin, as we have seen Olympic Games are symbolic of truths about the nature of human life which were to him transcendent. The Games were designed to provide ritual experiences of the unity of mankind, experiences of what the philosopher David Hume called "human-kindness" and what the anthropologist Victor Turner calls "egalitarian communitas" [11].

Turner has closely associated feelings of "communitas" with the structure and process of rites of passage, first outlined by Van Gennep [20]. The Olympic Games are organized like a rite of passage, with the Opening Ceremonies as rites of *separation* from "ordinary life," the athletic contests as rites of *selection*, the victory ceremonies as rites of *confirmation* and *initiation* and the Closing Ceremonies as rites of *reaggregation* with the "real world." The Games mark out in space and time a liminal arena in which the values and norms of ordinary life are reversed in sacred play. This is a formal, behavioral pattern familiar to anthropologists and students of religion from a wide variety of societies.* The difference in the Olympic Games is that here the process is expanded to the "meta-community" of mankind, providing it with compelling images of another world to live in. And as Santayana writes: ". . . and another world to live in — whether we expect ever to pass wholly over to it or not — is what we mean by having a religion" [11].

Religion or Religious . . . and for Whom?

I have tried to suggest that modern Olympism and the Olympic Games raise important and interesting questions for students of religious history and behavior and, in turn, that we cannot fully appreciate the phenomenon of Olympism without paying attention to the religious dimension of its genesis. I've tried to indicate that this dimension is historically substantial and that religious themes and structures are built into the ideology and design of the Games. In doing so, I've left two important questions untouched.

Henri de Montherlant wrote somewhere that "sport is not a religion, but what we do here, we do with a religious heart." He referred directly to the Olympic Games. Probably for Coubertin, as I've indicated, Olympism was sufficiently systematic, perennial and enduring that it constituted a religion for him. But for most others, we may well suspect, the Games may provide religious emotions, representations and experiences but in an occasional, spontaneous and ad hoc fashion, much too unreflective and unsystematic ever to merit the full status of a religion. Moreover, it may turn out that whatever religious dimension the Games may have is more dependent upon the religious symbol systems and belief systems participants and spectators bring with them, rather than to Olympism's own dogmas and symbols. And just how widespread are religious feelings and perceptions during the Games? Who has them? With what depth and frequency? Has this changed over time?

These are empirical questions which require empirical answers. This paper has attempted to indicate why the questions are worth asking.

---

*MacAloon, 1965; Geertz [11].

References

1. Bellah, R.: Beyond Belief: Essays on Religion in a Post-Traditional World. New York:Harper and Row, 1970.
2. Bowra, C.: The Odes of Pindar. Baltimore:Penguin Classics, 1969, pp. xii, xvi-xvii.
3. de Coubertin, P.: The Olympic Idea. Carl-Diem-Institut (ed.) Stuttgart: Verlag Karl Hofmann, 1967, pp. 1, 34, 87, 107, 109, 110, 118, 124, 131, 134.
4. de Coubertin, P.: Une campagne de vingt-et-un ans. Paris:Librairie de l'éducation physique, 1908, pp. 1-7.
5. de Coubertin, P.: La chronique de France. Auxerre:Ed. Albert Lanier, 3e année, 1902, pp. 142-145.
6. de Coubertin, P.: The Evolution of France under the Third Republic. Hapgood, I. (trans.). New York:Crowell, 1897, pp. 272-307.
7. de Coubertin, P.: Universités transatlantiques. Paris:Ed. Hachette, 1890, pp. 307-311.
8. de Lubac, H.: The Drama of Atheistic Humanism. New York:Meridian, 1950, pp. 79-159.
9. Durkheim, E.: The Elementary Forms of the Religious Life. New York:Free Press, 1965, p. 62.
10. Eyquem, M.: Pierre de Coubertin: l'épopée olympique. Paris:Calmann-Lévy, 1966, pp. 110, 288.
11. Geertz, C.: The Interpretation of Cultures. New York:Basic Books, 1973, pp. 98, 112.
12. La Capra, D.: Emile Durkheim. Ithaca:Cornell University Press, 1972, pp. 87-142, 243, 430ff.
13. MacAloon, J.: French aristocracy and the revival of the Olympic Games, 1870-1910. Paper presented to the Society for Social Research, Chicago, April, 1976, pp. 17, 34.
14. MacAloon, J.: Deep play and the flow experience in rock climbing. *In* Csikszentmihalyi, M.: Beyond Boredom and Anxiety. San Francisco: Jossey-Bass, 1975.
15. Mauss, M.: Oeuvres, Vol. 3. Paris:Ed de Minuit, 1969, pp. 573-639.
16. Turner, V.: Symbols in African ritual. Science 179:89, 90, 1973.
17. Turner, V.: The Ritual Process. Chicago:Aldine, 1969.
18. Turner, V.: The Drums of Affliction. Oxford:Clarendon, 1968.
19. Turner, V.: The Forest of Symbols. Ithaca:Cornell University Press, 1967.
20. Van Gennep, A.: The Rites of Passage. Chicago:University of Chicago, 1960.
21. Wallace, A.: Revitalization movements. Am. Anthropol. 58, 1956, pp. 100, 103, 125.

La vie et l'existence: Helmuth Plessner et Martin Heidegger

Jean-Claude Petit

> Der Forscher:
> "... mir ist es unerfindlich, wie das Wesen des Menschen je gefunden werden soll, indem man vom Menschen wegblickt."
> Der Lehrer:
> "Mir ist das auch unerfindlich; darum suche ich darüber Klarheit zu erlangen, inwiefern dies möglich oder vielleicht gar notwendig ist."
>
> *Martin Heidegger*
> *Zur Erörterung der Gelassenheit*

Cette question est celle qu'on appelle "la question de l'homme," c'est-à-dire la question qui questionne au sujet de ce qu'est l'homme. La question, donc, que l'homme pose lui-même à son propre sujet. D'une manière plus précise encore, il s'agit ici de la direction dans laquelle cette question devrait s'engager pour voir apparaître une réponse. Il s'agira donc de l'orientation de ce qu'on appelle dans certains milieux: une anthropologie philosophique.

Nous rappelons, pour ce faire, le débat qu'entretient depuis quelques années le philosophe et savant allemand Helmuth Plessner avec la pensée de Martin Heidegger.*

En référence à une étude de H. Farenbach sur M. Heidegger [2], Plessner écrit: "La question 'qu'est-ce que l'homme', c'est là l'avis de Heidegger, en un temps où elle ploit sous le fardeau d'une tradition séculaire de la philosophie, qui vit de cette question et qui fut depuis

---

Jean-Claude Petit, Faculté de théologie, Université de Montréal, Montréal, Canada.

*H. Plessner est né en 1892 à Wiesbaden en Allemagne. Avec Max Scheler [12], il est considéré comme un des fondateurs de l'anthropologie philosophique comme discipline particulière, dont il influença d'une manière décisive la problématique avec son étude "Die Stufen des Organischen und der Mensch" (1928).

toujours contrainte d'y revenir, ne peut être reprise aujourd'hui dans toute sa densité si la question au sujet du petit mot "est" n'est pas auparavant résolue" [8, p. 336]. Pour Heidegger, en effet, "la question de l'homme ouvre la question du sens de l' "être" ", qui, Plessner le rappelle bien, ne doit pas être confondue avec celle du sens de l'étant ni même avec celle du sens du monde.

Comme il l'écrit déjà dans son étude sur "Kant et le problème de la métaphysique" [5], Heidegger pense que "toute anthropologie, y compris l'anthropologie philosophique, a déjà posé l'homme comme homme," c'est-à-dire, pour expliciter cette affirmation en reprenant les termes de la Lettre sur l'humanisme, a déterminé l'humanitas de l'homo humanus en regard d'une conception déjà établie du monde et de la nature, i.e. "en regard de l'étant dans son ensemble" [1, p. 425; 6, p. 50]. Alors qu'il se serait agi, et précisément pour répondre à la question 'qu'est-ce que l'homme? ', de penser l'homme dans son rapport à l'être, et de telle manière que ce rapport apparaisse comme le rapport de l'être à l'homme (car ce rapport de l'être à l'essence de l'homme appartient à l'être lui-même [3], il est l'être lui-même [6, p. 80]), la philosophie a pensé l'essence de l'homme dans son rapport à l'étant et est restée préoccupée par la place qu'il tient au milieu du monde. Elle était tributaire en cela de la manière dont, depuis Platon et Aristote, la pensée a posé la question de l'être. Ce faisant, la philosophie a oublié en quoi réside précisément la dignité de l'homme, qui n'est pas d'être le maître de l'étant mais le "berger de l'être," c'est-à-dire "d'être appelé par l'être lui-même dans la sauvegarde de sa vérité" [6, p. 108]. C'est ce que Heidegger appelle l'ek-sistence, qui est pour lui le mode d'être propre de l'homme.

En orientant la pensée dans cette direction, Heidegger prenait consciemment ses distances à l'égard d'une subordination de la question de l'homme à une anthropologie biologique, ou, comme le rappelle Plessner, à l'égard d'une "discipline empirique" [8, p. 335]. La mise en contraste habituelle de l'homme avec l'animal n'opère pas seulement pour Heidegger, avec deux grandeurs inconnues mais simule une comparaison entre deux réalités données, alors qu'il s'agit précisément de dépouiller l'homme de son caractère de chose, d'objectivité, pour arriver à le considérer comme celui qui peut questionner à son propre sujet [8, p. 336].

Si la définition aristotélicienne de l'homme comme Zoon logon echon est encore bien accueillie chez nos contemporains, qui considèrent l'homme comme une espèce particulière de vivant douée du don de la parole, c'est que ceci correspond à l'expérience quotidienne qui se laisse conduire par la compréhension habituelle des mots. Mais qu'est-ce que le logos dont parle cette définition? Quel est ce don en la possession de l'homme? Pour obvier à une définition de cette sorte qui opère avec deux grandeurs inconnues, Heidegger n'amorce pas sa réflexion avec l'idée d'être vivant ou de vie, mais avec celle de Dasein qu'il réserve exclusivement à l'homme [8, pp. 336-337].

Or cette ontologie fondamentale qu'Heidegger a ainsi déployée en lieu et place d'une anthropologie philosophique pour répondre à la question de l'homme, s'est avérée, pour Plessner, incapable de prendre au sérieux ce qui, à ses yeux, reste constitutif de l'existence humaine, à savoir le mode propre d'existence corporelle de l'homme. Lorsque Heidegger parle de Dasein, il oriente la question de l'homme en direction de celle du sens du Dasein et la soumet ainsi à celle du sens de l'être purement et simplement. L'anthropologie supposerait ainsi une ontologie fondamentale. Si l'on ne veut pas aboutir dans les voies d'une telle argumentation, et pour éviter cette prédétermination ontologique, nous pouvons choisir le mot "vie," employé aussi bien pour ce qui est spécifiquement humain que pour ce qui est extérieur à l'homme [8, p. 342].

Avec ceci, poursuit Plessner, il n'est pas encore question d'aucune décision préalable en faveur d'un concept biologique de vie. Là-dessus, bien qu'il ne soit pas toujours facile cependant de faire ce partage dans la suite de son exposé, Plessner est assez ferme. Il y avait d'ailleurs insisté dans un texte publié l'année précédente: "Pour comprendre l'homme comme un être vivant, nous devons dépasser ses caractéristiques biologiques" [10, p. 51]. Il lui semble, en effet, que ce ne soit pas sans raison que le concept de vie se maintienne ouvert à l'égard de l'être et du devenir.

Quoiqu'il en soit de ce dernier point, ce qu'il importe ici de noter c'est la position que Plessner croit pouvoir formuler en alternative à l'entreprise heideggerienne: plutôt que de fonder la vie sur une de ses possibilités, en l'occurrence l'existence, il s'agit de faire exactement l'inverse; plutôt que de déployer, comme le fait Heidegger, la question de l'homme à partir de celui-là même qui questionne, il s'agirait de la faire "im Gesichtskreis des Lebens," dans "l'entourage de la vie," pour ainsi dire "par en-bàs" [8, p. 343]. Il faudrait en définitive une autre amorce, qui ne se laisserait pas égarer par le prétendu primat de la question du sens de l'être. Ce dont il s'agirait de s'enquérir ce sont bien plutôt des conditions qui doivent être remplies pour que la dimension de l'existence soit fondée sur celle de la vie [8, p. 344].

C'est pour répondre à cette exigence que Plessner développe son concept de "positionalité excentrique" (Exzentrische Postionalität) où l'accent porte évidemment sur l'excentricité de la position de l'homme au milieu des êtres de son monde, laquelle "excentricité," en définissant précisément le mode de la position de l'homme, a nom 'intelligence,' 'possibilité d'objectivation,' 'langage,' qui permettent à l'homme de vivre son corps dans la distance unifiante de l'instrumentalité et l'obligent ainsi, en quelque sorte, à se prendre en main pour réduire, sous l'intervention de toutes ses possibilités, les déficiences que portent sa "positionalité" [8, pp. 344, 350, 351; 10, p. 60]. C'est cette "excentricité" qui définit l'homme, cette distance pour ainsi dire entre son lieu d'insertion dans la chaîne biologique et la manière dont il s'y maintient, mais laquelle est à son tour enracinée dans la première. "La nature de l'homme, écrit Plessner dans un autre texte, ne se laisse cerner que comme une manière de vivre limitée mais en même temps rendue possible par sa base biologique; et c'est cela même qui soustrait l'homme à toute détermination définitive" [9, p. 49]. Une anthropologie philosophique doit donc ainsi se constituer comme une doctrine des conditions de possibilité d'une essence humaine de l'expérience totale dans la nature et dans l'histoire, "als Lehre von den Bedingungen der Möglichkeit eines menschenhaften Wesens der vollen Erfahrung in Natur und Geschichte" [8, p. 351]. Pour cette anthropologie, les recherches dans les domaines de la préhistoire et de l'histoire ancienne sont tout aussi importantes que celles sur le développement de l'embryon et de l'enfant.

Il ne fait pas de doute qu'indépendemment de la justesse de sa compréhension de Heidegger, les vues exposées par Plessner ne soient proches de la sensibilité de l'homme contemporain. Baigné dans un monde qui met à sa portée des connaissances chaque jour plus vastes et plus pertinentes pour la conduite immédiate de sa vie et la compréhension de sa situation dans le monde, il est aussi chaque jour livré de plus en plus à la menace d'une détérioration physique et psychologique qu'il éprouve douloureusement dans son corps: la faim et la fatigue, la solitude et l'anonymat, l'incertitude et l'angoisse, l'exploitation et la mort, tout cela lui parle viscéralement de sa fragilité et lui fait découvrir, dans la douleur, une illusoire grandeur: la fatigue parle en creux du repos; la solitude, de l'amour; la mort, de la vie . . . Toute tentative pour comprendre ce qui se joue ainsi au coeur même de cette expérience, qui aurait l'air de ne pas prendre au sérieux cet enracinement biologique de l'homme, qui semble bien expliquer à la fois ses limites ("Positionalität") et ses possibilités ("Exzentrizität"), une telle tentative doit appaître comme impertinente et inutile. C'est le verdict de Plessner à l'égard de la tentative de Heidegger. Pour être féconde, la question de l'homme doit regarder en direction de l'homme.

Revenons toutefois à Heidegger. Il faut d'abord remarquer qu'il ne récuse pas du tout la formule aristotélicienne qui fait de l'homme un Zoon logon echon. Bien au contraire: "une telle détermination de l'essence de l'homme n'est pas fausse, mais elle est conditionnée par la métaphysique. C'est son origine essentielle et non pas seulement ses limites qui toutefois sont devenues dignes d'être mises en question dans "Sein und Zeit." Ce qui est digne d'être mis en question est confié avant tout à la pensée comme ce qu'elle a elle-même à penser, et pas du tout livré à l'action dissolvante d'un scepticisme vide" [6, p. 52]. Cette formule n'est pas fausse, écrit donc Heidegger, seulement elle ne va pas assez loin. Elle pense bien, sans doute, la place de l'homme au milieu des étants, elle ne pense pas cependant l'essence de l'homme ainsi découvert. Ce qu'il faut dire c'est précisément l'essence de cet être qui existe comme "Zoon logon echon." Le terme d' "animal" en cette définition, "zoon," "implique déjà une interprétation de la "vie" qui repose nécessairement sur une interprétation de l'étant comme zoè et physis, à l'intérieur desquels le vivant apparait. Mais, en outre, et avant toute autre chose, reste à se demander si l'essence de l'homme, d'un point de vue originel et qui décide par avance de tout, repose dans la dimension de l'animalitas. D'une façon générale, sommes-nous sur la bonne voie pour découvrir l'essence de l'homme, lorsque nous le définissons, comme un vivant parmi d'autres, en l'opposant aux plantes, à l'animal, à Dieu? " [6, p. 55].

Il est bien certain que l'on peut toujours procéder ainsi, et, ce faisant, on pourra chaque fois dire des choses justes à propos de l'homme. "Mais on doit bien comprendre, poursuit Heidegger, que, par là, l'homme se trouve repoussé définitivement dans le domaine essentiel de l'animalitas, même si, loin de l'identifier à l'animal, on lui accorde une différence spécifique. En principe on pense alors toujours l'homo animalis, même si on pose l'anima comme animus sine mens, et celle-ci, plus tard, comme sujet, personne ou esprit" [6, pp. 55-57]. Au lieu de penser l'homme en partant de l'animalitas, ce qui est le propre de la métaphysique, il faut le penser en direction de son humanitas.

Plessner ne semble pas avoir compris la différence fondamentale qu'il y a entre ces deux questionnements. Nous pouvons le vérifier, semble-t-il, à la signification qu'il donne à son concept de "positionalité excentrique." Il écrit, en effet: "Ce qui est décisif, c'est ceci: la séparation intrasomatique du corps (biologique) (Körper) et du corps (-vécu) (Leib) force l'être vivant de positionalité excentrique à vivre sa vie; ainsi se trouve accompli le concept heideggerien de Dasein. Cet être vivant existe . . ." [8, p. 350]. Plessner comprend le Dasein de Heidegger comme une tentative malheureuse pour exprimer en termes ontologiques la situation particulière de l'homme parmi les autres étants et tout son effort tend à dégrever cette entreprise de cette hypothèque pour lui redonner des bases plus larges et plus solides, en l'occurence des bases biologique, qui intégreraient l'acquis des diverses sciences occupées depuis des décennies à mettre cette situation particulière de l'existence humaine en évidence: la paléontologie, l'archéologie, la biologie, la psychologie génétique, etc.

L'intention de Heidegger, c'est le moins qu'on puisse dire, n'est pas étrangère à ce souci de comprendre l'homme. Elle est cependant beaucoup plus vaste et plus radicale: ce qu'il poursuit, c'est le project de mettre à découvert les raisons qui nous amènent précisément à poser de cette manière la question de l'homme. Il les retrouvent dans le destin même de la pensée occidentale depuis Platon et Aristote, qui n'ont toujours pensé l'homme que dans son rapport à l'étant sans questionner sur le rapport de l'être à l'essence de l'homme. Or c'est ce questionnement qu'il faut reprendre; dans la voie qu'il ouvre, s'offre une possibilité de redonner à l'homme une dignité oubliée et de le soustraire à la main-mise d'une pensée qui, se le re-présentant, le situe et le place dans un monde qui n'a pas été préalablement soumis à la question de celui qui le pense.

Que l'essence de l'homme soit d'être le seigneur du monde et d'occuper ainsi une place particulière dans la nature, cela lui est devenu comme allant tellement de soi, qu'il y a longtemps déjà qu'il ne se demande plus comment il en est arrivé là. Mais l'homme peut-il ainsi toujours supposer son essence comme quelque chose qui ne pose pas de question? Et considérer comme allant de soi la manière dont, dans cette situation, il dispose des étants? Ne se pourrait-il pas que la nature cache précisément son être en ne présentant à l'homme qu'un côté techniquement manipulable? Ne se pourrait-il pas que l'homme méconnaisse précisément son essence lorsqu'il ne se comprend que comme le maître de la terre [11]?

Le physicien Werner Heisenberg écrit dans son étude sur "La nature dans la physique contemporaine:" "Autrefois, l'homme était face à face avec la nature; habitée par des créatures de toute espèce, elle constituait un royaume qui vivait selon ses propres lois; l'homme devait de quelque manière s'y adapter. Aujourd'hui, nous vivons dans un monde si totalement transformé par lui que nous rencontrons partout les structures dont il est l'auteur: emploi des instruments de la vie quotidienne, préparation de la nourriture par les machines, transformation du paysage par l'homme; de sorte que l'homme ne rencontre plus que lui-même" [7, pp. 28-29].

De sorte que, dans ce monde, l'homme ne rencontre plus que lui-même . . . Heidegger, dans sa conférence sur "la question de la technique," rappelle ce passage du livre de Heisenberg. Il commente ce dont ce texte parle: "Que l'envoi cependant règne sous le mode de l'arraisonnement, et alors c'est le plus grand danger. (. . .) . . . l'illusion se répand, que tout ce que l'homme rencontre n'a de consistance qu'en autant que cela est sous son emprise. Cette apparence temporalise une dernière illusion, selon laquelle il apparaît que l'homme ne rencontre plus partout que lui-même. C'est avec raison que Heisenberg a attiré l'attention sur le fait que pour l'homme d'aujourd'hui le réel ne peut que se présenter à lui de cette façon. *En cela l'homme d'aujourd'hui ne se rencontre plus nulle part en vérité, c'est-à-dire qu'il ne rencontre plus nulle part son essence.* Il se tient d'une manière si décisive dans la dépendance de l'exigence de ce qu'il a arraisonné qu'il ne le perçoit plus comme une revendication, qu'il ne se voit plus comme celui qui est interpelé et il n'entend plus ainsi la manière selon laquelle il ek-siste à partir de son essence dans le domaine d'une interpellation et qu'il *ne peut* ainsi *jamais* ne rencontrer que lui-même" [4].

Mais que l'homme ne croit plus rencontrer que lui-même, voilà le danger qui le menace. Ce danger, cependant, n'est pas une fatalité. De ce danger l'homme pourra être libéré s'il accepte jamais de faire "l'expérience de l'oubli fondamental qui règne dans le déploiement de l'essence de la technique" et d'éprouver celle-ci *comme* danger. "Car cet oubli concerne l'essence même de l'homme et celle de la vérité" [1, p. 475]. Il est le mode sous lequel l'être se décèle actuellement.

Pour répondre à la question de l'homme, il faut peut-être regarder ailleurs que dans la direction de l'homme.

Références

1. Couturier, F.: Monde et être chez Heidegger. Montréal:Les Presses de l'Université de Montréal, 1971.
2. Farenbach, H.: Heidegger und das Problem einer "philosophischen" Anthropologie. Dans: Durchblicke. Martin Heidegger zum 80. Geburtstag. Frankfurt:Klostermann, 1969.
3. Heidegger, M.: Einleitung zu "Was ist Metaphysik? ". Dans: Wegmarken. Frankfurt:Klostermann, 1967, p. 201.
4. Heidegger, M.: Die Frage nach der Technik. Dans: Vorträge und Aufsätze. Teil I. Pfullingen:Neske, 1967, p. 27.

5. Heidegger, M.: Kant und das Problem der Metaphysik. (1929) Frankfurt: Klostermann, 1965, p. 207.
6. Heidegger, M.: Lettre sur l'humanisme. Texte allemand traduit et présenté par R. Munier. Nouvelle édition revue. Paris:Aubier, Editions Montaigne, 1964.
7. Heisenberg, W.: La nature dans la physique contemporaine. Paris:Gallimard, 1962.
8. Plessner, H.: Der Aussagewert einer philosophischen Anthropologie. Dans: Wirklichkeit und Reflexion. Zum sechzigsten Geburtstag für Walter Schulz. Pfullingen:Neske, 1973.
9. Plessner, H.: Homo absconditus. Dans: Philosophische Anthropologie heute. (Beck'sche Schwarze Reihe, Band 89) München:Verlag C. H. Beck, 1972, p. 49.
10. Plessner, H.: Der Mensch als Lebewesen. Dans: Philosophische Anthropologie heute. (Beck'sche Schwarze Reihe, Band 89) München:Verlag C. H. Beck, 1972, p. 51.
11. Pöggeler, O.: Existentiale Anthropologie. Dans: Rombach, H., (ed.): Die Frage nach dem Menschen. Aufriss einer philosophischen Anthropologie. Festschrift für Max Müller zum 60. Geburstag. Freiburg-München:Verlag K. Alber, 1966, p. 453.
12. Scheler, M.: La situation de l'homme dans le monde. (Die Stellung des Menschen im Kosmos, 1929). Traduit et préfacé par M. Dupuy. Paris: Aubier, Editions Montaigne, 1951.

Du temps compétitif au temps réalisé: la fête comme mouvement

Maurice Boutin

Aujourd'hui plus que jamais auparavant peut-être, on associe très étroitement le temps et la vitesse jusqu'à les identifier parfois purement et simplement. Le rapport à l'espace est alors compris et vécu avant tout comme mouvement de déplacement. Dans cette association — ou même identification — du temps à la vitesse prédomine une 'lutte contre la montre' qui ne se limite aucunement aux activités du stade mais envahit tout aussi bien la vie quotidienne, au moins dans les pays hautement industrialisés. Le temps compétitif n'est donc pas un temps particulier, exceptionnel. Il n'est pas que le 'temps de la compétition' sportive. Ce dernier en est toutefois une manifestation privilégiée, car il oblige à tenir davantage compte de la structure fondamentale du temps compétitif.

Le temps dans lequel nous vivons toujours plus radicalement peut être sensément appelé *temps compétitif* parce que de fait il est temps de *libre concurrence*, bien qu'il comporte également des impératifs qui deviennent toujours plus contraignants surtout à cause du règne de la technique. Si la structure fondamentale du temps compétitif a rendu possible, en Occident du moins, l'advenance de la technique, celle-ci radicalise en retour les exigences propres au temps compétitif. D'où la question qui se pose existentiellement de plusieurs manières et qu'on pourrait formuler ainsi: est-il possible de se libérer du temps compétitif? Et si oui, comment?

Au lieu de dénoncer ici une fois de plus 'la Technique' en disant par exemple qu'elle révèle non seulement l'habileté et l'ingéniosité de l'esprit humain mais en même temps aussi sa folie, il est préférable de se demander ce que recèle cette suprématie du temps compétitif dans ce qui en est une manifestation à bien des égards privilégiée: la performance sportive en contexte de compétition. Dans quelle mesure ce contexte présage-t-il d'une évolution de la technique menant possiblement à l'impasse? Et en quoi consisterait la libération par rapport à cette évolution de la technique?

Maurice Boutin, Faculté de théologie, Université de Montréal, Québec, Canada.

Référons surtout, pour ne pas dire exclusivement, à des performances sportives qui ont à voir avec le temps comme dimension entrant *directement* dans l'objectif de la compétition et dans son appréciation. Ce qui va suivre sur le temps compétitif et la compétition concerne beaucoup moins ou même pas du tout des performances sportives dont le résultat visé s'obtient dans une période de temps toujours la même (au hockey par exemple), dans lesquelles donc l'idéal du 'moins de temps possible' n'entre pas dans l'objectif de la compétition elle-même et dans lesquelles le critère principal, sinon exclusif, d'appréciation de la performance n'est pas la vitesse. Personne ne songera à attribuer la victoire à l'équipe de hockey qui a patiné le plus rapidement.

Les disciplines sportives dans lesquelles la performance s'apprécie d'abord et avant tout en terme de vitesse dépendent plus étroitement que d'autres et l'équipement utilisé. C'est éminemment le cas dans des disciplines comme le patinage de vitesse, la luge et le ski alpin, à propos desquelles on multiplie les tests ces dernières années dans le but de confectionner un matériel de 'qualité supérieure,' c'est-à-dire pouvant faire gagner quelques centièmes de seconde de plus à son porteur, et au sujet desquelles on tente des essais comme celui du ski à spatule perforée susceptible d'augmenter quelque peu la vitesse du skieur.

Le sport de compétition, au moins dans certaines disciplines, devient ainsi plus dépendant non seulement des techniques d'entraînement et des techniques de 'concentration,' mais aussi des techniques d'équipement pour lesquelles certaines compagnies productrices d'équipement sportif consacrent des budgets de recherche assez importants. La compétition du marché commande un perfectionnement coûteux du matériel, et la compétition sportive est considérée quasi tout naturellement comme un banc d'essai privilégié de nouvelles techniques de fabrication du matériel d'équipement. Cette recherche et ces essais accentuent davantage encore la dimension compétitive du temps lui-même dans le sport, et manifestent à leur façon la suprématie de cette dimension dans la vie moderne.

Temps compétitif et mesure du temps-mouvement

Le temps compétitif est temps-mouvement mesurable, et sa mesure fonde souvent l'appréciation de la performance sportive. Ici la détermination aristotélicienne du temps comme "arithmos kinêseôs kata to proteron kai husteron" ("compte du mouvement selon l'avant et l'après") est primordiale, tout comme celle, philosophiquement fondée par Descartes, de la vitesse comme ce à partir de quoi le mouvement est compris.

La mesure ou le "compte" du mouvement nécessite une fragmentation, c'est-à-dire la détermination d'une unité de mesure du temps-mouvement. Dans la compétition sportive, cette unité n'appartient plus au domaine macrocosmique des sens. Elle échappe au contraire toujours plus à la perception directe, ce que seul le développement de la technique chronométrique permet: sans l'électronique, il est impossible de prendre comme unité de mesure du temps-mouvement le centième ou même, depuis tout récemment, le millième de seconde.

La recherche de l'unité fragmentaire la plus petite dans la mesure du mouvement favorise une appréciation plus 'objective' de la performance. Mais elle accentue aussi la portée compétitive du temps-mouvement lui-même. L'utilisation d'unités plus petites de mesure du temps-mouvement est très importante dans les compétitions où la différence de vitesse entre les participants n'est pas mesurée par la distance qui les sépare au point d'arrivée, dans lesquelles donc les différences de performance ne sont *pas spatialement* perçues. Dans une même compétition, une descente de ski par exemple, les participants ne sont pas plus ou moins distants du but de la compétition (la victoire *sur* le temps remportée par le skieur le plus rapide) parce qu'ils s'exécutent les uns après les autres. Et le skieur qui ne part pas le premier n'est pas pour autant en position de désavantage par rapport à ceux qui l'ont précédé dans la descente.

Cet état de fait est rendu possible seulement parce que le critère d'appréciation de la performance se prend alors en référence au compte enregistré du temps-mouvement *et non de l'espace*, bien que le rapport à l'espace demeure lui aussi déterminant. Ceci, on peut facilement le constater par exemple dans le phénomène du record sportif: celui qui établit un nouveau record est supérieur à celui qui le détenait jusque là, mais à la condition que la performance de vitesse des deux soit en rapport avec une même distance parcourue. Le rapport à l'espace compris comme distance mesurée reste donc déterminant, mais c'est pourtant la mesure du temps-mouvement qui est décisive dans l'établissement de nouveaux records.

Que l'espace soit lui aussi déterminant, quoique de façon seulement médiate, la spécialisation poussée de la compétition sportive permet de mieux le comprendre. En effet, il n'est aucunement absurde de se spécialiser comme coureur par exemple dans le 400 ou dans le 800 mètres. Cela ne veut pas nécessairement dire que le champion du 800 mètres pourra a fortiori être champion du 400 mètres, car il s'agit, à l'intérieur d'une même discipline, de spécialisations qui sont différentes précisément en fonction d'un espace déterminé à parcourir.

En tant qu'obstacle à surmonter qui est le même pour chacun et détermine ainsi *médiatement* l'appréciation de la performance, l'espace place les participants d'une même compétition dans une certaine condition commune. Cependant, l'obstacle commun à vaincre reste d'abord et surtout le temps-mouvement mesurable: le temps compétitif est le temps mis à leur disposition pour qu'ils en disposent le moins possible.

Pour être mesuré, le temps doit être arrêté dans sa plus petite partie possible: la seconde, le centième et même actuellement le millième de seconde. Sans cet arrêté on ne peut y recourir comme critère d'appréciation de la performance dans certaines disciplines compétitives n'exigeant pas des participants la simultanéité d'exécution.

Le compétitif permet donc une expérience particulière non seulement du mouvement (comme vitesse), mais aussi du temps. Mode de vivre ou de se comporter face au temps, le temps compétitif vise aussi à réduire le temps mis à la disposition, à 'faire l'économie' du temps, et la performance est appréciée d'après cet idéal minimalisant d'une disposition du temps inversement proportionnelle à la capacité de rapidité des concurrents. Ainsi le temps compétitif implique une décroissance constante du nombre de compétiteurs virtuels, il est l'expression d'un 'temps public' disponible de façon élitiste. Le 'temps public' est donc lui-même rejoint de plus en plus par ce que le biologiste américain Garrett Hardin appelle le "principe compétitif d'exclusion" ("competitive exclusion principle") déjà à l'oeuvre dans les divers secteurs de la vie moderne dont l'économique n'est sûrement pas un des moindres.

Temps réalisé et négation du mesurable

Le titre de cette communication réfère à la possibilité du passage du temps compétitif au *temps réalisé*, laissant entendre par là un mouvement opérant en quelque sorte un métabolisme de l'expérience même du temps.

L'expression 'temps réalisé' n'est probablement pas très heureuse. En effet, si elle veut dire que le temps se réaliserait dans le temps, elle semble contraire à l'expérience la plus élementaire pour laquelle le 'cours du temps' coule vers autre chose un peu comme le fleuve coule vers l'océan. Si elle veut dire que le temps courrait, jusqu'à l'épuisement de son mouvement, vers sa réalisation donnée dans l'absolu ou une quelconque fixité devenue une sorte d'idéal, elle semble entériner alors une distinction par ailleurs présente dans la pensée occidentale, et elle suscite la question de savoir si une telle signification ne serait pas le fait d'une pensée sans cesse guettée par le dualisme. L'expression 'temps réalisé' ne doit pas non plus être comprise à l'aide par exemple de la référence à l'"oeuvre réalisée,' c'est-à-dire terminée dans sa production. Si le temps est dans une certaine mesure l'oeuvre de l'homme, ce n'est pas au sens de l'oeuvre réalisée. L'expression ne renvoie pas ici à un quelconque point d'achèvement du temps-mouvement.

Parler de temps réalisé, ce n'est donc pas affirmer que le temps réalisé n'est pas du temps, ou que le temps compétitif n'est qu'une illusion, donc que le temps serait seulement ou bien mesurable et mesuré, ou bien non mesurable. Temps compétitif et temps réalisé ne sont pas deux temps qu'on pourrait distinguer, voire opposer, en identifiant par exemple le temps réalisé à ce que la métaphysique classique appelle l'éternité. Ils sont bien plutôt deux dimensions du temps-mouvement.

La préséance inébranlée du temps compétitif dans notre expérience quotidienne du temps contredit toutefois une telle affirmation. Cette préséance semble ou bien contraindre à l'identification pure et simple du temps au temps-mouvement mesurable, ou bien ne susciter qu'occasionnellement et en contrepartie une nostalgie vaguement romantique, plus ou moins directement apparentée à celle qui poussait Goethe dans son *Faust* à interpeller l'instant en disant: "Reste donc, tu es si beau!", et faisait entendre à Lamartine ces paroles qu'il rapporte dans *Le lac:*

O temps! suspends ton vol, et vous, heures propices!
    Suspendez votre cours:
Laissez-nous savourer les rapides délices
    Des plus beaux de nos jours!

Dans cette perspective, le temps réalisé serait donc un demeurer ou une suspension du temps, une négation du temps-mouvement et un repos provoquant un arrêt d'autant plus radical de la course commandée par l'emprise du temps compétitif que, suspendu au vide du 'ciel des valeurs', il participerait davantage de sa fixité.

Dans le temps réalisé, il s'agit essentiellement non pas de la négation du temps-mouvement, mais de la *négation de l'arrêté du temps* indispensable à la mesure du temps-mouvement. Cette négation, on peut la comprendre de deux manières: en rapport avec le temps compétitif — et dire alors que celui-ci cesse et même disparaît; ou positivement, c'est-à-dire en rapport avec le temps réalisé — et dire alors de celui-ci qu'il advient.

Si l'on comprend habituellement le temps compétitif en l'identifiant au temps et sans tenir compte de la possibilité du temps réalisé, peut-on à l'inverse comprendre vraiment le temps réalisé sans tenir compte de la réalité factuelle du temps compétitif? Il semble que non. Mais si l'on ne peut situer la négation de l'arrêté du temps-mouvement mesurable dans un 'ailleurs' extérieur au temps, quel sens comporte encore une telle négation advenant *dans* le temps-mouvement mesurable?

Négation de l'arrêté du temps-mouvement mesurable, le temps réalisé est tout le contraire du repos. Il est mouvement libéré de l'arrêté et de la mensurabilité. Le prix à payer pour une telle libération est assez haut aujourd'hui: c'est le renoncement non pas au mouvement, mais au mesuré comme critère dernier d'appréciation de toute activité. Le passage du temps compétitif au temps réalisé est donc passage du temps-mouvement mesurable et mesuré au temps-mouvement non mesurable, libération de l'emprise du mesuré (et de l'arrêté du temps qui le permet) au prix du renoncement à cet arrêté et au mesuré. Cette libération et ce renoncement font partie aujourd'hui d'une recherche diffuse dans plusieurs cultures occidentales, surtout dans les pays hautement industrialisés.

Le temps réalisé est mouvement dans lequel la vitesse, la compétition, la mesure, l'arrêté du temps-mouvement mesurable, le temps comme obstacle à défier et à surmonter et donc son expérience en terme de 'lutte' ou de 'course contre la montre,' n'ont plus de sens en eux-mêmes et pour eux-mêmes. Une telle affirmation n'a toutefois de sens que si le temps réalisé est expérimenté lui aussi comme temps-mouvement, bien que non mesurable. Le 'lieu' privilégié de cette expérimentation est ce qu'on désigne habituellement par *la fête*.

Fête et temps-mouvement

Le rapport entre temps compétitif et temps réalisé tel que précisé jusqu'ici dans une de ses dimensions fondamentales, est nécessaire à la compréhension de la fête comme mouvement. Celle-ci n'est cependant pas simplement le mouvement du passage du temps compétitif au temps réalisé, comme une sorte de troisième temps-mouvement quelque part 'entre' le temps compétitif et le temps réalisé, et dont il faudrait maintenant rechercher ce qu'il a à la fois de commun et de différent par rapport aux deux premiers comme dimensions du temps-mouvement. Le mouvement de la fête est précisément le mouvement du temps réalisé. La fête est temps réalisé et, comme celui-ci, négation de l'arrêté permettant la mesure du temps compétitif. C'est pourquoi la fête est sans cesse exposée à la démesure et dégénère d'autant plus en 'orgie' que le temps compétitif cherche à établir davantage sa domination sur elle.

L'espace festif ne médiatise pas un obstacle à vaincre dans une condition compétitive commune aux participants de la fête parce que ces derniers ne sont pas des concurrents. La 'performance' festive est autre que concurrentielle, et la solidarité advenant dans la fête n'est pas réponse à l'impératif d'une victoire *sur* le temps-mouvement, mais appel et préparation de la victoire *du* temps-mouvement non mesurable qui advient aussi en elle. D'où l'importance de la fête comme expérimentation d'une dimension fondamentale du temps-mouvement qui, si elle n'advient que trop rarement, sinon jamais, ne peut pas ne pas avoir de répercussions sur l'être-homme dans l'expérience et la compréhension de sa temporalité propre.

Lorsque l'occasion de la fête est le rappel d'un fait historique particulier, son caractère festif n'est pas un critère d'appréciation, mais une réalité d'avènement qui ne réfère pas à ce fait comme s'il s'aggissait seulement d'en reconnaître et célébrer la signification durable. La 'durabilité' d'un tel fait historique est bien plutôt intimement reliée au temps-mouvement non mesurable lui-même.

Ainsi pour la foi chrétienne, la référence à la personne du Christ est rappel du temps réalisée à vivre comme fête. Ce rappel est une exigence dont la foi chrétienne est, en même temps que 'memoria' du Christ, également la mémoire; une mémoire qui ne saurait être comprise par référence au simple souvenir, même pas au souvenir archétypal de quelque 'moment primordial' dans le temps lui-même, voire possiblement hors du temps. Pour suggestive qu'elle pourrait sembler à première vue, une telle référence laisse toute entière posée la question de la possibilité — et aussi du sens — d'un tel 'temps primordial' auquel la mémoire renverrait. Une telle référence suggère de plus une identification de la mémoire et du souvenir qui tombe facilement dans les ornières d'un soi-disant temps psychologique intériorisé, et fait ainsi de la 'memoria' de la foi chrétienne, autant vis-à-vis de la personne du Christ que du temps réalisé comme dimension du temps-mouvement, autre chose que ce qu'elle est: événement du temps dont le mouvement échappe à la mesure, c'est-à-dire tout le contraire de la réitération d'un fait de l'histoire auquel on accorderait par ailleurs un sens durable traduisible en 'valeur d'"éternité" abolissant le mouvement tout comme le temps.

La 'durabilité' du Christ indique bien plutôt dans le sens d'un mouvement qui ne se détache pas de lui, mais "demeure en lui," comme l'affirme expressément surtout l'évangile de Jean, dans une transformation reconvertissante du rapport à lui et au quotidien partagé par la communauté des croyants dans sa solidarité avec les autres hommes.

Etude historico-théologique sur la fête en Israël ancien

Jean Martucci

Après avoir fait un inventaire des fêtes d'Israël, cette communication proposera quelques hypothèses sur leurs origines et leur sens.

Les fêtes d'Israël

Il faut ici distinguer entre les fêtes anciennes, les fêtes tardives, les temps sacrés et la fête eschatologique.

Les fêtes anciennes

Les trois plus anciennes fêtes d'Israël sont: "La Pâque et les Azymes" (en hébreu: "Pesach" et "Mazzôt"), "la fête des Semaines" (en hébreu: "Shabu'ôt") et "la fête des Tentes" (en hébreu: "Sukkôt"). C'est surtout le Pentateuque qui nous permet de les connaître. Les couches de rédaction de cet écrit vont du Xe au Ve siècle, mais elles empruntent souvent à des traditions orales beaucoup plus anciennes.

"Pesach" et "Mazzôt," deux fêtes distinctes très tôt réunies, sont directement reliées par la Bible à la sortie d'Egypte. C'est entre la neuvième et la dixième plaie d'Egypte qu'a été inséré le principal témoignage du Priesterkodex à leur sujet (Exode 12, 1-20). Le mot "Pesach," dont l'étymologie est obscure et qui, manifestement, n'est pas un mot d'origine hébraïque, est interprété par Exode 12 dans le sens de "sauter, passer outre" par rapprochement populaire avec la racine "Pasach" qui a ce sens. C'est de là que l'anglais a tiré le mot "Passover" pour désigner la Pâque juive. Le français, avec le mot "Pâque" a hérité de la racine "Pesach" elle-même, à travers l'araméen, le grec et le latin. Pour la tradition biblique, "Pesach" rappelle "l'Ange exterminateur" qui, la nuit de la sortie d'Egypte, "passait par dessus" les maisons israélites. Jusqu'à la destruction du Temple de Jérusalem en 70 de notre ère, "Pesach" se célébrait par l'immolation d'un agneau ou d'une chèvre sans tares, mâle et agé

Jean Martucci, Sciences bibliques, Université de Montréal, Montréal, Québec, Canada.

d'un an qu'on devait faire rôtir et manger en toute hâte, les reins ceints, sandales aux pieds et bâton à la main. C'est sous le roi Josias (640-609) que "Mazzôt" fut réunie à "Pesach." Sept jours durant, on ne mange que des pains sans levain ("Mazzôt"). Le rattachement de "Mazzôt" à "Pesach" a entraîné une interprétation historicisante des pains sans levain: à la sortie d'Egypte, les pains n'eurent pas le temps de lever "car c'est en toute hâte qu'on a quitté le pays d'Egypte" (Deutéronome 16,3).

"Shabu'ôt signifie "Semaines." Son rituel le plus élaboré a été consigné en Lévitique 23,15-21. Le cinquantième jour (en grec: "Pentekostè"; d'où "Pentecôte" en français et "Pentecost" en anglais concurremment avec "Whitsunday") après "Mazzôt," soit "sept semaines complètes," on apporte, chacun de chez soi, des pains à offrir "à titre de prémices pour Yahvé." La fête est cependant peu mentionnée dans les textes bibliques. C'est une fête populaire et joyeuse qui n'allait pas toujours sans excès et on comprend que les disciples de Jésus, ce jour-là, aient encourru le soupçon d'être "pleins de vin doux" (Actes 2,13).

"Sukkôt" veut dire "huttes" en hébreu, et c'est pour cette raison qu'on parle de "La fête des Tentes." Mais il y a manifestement une différence importante entre la hutte, qui est faite de branchages et se réfère aux champs, et la tente, qui est faite de toile et se réfère au désert. On peut déjà soupçonner une historicisation de la fête à partir de l'expérience d'Israël au Sinaï. L'expression "fête des huttes" apparaît avec les traditions deutéronomiques (Déutéronome 16,13.16) et sacerdotale (Lévitique 23,34), mais on parlait antérieurement de "la fête de la Récolte" ("'asip'": Exode 23,16 et 34,22). "Sukkôt" s'accompagnait de dégustation de fruits, de musique, de chant et de danse: "Allez, mangez des viandes grasses, buvez des boissons douces et fraites porter sa part à qui n'a rien de prêt . . . Tout le peuple s'en fut manger, boire, distribuer des parts et se livrer à grande liesse (Néhémie 8,10.12).

Les fêtes tardives

"Rosh ha-Shana" (littéralement: "Tête de l'année," comme en italien "Capodanno") est aujourd'hui très connue et on en parle comme du Jour de l'an juif. La "Mishna" lui a consacré un traité, mais l'Ancien Testament ignore cette fête et Flavius Josèphe ne l'insère pas dans sa liste des fêtes juives.

Le "Yôm Kippur" ("Jour de l'expiation" appelé aussi "Jour des pardons") constitue une des grandes solennités du judaïsme d'aujourd'hui. Quelques textes bibliques (Lévitique 23,27-32; Nombres

29,7-11; et surtout Lévitique 16) relativement récents en parlent. C'est le jour où, pour la seule et unique fois dans l'année, le grand prêtre entrait dans le Saint des Saints pour l'aspersion du propitiatoire avec le sang du taureau immolé. C'est le jour aussi où un bouc émissaire, chargé de toutes les fautes d'Israël, même inconscientes, était mené au désert pour s'y perdre.

La "Hanukka," appelée aussi "fête de la Dédicace" et, par Flavius Josèphe, "fête des lumières," date exactement du 25 du mois de Kislev (novembre-décembre) de l'an 164 avant J.-C. Ce jour-là, le Temple de Jérusalem, souillé trois ans plus tôt, par l'introduction de la statue de Zeus Olympien imposée par Antiochus IV Epiphane, fut rendu au culte du Dieu d'Israël, grâce à l'action de Judas Maccabée (1 Maccabées 4,36-59). A l'occasion de cette fête, on portait des rameaux verts et des palmes ainsi qu'une sorte de "bâton de Bacchus" entouré de lierre et terminé par une pomme de pin (2 Maccabées 10,7), et on allumait les lampes (2 Maccabées 1,8).

"Purim" (c'est-à-dire "les sorts" parce que, d'après Esther 3,7 et 9,24, Aman avait tiré au sort la date à choisir pour l'extermination des juifs) est une sorte de carnaval commémorant avec humour et sarcasme la revanche des juifs de Perse contre leurs ennemis (épisode sans doute légendaire). Ce sont les écrits rabbiniques qui fournissent le rituel de la fête: on va à la synagogue, on lit le Livre d'Esther, on crie des insultes à Aman pendant la lecture, on loue Mardochée, on se fait des cadeaux, on offre des banquets où on peut boire, disent les rabbins, jusqu'à ne plus faire de distinction entre "Maudit soit Aman" et "Béni soit Mardochée"!

Les temps sacrés

Le plus important des temps sacrés d'Israël est évidemment le sabbat. Son institution est très ancienne. Le code yahviste en fait état dans Exode 34,21. Le code élohiste de l'Alliance en parle dans Exode 23,12. Les deux rédactions du Décalogue l'incluent dans les préceptes fondamentaux (Exode 20,8-10 et Deutéronome 5,12-14). C'est un jour de cessation absolue des activités serviles afin qu'on puisse rendre grâces au Dieu libérateur de la servitude égyptienne (interprétation deutéronomiste) ou au Dieu créateur de l'univers (interprétation sacerdotale).

Calquées sur le sabbat, l'année sabbatique (à tous les sept ans) et l'année du jubilé (à toutes les sept fois sept ans, donc à la cinquantième année) visait à libérer chaque israélite de ses dettes ou de l'esclavage où elles l'avaient réduit. Mais la législation de Lévitique 25,1-55 dans ce sens n'a jamais été intégralement respectée et on est même en droit de se demander si l'année du jubilé n'est pas une pieuse utopie.

La néoménie, célébrant le premier jour du mois lunaire, est attestée par la Bible (Nombres 28,11-15; Esdras 3,5; Néhémie 10,34; 1 Chroniques 23,31; 2 Chroniques 2,3; 8,13; 31,3; Colossiens 2,16), mais elle s'est complètement perdue dans le judaïsme postérieur.

La fête eschatologique

Le goût pour la fête en Israël devait presque nécessairement entraîner qu'on vît comme une fête l'avenir de bonheur que Yahvé promettait à son peuple. Il semble que ce soit surtout la grande épreuve de l'Exil qui ait amené Israël à voir sa restauration, prochaine ou lointaine, comme une grande fête préparée par son Dieu. Les textes dans ce sens, souvent des ajouts à des écrits plus anciens, datent des périodes exilique ou post-exilique (Sophonie 3,14-18; Amos 9,13-14; Isaïe 25,6; Malachie 3,20).

Cet inventaire des fêtes d'Israël, qui laisse évidemment de côté toutes les fêtes spontanées mentionnées par la Bible, ne fait état que des points d'arrivée d'une évolution beaucoup plus significative qui va nous faire voir comment Israël a transformé des fêtes déjà existantes par un admirable pouvoir de réinvention.

Leurs Origines

Il n'est pas facile de découvrir comment Israël a réinterprété les fêtes qu'il a trouvées au fur et à mesure de son expérience historique. Certaines hypothèses sont généralement admises, mais parfois il faut se contenter de simples conjectures.

Les hypothèses reçues

L'origine étrangère du mot "Pesach" amène déjà à penser que la Pâque juive a d'abord été une fête étrangère. Il ne fait maintenant plus de doute qu'elle vient d'une célébration printanière des tribus nomades du Sinaï. Même si elle a été, avec le temps, confinée au Temple de Jérusalem, pour l'immolation de l'agneau du moins, "Pesach," à l'origine, se célébrait sans prêtre, sans autel et en dehors de tout sanctuaire, comme une fête familiale. Les sanctuaires, les ministres et les autels caractérisent une religion de sédentaires. "Pesach," qui n'a pas toujours eu besoin de tout cela, pourrait donc avoir été une célébration de nomades. L'hypothèse se confirme quand on s'aperçoit que les Arabes pré-islamiques ont conservé un rite sacrificiel du même genre placé justement au printemps. Certains rites secondaires de "Pesach" pointent dans la même direction: les pains sans levain (Exode 12,8) sont le pain ordinaire des nomades; les herbes amères (Exode 12,8) sont les herbes du désert; les sandales aux pieds et le bâton à la main (Exode 12,11) constituent la tenue habituelle des bergers; la célébration en pleine nuit coïncide bien avec le temps où on n'a pas à faire paître le troupeau; la date fixée à le pleine lune pourrait venir de la nécessité d'avoir assez de lumière; "l'Exterminateur" (Exode 12,23) pourrait être la personnification des dangers qui menaçaient les jeunes bêtes, que les brebis et les chèvres venaient de mettre bas, au moment difficile de la transhumance. D'ailleurs, l'ordre donné à Moïse d'aller "immoler la Pâque" (Exode 12,21), sans plus d'explication, laisse entendre que le rite était déjà connu.

Les clans qui suivaient Moïse ont dû sortir d'Egypte au moment même où se célébrait le rite de l'immolation d'un agneau chez les tribus nomades du Sinaï. C'est peut-être même pour aller célébrer cette fête que Moïse demandait de pouvoir quitter le travail forcé auquel les Hébreux étaient astreints: "Laisse partir mon peuple pour qu'il me rende un culte au désert," dit le Seigneur (Exode 7,16). La coïncidence chronologique a permis à Israël d'établir un lien théologique. La fête fut réinterprétée. Ce n'est plus le troupeau mais le peuple que l'immolation d'un agneau préservait du danger. L'épreuve de la transhumance fit place, dans la mémoire collective, à l'épreuve de l'esclavage en Egypte. On historicisa certains détails: les pains non levés dirent la hâte de la fuite au lieu de rester prosaïquement la nourriture des Bédouins; les herbes amères devinrent le souvenir d'une amère servitude au lieu de rester l'assaisonnement préféré des Bédouins; sandales et bâtons rappelèrent la marche dans le désert au lieu de rester le simple costume des Bédouins; la consommation de la victime avec les doigts et sans ustensiles devint le symbole de la hâte de partir au lieu de rester la façon habituelle de manger des Bédouins. Israël a complètement réinventé une fête qui n'était pas sienne à l'origine.

"Mazzôt" est d'origine sédentaire. Il s'agit encore de pains sans levain, mais ce n'est plus la nourriture des nomades. Il s'agit de pains dont la fabrication s'est faite à partir de grains nouveaux, sans que rien n'y entre de l'ancienne récolte. "Mazzôt" fut d'abord une fête d'agriculteurs dont Lévitique 23,9-14 souligne le caractère sédentaire en parlant de l'offrande de "la première gerbe" entre "Mazzôt" et "Shabu'ôt." C'est une fête des prémices. Elle ne pouvait pas se célébrer à date fixe puisqu'elle dépendait de l'état de la moisson, mais elle tombait toujours au mois de Nisan (mars-avril), comme "Pesach." Empruntée sans doute à la religion cananéenne et trouvée sur place par les Israélites au moment de leur installation, "Mazzôt" ne fit plus qu'un avec "Pesach," venue, elle, d'un milieu nomade.

"Shabu'ôt" est explicitement désignée par Exode 34,22 comme la fête "des prémices de la moisson des blés." C'est donc une fête d'agriculteurs. Les cinquante jours de la Pentecôte constituent le temps normal qui s'écoule entre le début de la moisson des orges, marquée par la fête de "Mazzôt," et la fin de la moisson des blés, marquée par la fête de "Shabu'ôt." La célébration de "Shabu'ôt" vient sûrement d'un usage cananéen.

Comme "Pesach" et "Mazzôt," "Shabu'ôt" a été historicisée par Israël, quoique plus tardivement. A partir d'Exode 19,1, on calcula que c'était "au troisième mois," donc vraisemblablement au "cinquantième jour," après la sortie d'Egypte que la Loi fut remise à Moïse au sommet de la montagne du Sinaï. "Shabu'ôt" devint donc pour Israël le mémorial du don de la Loi.

"Sukkôt" aussi a d'abord été une fête agricole. Au passage d'une année à l'autre, là où se situe justement "Sukkôt," les agriculteurs de Canaan estimaient que des esprits malins s'attaquaient aux habitations et, pour leur échapper, ils se réfugiaient dans les huttes. La Bible n'a rien conservé du caractère superstitieux de ce rite. Elle invite plutôt à penser que les huttes de la fête de "Sukkôt" ne sont que les abris de branchage dressés dans les vignes et les vergers pour abriter vaille que vaille les ouvriers travaillant à la vendange et à la récolte. Elle parle même de "Sukkôt" comme étant tout simplement "la fête de la Récolte" (Exode 34,22). Mais, Israël, là encore, a historicisé la fête: "Vous habiterez sept jours dans des huttes. Tous les citoyens d'Israël habiteront dans des huttes, afin que vos descendants sachent que j'ai fait habiter sous des huttes les enfants d'Israël quand je les ai fait sortir du pays d'Egypte" (Lévitique 23,42-43). Les huttes des champs sont devenues les tentes du désert.

Les conjectures

La "Hanukka" est clairement rattachée par la Bible à la restauration du Temple au vrai culte sous les Maccabées. On est cependant tenté de voir un lien entre les lampes de la "Hanukka," qui augmentent graduellement en nombre chaque jour pendant neuf jours, et les fêtes du solstice d'hiver qu'on célébrait dans l'empire romain en l'honneur du "Sol invictus." L'insistance que met 1 Maccabées 1,18-36 à parler du feu "caché," puis "manifesté," et du brasier qui s'alluma "le moment venu où le soleil, d'abord obscurci par les nuages, se mit à briller" peut pointer dans la même direction. Le 25 Kislev, date de la fête de la "Hanukka," obéit, il est vrai, à un calcul lunaire tandis que le 25 décembre, date de la "Natalis solis invicti," obéit à un comput solaire, mais le choix du 25 du mois dans les deux cas n'est peut-être pas une simple coïncidence ou, s'il s'agit d'une coïncidence, il est assez probable que la fête païenne ait eu, avec le temps, une influence sur la fête juive. Même si la "Hanukka" a été, à l'origine, une fête essentiellement anti-païenne, célébrant la victoire des Maccabées sur l'hellénisation forcée de leur pays, on peut concevoir que, une fois la tourmente passée, des éléments de la fête païenne de la lumière soient passés à la fête juive "des lumières." On voit, d'ailleurs, comment Jonathan, devenu grand prêtre, se met lui-même à porter un nom grec: Alexandre Jannée. Et ce, une cinquantaine d'années à peine après la révolte des Maccabées.

"Purim" vient sûrement de l'étranger. On a pensé à une origine babylonienne et il faut bien avouer que le rapprochement linguistique entre "Marduk" et "Mardochée" et entre "Ishtar" et "Esther" a quelque chose de séduisant. Marduk et Ishtar (d'où "astre" en français et "star" en anglais, Ishtar étant l'équivalent de Vénus) personnifient la lumière prenant le dessus sur les ténèbres. L'histoire du Livre d'Esther prend occasion d'un récit légendaire pour évoquer la victoire d'Israël sur tous ses ennemis à travers les siècles. Ester 3,7 et 9,20-32 constituent des gloses qui rattachent artificiellement la fête de "Purim" à cette légende. Il se pourrait que "Purim" démythologise et historicise une fête étrangère.

"Sabbat" n'est pas un mot hébreu. La Bible (Genèse 2,2-3) établit un lien entre le mot "sabbat" et le verbe "shabat" qui signifie "cesser de travailler," mais il faut faire bon marché des règles ordinaires de la formation des noms pour finir par faire dire à "sabbat": "jour où l'on cesse de travailler." Par ailleurs, le sabbat est sûrement antérieur à l'installation en Canaan et ce n'est peut-être pas par simple anachronisme qu'Exode 16,22-30 affirme qu'on observe le sabbat lors de la cueillette de la manne. Parce que le sabbat impose qu'on n'allume aucun feu ce jour-là, on a pensé à une origine du côté des Qénites dont l'ancêtre éponyme, Tubal-Caïn, était "l'ancêtre de tous les forgerons" (Genèse 4,22). L'interdiction de faire du feu (Exode 35,3) viendrait du repos des forgerons génites. L'hypothèse peut être, cependant, plus ingénieuse que solide. Du côté des Cananéens, on trouve bien peu de chose puisqu'il n'est même pas prouvé qu'ils aient connu une division hebdomadaire du temps. Du côté de Babylone, on trouve les "jours néfastes" qui sont justement les septième, quatorzième, vingt-et-unième et vingt-huitième du mois où le roi ne pouvait pas manger de viande, changer de vêtements, offir des sacrifices, monter sur son char etc. et où il était interdit aux prêtres et aux médecins d'exercer leurs fonctions. Mais il faut avouer que ce n'est pas parce qu'il serait "néfaste" que le septième jour est chômé en Israël. D'où qu'il vienne, le sabbat est jour de louange en Israël et la tradition deutéronomiste l'historicise radicalement en le rattachant à la libération d'Egypte (Deutéronome 5,12-15).

Pour avoir aussi souvent réinventé la fête et réinterprété des fêtes, Israël devait sentir un irrésistible besoin de fêter. Israël a vu la fête comme un moyen d'identification et de survie. Elle n'a été pour lui ni un amusement ni un spectacle ni une corvée rituelle. Par ses fêtes, Israël devenait toujours plus lui-même et redisait sans cesse son espérance. C'est à ce sens des fêtes d'Israël que nous allons maintenant nous attacher.

Leur sens

Les fêtes d'Israël sont libération, contestation, rassemblement et cohérence. On peut, en effet, ramener sous ces quatre chefs le sens profond des fêtes d'Israël.

Libération

L'histoire ancienne d'Israël est un lutte continuelle pour la liberté que ce soit contre les Egyptiens, les Assyriens, les Babyloniens, les rois hellénistiques ou l'empire romain. Ce sont les peuples épris de liberté qui savent le plus et le mieux fêter. Israël a vécu ses fêtes comme autant de célébrations de la délivrance de toute servitude. En libérant de tout travail, le sabbat rappelle le jour où Israël, esclave en Egypte, fut libéré de la servitude (Deutéronome 5,12-15). "Pesach" a le même sens et célèbre, comme dit la Haggada de la Pâque, "celui qui tira Israël de la servitude vers la liberté, de la détresse vers la joie, du deuil vers la fête et des ténèbres vers la grande lumière." Reliées aux événements de l'Exode, "Mazzôt" et "Sukkôt" prennent ausi des allures de célébrations de la libération. La "Hanukka," enfin, célèbre le combat des Maccabées contre le joug hellénistique.

Contestation

Israël avait également besoin de ses fêtes pour contester la dureté de sa vie et, même, pour contester l'ordre établi. Seuls les peuples pauvres et malheureux sont capables d'un brin de folie quand vient la fête. "Shabu'ôt," "Sukkôt" et "Purim," avec leurs danses, leur musique, leurs repas joyeux et leur vin versé à profusion, contestent la dureté de l'histoire d'Isrël. Aujourd'hui encore, la "Simhat Tora," au huitième jour de "Sukkôt," dit, souvent chez les juifs les plus simples et les plus pauvres, le besoin de rompre avec la dure condition présente. Les quatre coupes rituelles de vin du rite rabbinique de "Pesach" invitent encore à la contestation de l'indigence.

Mais, par ses fêtes, Israël contestait aussi l'ordre établi. Il y a, dans toute fête, une volonté de subversion, un désir de révolution. Au "Séder" de la Pâque juive, les enfants lancent des gouttes de vin sur la nappe à l'évocation de chacune des "plaies d'Egypte" où s'exprime, dans la Bible, la rébellion de Moïse.

La "Hanukka" rappelle la révolte des Maccabées. Mais c'est sans aucun doute "Purim" qui est la plus subversive des fêtes d'Israël puisque c'est alors le désordre absolu, le désordre voulu et devenu vertueux parce que, en sapant l'ordre humain, il veut renvoyer à l'ordre divin. Même le "Yôm Kippur," qui n'a pourtant rien d'un débordement de joie, exprime une volonté de re-création. Par des bains de purification, les prêtres deviennent des êtres neufs et, par le jeûne, le peuple exprime son désir d'évacuer l'ancien pour repartir à zéro. Le lien chronologique entre le "Yôm Kippur" et le "Rosh hashana" montre le nouvel an juif comme une occasion de renouvellement. Pour certains rabbins anciens, c'est d'ailleurs au mois de Tishri que le Dieu d'Israël aurait créé le ciel et la terre et, pour d'autres, c'est au premier jour de ce mois qu'Adam aurait été créé. Ces calculs peuvent nous faire sourire, mais ils disent comment "Rosh hashana" et "Yôm Kippur" veulent effacer l'ordre établi pour reprendre à zéro l'homme et l'univers.

Rassemblement

La fête abolit les barrières sociales. Elle rassemble les gens de toutes les classes. Elle fait disparaître les étiquettes. Elle supprime la solitude et amène tous les hommes à se rencontrer dans une communion de sentiments. La fête ne se limite pas à récréer le peuple: elle re-crée la communauté en répondant au besoin inné de vie collective. Composé en bonne partie d'éléments disparates et souvent divisé par des tensions internes, le peuple d'Israël a sans cesse refait son unité par ses fêtes. Sans magistère et sans dogmes, ce peuple profondément religieux a vécu ses fêtes comme autant de rassemblements autour de la Loi de Moïse et de la fidélité commune à l'Alliance du Sinaï. Autour du père de famille et, plus tard, autour du Temple de Jérusalem, Israël a vu dans ses fêtes un principe de cohésion.

Cohérence

L'histoire des religions et l'histoire tout court nous apprennent que les fêtes deviennent plus nombreuses, ou sont plus intensément célébrées, aux époques de changement de civilisation. C'est sans doute à cause des changements si nombreux de condition culturelle à travers son histoire qu'Israël a tant ressenti le besoin de célébrer. Passant du sédentarisme égyptien à la vie nomade du Sinaï, Israël célèbre "Pesach." Quand arrive la réforme de Josias, Israël donne même une dimension nouvelle à cette fête en en faisant une célébration nationale. Passant du nomadisme à la vie sédentaire de Canaan, Israël célèbre "Mazzôt," "Shabu'ôt" et "Sukkôt." Passant de l'Exil à la restauration, il insiste sur le "Yôm Kippur." Passant de l'hellénisation forcée à l'autonomie, il se livre aux célébrations de la "Hanukka." C'est pour prendre collectivement conscience de sa cohérence historique qu'Israël a tant eu besoin de ses fêtes.

Mais il y a plus. La fête fut, pour Israël, une façon de réconcilier les temps. Ce peuple aurait pu se réfugier dans le passé et ne vivre que de nostalgie. Il aurait pu se donner entièrement au présent et se construire une grande civilisation matérielle. Il aurait pu se livrer exclusivement à l'utopie en ne pensant qu'à l'avenir promis en fonction du messianisme et de l'eschatologie. Au lieu de tout cela, Israël, par ses fêtes, réconcilie le passé, le présent et l'avenir. Chaque fête devient pour lui un "mémorial." Contrairement à ce que le mot "mémoire" évoque en Occident, l'acception biblique du mot "mémorial" suupose qu'on fait appel au passé comme point d'appui pour une appropriation actualisatrice et une espérance créatrice. Le célèbre "poème des quatre nuits," qu'on trouve dans le Targum d'Exode 12,42, voit dans l'unité la plus parfaite les quatre grands moments de l'histoire d'Israël: "La première nuit, quand Yahvé se manifesta sur le monde pour le créer . . . La deuxième nuit, quand Yahvé apparut à Abraham . . . La troisième nuit, quand Yahvé apparut aux Egyptiens . . . Et la quatrième nuit, quand le monde arrivera à sa fin pour être racheté et que les jougs de fer seront brisés." C'est autour de la nuit pascale que sont rassemblées ces quatre nuits. "Pesach" célèbre et relie toutes les libérations d'Israël: libération du chaos par la création, libération de l'ignorance par la foi d'Abraham, libération de l'esclavage par la sortie d'Egypte et libération de la condition présente par la fin des temps. Un proverbe rabbinique établit clairement le fondement de ces liens: "Cette nuit-là ils furent sauvés; cette nuit-là ils seront sauvés." Assez paradoxalement, c'est par la fête, qui est pourtant un arrêt dans le temps, qu'Israël a pris conscience de la cohérence de son histoire.

Conclusion

Israël s'est façonné par ses fêtes en donnant très souvent un sens nouveau à des célébrations anciennes. Les jeux olympiques peuvent devenir, si nous le voulons, "la fête olympique," célébrant la délivrance de l'homme à l'égard des servitudes du corps et de la matière, la contestation des peuples face à la dureté du monde, le rassemblement des nations dans un monde marqué par la violence et la réconciliation des temps par le jeu.

The Human Body: Temple, Cage or What?

Adrian C. Kanaar

Introduction

As a physician, my work is largely concerned with physical treatment and counseling of the handicapped. This paper draws largely upon my clinical experience. In the title "The Human Body — Temple, Cage or What?" there is both a psychological and a theological sense in my use of the word "cage." Many patients feel trapped in a handicapped body which limits them physically, mentally and emotionally and may jeopardize their career and family life. However, the concept of feeling caged is also typical of millions in relationship to their Creator. Some express it in fatalism, whether through Kismet or Karma, or the predestination aspects of Puritanism and the Jehovah Witnesses. Others feel like expendable pawns in a meaningless cosmic or earthly game of chess. It will be my purpose to show how some have escaped from the "cage complex."

The Self-image of the Handicapped

This, of course, varies as much as it does with the able-bodied. However, there is sometimes added reason for self-pity, anxiety and depression.

Case 1

A middle-aged patient of mine who had been very active in the community had a stroke. Physically, her recovery would have permitted resumption of most of her activities. Psychologically, she was finished. She had felt herself to be a whole person before the stroke. To her, wholeness meant complete physical function. Rather than continue to be active, using a drop foot brace and limping a little but with perfect speech, she withdrew from all her previous interests and spent her time at home doing virtually nothing.

Adrian C. Kanaar, Poughkeepsie, New York, U.S.A.

Case 2

By contrast, a young IBM engineer, who developed a similar cerebral thrombosis, doggedly fought his way back to full activity. Specific exercises for coordination, walking, swimming and finally golf helped him back to practically complete recovery, despite his justifiable fear that another stroke might at any time take his life or make him unable to support his young family.

Both patients had equal encouragement and guidance, and the real difference did not lie in their age, sex, physical weakness or deformity, but in their self-acceptance.

Case 3

Another hemiplegic lady was left with almost total aphasia and could not use her right arm and leg. She recognized no numbers or letters, yet she returned to her work as a housewife and was even able to set the oven temperature correctly. Her spirit triumphed so greatly over her bodily weakness that she was actually cheerful, even without speech.

Habilitation and Rehabilitation

All people, whether handicapped or not, may need to be helped in order to do the *best* with what they have, seeking goals which serve the spirit as well as the body. Early referral of all potentially disabled persons for complete evaluation is most desirable before they become despondent. The man who has just lost a leg in an accident should see another amputee who is walking, working and happy and see him within hours, while he still feels lucky to be alive.

Behavior Modification

These techniques may overcome addiction, persuade the lazy to work, decrease complaining and promote positive thinking. However, if the rewards from improved behavior cease, there is frequently relapse. One cannot consider a patient as rehabilitated until he understands his disability as realistically as he is able, has done what he can to regain function, lives as normal a life as possible and accepts his limitations — if not with enthusiasm, at least without resentment.

Case 4

A farm girl in her late teens developed polio in the 1952-1953 epidemic in Western Canada. After months of physical treatment, she became a secretary in a rehabilitation center in Saskatchewan. She was permanently confined to a wheelchair. One day, in a thoughtful mood, she said, "I sometimes think that the best thing that ever happened to me was when I got polio." Answering my gasp of amazement, she added: "If I had not had polio, I would still be on a farm, far out in the country without the interesting work I now have to do." She had developed a positive change in her self-image — not that her farm duties had been unimportant, but that the new duties meant more to her as a person and so made all her physical loss more bearable. Her philosophy was reinforced when she met and married a like-minded person at her new job.

Case 5

In Hamilton, Ontario, a young man became paraplegic in an accident. After hospital care he went home where he wallowed in self-pity and idleness for five years. One day an old friend heard of his plight and paid him a visit. The patient later said that his friend spent nearly two hours telling him reasons why he should be ashamed of himself. "With your brains, you could be an accountant," his friend concluded. When I first met the "patient" several years later, he was a public accountant, doing well, with five employees. He spent a good deal of time traveling and lecturing on the *abilities* of the handicapped. For years, he had a weekly one-half hour radio program for the handicapped entitled "At Home with Lew Roach." When he died, about eight years ago, he was widely known and admired. His wheelchair had become a means of self-fulfillment and he had done great service to the cause of the handicapped — thanks to the frankness of a true friend.

Overcoming Pain

Case 6

A middle-aged Yugoslavian mechanic came to see me about two years after an injury at work which amputated all but a short stump of his right index, middle and ring fingers. He complained of constant pain and would not allow the hand to be touched. Despite counseling and physical therapy, he refused to use his right hand. Finally, a deadlock was reached and he promptly stopped coming to see me. A few months later, a friend persuaded him to return. After progressive resistance exercises, I had him doing repair work around my office. Several months later, he returned to work as a mechanic, using his injured hand which now had a remarkably good grip. He has worked steadily ever since. Ninety percent of his pain was "bereavement" for his lost fingers. Once he had decided to face up to the responsibility to resume the support of his family, he regained physical strength, self-confidence and a good job. He ignored his residual pain.

Overcoming Fear

Case 7

A 60-year-old factory worker who had recently migrated from Poland came to see me at almost the same time as Case 6, also after a two-year period off work. His right arm had undergone traumatic above-elbow amputation when caught in a defective roller at work. He requested a prosthesis, evidently expecting a virtual replacement of his own arm. With considerable misgivings, I ordered the prosthesis, despite the bad omen that he had managed partial self-care without it for years. The day the prosthesis came, I tried for 1½ hours to get him to understand the controls. He spoke no English and his daughter interpreted. Finally, he seemed to have grasped it, but was still in a bad mood. I allowed him to take it home for practice that night. The next day he was all smiles. Basically a good technician and encouraged by his daughter, he had learned the shoulder movements to operate the elbow and hook. "Me professional," he said with pride. He soon passed all the efficiency tests but was not willing to return to his job. He had been employed at a factory where Polish was understood. Because of his technical experience, his old job was also the easiest for him to resume. His age and the language barrier almost eliminated other possibilities. The whole family was solidly opposed to his risking further injury — as they put it. I reminded him that an air pilot who has a crash needs to fly again soon, lest he lose his nerve. He was unimpressed. He admitted that the defective roller had been repaired. ("Why wasn't it done earlier?" he wanted to know.) He agreed that he had been acting against the rules when his arm got caught. Would he break the rules again? "Never." "Then," I said, "you would be in less danger than any of the other employees, would you not?" He returned to the job and was a steady, reliable employee.

Overcoming Secondary Gain ("Compensationitis")

This is a problem which some humanitarian societies have brought upon themselves. When a patient receives about as much from some type of compensation as he would be paid for work, he is sorely tempted to emphasize his disability. Such "generosity" makes sluggards and deceivers out of many previously good workers. Every society should make sure that compensation is high during obvious total disability, but *promptly* reduced if the patient does not cooperate to achieve reasonable rehabilitation goals. Failing this, rehabilitation may prove impossible, especially if the patient has a poor self-image and has only been a marginal worker.

Case 8

A 26-year-old lady presented with persistent low back pain after a sprain at work and was on compensation for many months. There was obvious hysterical overplay and she was full of self-pity, long after the organic aspects of her problem had subsided. She and her husband had several young children, and both parents had been working. Now he had to do housework too, while she relaxed. Eventually, he rebelled, and left her. Suddenly she found herself responsible for her children, with too little money to live on. Her previously intolerable pain did not prevent her immediate return to work. Her husband eventually returned. From time to time, her pain worsened, but I have managed to persuade her to resume work fairly soon, but under protest. Her self-image as a wife did not prevent her from loading all her duties on her husband, but her self-image as a mother enormously increased her pain tolerance.

When the Experts Have Already Failed

Sooner or later, the specialist in medical rehabilitation sees a patient who has been treated unsuccessfully by the big-named specialist or rehabilitation centers and has given up hope.

Case 9

Some years ago, when I was living in Buffalo, N.Y., I inherited such a case. She had spent 3½ years in hospital continuously since sustaining traumatic paraplegia and was certain that she was to be hospitalized for life. Her husband had been estranged from her before the accident and she never saw him again. Her injuries had included a compound fracture of the left femur which took many months to heal. Meanwhile, her knee became stiff. A physical therapist, in attempting to regain movement, refractured her femur! Now she had the law on her side — or believed so! "Send me out, and I'll sue the hospital for negligence," she warned. So there she sat in her wheelchair on top of a huge decubitus ulcer, in a pool of urine. With both hips dislocated, even the largest catheter could not prevent leakage from her stretched urethra. Her self-image was so poor that she transferred care of her 7-year-old son to her sister so that he called her "mother." Rehabilitation was a meaningless word to her. In vain, I told her of a possible bright future, earning her own living, supporting her son and driving her own car. She had to be shown. I forbade her ever to lie or sit on her sore. In a few months, it was practically healed, without surgery. An artificial bladder was constructed by isolating a loop of small intestine and diverting the urinary stream from the kidneys to the loop and thence to an opening onto the abdomen, where it could be collected into a bag without leak or odor. Within six months, she *asked* to go into training as a medical secretary! She was allowed to attend evening classes from the hospital and worked by day as a secretary in my office. Since her discharge, she has driven her own car, worked as a medical secretary and supported her son who came back to live with her. No longer was a damaged body acting as a cage to her spirit. She could even laugh at herself as a "poor little crippled girl." Indeed, her self-image was better than before her accident, and she also acted more responsibly.

Sports for the Handicapped

Not only the self-image but the public image of the handicapped has been immensely improved by sport. Who can deny social acceptance and work to someone who can race in a wheelchair, do weightlifting, play basketball or table tennis? The handicapped of many countries now participate in local, regional, national and international competitions, including the paralympics held every fourth year in the vicinity of the Olympic Games. A wheelchair need no longer be regarded as a restriction, but as a useful means of transportation and a first rate piece of sports equipment.

Case 9 (Continued)

At my invitation, my paraplegic wheelchair secretary became a charter member of the Buffalo Boosters Wheelchair Athletic Club. With expert and free instruction, she soon demonstrated remarkable ability, becoming national Wheelchair Archery Champion of the United States in 1961 and National Wheelchair Bowling Champion in 1962. She also won four state or multistate archery championships in 1963 in open competition against the able-bodied. She was a member of the U.S. paralympic team, competing in Britain in 1962 and 1963 and in Tokyo in 1964. While in Britain, she was the only member of the team who took a side trip to see Paris — this "little crippled girl" who had been afraid to leave hospital. Good health, sport, travel, social acceptance and the spice of success, added to her new capacity of economic independence, had brought a transformation in her "joie de vivre."

Rehabilitation by the Handicapped

Sometimes the best rehabilitators are those who have overcome disability themselves. I know of several who work at rehabilitation centers from a wheelchair. An outstanding achievement is that of Ed J. Desjardins, Director of the G. F. Strong Memorial Rehabilitation Center in Vancouver, British Columbia. At 57, despite his quadriplegia which allows limited use of his hands, he has just completed a $7 million expansion program. Several years ago, he served a term as President of the Association of Rehabilitation Centers, and, with willing help from his beautiful wife, has met problems of travel and long hours of work with cheerfulness, wisdom and success.

Realism and Faith

Since every physical handicap tends to have an emotional counterpart, the latter must be dealt with just as much as the physical need. There is great value in facing the immediate personal cause of problems, rather than utilizing a lengthy process of analysis. If the patient does all that he can to put matters right, he may well find he can tolerate the problems which remain. However, reality therapy like psychoanalysis may fail if it weakens rather than strengthens the person's self-image. Alcoholics Anonymous discovered that it was not enough for a member to admit he had a drinking problem but to attempt to change his habits, with support from other members, as well. For long-term success, it was also necessary for him to recognize continually his need of help from a "Power Greater than himself." If this idea is too shattering to his self-esteem, the likelihood of failure or relapse increases.

Case 10

A 19-year-old patient with quadriplegic cerebral palsy had a 125° angular curvature of the spine. She could speak, breathe, swallow, blink and move her head slightly but had no control of her trunk or limbs. She underwent corrective spinal fusion and was put in a cast. She knew how to read, but there was no one to turn the pages for her. We obtained a special page turner and had it modified so that it would function in any plane and could be placed in alignment with her eyes, over her bed or over her chair. She operated it electrically by a slight head movement. She was delighted when she read a whole book, the first day that she had the appliance.

Soon afterwards, she had a visit from members of a Christian church. For the first time in her life, she saw herself as a person whom God loved. She accepted the good news that God had sent his Son Jesus to live and die for the world. She prayed a prayer of thanks and asked God's forgiveness for all her faults, especially the resentment which she had felt for years. She asked God to put his Holy Spirit within her, making her almost useless body His temple.* From that day on, other patients were constantly at her bedside, not to help her but to be helped. She gladly shared her new-found joy. She escaped from her caged feeling by a tremendous change, called Christian conversion.

Theological Implications

In all of these cases, there were problems of the self-image, but most of them responded satisfactorily to a rehabilitation milieu. While facilities to help all patients who verbalized spiritual problems were available through contacts with hospital chaplains or people of their own religious background, no specific information was routinely sought by the rehabilitation team regarding this aspect of their self-image. The experience of the quadriplegic girl suggested that such exploration, while a delicate matter, should be regarded as most important. Clearly, her experience had an excellent therapeutic effect. I believe that it accomplished a genuine new relationship between her and Her Creator. Those of a different persuasion may offer some other explanations, pointing out that courage in adversity has cultural and ideological as well as religious determinants. Since I spent 27 years as a British citizen, was then 10 years in Canada and settled in the United States 17 years ago, those with a different background may reasonably claim that my own views are culturally biased toward Christianity. However, in partial rebuttal, I would mention that I was a rebellious teenager when I was led by a Christian athlete to a life-changing commitment to Jesus, as the Christ. I immediately lost my well-earned feeling of guilt and gained a new consciousness of God's presence within me. I was inspired to

*In the New Testament, St. Paul, writing to Christians at Corinth, said: "Do you not know that your bodies are the Temple of the Holy Spirit who dwells in you?" (1 Cor. Ch. 3, Verse 16). Jesus Christ had said that His Spirit would indwell all his true followers (Gospel of John, Ch. 14, Verse 22).

regard my body as His temple, to strive toward my highest potential and to choose a life of service. As a medical student, I made two attempts to swim the English channel, coming within 1¼ miles of my goal. Early in my 42 years of medical practice, I spent six years in the British Army in World War II. I have had the privilege of seeing a number of patients and friends find in Christ the answer to seemingly insoluble problems. My concepts have matured over the years since I have remained open to evidence from my many friends from other countries and faiths.

The following four questions are posed for those who would give further thought to the vital question "Is the Human Body a Temple, a Cage or What?" By answering these, there is a good hope that an open-minded person can make a choice between these three fundamental concepts and do it with minimal bias and great advantage.

1. Which is best supported by religious, philosophical and scientific literature?
2. Which is most likely to lead to *positive achievement* which tends to make the world a better place for everyone?
3. Which is most likely to encourage good relationship between competitors?
4. Which is the most likely to develop the personality of the competitior as a friendly, outgoing person, by whose presence the world is enriched?

Conclusions

There are many standard means by which a handicapped person may escape the "caged" feeling. High on the list are expert medical care, establishment of feasible and attractive goals, strong emotional support and retraining.

Appropriate competitive sports are of outstanding value in rehabilitation, and lifelong physical fitness should be a goal for the handicapped as for the able-bodied.

If deep personal spiritual needs are met, even the severely handicapped patient can be really happy and exert a positive influence over others.

To be consistent as a science, any theology which applies to sport should also be applicable, in some appropriate sense, to the handicapped, including the retarded, the old and the dying.

Christianity can be a liberating and motivating force leading to a lifelong goal of maximum achievement with concern for the good of all mankind.

Bibliography

Kanaar, A.C.: Some important psychiatric complications of injury. Ontario Med. Rev., Aug. 1952.

Kanaar, A.C.: Life long fitness: A positive approach. J. Assoc. Phys. Mental Rehabil. 16(6):169-173, 182, 1962.

Kanaar, A.C.: Rehabilitation of the Handicapped Adolescent. Rehab. Counseling Bull. 6(2):69-75, 1963.

Kanaar, A.C.: Long distance swimming. *In* Frazier, C.A. (ed.): Games Doctors Play. Springfield, Illinois:Charles C Thomas, 1973.

Kanaar, A.C.: Moral issues in sports. *In* Frazier, C.A. (ed.): Is it Moral to Modify Man? Springfield, Illinois:Charles C Thomas, 1973.

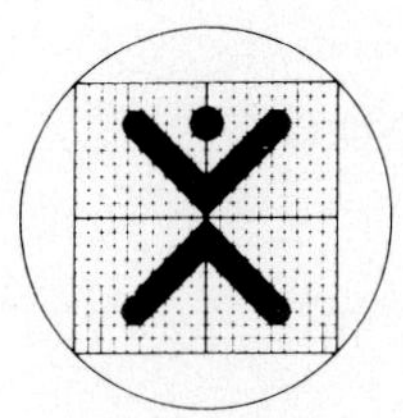

History

Histoire

Historiography of Modern Olympism: Emphasis on the Works of the Socialist States of Europe

K. A. Kulinkovich

The author sees Pierre de Coubertin as one of the first and talented historiographers of Olympism. He follows with a listing of the names of authors from the socialist countries of Europe, along with the titles of their works, underlying their contributions to the historiography of the Olympic Games and of the Olympic Idea, particularly under the aspects of official results and reports, educational, social, scientific and cultural influences.

The international Olympic movement has become an important phenomenon of social life, a factor of strengthening the mutual understanding of peoples and one of the trends in the Peace movement.

The historiographic analysis of literature devoted to the Olympic Games is of great importance in comprehending the role of this phenomenon. The analysis enables one to conclude that the historic knowledge of the development of the social phenomena has kept up with the growth in popularity of the modern Olympic movement and in a close relationship with it.

At the very outset of modern Olympism the reports and publications of Baron Pierre de Coubertin, the founder of the Olympic Games and a talented propagandist of the Olympic ideas, were of particular importance. Suffice it to say that 225 of his official reports, letters and articles are known to us. Under his influence the first works in the history of the Ancient Olympic Games, the revival of the Olympics at the end of the last century and in the history of the Modern Olympic Games were published in a number of European countries. For example, the work of A. D. Butovsky, the IOC member, the participant of the Constituent Session and of the first Olympics — *Athens in Spring of 1896* — was

K. A. Kulinkovich, High Institute of Physical Culture, Minsk, U.S.S.R.

published in Russia in 1896. The same year the book *The Stories About Olympia* by Dittenberger was issued in Berlin.

In the following years the books of great historiographic importance appeared (Vernatsky, Warsaw, 1916; V. E. Ignatyev, Moscow, 1918; Dupperon, Moscow, 1909, 1913, 1915; Gardiner, Oxford, 1925). And in 1928, Doctor Ferenc Meze, a Hungarian historian of Olympism, was awarded a Gold Medal for his work *The History of the Olympic Games* at the literary competition of the IXth Olympics. There were still only a few works dealing with the history of the Olympic Games when the Olympics themselves began to grow in popularity and created their history. For example, athletes from 46 countries participated in the IXth Olympic Games, many of the nations being represented by four or five athletes.

The popularity of the Olympics increased greatly after World War II. The ideas of the struggle for peace opposed to the new war was espoused by various sports organizations and by every athlete. It was because of this that the appeal of the World Peace Council to hold the XVth Olympic Games (1952) in an atmosphere of friendship. It was a warm meeting of friends as was attested to by many international federations, sports organizations of many countries and by sports officials and athletes. Since then, the sports organizations in the socialist countries began to participate more actively in the Olympic movement and the tendency of the Olympics as a factor in promoting and strengthening peace became more evident.

All this found its expression in the considerable increase of literature devoted to various aspects of the Olympic movement. The book *Sixty Years of the Olympic Games* by Ferenc Meze, published in 1956 under the patronage of the IOC in Hungarian, German, French and English, was of great historiographic importance. In 1959 the book was translated into Russian, edited in 150,000 copies and in a short period of time became a rare book. The book is a rich source of reliable data and is an invaluable treasury for all those who are interested in the Olympic movement.

After the XVth Olympic Games a vast amount of literature dealing with the problems of Olympism appeared in the socialist countries of Europe. By its trends the materials can be divided into publicistic, educational, scientific and official literature.

The publicistic literature appeared in response to the growing interest of various strata of the population for the results of the Olympics, their organization, social significance, the role in the fight for peace, for romanticism and dynamism of sports struggle.

In the U.S.S.R. the first publicistic work was the book by N. I. Lubomirov *The XVth Olympic Games* (1955). On the basis of personal observations, the analysis of official documents and foreign periodicals the author describes in his essays the course of the Olympics, the peculiarities of contests, the atmosphere of warm and friendly relations between the athletes from different countries. In the subsequent works (1957, 1960, 1967, 1970) Lubomirov expands the object of his writings and gives the history of the Ancient and Modern Olympic Games.

Many publications dealing with the Olympics were authored by a well-known Soviet sports journalist P. A. Sobolev who wrote a number of interesting and valuable works. In 1955 together with N. Kalinin he wrote a book *The Olympic Games* in which he related the history of the Ancient and Modern Olympic Games in a popular and attractive manner. Essays, sketches and impressions of the Winter Olympic Games were collected in co-authorship with A. Kuleshov in the book *Snowy Olympics* (1956). Still more thoroughly and attractively the history of the Olympic Games was described in the book *Olympia, Athens, Rome* by Sobolev (1960).

The Soviet publicistic literature about the Olympic Games is very extensive (more than 150 books, booklets, essays were published). The authors of these works are mainly sports journalists (N. Lubomirov, P. Sobolev, A. Kuleshov, N. Kiselev, B. Khavin, Y. Lukashin, I. Nemukhin, V. Novoskoltsev, A. Kiknadze, M. Shishigin, etc.). However, the Olympic theme draws the attention of many prominent writers (L. Kassil, A. Sofronov, R. Rozhdestvensky and Z. Solodar).

In Bulgaria, Poland, Hungary, Czechoslovakia and the GDR considerable publicistic literature concerning the Olympic Games was published and enjoys great popularity. For example, the book *The Olympic Trumpets* by V. Golebnevsky and Stroinovsky was edited in Warsaw in 1957. It contains the history of the Ancient and Modern Olympic Games up to the XVIth Games. Many essays were published in Czechoslovakia by F. Kratky, V. Kotsourek, Y. Zhak, F. Kozhik and others. In Bulgaria, an interesting book *From Athens to Melbourne* by A. Vlasev and D. Mishev was published (Sofia, 1957) which includes essays in history of the Olympics and the data concerning the performance of Bulgarian athletes. *The Modern Olympic Games* (Budapest, 1961) aroused great interest among Hungarian readers.

The treatment of the Olympic Games in textbooks on the history of physical culture is of great historiographic significance. In all the socialist countries the students of physical training institutions study the history of physical culture, including the history of the Ancient and Modern Olympics, their significance, results and prospects of further development. Great contributions to the composition of textbooks and other materials for teaching the history of physical culture were made by the Soviet historians: F. Samoukov, V. Stolbov, N. Bugrov, K. Kulinkovich, Y. Talalayev, A. Romanov et al; Bulgarian scientists: V. Zonkov, X. Meranzov, N. Petrova; Hungarians: L. Kutashi, F. Meze; the historians of the GDR: V. Eichel, G. Wonneberger, G. Simon et al; Czechoslovakian scientists: F. Kratky, A. Himl, V. Perutka.

In the postwar years different problems of modern Olympism became a subject matter of profound scientific investigations. The second International Symposium in the history of physical education and sport held in Sofia in 1972 revealed a particular interest of the scientists in the history and the actual problems of the modern Olympic movement. Two problems were undertaken at the symposium: "The Role of Regional Games in the Development of Sports and International Olympic Movement" and "International Olympic Movement." Twenty reports of European scientists mainly were heard and discussed. The reports and discussions demonstrated a great interest of the participants in the problems mentioned above and revealed the profundity, objectivity and reliability of the research. The collected materials of the symposium edited in Sofia enjoyed great popularity in many countries.

It was also demonstrated in a number of reports of sport historians made at the International world Congress "Sport and Modern Society" (1974).

In the works of the Soviet scientists V. Stolbov, A. Romanov, N. Bugrov, K. Kulinkovich, F. Samoukov, Y. Talalayev et al such important problems as the genesis of modern Olympism, its social essence, the peculiarities of the postwar development and its role in the consolidation of peace were treated. Thirty-six works dealing with the social essence of modern Olympism were published. The historians of the GDR (G. Vestfal, E. Emigen, V. Shreder, V. Eichel) dealt with a number of historical problems as well as the relationship of the national and international problems in the Olympic movement, the role of socialist countries in the development of modern Olympism.

The official publications which include the results of the Olympic Games, reference books, reports of the officials are of great historiographic and bibliographic importance. Special mention should be made of the series "The Olympic Year," published in the U.S.S.R. It is a basic book devoted to the results of the Winter and Summer Olympic Games (1956, 1960, 1968, 1972). Each book of the series was written by many authors — coaches, experts, officials — contains extensive, multifaceted information on the peculiarities of specific sports, on competitions and defines their role in the development of international sports movement.

Similar books are published after every Olympic year in Bulgaria, Hungary, the GDR, Poland and Czechoslovakia.

Conclusion

A review of the literature published in the socialist countries of Europe which have investigated the many processes taking place in the International Olympic Movement and referred to above would enable one to conclude that this literature has played an important role in the propaganda of the Olympic ideas, upholding their purity and in spreading the knowledge of Olympism. A review of the literature would show that the Olympic Games promoted the popularization of the Olympics and the formation of positive social opinion. Its cognitive and educative significance is obvious.

L'historiographie de l'olympisme: emphase sur les ouvrages de l'U.R.S.S. et des autres pays socialistes de l'Europe

L'auteur place Pierre de Coubertin en tête de liste des historiographes talentueux de l'Olympisme moderne. Il donne une liste de noms d'auteurs en provenance des pays socialistes de l'Europe et souligne, par le truchement des titres de leurs ouvrages, leur contributions a l'historiographie des Jeux olympiques et de l'Idée olympique, plus particulièrement sous les aspects des résultats et rapports officiels, ainsi que des influences éducatives, sociales, scientifiques et culturelles.

Historiography of Modern Olympism: Emphasis on Historical Works of Western Europe

Horst Ueberhorst

The author contends that literature on Olympism has increased considerably since the 1960s, particularly as concerns works based on scientific research. Comments are made on a certain number of works published or edited in Western Europe and that have dealt with descriptions and criticisms of modern and ancient Olympic Games from the perspective of their organization, objectives, contents as well as sociocultural and artistic aspects and values.

Literature on Olympism, even in German-speaking countries, is so comprehensive that a complete survey is nearly impossible. Lennartz, for example, has listed more than 500 titles in his bibliography. Being confronted with the difficult task to offer a historiography of Olympism in Western Europe, it is necessary — in regard to the complexity of this subject — to come to a temporal and material limitation. Most publications which are based on scientific research were published after 1960. That is why I tend to examine mainly the past 15 to 20 years. Concerning the method of application, the presentation, oriented on problems, will be preferred to official and semi-official reports. Publications from the GDR (German Democratic Republic) are not included in my paper for reasons of methodology.

The Olympic movement, after the Games of Rome in 1960, was first harshly criticized by authors in the Federal Republic of Germany. The Games were accused of being the organization of a superbusiness, in which only a fool could deceive himself as far as finding the presence of a humanistic ideal. Lenk showed in his research — *Values, Aims and Reality of the Modern Olympic Games* — that Olympic aims and fundamental values are realized for the

Horst Ueberhorst, Institute of Sports Sciences, Ruhr University, Bochum, Federal Republic of Germany.

greater part. The athletes, the officials and the organizers of the Olympic Games of Rome have actualized to a high degree the goals occupying a strategic focal point in the value system. It would be wrong to say that the Olympic idea has been corrupted. Lenk further mentioned that the Olympic Games gave impetus to many undeveloped countries in building up their own national sport organizations. The organization of the Olympic Games or the participation in the Games had enriched or highly stimulated sport in all countries.

Between 1968 and 1972, between the Mexican and the Munich Olympics, the interior political situation in West Germany changed fundamentally. The "New Left" tried (influenced by the ideas of Marcuse) to attack society and its system of knowledge and education which it described as a late capitalistic authoritarian and repressive achievement society. Sport was discriminated against as conforming to that system and serving to stabilize it. It is evident that they mocked the Olympic movement and the Olympic idea as being a product of late capitalistic influence. Prokop (*Sociology of the Olympic Games*, 1971) believed that she unmasked the "festival character" of the Olympic Games by writing:

> The structure of the Olympic Games, the perfect organization, the cheerfulness, the cult and the individual self-denial, manifestly fetishlike, the service-taking, rule-implicating relationship of men.

Sportsmen conforming with the system prevent mass mobilization. Especially Olympic competitive sport seemed to be an integrative and system-stabilizing institution which drills technocratic conscience. Therefore, it helps cementing hierarchical structures.

Against these viewpoints there has been such strong argumentation (Lenk, Krockow, Linde, Heinemann, Grupe, Schmitz) that their absolute pretension is disproved. Nevertheless, the whole argumentation has brought new insights in the problems of high-performance sport.

A few months after the Munich Olympics the well-known sociologist Schelsky tried to give an interpretation of the great world festival focused on the idea of partial peace-establishing. He examined the Games from the approaches of political science and sociology in order to analyze special fields of problems and confrontations. On the basis of this examination he saw a future for the Olympic Games.

At the time that Munich was chosen to host the Games, the discussion about the Berlin Olympics (1936) was revived. Special attention was given to the problem of the misuse of the Games by the Nazi regime. Krüger gathered heretofore unknown material in the United States and could demonstrate the magnitude of the American boycott movement. In his opinion the Berlin Olympics were an example of the interference of politics in sport. In his biography on Lewald he pointed out how the honorable president of the Organizing Committee contributed to make the Berlin Olympics an extraordinary propaganda success, thereby increasing the prestige of the NS regime in the international sport movement. In his study "Sport-politics in the Third Reich" Bernett dedicated his greatest interest to the Berlin Olympics also. As is Krüger he is working on archive material (Files of the Reichskanzlei) now part of contemporary historical literature. He particularly examined Lewald's endeavors to gain protection of the "Reich," the demands of IOC president de Baillet-Latour toward Hitler, the boycott movement in foreign countries and the intervention of General Sherill from the United States. In his "Studies on Contemporary History" there is one chapter analyzing the Riefenstahl film of the Berlin Olympics. Jahnke in 1972 published material that demonstrated the extent and intensity of the socialistic boycott movement prior to the Olympic Games of 1936.

The main goal of the Carl-Diem-Institute in Cologne is a systematical adaption from the Olympic literature. Under the title *Olympic Thought* (1966), speeches and essays of Coubertin were published. Coubertin's *Olympic Memories*, translated into German, were put on the market in 1961. At the 75th anniversary of the inauguration of the Olympic movement in Germany (December 13, 1895), in 1970, *Documents of the Early History of the Modern Olympics* was published. Coubertin's endeavors to start the Athens Olympic Games, as well as Gebhardt's successful attempt to unify the German sport associations and to participate in the Games of Athens are properly valued. The letters, which heretofore were mostly unpublished, as well as the reports and essays were gathered in the archives of the International Olympic Committee or of the German Reichsausschuss für Leibesübungen.

A careful study on Gebhardt appeared in 1971, written by Hamer. At the same time the Carl-Diem-Institute published further contributions to the Olympic idea such as, in 1969, Malter's critical studies on the idea and ideology of sports and modern Olympics and Hojer's *Olympia — or Sport Between Pedagogy and Ideology*. These studies are a valuable addition to the remarkable publications on Coubertin and Diem. Of particular interest is the official report on the first Olympic Games of Athens (1896), a reprint of the original text of 1897 published by the Diem-Institute.

By commission of the German Olympic Society Umminger, in 1969, published an illustrated cultural history of the modern Olympic Games. This volume shows instructively the relationship between the Olympic world festival and the complex development of civilization in the past eight decades.

The scientific literature on the Olympics has also been enriched by research in the field of ancient history. Generally well respected is Bengtson's work on *The Olympic Games in Antiquity* (1971). Without speculations and strongly orientated on sources, the outstanding historian has painted an impressive picture of the ancient games in the Alphaios valley. Drees in his book about the origin of the Olympic Games (1962) has too keenly drawn some perspectives and overinterpreted the mythological background; however, to his merit, he recognized the great importance of cults in the early period of the games. His main work *Olympia* and his *100 Years of German Excavation at Olympia*, edited by the Organizing Committee of the Munich Olympics in 1971, are together with Bengtson's book the best representations of ancient Olympia in West Germany. Other interpretations are also worthy of mention: Lämmer's *Olympics and Hadreanees in Ancient Ephesos* (1967), Körbs' *Dispositions of Interpreting Ancient Gymnastics and Agonistics* (1967) and Wil-limczik's study on physical exercises in the works of Homer (1969). Last, but not least, two other books are highly recommendable: Popplow's *Physical Exercises and Physical Education in Greek Antiquity* and Zietschmann's *Sport-grounds for Competition and Training in Greece.* Popplow's book should not be overlooked in sport studies. Zietschmann, an archeologist, gives for his part a vivid, exact and instructive description of palästra, stadia and gymnasia in ancient Greece. Lennartz has gathered material, showing that knowledge and ideas on the Olympics remained alive between 393 B.C. and 1896 A.D.

Since 1962, the Hellenic Olympic Committee has published annual reports of the sessions organized by the International Olympic Academy at Olympia. The contributions of the invited speakers differ according to the unequal level of sports sciences in the world; however many papers are of high quality and should be mentioned in a historiography of modern Olympics. Contemporary Greeks have themselves presented lectures in every session, more specifically, on the Olympic idea (Symiczek), amateurism (Tzart-zanos) and ancient and modern games (Paleologos). In 1964, Paleologos lectured on the ancient Olympics, the truce, the organiza-tion and the events. Then in 1966 he brought new interesting information on the first modern national Greek Olympics held in the second half of the 19th century in Athens. In the following year (1967) he spoke about the "position of the athletes in society in ancient Greece" and pointed out that by primarily utilizing the forces of intense movement and activity and by showing the spirit of heroism and sacrifice, the spirit of contest and rivalry, the athletes of antiquity were outstanding personalities in the society of ancient Greece and were greatly honored by the city-states of that period. These and other representations such as *Ancient Olympics and their Moral Teaching* (1969), *Preparation for the Olympic Games in Ancient Greece* (1970) and *The Olympics of 512 BC* (1972) demonstrate that Paleologos should be respected as an expert of Greek antiquity, although his historical interpretation is rather idealistic. Besides Paleologos, Yalouris, the director of the archeological museum in Olympia, must be mentioned. His contributions *The State of Elis and the Sanctuary of Olympia* (1970) and *La guérison et l'art au sanctuaire d'Asclepios in Epidauros* (1968) demonstrate the mutual relationship of physical and moral education in ancient Greece. Yalouris showed how Elis protected the truce and organized the Olympic Games and how it offered an amazing contribution to the awakening and cultivating of the idea that all the Greeks, though scattered in small states and opponents of one another, formed a unique race with a common language and basically common ideas.

Pouret from France has several times presented remarkable papers. In *Pierre de Coubertin — Aspects méconnus ou oubliés de sa vie et de son oeuvre* (1966) he introduces the main lines of Coubertin's World History (*L'histoire universelle*). Here encyclopedic traditions of enlightenment and modern social ideas, for instance the foundation of a Workers' University, are brought to a synthesis. The contemporary *Olympic Games and Arts* (1969) offers an analysis of Coubertin's concepts and gives a survey of cultural competitions in the modern Olympics. His question, who are the "Men, who influenced Coubertin's thought" (1973) is answered by the names of Father Caron, Hyppolyte Taine and Le Play. Pouret obtained good information for this subject from Eyquem, author of a respectable biography on Coubertin which was translated into German by Kreidler in 1972. Eyquem skillfully worked into her biography letters, speeches and essays of Coubertin. We regret that there are no notes or a register; nevertheless, in this biography, we find valuable information on Coubertin's evolution. Especially in two chapters ("A revolutionary pedagogy" 1. From high-school to a labor university;

2. From physical education to Olympism) the leading cultural, historical, social and sportive reform ideas of Coubertin are clearly revealed. In the opinion of Coubertin, history is of the greatest importance and value in an educational process. Political and moral progress is seen as dependent on it.

Interesting is Coubertin's campaign in favor of educating the proletarians. Already in 1891 he called for the foundation of a university for workers; this is the theme of one of his books published in 1921. This institution should be run by worker-students, that is to say, by adults, who have a profession. Coubertin expected very much from this institution. Verhaegen from Belgium, in 1971, added new material on this subject when he published three letters of Coubertin written to the Belgian labor sport leader Devlieger in 1926. Coubertin had been highly impressed by the Worker Olympiad at Frankfurt in 1925. He asked Devlieger to support him to realize the pedagogical aims of the newly founded society "Union pédagogique universelle." Sending two of his brochures, Coubertin expressed his wish that they might help the working class to find a new pedagogy because the old bourgeois one had failed. The world, to Coubertin, expected such a renewal.

Berlioux of Lausanne has given several reports on the work of the International Olympic Committee (1968, 1970, 1973) when she participated to the sessions of the Olympic Academy. So did Vind, IOC member for Denmark. The most fundamental presentation of the IOC work, however, was done by Mayer from Switzerland in his book *A travers les Anneaux Olympiques.* The history of the IOC is carefully traced through the official minutes of this organization.

At the 13th session of the Academy in 1973 Seurin of France presented a paper entitled "Contributions of Education to the Olympic Movement," in which he tried to demonstrate that the modern Olympic movement had been influenced by the generous educational concept of Coubertin. Diem examined the pedagogical value of rules in the play of children and in the Olympic Games (1969), Henze reported on the pentathlon as an ideal event in the ancient world and in modern times (1967) and Körbs (1963) gave an interpretation of the *gymnasion* based on material that had been gathered from hellenistic papyri of the early Ptolemaic period. Pikhala from Finland, in 1966, discussed Gardiner's interpretation of the ancient pentathlon and Staubo, IOC member for Norway, gave a talk on the Winter Olympic Games (1973).

McIntosh, speaking about *Fitness and Prowess* (1963), pointed out that payment to the athletes, commercialization and political exploitation changed the character of the ancient Olympic Games, from genuine contests between ordinary citizens to entertainment conducted by professional performers who had been undergoing intensive and specialized training and were organized into guilds and unions. He then built a bridge over centuries to our time, showing that the worldwide participation in competitive sport as now a factor in civilization a fact never readily admitted before. In his book *Sport in Society* (1963) the sport-historian posed the question on the future relations between amateurism and professionalism. He answered as follows:

> The Olympic Movement cannot be more amateur than the organization which support it, and the enforcement of part-time training and competition is likely to prove as difficult as the prevention of athletes receiving direct or indirect rewards for their prowess.

Sayer in his presentation at the Olympic Academy (1966), entitled "English Sport and the Olympic Ideal," showed, by examining the nature and purposes of contemporary sport in England, the extent to which it seeks to develop much of those characteristics of the Olympic ideal which have a special significance in the individual and the community. The two Englishmen Hartmann (1972) and Masterson (1973) spoke about the "Environment of a Woman Olympic Competitor" (1972) and about "Contributions of Fine Arts to the Olympic Movement" (1973). In the opinion of Masterson, the art competitions, inaugurated in 1912 and terminated in 1948, were a failure, because it was impossible to translate the language of sport into the language of plastic forms.

The late Harris, an outstanding British scholar, was the editor of two standard works dealing with Olympic events: *Greek Athletes and Athletics* (1966) and *Sport in Greece and Rome* (1972), hereby continuing the work of Gardiner (*Athletes of the Ancient World* [1925]). Harris' work is based on original sources, on special studies of Greek and Roman stadia and on the analysis of antique vases which show sportive motifs.

From Austria we possess several documents on the Olympic movement assembled by Recla. His compatriot Kamper is the editor of a lexicon on the Winter Olympics and of an encyclopedia of Olympic champions. Invited as a speaker to the Academy in 1966, the title of his talk was "Analysis of Age of Competitors of the Olympic Games." It is interesting to note that the span of ages of Olympic competitors is from 11 to 73 years. Brein is the editor of the revised work of Jüthner (*Gymnastic*), published in two volumes

1965 and 1968 under the title *Athletics of the Greeks*; this work is considered a masterpiece of sport history. Finally, the Austrian Andrecs is worthy of mention; in 1973, he lectured at the Academy on "The Olympic Idea and its Realization in Schools." He demonstrated the relationship between Coubertin's and Gaulhofer's ideas. The founder of the modern Olympic Games was in Andrecs' opinion concerned first and foremost with formative objectives, ennobling and renewal of the individual and at the same time with a reshaping of society, equality among men, equality of opportunity. This, to Andrecs, would conform to the goal and objectives of the Austrian school today; these are based on Gaulhofer's concept "Bildung vom Leibe her," divided into four categories: maintenance of health, development of capacity of achievement, imparting of joy, harmony and love of nature. Dangers for the Olympic movement, according to Andrecs, appear to be isolation of the achievement principles (victory at any cost); discrimination against financially weaker states; avalanche of the commercialization and gigantic dimensions of the games.

For more than 20 years, Favre from Italy is an enthusiastic herald of Olympism. Member of the Italian Olympic Committee and author of the book *Civilization, Art and Sport* (Rome, 1969) he has repeatedly been one of the key speakers of the International Olympic Academy. In *Olympism and Civilization* (1964) he showed that Greeks' thoughts were at the onset directed at achievements, that is to say in nature and characteristics, they were preeminently sporting. Then Olympism had formed itself as a social and idealistic expression tempering the civilization of the past and of the present. According to his papers "Philosophy of the Modern Olympic Movement" (1969 and 1970), philosophy in Greece arose with the myth of Heracles, long before the Seven Sages, Plato and Aristotle. Favre then pointed out how the Olympics and other Games were factors which helped to promote Mediterranean and European evolution. He is probably too idealistic when he contends that no organization, whether political or social, has power to unite all peoples and all races in brotherly understanding as has the sporting ideal at its most constructive expression, the Modern Olympic Games, and, along with them, their radiant philosophy. Zauli, General Secretary of the Italian Olympic Committee, in 1963, ('Law of Sport') expounded some fundamental principles, inherent in the philosophy of sport, impressing human freedom.

Cagigal began in 1971 a very interesting research on the pedagogical evaluation of the Olympic Games in the opinion of the

Spanish people. The results of study are data, which illustrate the Olympic values and aims, as seen by Spanish sportsmen. There is an astonishing coincidence with Lenk's research: 18 of the 19 analyzed values were positive. His compatriot Hombrevella (*Preparation of Olympic Candidates from the Psychological Point of View*) in 1970 at the Academy outlined a plan for psychological preparation of the Olympic athletes. His proposal is that the psychological preparation of the athletes should be based on a pedagogical synthesis of sports sciences.

Weaknesses and strengths of the Olympic movement were discussed by van Ziyll of Holland in 1964. Weaknesses, in his opinion, are amateurism, nationalism, political influences and organization (size of program); they show the vulnerability of the Olympic Movement in general and of the Olympic Games in particular. Strengths of the Olympic Movement are its contribution to the expansion and popularization of the worldwide practice of sport, to the regulation of the practice of sport, to the improvement of achievements, to the promotion of sporting and physical training. The influence of the Olympic Movement on thought lies particularly in the recognition and in the development of the recreational and educational possibilities of sport.

As I pointed out at the onset of my presentation, the rapid increase of Olympic literature made it difficult for me to select the material. However, the growth is an impressive example of the vividness of the Olympic idea even with all its contradictions. We could recognize, in this short historiography of Olympism, the growing endeavors to work more and more scientifically and to further one's strong personal engagement for the Olympic idea. There are in my opinion two good reasons for this: first, the fascination of modern sport and, second, the hope and desire that in our world so full of conflicts there remain high goals for the often blocked up, but always through-coming humanity. Even those who strongly criticize the Games and the Olympic movement mostly want to solve the contradictions between idea and reality and do not wish to destroy their existence.

Bibliography

Bengston, H.: Die Olympischen Spiele in der Antike. Stuttgart, 1971.

Bernett, H.: Sportpolitik im Dritten Reich. Schorndorf, 1971.

Bernett, H.: Untersuchungen zur Zeitgeschichte. Schorndorf, 1973.

Cagigal, J.M.: Pädagogische Bewertung der Olympischen Spiele in der Volksmeinung. Unpub. Manuskript. Madrid, 1971.

Coubertin, P. de: Olympische Erinnerungen. Frankfurt, 1961.

Coubertin, P. de: Der Olympische Gedanke, Reden und Aufsätze. Hersg. vom Carl-Diem-Institut an der Deutschen Sportchochschule. Köln. Schorndorf, 1966.

Coubertin, P. de: Bibliography of the Works of Baron Pierre de Coubertin (1863-1937). Schorndorf:Carl-Diem-Institut, 1967.

Coubertin, P. de: Einundzwanzig Jahre Sportkampagne (Une campagne de vingt-et-un ans). Ratingen:Carl-Diem-Institut, 1974.

Diem, C.: Der Olympische Gedanke, Reden und Aufsätze. Schorndorf, 1967.

Drees, L.: Der Ursprung der Olympischen Spiele. Schorndorf, 1962.

Drees, L.: Olympia: Götter, Künstler und Athleten. Stuttgart, 1967.

Drees, L.: Dokumente zur Frühgeschichte der Olympischen Spiele. Köln:Carl-Diem-Institut, 1970.

Drees, L.: Die Olympischen Spiele 1896. Offizieller Bericht. (Nachdruck des Textes von Athen 1897). Köln:Carl-Diem-Institut, 1971.

Eyquem, M.T.: Pierre de Coubertin, l'épopée olympique. Paris, 1966.

Eyquem, M.T.: Pierre de Coubertin — Ein Leben für die Jugend der Welt. (Ubersetzung von H. D. Kreidler). Dortmund, 1972.

Favre, S.: Civilization, Art and Sport. Rome, 1969.

Göhler, J.: Olbaumzweig und Goldmedaille. Würzburg, 1968.

Hamer, E.: Willibald Gebhardt 1861-1921. Köln:Carl-Diem-Institut, 1971.

Harris, H.A.: Greek Athletes and Athletics. Bloomington, Ind., 1966.

Harris, H.A.: Sport in Greece and Rome. Ithaca, N.Y., 1972.

Hellenic Olympic Committee (ed.): The International Olympic Academy Reports of Second to Thirteenth Summer Sessions. Athens, 1962; Athens, 1973.

Hojer, E.: Olympia — oder: Der Sport zwischen Pädagogik und Ideologie, Köln:Carl-Diem-Institut, 1969.

Hörrmann, M.: Religion der Athleten. Stuttgart, 1968.

Hundert Jahre deutsch Ausgrabung in Olympia. (Hrsg. vom Organisationskomitee der Olympischen Spiele von München.) München, 1972.

Jahnke, K.H.: Gegen den Missbrauch der olympischen Idee. Sportler im antifaschistischen Widerstand. Frankfurt, 1972.

Jüthner, J.: Gymnastik. Bd1 und Bd.2 Hrs. von F. Brein. Die athletischen Leibesübungen der Griechen. Bd. 1 Geschichte der Leibesübungen, Bd. 2 Einzelne Sportarten. Osterreichische Akademie der Wissenschaften Bd. 249 1965 und 1968.

Kamper, E.: Enzyklopädie der Olympischen Spiele. Daten — Fakten-Namen. Stuttgart, 1972.

Körbs, W.: Interpretationsansätze der antiken Gymnastik und Agonistik. Köln, 1967.

Krüger, A.: Die Olympischen Spiele 1936 und die Weltmeinung. Berlin, 1972.

Krüger, A.: Theodore Lewald — Sportführer im Dritten Reich. Berlin, 1975.

Lämmer, M.: Olympien und Hadrianeen im antiken Ephesos. Diss. Köln, 1976.

Lenk, H.: Werte, Ziele und Wirklichkeit der modernen Olympischen Spiele. Schorndorf, 1972.

Lennartz, K.: Kenntnisse und Vorstellungen von Olympia und den Olympischen Spielen in der Zeit von 393 — 1896. Schorndorf.

Lennartz, K.: Bibliographie. Geschichte der Leibesübungen. Band 5: Olympische Spiele. Köln, 1971.

Malter, R.: Der 'Olympismus' Pierre de Coubertins. Köln:Carl-Diem-Institut, 1969.

Mayer, O.: A travers les anneaux olympiques. Genève, 1960.
McIntosh, P.: Sport and Society. London, 1963.
Megede, E.: Die Geschichte der olympischen Leichtathletik, Bd. 1, Berlin, 1968; Band 2, Berlin, 1969.
Moretti, L.: Olympionikai —i vincitori negli antichi agoni olympici, Roma, 1957.
Nationales Olympisches Komitee (Hrsg): Innsbruck 1964. Offizielles Standardwerk. Stuttgart, 1964.
Nationales Olympisches Komitee (Hrsg): Tokio 1964. Offizielles Standardwerk. Stuttgart, 1965.
Nationales Olympisches Komitee (Hrsg): Mexiko 1968. Offizielles Standardwerk. Dortmund, 1968.
Nationales Olympisches Komitee (Hrsg): Grenoble 1968. Offizielles Standardwerk. Dortmund, 1968.
Nationales Olympisches Komitee (Hrsg): Sapporo 1972. Offizielles Standardwerk.
Nationales Olympisches Komitee (Hrsg): München 1972. Offizielles Standardwerk.
Popplow, U.: Leibesübungen und Leibeserziehung in der griechischen Antike. Schorndorf, 1972.
Prokop, U.: Soziologie der Olympischen Spiele. München, 1971.
Recla, J.: Bibliographie zur Internationalen Olympischen Akademie. Graz, 1970.
Recla, J.: Die Olympischen Spiele in der Gegenwartsliteratur. Eine Literaturstudie. Graz, 1969.
Rösch, E.: Ist das noch Sport? — Kritische Anmerkungen zum Sport und zu den Olympischen Spielen. Freiburg, 1972.
Schelsky, H.: Friede auf Zeit. Die Zukunft der Olympischen Spiele. Osnabrück, 1973.
Scherer, K.H.: 75 Olympische Jahre. NOK für Deutschland. Eine Dokumentation über die olympische Bewegung in Deutschland. Hrsg. NOK für Deutschland. Frankfurt, 1970.
Scherer, K.H.: Männerorden. Die Geschichte des Internationalen Olympischen Komitees. München, 1974.
Seurin, P.: L'éducation physique dans le monde. Bordeaux, 1961.
Ueberhorst, H.: Von Athen bis München. Die modernen Olympischen Spiele. Der olympische Gedanke. Der deutsche Beitrag. Berlin, 1971.
Umminger, W.: Die Olympischen Spiele der Neuzeit. Eine illustrierte Kulturgeschichte der O.S. von Athen bis München. Offizielles Standardwerk des NOK. Hrsg. Deutsche Olympische Gesellschaft. Dortmund, 1969.
Verhaegen, M.: Quelques aspects de la pensée de Pierre de Coubertin sur le sport des travailleurs. Symposium CIEPS, 1971, Madrid.
Willimczik, K.: Leibesübungen bei Homer. Quellen zur Geschichte der Leibesübungen in der Antike. Schorndorf.
Zietschmann, W.: Wettkampf-und Ubungsstätten in Griechenland. I. Das Stadion; II. Palästra und Gymnasion. Schorndorf, 1960 und 1961.

L'historiographie de l'Olympisme moderne en Europe de l'ouest

L'auteur se dit d'avis que la littérature sur le phénomène olympique s'est considérablement accrue depuis les années 60, en raison principalement de

l'apport des travaux à caractère scientifique. Il donne les titres de certains ouvrages publiés ou édités en Europe occidentale et qui ont trait à l'olympisme dans les Jeux anciens et dans les Jeux modernes plus particulièrement sous les aspects de valeurs d'ordre sportif, socio-culturel et artistique.

A Survey of the Historiography of Olympism in North America

Jean M. Leiper

Four facets of Olympism in North America are examined using three categories of sources. The four aspects investigated are amateurism; physical and "moral" health; international understanding and goodwill; and culture. The source material used included magazines, newspapers and commentaries; books; and academic works. The author contends that North American writers generally have paid little attention to the concept and facets of Olympism and of the Olympic Idea.

Introduction

First, I must explain that I am concentrating my presentation on works of North Americans, and I wish to apologize to those writers whose work I do not mention. The time limit permits only a brief examination, not an extensive survey.

The second point to be made is, "What are we talking about?" The given topic is "Olympism" but do we know what that means? My research over the past three years suggests that "Olympism" is an obscure term not specifically defined anywhere in the English language, possibly not in French and certainly not by the promoters of the Olympic Movement — which encompasses Olympism — the I.O.C. Occasionally, it is used as a substitute for the "Olympic Ideal," a more common appellation but equally misunderstood. Meaning seems to depend upon whatever the speaker wants it to mean. Little has been written to enlighten North Americans about this philosophy of sport which surrounds the Olympic Games. In this paper I am using "Olympism" "the Olympic Idea" and "the Olympic Ideal" as having very similar meanings. Three aspects of the Olympic Idea, however, have received relatively wide recognition:

1. Coubertin's borrowed aphorism "It's not the winning but the taking part that's important" — to paraphrase the original

---

Jean M. Leiper, Faculty of Physical Education, University of Calgary, Calgary, Alberta, Canada.

2. Amateurism — sport for love not gain — as a requirement for participation in the Olympic Games

3. The Olympic Games are supposed to promote international understanding.

But are these synonymous with Olympism? I have developed an interpretation of Olympism, based on a study of Coubertin's statements. I postulate Olympism to be a philosophy of sport in life, which has four facets:

1. Amateurism — sport as an avocation, not a vocation

2. Creating physical and moral health through sport training and competition

3. The Olympic Games as a means of increasing international respect and therefore developing peace and goodwill in the world

4. Emphasizing sport as an element of culture involved in arts and letters

For this paper I have investigated three categories of works and have selected a few representative samples of what has been written in North America about the Olympic Movement as compared with the definition just given. Recent examples have been emphasized.

Material in Magazines, Newspapers and Similar Commentaries

The area of emphasis in this category of work is heavily on amateurism, although the last ten years has seen a growth of concern with the internationalism factor. Also, there appear to be more critical positions than ones supportive of the idealistic aims of the Olympic Games. In the early years, however, support for idealistic stances was much more prevalent. For example, Sloane, writing in 1912, incorporated all four of the facets of Olympism in his article, but it must be remembered that Sloane was a charter member of the I.O.C. and had much close contact with Coubertin [18].

Avery Brundage, the American president of the I.O.C. from 1952 to 1972, was the most knowledgeable and biased advocate of Olympism but his philosophical words were less likely to reach the pages of the press than were his criticisms of nonamateur competitors. In a speech to the I.O.C. in 1958 he outlined the purposes of the Olympic Games and the points made sound like a definition of Olympism, except that amateurism is not included.

> a. To stimulate interest in physical education and physical training and thus to contribute to the strength and health of mankind.

b. To establish standards of fair play and good sportsmanship, which might eventually be adopted in other fields of endeavour.

c. To promote peace and international good will by bringing the youth of the world together in friendly competition under the proper idealistic sponsorship.

d. To give emphasis to the desirability of a well rounded life such as prevailed in the Golden Age of Greece, in the days of Pericles, when the ancient Olympic Games were at their perihelion, by combining a program of Fine Arts with athletic contests [1].

Physical education teachers, people who might be concerned with sport benefits beyond the purely physical, heard from Goodwin of the Canadian Olympic Association and Canadian Broadcasting Corporation, at the C.A.H.P.E.R. convention in 1965. Although Goodwin's title was "The Much Misunderstood Olympic Ideal," the burden of his remarks stressed only one factor of Olympism — a healthy moral attitude that should be developed by sport participation [6].

Much ink has been expended on the Montreal Games — but not much has mentioned the philosophy of sport which the Games celebrate. Kidd endorsed the "international brotherhood (or sisterhood)" possibilities engendered by the Olympic Games, the spread of sport participation and the "association of sport with other art forms" [10]. He was not too enthused about the structure under which these great goods are supposed to develop, but he was in favor of finding a better way for people to obtain such benefits through the Olympic Games.

Even McMurtry presents portions of Olympism in his paper [13]. His argument is that the Olympics cost too much money that could benefit needy Canadians for us to support a festival that not only does not achieve its golden purposes, but even distorts them to chauvinistic ends. But, if one looks closely, his contentions are based on several of the facets of Olympism. On the other hand, Rowan [14] never mentions Olympism or anything close to it. But, considering her expose of the cost in human terms to low income Montrealers, it's not surprising that she ignores the idealistic aims of the Olympic Movement. However, it might be wise to avoid including in this survey further discussions relative to the Montreal Olympic problems or there will be no end to this presentation.

It must be admitted that the majority of working sports press have not lined up beside Olympism in their writings. The responsibility they seem to feel for "telling it like it is" prohibits their support for the idealistic values of Olympism. Heywood Broun, Howard Cosell, Paul Gallico, Dick Beddoes and legions of others have all found reason for strong criticism of the amateur and internationalism factors of Olympism while largely ignoring the remaining points.

Books

This is not a rich field for exploration. Most publications in North America have been produced in the last 20 years, and most are a summary of the events of the Olympic Games, preceded by a brief outline of the history of the Games, ancient and modern. The Olympic Ideal is sometimes mentioned, Olympism almost never. In 1948 Henry produced one of the few comprehensive such books with an excellent section on the founding of the modern Games [8]. Although Henry never says Olympism is - - - -, his extensive discussion of Coubertin's purposes in reestablishing the Olympic Games and the numerous quotations from Coubertin's writings expose the content of Olympism rather thoroughly. Roxborough [15] never mentions it, and diligent searching reveals only passing references in Grombach [7] and Mandell [12]. Johnson evaluates the "synthetic mythology" of Olympism which seems to cause the cynicism and hypocrisy in which he sees the Olympic Games clothed [9]. In the process he, at least, makes reference to each of the factors, possibly excepting the sport and culture marriage. He, again, is an example of the sport journalist presenting reality, not dreams. Fisher and Wise [2] appear to follow the press writer's penchant for emphasis only on amateurism and even that is just a brief sentence or two. Gallico [4] is another who finds fault with the amateur requirement for participation and also with the aim of international peace through the Olympic Games. Gallico insists that much more damage than good is done to international relations through the medium of the Olympic Games.

In contrast to these positions, Schaap [16] presents a much more optimistic mood. Either directly or indirectly he displays, in pictures as well as in words, all of the faces of Olympism. In his introduction he suggests that the Olympics hold a potential for rich experiences:

> For the observers and the observed, the Olympic Games are the most compelling spectacle in sports.
>
> Yet the Olympics go beyond sports. They approach art. They offer ritual in the symbolic freeing of the pigeons, the solemn lighting of the Olympic flame, the

> quiet dignity of the Olympic oath. They offer competition, with the animal excitement of physical combat, strength matched against strength, style against style, stamina against stamina, courage against courage. And, above all, they offer a singular spirit of a camaraderie born of shared victories, an understanding born of shared defeats.

What have past medal winners had to say? One athlete-writer who presents a much wider picture than most of the comments just mentioned is Don Schollander, the swimmer who collected five Gold Medals in 1964 and 1968. In his book [17], Schollander told of almost quitting the Olympic Games the day before they were to open in Mexico City. His reason — the deterioration of the Olympic Ideal. In the retirement speech he wrote, but never gave, Schollander does as complete a job of identifying the facets of Olympism as can be found. He even mentions the cultural aspect. He did not personally subscribe to items such as amateurism, but there was no doubt that he was a strong believer in the potential of the Olympic Movement for individual and international good.

There really is not much point in perusing the official publications of the various Olympic Committees. When they do interrupt the account of performance achievements to mention Olympism, the accent is only on the international contact point of view and, predictably, is utopian.

The Academic Area

Considering the impact of the Olympic Games — certainly since World War II — little research has been produced. The most complete, as far as Olympism is concerned, is John Lucas's dissertation [11]. Two other theses have concentrated on factors of Olympism — amateurism and internationalism. Glader [5] explored the history of amateurism and did a comprehensive job, but he did not seem to identify amateurism as anything with a deeper significance than a rule of qualification for the Olympic Games which was rapidly becoming outmoded. Fuoss investigated the goal of international peace and goodwill as representating the Olympic Ideal [3]. His thesis dealt with uncovering all the incidents of friction in the Games that would refute the contention that international friendship was a more common outcome than international dissension. He also presented events of noticeable sportsmanship and fair play which had been reported over the same span of Olympic Games. Although the negative incidents much outnumbered the positive behaviors, Fuoss commented that that could be because conflict is much more likely to be reported in the press. Fuoss's conclusion was that the Olympic Games do serve a valuable purpose of making people aware of those of other nationalities and most often the reaction is favorable. Fuoss also mentions the connection of amateurism and the fine arts with the Games but this is an added section exploring "Other Problems facing the Olympic Games," not part of any investigation of Olympism.

There can be little doubt that the most extensive examination of Olympism and its sources is John Lucas's dissertation mentioned previously. He interpreted Olympism as a world philosophy of sport celebrated every four years by the Olympic Games — just as Coubertin appeared to intend that the world should so understand it. One must thoroughly agree with Lucas that "a definition of the term 'Olympism' is made difficult by the extreme diversity of the ideas which may be subsumed under it." Lucas then identified three *characteristics* of Olympism, using a radio broadcast by Coubertin in 1935 as his major source. He said that the Baron "portrayed the characteristics of Olympism as 'religion first, then peace, and finally beauty.' " The amateur ideal and the values of physical and moral development are excluded from this version of Olympism, and religion is included. Lucas went on to explain in greater detail Coubertin's beliefs about each of these characteristics. Whether Lucas's interpretation of Olympism is correct, it would appear, to this time, that only he has made a thorough attempt to analyze the complexities of Olympism.

The most unfortunate aspect of this confusion about the meaning of Olympism is that it prevents the proliferation of the philosophy of sport celebrated by the Olympic festival. Canada and the United States, for the last few months, have been inundated with words, written and spoken, about the Olympic Games. The lack of understanding of columnists and script writers is most evident in the frequent interchange of the word "Olympiad" for "the Olympic Games." Mistakes such as this illustrate the widespread ignorance of Olympism.

In summary, it is evident that, in general, North American writers have paid little attention to Olympism, allowing it to remain as a shadowy backdrop to the spectacle of the Olympic sport competitions.

References

1. Brundage, A.: The Speeches of President Avery Brundage, 1952-1968. Lausanne:The International Olympic Committee, 1968 (?), p. 37.

2. Fisher, D. and Wise, S.F.: Canada's Sporting Heroes. Don Mills, Ontario: General Publishing, 1974.
3. Fuoss, D.E.: An Analysis of the Incidents in the Olympic Games from 1924-1948, With Reference to the Contribution of the Games to International Good Will and Understanding. Unpublished Doctoral Dissertation, Columbia University Teacher's College, 1952.
4. Gallico, P.: Farewell to Sport. New York:Alfred A. Knopf, 1938.
5. Glader, E.A.: A Study of Amateurism. Unpublished Doctoral Dissertation, University of Iowa, 1970.
6. Goodwin, D.: The much misunderstood Olympic Ideal. J. Can. Assoc. Health Phys. Educ. 32(1):9-10, 50, 1965.
7. Grombach, J.V.: Olympic Cavalcade of Sports. New York:Macmillan, 1971.
8. Henry, B.: An Approved History of the Olympic Games. New York: Putnam's Sons, 1948.
9. Johnson, W.O.: All That Glitters Is Not Gold. New York:Putnam's Sons, 1972.
10. Kidd, B.: Confronting the Olympic Dilemma. Mimeographed paper.
11. Lucas, J.A.: Baron Pierre de Coubertin and the Formative Years of the Modern Olympic Movement, 1883-1896. Unpublished Doctoral Dissertation, University of Maryland, 1962, p. 139.
12. Mandell, R.D.: The Nazi Olympics. New York:Macmillan, 1971.
13. McMurtry, J.: A Case for Killing the Olympics. Maclean's (January, 1973), pp. 34, 57-58, 60.
14. Rowan, M.K.: The Real Losers. Canadian Magazine (June 9, 1975 (?)).
15. Roxborough, H.: Canada at the Olympics. Toronto:Ryerson Press, 1963.
16. Schaap, D.: An Illustrated History of the Olympics, ed. 3. New York: Ballantine, 1976, p. ix.
17. Schollander, D. and Savage, D.: Deep Water. New York:Crown, 1971.
18. Sloane, W.M.: The Olympic Idea. The Century Magazine, 84 (July, 1912).

L'olympisme dans les ouvrages historiques des Amériques

L'auteur discute du concept de l'Olympisme sous quatre rubriques: l'amateurisme, la santé physique et "morale," la compréhension et la collaboration internationales, les aspects culturels. Les sources consultées comprennent des revues périodiques, journaux, volumes et autres ouvrages à caractère académique. L'auteur se dit d'avis que de façon générale, les écrivains et auteurs Nord-américains ne se sont que très peu penchés sur le concept et sur les facettes de l'Olympisme et de l'Idée olympique.

R. Tait McKenzie: The Scientist

C. R. Blackstock

The manner in which McKenzie applied his medical knowledge to his works of art and how his interest in physiotherapy and prescribed exercise led him to become an authority in physical medicine is presented. His career and works during World War I are reviewed, underlining his contribution to the recognition of the importance of physical activity in the growth, development and education of youth.

In 1962 Dr. A. D. Kelly, General Secretary of the Canadian Medical Association, presented a Resolution of the Association to the federal Department of National Health and Welfare urging the Minister to put the Mill of Kintail at Almonte into the public domain as a memorial to R. Tait McKenzie. Justification was put in these words: "*Exercise in Education and Medicine* (3rd edition, 1923 by R. Tait McKenzie) reflects the concentration, in one man, of the knowledge and skills of the physician, surgeon and psychiatrist, and the techniques of the physio- and occupational therapist." . . . "His early studies in the treatment of deformity by exercise were expanded into methods of rehabilitation of the shattered minds and bodies of the wounded by physical means" . . . . "In medicine, he pioneered in setting down much of the beginnings of a new specialty, physical medicine."

It is appropriate that his career in medicine should be considered first, since medicine provided the foundations on which McKenzie built his life work. The medical education he received at McGill, the lecturing he did there in anatomy and his private practice in orthopedics in Montreal were excellent preparation for the future. His personal experiences in sports and gymnastics when he was a student and then as an assistant instructor and coach of physical activities were combined with those in medicine.

It was at this point he decided to combine medical science with physical education for a career. He believed everyone should have the opportunity to develop his full potential for a healthy, active life. He was unalterably convinced that there was a wisdom of the body that

C. R. Blackstock, Vanier City, Ontario, Canada.

could be developed by progressive physical activity learning experiences as well as those for the mind. Any study of his life reveals him as a multifaceted, learned, broadly concerned person who lived life to the full. His first concern was his fellows, his neighbors — marks of a true professional. He was a scientist and a practitioner; a scholar and an artist; an idealist and a poet.

Medical Director of Student Health and Physical Training at McGill in 1894, succeeding the former director, Naismith, McKenzie immediately instituted the plan which had been accepted by the University. (It had been vehemently opposed by a number of faculty and some students because it was not academic.)

McKenzie went to Harvard in 1890 to the summer school offered for teachers by Dr. Dudley Sergent, the school director. The Harvard plan to monitor the health and development of the students was based on the Amherst plan initiated in 1861 by Dr. Edward Hitchcock. The use of anthropometry for this purpose was adopted by many eastern U.S. universities.

McKenzie's plan was a modification of it to suit the conditions at McGill. These medical and physical examinations were the first use of anthropometry in Canada. In succeeding years it became common practice in universities and private boarding schools in the country.

He knew from his own experience as an athlete the personal satisfactions and feelings of well-being that come from developing the physique, physical condition and skills through participation in directed physical activities and sports. He wanted all students to have these experiences. He applied his medical knowledge, especially that of anatomy and physiology, to the scientific study of the athletes he instructed and coached. He applied his knowledge and skill in orthopedics to the treatment of the defects. In both situations exercise and physical activity played major roles.

McKenzie became involved with the Society of College Gymnasium Directors. (It is interesting to note that many of the pioneers engaged in physical education and athletics in educational institutions made their entry into the academic community as medical doctors.) The Society commissioned McKenzie in 1902 to model the "Athlete." The physical proportions of the typical man and the physical characteristics of the athlete had been derived from averaging the anthropometric measures and tests that the members of the Society had collected on their students.

The models used to do his first figure in the round, "The Sprinter," were people at McGill. McKenzie described how he got the proportions for "Athlete"; . . . "I obtained the average measurements of four hundred Harvard men, all of whom came from within the first fifty strongest over the last ten years" (1894-1904) . . . "Taking this set of measurements and proportions as basic, I modelled the figure of this ideal young man of 22 years and having a height of 5′9″, so the linear measurements of the statue were exactly one fourth life size." . . . "The athlete is about to try his right forearm by the oval dynamomenter." The Society expressed its appreciation for its "scientific truthfulness and artistic excellence."

Studies of the physiological effects of exercise and performance were begun at McGill. To more clearly illustrate these, McKenzie made plasters such as the Masks. He had a knack of discerning the critical moment in the action that caught up the underlying emotional or psychological responses as well as the physiological effects on the body. Many of the athletic sculptures show these.

All of these studies helped to provide a standard or scale against which to compare the individual. The exercise and remedial prescriptions were made which would get the student up to the "norm or beyond."

The appointment to the full professorship of physical education at the University of Pennsylvania in 1904 gave McKenzie the opportunity to expand and refine the ideas and methods he began at McGill. It put him in closer contact with others similarly engaged such as Director of Physical Education and Hygiene Dr. Edward Hitchcock. Many other universities set up the same kind of programs during the last quarter of the 19th century. All of them, with the exception of Harvard, had a physical education requirement of two periods a week for at least two years.

Equally important were the programs provided or prescribed for those who were found to have defects, illnesses, injuries and malfunctions which restricted or limited normal function. Remedial programs suited to the individual were instituted. They could include surgery, supportive apparatus and such things as eye glasses. Always they included physical activity and corrective physical exercises, often special apparatus and gadgets to exercise a muscle or joint.

McKenzie, along with Sargent, Hitchcock and Seaver, combined physiotherapy treatments with the prescribed exercises. Massage, hydrotherapy, electrotherapy and mechanotherapy were used. There was a great exchange of experience among these pioneers in physical education. Most of them had rejected the various "systems" which had been transplanted from Europe during the mid 1800s. They went back to the study of the human body. They sought to provide an environment and a learning program which would effect the individual's best growth and development.

These experiences became the base on which McKenzie, in the next phase of his career, built the methods and techniques of physical medicine. He didn't do it alone. Other orthopedic specialists were involved. McKenzie happened to land in a situation in which he provided the necessary leadership to apply the principles, methods and techniques of this emerging specialty, physical medicine. The situation was England 1915 during World War I.

In 1914, McKenzie had been ten years at Pennsylvania. He was at one of the many peaks he achieved in his life. Recognition had come to him from the physical education professional associations in which he was one of the originators and leaders. His sculpture had established him in the international art world as a classicist. In medicine, his textbook *Exercise in Education and Medicine* (1st edition, 1910) had made him an authority on preventive and remedial practice. Then came the war!

McKenzie arrived in England early in 1915. He applied to the Canadian Army Medical Corp, already over there, but was not accepted because he had not followed the proper procedures. Impatient, he went to the British Royal Army Medical Corp and was accepted with a rank of lieutenant attached to the Connaught Hospital at Aldershot. He was moved to the Physical Training Headquarters staff and for his own edification took the course. It so happened that his book was in the Mess and was being used by the instructors. There was some curiosity about the similarity of names but McKenzie did not reveal, until the end of the course, that he was indeed the author of the text. Things changed rapidly when this became known.

His Colonel quickly picked him out and together they did a tour of the convalescent hospitals and training camps. This inspection grouped the men into two general categories: those who were unfit for service because of lack of condition and those who were in need of remedial treatment.

The plan proposed by McKenzie for the rehabilitation of these men was readily accepted and he was posted to the staff of the War Office in charge of putting it into action. His title was Inspector of Physical Therapy and Remedial Surgery in the military hospitals and depots of Great Britain and Canada. When the United States came into the war he was the adviser to its Army too.

The first depot was set up at Heaton Park in the fall of 1915, with McKenzie in medical charge. It was here that he set out the treatment principles, the methods and techniques for the reeducation and training of the physically unfit soldiers. In four months over

1200 men had been returned to service. Other similar command depots were set up and followed the same plan, successfully returning hundreds of soldiers to active duty. For the most part these were men who had not suffered severe wounds.

A surgeon, Sir Robert Jones, Inspector of Military Orthopedics, was setting up a chain of orthopedic centers. McKenzie and Jones toured the convalescent hospitals where surgical cases were being treated. They sorted out those for whom remedial procedures would work from those requiring further surgery. These were sent to the orthopedic centers. What McKenzie called "curative workshops" were added to these orthopedic centers and it was in these the physiotherapy methods of treatment were applied.

The Macmillan Company (1918) published *Reclaiming the Maimed, a Handbook of Physical Therapy* in which McKenzie describes in detail with photos and diagrams the kinds of treatment and apparatus used. In the first chapter he wrote:

> Old conditions have come up with new names, and new conditions have had to be met by a rearrangement and application of old means. We must reconsider at this time the whole field of physical therapy as applied to and affected by the great war.
>
> This Cinderella of the therapeutic family may be said to include the application of Electricity in its many forms, Radiant Heat, Water, Hot and Cold, Massage, Passive Movement, Muscular Reeducation, and Gymnastics Exercises.

This general plan worked. The command depots were turned into training camps. It was used in India, in Canada, in the United States and in France. The Heaton Hall procedures became the textbook and resulted in the Handbook *Reclaiming the Maimed* authored by R. Tait McKenzie.

Early in the winter of 1916-1917, McKenzie had to put in an appearance at his University in Philadelphia. From there he went to Canada where he did a survey of the Canadian military convalescent hospitals. McKenzie teamed up with Dr. Edward Bott, head of the psychological laboratory, University of Toronto, to set up the principles of reeducation of the wounded. Such hospitals were established all across Canada. Their purpose was "the placing within the patient's reach the proper apparatus, assistance and encouragement for practising such physical movements or mental processes as may have been interfered with or have entirely disappeared, through injury or shock. Individual attention is the keynote throughout, each case being a study in itself."

Hart House, a large gymnasium and social center, on the University of Toronto campus, a gift of the Massey Foundation, had been opened in 1917. Lt.-Col. Vincent Massey approved the use of the facilities as a training center for the staffs for the Canadian military convalescent hospitals. The Manual was used as the basic text.

McKenzie did the same thing in Washington once the United States entered the war in 1917. As so often happens under the pressure of war, developments are speeded up, take place in a compacted time space. McKenzie was in the right spot to lead the way for many countries in the establishment of physical medicine among the specialties in medical science.

Physical medicine has grown quite rapidly in the past 20 years. The physiatrist is a recognized specialist in charge of the rehabilitation service of most of the health sciences centers at universities. The various physiotherapies play a larger and larger role in the treatment of injury and disease.

It has taken over 100 years to reestablish physical activity as a basic, essential, vital part in the good growth and development and education of humans and that it has such a place in the restoration of health and fitness following injury or disease. The time could have been shortened had we looked into, not back, but into what McKenzie had discovered and the courses of action to follow. Certainly he tried to share his experiences, especially by his writings in the professional journals; his widely reported research; his catholic interests in so many of the arts and crafts. This International Congress is a good occasion to reexpose what he learned about the place of physical activity in the evolution of man. Once born we have to move. We might as well learn to move in such a manner as will give us the best of living, health and joy.

There is a story about a species of bird that existed long ago that flew backwards. It didn't care where it was going but it sure wanted to know where it had been. We in history have been doing a lot of this. It is time to turn around and see what is coming because we will have to deal with it and that is better done head on than tail on. You can see that this will require a change of attitudes for many of us.

The findings from the use of the electron microscope in the last ten years are, to say the least, revealing. Hear what Lewis Thomas has to say in *The Lives of a Cell.*

> We are told that the trouble with Modern Man is that he has been trying to detach himself from nature. He sits in

> the topmost tiers of polymer, glass and steel, dangling his pulsing legs, surveying at a distance the writhing life of the planet. In this scenario, Man comes on as a stupendous lethal force, and the earth is pictured as something delicate, like rising bubbles at the surface of a country pond, or flights of fragile birds.
>
> But it is illusion to think that there is anything fragile about the life of the earth; surely this is the toughest membrane imaginable in the universe, opaque to probability, impermeable to death. We are the delicate part, transient and vulnerable as cilia. Nor is it a new thing for man to invent an existence that he imagines to be above the rest of life; this has been his most consistent intellectual exertion down the millennia. As illusion, it has never worked out to his satisfaction in the past, any more than it does today. Man is embedded in nature.
>
> The biologic science of recent years has been making this a more urgent fact of life. The new, hard problem will be to cope with the dawning, intensifying realisation of just how interlocked we are. The old, clung-to notions most of us have held about our special lordship are being deeply undermined.

S. E. Luria in *Life the Unfinished Experiment* tells us once we have become aware of the fact that we "have not arrived" at the ultimate peaks in our field, of the scientific paths which lie before us.

> Life has two scientific aspects: life in action and life in time. Life in action is the functioning of living organisms, the molecular and atomic events brought about by the presence of life, and is the subject matter of biochemistry Life in time is the persistence and disappearance and replacement of organisms, by individual death as well as the generation and differential proliferation of new species — in one word, evolution. These two aspects, biochemistry and evolution, make life a unique phenomenon in the history of the earth, one that long before the coming of man had impressed its profound mark on the features, the climate, the very structure of the planet earth. Life is distinct from all other natural phenomena in one feature: it has a program.

What has all this to do with McKenzie, one of the pioneers in physiatrics-physical medicine? Certainly, to show again what one medical scientist did to apply that science in the field of physical education, human physical activity. Until the day he died, after 70 years of living, he looked ahead to see what was coming. Six days before he died, speaking as president of the American Academy of Physical Education at Atlanta in 1938, he said:

> We need people not just to gather data and publish it, but to think through the results and their implications. . . . We need a group that will make authoritative statements and be didactic about it. . . . It is not the function of the Academy to do only hard physical labor, but it is its function to look for and recognize the ultimate milligram of truth that results from it. . . . If we can bring about the discovery of one truth about physical education that is at all comparable to these discoveries (in science), the Academy will not have been founded in vain. . . . We may not be able to give material assistance to those working toward this end, but we can pay with the more valuable coin of appreciation and understanding to the workers in the field.

As he did so often in his art, he created with and in his own life a model for us to which to shape our lives as humanists, as physical activity scientists, as physical educators. But we have to keep that model before us, in our view.

May each of you have the curiosity of a hungry raccoon, the persistence of a beaver rebuilding its dam and the vision of the soaring eagle all the days of your life.

Robert Tait McKenzie, le scientifique

L'auteur montre comment la formation et l'expérience médicales du canadien Robert Tait McKenzie lui ont servi dans la création de ses oeuvres d'art et dans ses travaux de physiothérapie et de réhabilitation physique, tout particulièrement au cours de la première guerre mondiale. Il montre également comment l'oeuvre de McKenzie a influé sur le cours des événements dans le monde de l'éducation au Canada par la reconnaissance progressive de l'importance de la place de l'activité physique comme moyen favorisant la croissance, le développement et l'éducation générale de la jeunesse.

Sculptor of Athletes: Tait McKenzie

Andrew J. Kozar

The life of Robert Tait McKenzie is examined focusing on the influences making him the foremost sculptor of athletes. His early association with artists, knowledge of anatomy and involvement in athletics provided the foundation of his first works. The anthropometry, for which he was criticized, yielded to the traditional European masters although the dominant theme of his works remained the concept of the athletic ideal.

R. Tait McKenzie immortalized our Golden Age of Sports in bronze. His work captured both Jesse Owens and David Cecil (Lord Burghley) as well as dozens of athletes less well known, and it established him as America's foremost sculptor of sports. Medals designed by him have been treasured by champion athletes throughout the world, and many of his pieces stand as monuments to courage and effort.

On the occasion of his 70th birthday, May 26, 1937, R. Tait McKenzie was toasted by his colleague at the University of Pennsylvania, E. W. Mumford. During the course of a lengthy offering at the Franklin Inn Club meeting at Valley Force, Pennsylvania, Mumford regaled his listeners with an imaginary vignette from his subject's earliest days:

> On the morning of his first anniversary, his parents decided it was time to find out what Rab was good for. They set him in the middle of the floor, and put near him a Bible, a bottle of pills, and a lump of clay. He swallowed the pills, seized and squeezed the clay, set the Bible up on edge and jumped over it. They couldn't make up their minds what this portended, but Rab knew. He had already decided

---

Andrew J. Kozar, Department of Health, Physical Education and Recreation, The University of Tennessee, Knoxville, Tenn., U.S.A.

This paper was prepared with material from the author's book *R. Tait McKenzie: Sculptor of Athletes* published by The University of Tennessee Press in 1975.

> that for a man of his parts at least three professions were indicated. He was on his way to becoming a physician, a sculptor, and a professor of physical education [3].

When McKenzie suffered a fatal heart attack in his Philadelphia home on April 28, 1938, he was still actively involved in all three professions. As physician, he had been honored by the Academy of Physical Medicine, having been elected its president for 1938. As sculptor, he was working on the memorial to Sir Arthur Doughty, Canada's distinguished archivist, and he had just completed a sketch statuette of Duke Kahanamoku, the great Hawaiian swimmer. As a physical educator, he had been re-elected president of the American Academy of Physical Education during the week prior to his death; at the same time the membership presented him with a beautiful scroll of highest tribute.

Moreover, McKenzie had been asked to visit St. Andrews University in Scotland that fall to receive his third honorary doctorate.* In a memorial address presented at a St. Andrews Society meeting in Philadelphia, J. Norman Henry recalled cruising the Bahamas in March with his dear friend when news of the degree arrived by telegram; at the same time, McKenzie received the final agreement on his commission for the Kahanamoku statue. Henry reported McKenzie said that he "needed to live two years and believed such expectation likely."† He began to plan these two trips — the one to Scotland, the other to Hawaii — journeys that unfortunately never materialized. Yet his life had been full, constructive and happy.

Indeed, McKenzie was so brilliantly endowed that he distinguished himself in each of his chosen callings. Without neglecting altogether his roles as physician and physical educator, this brief paper will center on his life as a sculptor of athletes.

McKenzie's remarkable achievements in medicine and physical education found a common medium of expression in his sculpture of athletes. His sculptures catch human beings in moments of physical stress, intense concentration and relaxation; he had a way of choosing the exact pose to express a beautiful movement in a motionless, sculptured figure.

---

*This degree was not awarded posthumously. Early correspondence indicated that McKenzie must have been present to receive the honor — a fact confirmed by a St. Andrews official. R. N. Smart to Andrew J. Kozar, September 16, 1970.

†Undated address, 1938. Copy in McKenzie Papers.

Interested in the perfect body as the Greeks were, McKenzie began his art career with the modeling of athletes for clinical study. The intense interest of physical educators in the late 19th and early 20th centuries in anthropometry as related to ideal man inspired his first well-known sculptures, "Masks of Facial Expression," "Sprinter" and "Athlete." After completing these anatomical, anthropometric pieces, he branched out into the wider field of sculpture, establishing his place in the art world with his statues and works of relief dealing with athletes.

The Golden Age of Sports he lived in, unparalleled since ancient Greece, became the inspiration for his sculpture. Not confining himself to the champion athlete, he treated all athletes in the glorious period of athleticism he observed. He personally experienced the revival of the ancient Greek Olympics initiated by Pierre de Coubertin, a man whose ideals he admired. He actively supported these amateur games throughout his life — speaking, competing in art and serving on committees. The modern Olympics, together with his total devotion to immortalizing the athlete, helped establish him as America's foremost sculptor of athletes. Medals he created in the early part of the century (1906, 1916, 1917) are still used and valued by various athletic organizations, not only for the appropriateness and beauty of design of the medals, but also for the high athletic and academic standards advanced by their designer.

In his life, as in his art, McKenzie embraced the classic ideal of the well-rounded man — "the eager mind in a lithe body."* Mr. Blackstock earlier told us that McKenzie as a physician played a prominent role in the rehabilitation of wounded and disabled veterans in England, Canada and the United States, both during and following the First World War. His books dealing with rehabilitation were adopted for use in the military forces of these countries. As a scholar and teacher he fought, and won respect, for physical education as a serious academic discipline.

In the world of art, however, McKenzie must have felt that the worth of his sculpture was not properly recognized. He continued to attract a number of sizable commissions for his work from 1921 until his death in 1938, but he was then, and still is, virtually ignored by the art world. Although he had a gift for successfully promoting his ideals of health and bodily exercise to reluctant Americans, his work never won the unreserved acceptance of arbiters of art.

---

*An inscription McKenzie used on the 1928-32 Olympic Shield — his "Shield of Athletes" — designed and entered into the sculpture in relief competition at the 1932 Olympics in Los Angeles.

While McKenzie was achieving eminence as a physical educator in his early professional life, he also maintained an abiding interest in the humanities. In his college days he belonged to an artistic group of university men in Montreal — men with a bent toward art and literature who made his home their center of activity. Early association with artistic friends, together with his lectures in anatomy and his involvement in athletics, seems to have provided the foundation for one of his first attempts at sculpture, the "Masks of Facial Expression." In his unfinished manuscript, "The Measured Mile: Fifty Years of Athletics and Physical Education," McKenzie credits his friend George W. Hill (1861-1934), a sculptor, with assisting him in his first attempt at modeling.

In "The Measured Mile," McKenzie told of his gradual movement away from medicine and anatomy into physical education. By 1903, as a direct result of his affiliation with a group of physical educators, characterized by its particular interest in body types, McKenzie, as Dr. Davidson clearly indicated in his paper, had created two pieces of sculpture, the "Sprinter" and the "Athlete." Discussing these works later, McKenzie remarked that they were "more or less inspired or encouraged by and grew in the atmosphere of this small group of enthusiasts who felt that they were missionaries in the education world." Actually, the physical culturists' fad of anthropometry which influenced McKenzie's "Sprinter" and "Athlete" was extremely short-lived; with the general abandonment of anthropometry, the sculptor would soon turn to the more traditional study of European masters. The early success of these pieces and his technique in creating them caused him to be criticized during his entire career as using anthropometry and anatomical knowledge to the detriment of good art. This criticism may have been valid, but was partly due to the wide publicity given his art work — publicity which emphasized his unusual background in medicine as well as his excellent knowledge of anatomy and his work in anthropometry.

During the summer of 1904, between jobs, McKenzie began the serious study of sculpture in the hope of rectifying the use of anthropometry in his work. These efforts were recorded in his manuscript entitled "Journal of the Tour in England and France, 1904." That summer he came into contact with a great many artists, including John Macallan Swan and Auguste Rodin, and studied both their approach to art and their working conditions.

After his brief stay in England, McKenzie traveled to Paris in search of a studio. During that summer in Paris, McKenzie expressed confidence in the progress of his work; he felt that it was becoming much stronger artistically. In Paris, he began work on the "Boxer";

he completed the piece later that year, and placed it on public exhibition, after returning to a new job.

In 1904, McKenzie reached a significant stage in his career when he left McGill University for the University of Pennsylvania, where he was presented expanded opportunity and outstanding support in pursuing his interest in physical education and art.

McKenzie traveled extensively throughout his life. In 1907, during one of his early trips abroad, he married Ethel O'Neil in Dublin. In a Philadelphia *Ledger* news report of their wedding she was quoted as saying, "Dr. McKenzie and I hope to make our house the centre of a large circle of musical and artistic people." Their interest in the arts made them friends around the world; throughout their marriage their talents complemented each other.

McKenzie's summer trip abroad in 1910 had an especial import, for it was then he met E. Norman Gardiner and Percy Gardner, noted researchers and writers on Greek sculpture. McKenzie's meeting with these scholars at Oxford proved to be highly significant to his future success as a sculptor of athletes [2]. These experts expressed their admiration of McKenzie's work in their studies of ancient Greek athletics, and Percy Gardner eventually drew a favorable comparison between the "Athlete" and the art of Greece. Unquestionably this long-standing friendship with Percy Gardner and E. Norman Gardiner and their comparison of his work with that of classic antiquity did much to shape McKenzie's image as a sculptor.

His growing reputation was also enhanced by exhibitions overseas. In a collection of American art shown at the Roman Exposition of 1911 and intended to be, as the catalog said, characteristic of the prevailing tastes and ideals in the United States at this day, McKenzie had five pieces of athletic sculpture displayed: the "Athlete," the "Supple Juggler," the "Competitor," the "Relay Runner" and the recently completed football group, the "Onslaught." Exhibiting by invitation in this important show established a period characterized by a strong tendency to reproduce nature in accurate detail and to revert to the ideals of Greek and oriental art. This was also a time in which American sculpture cultivated the form for form's sake, producing studies as esthetic ends in themselves. McKenzie adhered to this practice and devoted himself to sculpture in the nude — thus giving classic permanency to various phases of modern athletics that he considered so eminently important throughout his life.

Although his sculpture of athletes in the round continued to receive attention during this period of his life, McKenzie's portraits in relief also began to be noticed. Charles Wharton Stork, a poet and professor at Penn, writing in the *Old Penn Weekly Review*, compared his work to that of Franz von Lenbach, the "modern master painter" who studied and rendered each person individually [4]. Indeed, claimed Stork — and later critics echoed him — McKenzie's reliefs are his most perfect achievements and it is in portrait reliefs he is most successful [4]. At this juncture in McKenzie's art career, when several recognized European exhibitions had begun to display his work, the New York Metropolitan Museum of Art purchased two pieces, the "Supple Juggler" and the "Competitor," for its permanent collection.

Shortly thereafter McKenzie completed what many critics consider his finest work in relief, the "Joy of Effort," which was set into the wall of the great stadium at Stockholm on the occasion of the 1912 Olympics. The piece, showing three runners clearing a hurdle, was altered in design two years later, the most notable change being seen in the position of the hurdle.

Colonel Robert M. Thompson, then president of the American Olympic Committee, officially presented the "Joy of Effort" to Crown Prince Gustaf Adolph of Sweden. McKenzie must have been plased to have the medallion associated with the Olympic Games which he so enthusiastically supported.

In 1911, only seven years after he had come to Philadelphia, McKenzie received his first commission for a statue, one of Benjamin Franklin ordered by the Class of 1904 of the University of Pennsylvania. Called the "Youthful Franklin," it depicts its subject as "the poor boy, coming almost in the guise of the tramp to the city where he was to win fame and fortune."

In 1911 McKenzie also created a number of sculptural sketches of athletic figures. Such sketches include "Diver," "Watching the Pole Vault," "Discobolus Forward Swing," "Shot Putters: Preparing, Resting, Ready," "High Jumper Cleaning Shoe Number One," "High Jumper Cleaning Shoe Number Two," "Winded," "Wounded," "Tackle" (also known as "Head-on Tackle") and "Shot Putter, Hop."

McKenzie's football group, the "Onslaught," was his last sculpture depicting athletes in the round completed before World War I. He did not return to this particular way of immortalizing the athlete of his time until 1919, when he executed the "Flying Sphere," a classic study of a left-handed shot-putter following through after his release of the iron ball.

It was after World War I that McKenzie enjoyed his most successful exhibition, when 60 of his works were on display from

July 1 to August 21, 1920, at the Fine Arts Society, New Bond Street, London. As a result of McKenzie's fine showing in the London exhibition, he was asked to design the Cambridge memorial "Homecoming" — an honor which could be interpreted as a seal of merit on his work.

Still other honors came to McKenzie during these postwar years. In 1923 he was invited to the University of California to give two summer courses; while at Berkeley he lectured in Wheeler Hall and also had a show of his sculpture at Gump's in San Francisco, from July 23 to August 4 (Berkeley *Gazette*, July 16, 1923). The exhibition of approximately 60 pieces was well received in California. Laura Bride Powers, reviewing for the Oakland *Tribune*, fulsomely interpreted the meaning of his work in California. Her interpretation of McKenzie's work, reflecting the general sense of the times, had been expressed several years earlier by Frances Fisher Dubuc in a *New York Times* article (August 24, 1919). Dubuc believed that McKenzie's sculptured expression of his love of health, of its symptoms and of sane pleasures and activities expressed most successfully the prevailing sentiment of that era.

During the last five years of the decade, McKenzie's involvement in art intensified. His earlier successes had brought some lucrative commissions that required more of his attention,* leaving him increasingly less time for the heavy load of administrative work as the University of Pennsylvania's director of physical education. These diverse pressures prompted his decision to leave his academic post. Finally announcing his resignation in late May 1931, he remarked in an interview with the Philadelphia *Public Ledger* that "my work as a sculptor demands more time than I can give to it and retain my office at the University." The University officials, however, would not permit the distinguished sculptor, physician and physical educator to resign; instead they created a new post for him,

---

*These commissions included the following: (1925) "Victor," an 8-ft war memorial statue at Woodbury, New Jersey; (1926) "Dr. Edgar Fahs Smith," an 8-ft memorial on the University of Pennsylvania campus; (1927) "Percy Haughton" memorial, consisting of three plaques for a Soldiers Field monument at Harvard University; the "Call," an 8-ft figure combined with a 25-ft frieze representing a recruiting party which comprised his Scottish-American war memorial at the Princes Street gardens, Edinburgh; "Dean Andrew Fleming West," an 8-ft memorial statue at the graduate school, Princeton University; and "General James Wolfe," a 10-ft figure in Greenwich Park, London; (1931) the "Girard" memorial, an 8-ft statue at Girard College, Philadelphia; and the "Jane A. Delano" memorial, a 7-ft statue honoring World War I nurses at the Red Cross Building, Washington, D.C.

the J. William White Research Professor of Physical Education, "the first of its kind in the country." President Thomas S. Gates told the *Ledger* (May 30, 1931) that McKenzie's new assignment would "enable him to contribute through his research work, writings and sculpture to a field in which he already has made notable contributions."

At the opening session of the International Congress on Physical Education and Sport at Amsterdam in 1928, McKenzie discussed "Athletic Sports as an Inspiration for Art." The 28 years preceding these Olympic games and this speech had been called the golden age of modern athleticism, unparalleled since ancient Greece. McKenzie's total involvement with exercise and sports as a physician, physical educator and sculptor established him as an expert observer and interpreter of this phenomenon. Sports and games had greatly increased in number since the early Olympic Games of Greece, said McKenzie, adding that the current interest in athletic sports had no parallel in history. In words that seemed a directive to himself, he remarked in his opening session speech at Amsterdam that Greek athletics were brought to us "from their poets and sculptors and it now remains for the modern artist to put into imperishable form the power, beauty and virility of this great athletic revival in the midst of which we live." Although many sculptors contributed to the recording of sports of that golden age, McKenzie alone perpetuated it as the dominant theme of his labors.

In 1932, McKenzie had one of the largest displays of his work — a total of 67 pieces — at the Olympic art exhibition in Los Angeles. Some of the McKenzie entries had not been shown previously; among them was "Shield of Athletes," awarded the Olympic Games third prize in the medals and reliefs competition.* A great number of athletes are depicted on this beautiful medallion, which appears to represent a summary of his study of track and field athletes in action.

During his preparation of the Olympic art competition display, McKenzie also composed a lecture, "The Athlete in Sculpture," for the International Olympic Conference on Physical Education held at the University of Southern California from July 25 to August 5,

*Prize Winners in the International Olympic Competition and Exhibition of Art as Related to Sport. Los Angeles *Saturday Night*, August 6, 1932. See Mechlin, L.: Olympic Art Exhibition. *The American Magazine of Art*, 25:136-150, 1932. Awards in Sculpture of Medals and reliefs: first prize, Joseph Klukowski (Poland) for "Sport Sculpture II"; Second Prize, Frederick MacMonnies (U.S.A.) for his "Lindberg Medal."

1932. He called attention to the role of athletic action as a potential influence on art in the future, not a novel idea for McKenzie, but one which he seemed to voice more frequently after his appointment as research professor. Describing sculpture as "the medium peculiarly suited to portray athletic action," he added that "sculptors have always chosen the human body at rest and in action as the instrument for expressing their ideas, and nothing is more beautiful than the figure in the flower of its youth showing its strength, grace, and agility in the sports and games of the playing field, swimming pool and gymnasium."

In "Some Studies in the Sculpture of Athletes made during 1933-1934," a report concerning his research for the Department of Physical Education under the J. William White Foundation, McKenzie repeated his contention that "the artistic side of this great athletic revival has been comparatively neglected." He felt that sports and athletics were a vital phase of modern life — a phase which urgently needed interpretation in sculpture so that sports of his time could be preserved for the future.

There is no evidence of any formal showing of McKenzie's work after the 1936 Olympics in Berlin, where the "Invictus" and four other pieces were on display [1]. Subsequently a number of exhibitions were held, the most extensive of which was a posthumous showing of McKenzie's sculpture by the Philadelphia Art Alliance's University of Pennsylvania Bicentennial Celebration Memorial Exhibition, September 16-27, 1940. The showing consisted of 70 items.

The respect and affection expressed by so many of his friends and admirers during his lifetime were repeated in the many letters which came to his widow from all over the world after his death. McKenzie had achieved international fame not only as a sculptor but as an authority on health as related to physical activity. His career was "a triumph in industry, devotion and knowledge" wrote Sir Andrew McPhail, professor of the History of Medicine, to Mrs. McKenzie. He possessed a cultured and polished personality with the endearing qualities of humor, friendliness and fairness. Almost everyone who knew the man reported that along with his artistic ability, he had a manner that was simple and sincere, with an enormous capacity for friendship with all he met.

For decades R. Tait McKenzie worked with eager hands to interpret in sculptural form the splendid young athletes by whom he was surrounded. Posterity must be forever thankful for the industry, devotion and knowledge of the man who gave the world a sculptured concept of the athletic ideal.

References

1. Katalog der Olympischen Kunstausstellung. Olympisch Kunstausstellung, Berlin, July 15-August 16, 1936, p. 38.
2. McKenzie, R.T.: Diary of Summer, 1910. Entry of July 11. Copy in McKenzie Papers.
3. Mumford, E.W.: A Toast to McKenzie, 2, 3. Copy in McKenzie Papers, University of Pennsylvania Archives (unpublished manuscript).
4. Stork, C.W.: R. Tait McKenzie: Sculptor. Old Penn Weekly Review (University of Pennsylvania) 9:327-329, 1910.

Robert Tait McKenzie, le sculpteur

L'auteur traite des influences diverses qui ont amené le canadien Robert Tait McKenzie à s'intéresse aux arts et à devenir par la suite un sculpteur réputé. Le fait qu'il ont eu des amis artistes, ses connaissances de l'anatomie et son implication dans le sport ont influé sur ses oeuvres comme d'ailleurs l'ont fait les maîtres européens. L'aspect anthropométrique de ses sculptures illustre une recherche concentre des proportions ideales chez l'athlete.

Robert Tait McKenzie: Physical Educator

Stewart A. Davidson

The author analyzes the writings of Robert Tait McKenzie and underlines the contributions of this Canadian physician, physical educator and artist to sport, physical education, student health care, teacher training and professional organizations.

It is an honor and a privilege to present a paper at this International Congress of Physical Activity Sciences 1976. To warrant this honor it is essential that the paper be scholarly, historically valid and relevant to the international preoccupation of the Congress. I am certain that my fellow panelists would agree with this definition of our responsibility in this disciplinary seminar and I wish to express my personal appreciation to the organizing committee for asking me to join these illustrious gentlemen, Dr. Blackstock and Dr. Kozar, in attempting to place before you the inspiration of this great Canadian, Robert Tait McKenzie.

There is a great temptation, on an occasion such as this, to claim for Canada those accomplishments of McKenzie which we are hearing today. As a nation seeking its national identity and attempting to define its bicultural heritage, it is indeed tempting to reflect upon the talents of a native son and to ascribe to those talents something which is uniquely Canadian.

This approach would be, I suggest, not only contradictory to the theme of this International Congress, but would do a great disservice to the memory of Robert Tait McKenzie whose contribution to society through his practice of medicine, as an educator and as an artist, transcended all national boundaries and made him truly a citizen of the world. Our pride in McKenzie as a Canadian can be for the inspiration which his work as a healer, as a humanitarian and as a sculptor has provided for all who have come to know of him.

I would submit that it is, therefore, our professional obligation as physical educators to spread the message about this great man

Stewart A. Davidson, School of Human Kinetics, University of Ottawa, Ottawa, Ontario, Canada.

McKenzie. From a simple, rural community he moved out into the world and achieved fame and international recognition in *three* professions. His accomplishments in any one of these would be considered as more than could be expected for any one individual.

It is more than coincidental that it requires three speakers now to recount McKenzie's life; no one author could do it justice.

My particular responsibility on this panel is to present Robert Tait McKenzie, the physical educator.

I have drawn heavily upon McKenzie's own writings, from articles in professional journals and extracts from his books to identify those elements from his philosophy and his practice of physical education which are significant indicators of his inspirational impact upon our field.

McKenzie was one of the pioneers in the establishment of physical education in North America and the many letters he received from his colleagues in the field and the many articles written about him attest to the respect in which he was held in matters of research, teaching and organization of physical education programs.

His career as a sculptor coincided with the period of rapid increase in popular interest in physical education and his highly trained scientific eye made him a very competent recorder of the movements of athletes.

An article in the periodical *Saturday Night* (May 7, 1938) reporting on the death of McKenzie stated:

> It is possible that he will be known to posterity less as a sculptor than as the personification of the 20th Century movement towards the physical betterment of the human race.

As a youth in Almonte, Ontario, where he was born on May 26, 1867, McKenzie was himself athletic. He took part in gymnastics, football, skating, swimming, fencing and track and field. Possibly his greatest interest was in gymnastics and he shared this interest with his boyhood friend from Almonte, James Naismith, who later became famous, as surely you all know, as the inventor of the game of basketball.

Not a bad record, incidentally, for a little town like Almonte — producing two such famous men as Naismith and McKenzie — whose similar interests would have such international impact.

McKenzie looked upon the older Naismith as a brother. He was a boyhood hero of McKenzie's during their school days in Almonte and McKenzie credits Naismith for his interest in gymnastics and athletics [9].

Naismith won the Wickstead Silver Medal for Junior All-round Gymnastic Championship at McGill in 1884 and McKenzie subsequently won the same medal in 1887 when Naismith won the Gold Medal for Senior All-round Championship. Their teacher of gymnastics at McGill was Frederic S. Barnjum and when he died in 1889, Naismith was asked to take charge of the classes in gymnastics. This he agreed to do but only if McKenzie would agree to assist him in this work.

Naismith later went on to teach at the YMCA Training School at Springfield, Massachusetts, which was under the direction of Luther Gulick. Possibly as a result of Naismith's recommendation Gulick offered McKenzie a position on the staff at Springfield in 1893. There he gave an exhibition of high jumping "at which I was at that time an expert," and he wrote his very first paper "Hints on Teaching the High Jump" for *The Triangle* as a result of that experience [12].

Although McKenzie did not accept the staff position at Springfield his friendship with Gulick continued and, during the Olympic Games of 1904 in St. Louis, they worked together on observations of the temperature of athletes after the strenuous competition of the marathon race.

McKenzie was also strongly influenced by the work of such outstanding physical educators as Dr. Edward Hitchcock of Amherst, who was the first to use anthropometry in physical education; Dr. Dudley Allen Sargent of Harvard, an innovative inventor of gymnastic apparatus; and by Dr. Ernest Herman Arnold of the Anderson Normal School of Gymnastics, as a teacher.

It was Hitchcock's work in anthropometry which so influenced McKenzie's sculpture of "Sprinter" which he designed in 1902 and which was his first figure in the round. He used charts of anthropometric measurements of John D. Morrow, a McGill runner who was a Canadian Intercollegiate record-holder in the 440-yard run from 1903 until 1912. These charts included the measurements of other McGill track athletes such as Percy Molson, B. Howard and Dr. Fred J. Tees, and the composite became "Sprinter" [4].

McKenzie later reported in his book [13] how anthropometric measurement was employed in the search for a physical ideal as commissioned by the Society of Directors of Physical Education in Colleges in 1902.

> The Society . . . commissioned the modeling of a statuette embodying the average measurements and proportions of the pick of the student body, selected by taking the best

> fifty men in the all-round strength test (Sargent's strength test) for a period of eight years. These 400 sets of measurements were used to determine the proportions of the typical college athlete, who is represented as placing in his right hand the spring dynamometer with which he is about to test his grasping muscles. This youth may be said to embody the proportions and girths of the physically ideal American student of twenty-two. With a height of 5 feet 9 inches he carries a weight of 159 pounds. The girth of his neck, knee, and calf are the same, with the upper arm of 1½ inches less. The girth of his thigh is ½ inch less than that of his head. His expanded chest is 40 inches, the girth of his waist 10 inches less, his hip girth almost the same as his unexpanded chest, while the breadth of his waist barely exceeds the length of his foot, and the stretch of his arms measures 2 inches more than his height.

More than an interest in scientific investigation grew from McKenzie's association with Hitchcock. The "Amherst Plan," which Hitchcock initiated in 1861 and which included measurement, health supervision and regular exercise for students, was modified by McKenzie and put into effect at McGill University when he succeeded Naismith as physical training director in 1892 [7].

McKenzie's perception of the human body went much beyond mere scientific measurement. He was able to visualize the beauty of human performance and to transform that vision into clay through his gifted fingers. In an address which he delivered in Los Angeles during the Olympic Games of 1932 he expressed his feelings in these words:

> Wherever untrammeled youth is found, in camp, field, beach, or gymnasium; on land or in the river, lake, sea or swimming pool, there should be the sculptor with his appraising eye, his cunning hand, and his will to record his impressions, if an adequate interpretation is to be made of this great renaissance of athletic competition in which we are living for the most part unconsciously and too often with an unseeing eye [11].

He supports this position with reference to Greek artists who depicted athletes in action to give us an inspirational and historical record as well as an example for mechanical analysis.

In this same address, McKenzie deplored the fact that there was so little expression available from the painters and sculptors of the 1930s. He claimed:

> Sculpture is the medium peculiarly suited to portray athletic action. Sculptors have always chosen the human body at rest and in action as the instrument for expressing their ideas and nothing is more beautiful than the figure in the flower of its youth showing the strength, grace and agility in the sports and games of the playing field, swimming pool and gymnasium [11].

It is little wonder, then, that so much of McKenzie's sculpture depicted the athlete in a variety of sports and poses. A review of the sports sculpture illustrated in Dr. Kozar's excellent text, "The Sculptor of Athletes," shows the following sports to be represented: baseball, boxing, fencing, football, golf, gymnastics, rowing, skating (both speed and figure), swimming and diving, tennis, track and field (including the sprint, hurdles, relays, shot put, discus, javelin, pole vault, long jump and high jump) and wrestling.

To this list could be added the various figures depicting stunts requiring suppleness, dexterity or balance.

As it is to this aspect of McKenzie's life that Dr. Kozar will address his remarks, I shall resist the temptation to dwell at length on McKenzie's artistic works.

I must, however, speak of one piece which, in my opinion, is the best known and most inspirational of his sculpture for physical educators throughout the world.

I speak, of course, of the "Joy of Effort" which, I submit, resulted from McKenzie's ability to see beyond the actual performance of an athletic skill to a higher, more idealistic perception of man and competition.

The original of this medallion was placed in the wall of the stadium at Stockholm, Sweden to commemorate the Olympic Games of 1912. Small replicas are presented to professionals in the fields of sport and physical education in recognition of outstanding service and a graphic reproduction of the medallion appears on the cover of the *Journal of the Canadian Association for Health, Physical Education and Recreation.*

There is some controversy concerning what inspired McKenzie to create this sculpture. Mrs. McKenzie has been understood to say that the true inspiration came to the sculptor during an ocean trip as he watched a school of porpoises leaping through the waters. McKenzie's friend, Charles Wharton Stork, on the other hand, thought it was suggested by a Greek coin representing a chariot of the day.

Whatever the initial inspiration which caused McKenzie to create the medallion, the effect upon McKenzie's poet friend, Stork, was itself inspirational and caused him to write a beautiful poem which even today carries a message for all athletes:

The Joy of Effort

Eager as fire, impetuous as the wind,
  They spurn the ground and lightly clear the bar.
Three racers? Nay, three strong wills unconfined,
  Three glad, contending swiftnesses they are:
Three dolphins that with simultaneous leap
  Breast the high breaker of a tropic surge,
As flashing silvery from the purple deep
  And scattering foam, their curving backs emerge?
Three agile swallows, skimming near the ground
  That give their bodies to the buoyant air;
Three roebucks fleet that through the forest bound,
  Yet how can even such with men compare?
Not with mere pride of strength are these alive;
  The noblest joy of being is to strive [11].

What greater inspiration could we have who profess to serve mankind through sport and physical activity.

McKenzie had very strong feelings concerning sportsmanship and fair play in sports and games and this philosophy comes through clearly in a paper which was reported in the *American Physical Education Review* of February 1911 and in which he identified the Greek word Aidos as the spirit that should govern amateur competition. In this paper he described Aidos in these words:

Aidos is opposed to violence and servility.

Aidos puts into a man's heart the thrill and joy of the fight; restraining him from using his strength like a brute or from cringing to a superior force.

Aidos wins for him honor and respect in victory or in defeat, instead of terror from the weak and contempt from the strong.

Aidos includes scrupulous respect for personal honor and fairness that would make a team elect to risk defeat rather than win through the services of those who do not come within the spirit of a gentleman's agreement.

> *Aidos* is a spirit of modesty and dignity that obeys the law even if the decision seems unjust, instead of vocal protestations.
> *Aidos* cultivates in player and spectator alike wholesomeness of mind to be found best in clean manly sport.
> With *Aidos* in the hearts of the competitors, a sport which at first seems rough and brutal becomes a school for those manly virtues of self-control, courage and generosity [8].

Worthy indeed for our immediate reflection are these words of inspiration from the pen of McKenzie, for all men of whatever race, color or creed, of whatever nationality, to the end that the spirit of Aidos might permeate our athletic competitions.

It was during the late 1800s that the universities in North America began to play an important role in sports and athletics. While director of physical education at McGill University from 1892 to 1904 he fought hard for his belief that all students should be given a complete physical examination in order to determine the type and amount of physical activity in which they should engage. In a presentation to the Board of Governors at McGill in 1894 he stated:

> One half of the fight for physical training is won when the student can be induced to take a genuine interest in his bodily condition; want to remedy his defects, and to pride himself on the purity of his skin, the firmness of his muscles and the uprightness of his figure.

It was also during these formative years, in 1894, that McKenzie organized McGill's Athletic Association for intercollegiate competition. One of the association's responsibilities was to insure that any student who took part in football or "other violent athletic games" was given a thorough medical examination [5].

McKenzie carried his belief in physical exercise and medical examinations for all students with him on his new appointment in 1904 as a professor on the medical faculty of the University of Pennsylvania and director of physical education. He immediately brought into effect a physical examination and physical education classes were required for all students twice a week for four years, with credit toward graduation for successful participation and penalties for failure. He put forward his belief in this regard in a lecture he presented to the American Association for the Advancement of Science in 1909.

> The average man may be taken in classes which should begin by exercises of discipline, marching and setting-up movements to word of command. They should then be examined to find their ability to perform exercises of skill and classified according to their proficiency. A course of graded exercises should follow, closing with a re-examination [14].

In this same address, McKenzie attempted to distinguish between physical training and athletics.

> In physical training, the object is to bring the standard of health up to its highest level, and all excessive strain or exhaustion is avoided while all the activities are exercised.
>
> In athletic training, the object is to bring the human machine to its highest point of efficiency to perform a definite feat, and everything that is useless or detrimental is sacrificed . . . the object is not primarily health but superlative ability [14].

McKenzie also had a clear perception of the academic direction which university departments of physical education should follow. Soon after becoming director of physical education at the University of Pennsylvania, he submitted an article to the University's weekly revue known as *Old Penn* where he put forward his belief in these words:

> . . . the policy of the department (of physical education) may be said to contain something of the hospital clinic, a great deal of the classroom and laboratory, and a little of the arena [15].

McKenzie retired in 1931 and became research professor of physical education, but before retiring he presented the President of the University of Pennsylvania with a long-range plan for physical education at the university. One of the chief provisions of the plan was for a department of physical education composed of divisions of student health, physical instruction and intercollegiate athletics, all under a single dean and with a single budget.

The so-called "Gates Plan" was adopted in 1931 and this comprehensive department served as an administrative model for many colleges and universities which were attempting to find some way to control athletics and to insure that they became educational in nature [3].

Robert Tait McKenzie was a prolific writer. He published more than 100 articles in medical, educational and art journals. He edited a series of textbooks for the publishers Lea and Febiger. He contributed chapters on physical therapy to several medical books and even found time to write two books of his own which are classics in our field: Exercise in Education and Medicine, published by the W.B. Saunders Company in 1917 and *Reclaiming the Maimed*, published by the MacMillan Company in 1918.

McKenzie was truly a practicing professional in the field of physical education for 50 years of his life, from his first involvement as an instructor in gymnastics at McGill in 1888 until his untimely death in 1938. He practiced his profession as an athlete, as a teacher, as an administrator and as a writer. He also provided outstanding leadership through his active involvement with various professional organizations dedicated to the advancement of physical education.

He was the second of five Charter Fellows of the American Academy of Physical Education, which was organized in 1926, joining Clark W. Hetherington, who was number one, William Burdick, number three, Thomas Storey, number four, and Jay B. Nash, number five.

Hetherington, Storey and McKenzie had been members of an earlier Academy of Physical Education which had been organized by Luther Gulick in 1904. This had been an informal group that met for discussion for an entire week each year at a summer camp on Sebago Lake in Maine.

The new Academy was formally constituted in 1930 with McKenzie as president, a post he held until his death. The purpose of the Academy, as stated within its constitution, was clear and specific as outlined by McKenzie in an article he wrote for the AAHPER Journal in 1932:

> To advance knowledge in the field of physical education, to uplift its standards, and uphold its honor by:
>
> 1) selecting those who have made or are making significant contributions to the subject
> 2) making available trust funds for the purpose of research in physical education
> 3) encouraging promising students to enter this field of investigation
> 4) recognizing work of high merit and scholarship by appropriate awards
> 5) publishing results of investigation
> 6) furthering legislation in local, state and federal circles

7) keeping informed of significant work being done outside America [10].

McKenzie also served as president of the American Physical Education Association from 1912 to 1915. This organization, of course, was the forerunner of the American Association for Health, Physical Education and Recreation, which has subsequently become the American Alliance for Health, Physical Education and Recreation.

McKenzie was also president of the Society of Directors of Physical Education in Colleges in 1901, 1904 and 1909.

Some measure of the esteem with which McKenzie was held by his colleagues in physical education is illustrated by his commission by AAHPER in 1937 to design an official seal for the Association [1].

McKenzie conceived the idea of showing together the profiles of a typical American college boy and college girl. Typical of his dedication to scientific precision, he drew upon his past series of athletic figures which he had fixed in bronze as his guide for the man's profile. For the woman's profile he wrote to a large number of women's colleges for photographs of girls whom the various physical directors considered representative of the college girl of the day. After study of these photographs and posing by models who came nearest to the type, he completed the desired design.

The recognition by physical educators of McKenzie as a man dedicated to the education of youth culminated after his death in the purchase by AAHPER of the bronze "Column of Youth" which was suitably inscribed, mounted on a pedestal and placed in a prominent location in the National Education Association headquarters building in Washington, D.C., as a lasting memorial to Robert Tait McKenzie.

It also seemed appropriate that recognition of McKenzie should be demonstrated at his death by the very youth he had lived to serve. The famous Penn Relays had developed under McKenzie's administration of the athletic program at the University of Pennsylvania and it was in Philadelphia where McKenzie died in 1938. On the Saturday following his death, those same Penn Relays were being held at the very hour of his burial. With the flag at half-mast at Franklin Field in Philadelphia, three minutes of silence was observed by the youthful track athletes and then the relays continued. "The last race run, the final trophy won" [2].

Robert Tait McKenzie's overall philosophy was ageless and without constraint by international boundaries. His faith in youth and the value to be derived from physical activity permeated his every activity as physician, artist and physical educator.

He maintained that physical educators had a mission in life, to teach their students to preserve their health and physical efficiency, to learn certain muscular skills and to conduct themselves like gentlemen in the social relationships of competitive games. He believed that physical educators should use exercise as a means of keeping human beings well, rather than attempting to "cure and patch them up after they become ill" [6]. Surely this mission has international implication.

In conclusion, it seems most appropriate to note the perceptiveness of the organizers of this International Congress of Physical Activity Sciences in including this historical treatise on the life of Robert Tait McKenzie, for there is record of McKenzie's own participation in the International Congress of Physical Education in Paris in 1900, a Congress initially organized by Pierre de Coubertin in conjunction with the Universal Exposition in Paris in 1889 [16].

There is much more that has been recorded about Robert Tait McKenzie, as humanitarian, as valued contributor to the art and science of human movement. The words of your panelists today cannot do full justice to the accomplishments of McKenzie. It is to be hoped, however, that the inspiration of his example will provide added incentive for those of us who labor in his shadow in the field of physical education, in whatever country we might practice our profession.

References

1. Crapser, A.L.: The seal of the American Physical Education Association. CAHPER 3(4):203, 1937.
2. Day, J.: Robert Tait McKenzie: Physical education's man of the century. CAHPER 33(4):4, 1967.
3. Gerber, E.: Innovators and Institutions in Physical Education. Toronto: MacMillan Company, 1971, p. 345.
4. Howell, M.L. and Howell, N.: Sports and Games in Canadian Life. Toronto: MacMillan Publishing Company, 1969, p. 263.
5. Howell, M.L. and Howell, N.: Sports and Games in Canadian Life. Toronto: MacMillan Publishing Company, 1969, p. 82.
6. Kozar, A.J.: R. Tait McKenzie: Sculptor of Athletes. The University of Tennessee Press, 1975, p. 5.
7. Leys, J.: Theirs be the glory. From Tait McKenzie Memorial Address at McMaster University, Hamilton, Ontario. CAHPER 29(5):9, 1963.
8. McKenzie, R.T.: Aidos — A guide to fair play. CAHPER 31(5):3, 1965.
9. McKenzie, R.T.: Reminiscences of James Naismith. J. Am. Phys. Educ. Assoc. 4(1):21, 1933.

10. McKenzie, R.T.: The American Academy of Physical Education. J. Am. Phys. Educ. Assoc. 3(6):14, 1932.
11. McKenzie, R.T.: The athlete in sculpture. J. Am. Phys. Educ. Assoc. 3(9):41, 1932.
12. McKenzie, R.T.: Pioneers in physical education and the lessons we may learn from them. J. Am. Phys. Educ. Assoc. 2(9):6, 1931.
13. McKenzie, R.T.: Exercise in Education and Medicine, ed. 2. Philadelphia: W.B. Saunders Company, 1917, p. 269.
14. McKenzie, R.T.: The regulation of physical instruction in schools and colleges from the standpoint of hygiene. Science, March 1909, p. 481.
15. McKenzie, R.T.: Gymnasium dedicated. Old Penn 3:5, 1904.
16. Van Dalen, D.B. and Bennett, B.: A World History of Physical Education, ed. 2. Englewood Cliffs, N.J.:Prentice-Hall Publishing Company, 1971, p. 644.

Robert Tait McKenzie, professeur d'éducation physique

L'auteur analyse les écrits et les autres oeuvres de McKenzie et fait état de la contribution de ce médecin, éducateur physique et artiste canadien à l'avancement de l'éducation physique, du sport, des services de santé, de la formation des cadres et des groupements de professionnels.

The True Course Run by the Marathon Messenger: An Appeal to the International Olympic Committee for a Change

Ion P. Ioannides

Before proceeding to the object of my presentation, it is necessary to go back to the story of Marathon. It was toward the end of August 490 BC when the Athenians were informed that vast Persian forces had landed on Attic soil, at Marathon. The moment was most critical and a messenger named Pheidippides was sent to Sparta to ask for help, while the Athenian army marched in haste over the Pentele heights to meet the enemy.

The messenger, who was back at Athens after having covered the 450 km-distance in four days [5], set out without delay to Marathon to carry the answer to headquarters. When the Athenian generals received the negative answer of Sparta, they decided to face the enemy alone [7], and the next day, before daybreak, they lined up their men and moved against the foe.

Any reasonable voice would have said that this action of so few against so great a multitude of yet unbeaten Persians was an insane march to suicide. Yet, the Athenians ventured upon it; it was the spirit of the free man's inborn dignity and the thought that they were fighting for their homes and their temples that gave them the will for this action.

When the Athenians came within range of the Persian arrows, they started advancing at a run [5]. The enemy was caught by surprise; the appearance of the onstorming men from the hilltops, with shield and lance in thundering crash, was more than the Oriental soldiery could stand. They thought their opponents were possessed by demons. Soon in panic and confusion they ran back to the shore, where those who had escaped the slaughter were picked up by those on the ships.

Ion P. Ioannides, Ministry of Education, Athens, Greece.

The violent, hand-to-hand fighting, where the free man's courage, the well-trained body and the mighty force of the long lance had the decisive word, thus lasted only a few hours. Before noon the great battle was over.

I have paused over the Marathon episodes for two reasons: First, it is worth knowing the circumstances of a battle which represents the triumph of freedom and dignity over despotism and tyranny and, in Bury's words [2], is a turning point in humanity's destiny. Second, in the details of this battle one can trace the background of the marathon race.

History always looked on Marathon as marking an epoch: the feat of the 10,000 men running a distance of over 1500 meters to attack the enemy; their courage in engaging in such an uneven fight; the story of Pheidippides [1, 8-10], the heroic messenger delivering the news of the victory from Marathon to the Athenians* — all manifestations of an unusual human power and will — must have fired the imagination of men in later times very vividly and thus created the ideological climate which gave birth to the marathon race.

The new athletic event was introduced into the program of the Olympic Games in 1896, after an appeal by the scholar Michel Bréal of the Sorbonne, a friend of Coubertin, to commemorate the historic battle and at the same time to revive the memory of the legendary messenger.

Bréal, deeply impressed by the spirit of Marathon, wished to link its memory with the newly revived Olympic Games [3, 4]. The appeal was readily accepted by the Organizing Committee, and the Games technicians drew up the plans, made the village of Marathon the starting place, measured the road to Athens and on the given day the marathon race took place, becoming the greatest success of the Games. The memory of the historic battle, the beauty of the surroundings and the idyllic country road gave a special charm to the race.

---

*There is no clear historical evidence about this messenger. However it was very natural, after such a critical battle, for someone to run to Athens. Messengers who ran to their home cities to carry the news of victory are often mentioned, even in earlier times, i.e., in the 28th Olympiad, 668 BC, when the Eleans were engaged in war with the Dymaians and the decisive battle took place on the day of the Games. The Eleans won and an opletes ran to Olympia to tell the news to the archons.

We have a similar case in Delphoi during the first Holy War (Philostr. *Gymnastikos*, 7).

Eusebios: *Cronicle*, 113th Olympiad, "Argeus, winner of the Dolichos race, announced his own victory in Argos on the same day."

As time passed, the humble village of Marathon grew into a small town, the surroundings and the road to Athens lost their beauty and with the development of high-performance athletics* and the ever growing urge for records a change came over the character of the marathon race; it became exclusively an athletic event.

Efforts have been made by the Hellenic Olympic Committee to restore Bréal's original vision of the race by issuing pamphlets about its origin and by calling it "classical." The efforts, however, have so far been ineffective, and it remains the general belief that the marathon race has come to be considered as no more than a stop-watch event. No serious interest has been given to its cultural background, and this becomes more evident from the fact that the starting place of the race continues to be the entrance of a village (a modern village called Marathon) instead of the Tymbos, the burial place of the Athenian soldiers [11], and that the athletes still run on a road which is not the actual route taken by the ancient [2] messenger.

This last thought somehow attracted my interest, and two years ago, at a seminar in Vienna, in giving a paper on the Cultural Background of the marathon race [6] I also referred to the probable route taken by the messenger to Athens.

Recently, I set out to study further all the evidence related to the battle of Marathon, the camping grounds of the armies, the topography of the area and, more extensively, the various pathways leading to Athens. Often in the company of E. Vanderpool of the American School of Classical Studies and with veteran marathon race champions (Stelios Kyriakides, the winner of the 1946 Boston Marathon, and Chr. Varzakes), I walked all these paths to get a direct personal perception of the problem.

My conclusion is that the most probable route must have been the road which, starting from the Tymbos, passes near the Temenos of Heracles Sanctuary, crosses the Vrana stream, ascends past the monastery of Agios Georgios and along a narrow pass between the heights of Agriliki and Aphorismos and arrives at the Dionysos stream.† It then continues its ascent through a dense pine forest and

---

*In 1896 there were 13 nations participating in the Games and 285 athletes. Today there are more than 122 participating nations and about 10,000 athletes.

†In an article about *the Marathon Messenger* by Prof. A. Katsouros, analyzing the local folklore tale, the track is located between Aphorismos and Kotroni heights, that is, in the next pass which leads to Stamata village. I have been informed that Emil Zatopek, *in search of the trail of Pheidippides*, ran from Tymbos along the same pass.

joins a forest road which leads to the famous Dionysos Sanctuary. At this point the distance from the Tymbos is 9 km and the altitude about 350 meters above sea level. The greatest altitude of the official route is 250 meters at Stavros.

From the Dionysos Sanctuary onward the road is asphalt, still steep for about half a kilometer and then it descends gently through the beautiful suburbs of Ekale, Kephisia, Marousi* and Psychiko to the Panathenaic Stadion. The total distance is about 34 km, about 8 less than the distance of the now official marathon route.†

The arguments in favor of this route over the Pentele heights are the shortness of the distance and, above all, the safety which it secured for the messenger, a safety not afforded by the route along the coast. Particularly in favor of the path leading from the Tymbos to Dionysos is the fact that it is an easier ascent and that it passes by the great Sanctuary; this last factor alone makes it almost certain that this path was the one most used and consequently the shortest in the area.

As for the difficulty that this route might present, the opinion of athletes, who ran along the path from the Tymbos to the Dionysos Sanctuary,‡ is that the fresh air and the passage over beautiful mountainsides and through shaded forests greatly diminish the strenuousness of the effort. Besides, the ascent is only on the first third of the route, while the remaining two thirds are all downhill. Furthermore, the distance of the ancient route is shorter and this makes the race more humane.

In closing, I would like once again to urge the view that the significance and the beauty of the marathon race will be fully revealed and appreciated and thus link the spirit of classical Greece with the modern Olympic Games more strongly, when this race, held in memory of the ancient Marathon messenger, follows the true route run by him and when it has its starting line at the Tymbos.

With these thoughts in mind, I would like to add most warmly that a bold but very justified decision of the International Olympic Committee would be, in future Olympiads, to hold the marathon race at its classic birthplace. The event could be held very fittingly on the day of the lighting of the torch at Olympia. The change would

---

*The home village of Spyridon Loues, the Marathon Race winner of the first Olympic Games 1896.

†The distances and the altitudes have been kindly calculated, on special topographical maps and air photographs, by the engineer Nikos Donkakes of the Ministry of Public Works.

‡They were student-athletes of the Academy of Physical Education, Athens.

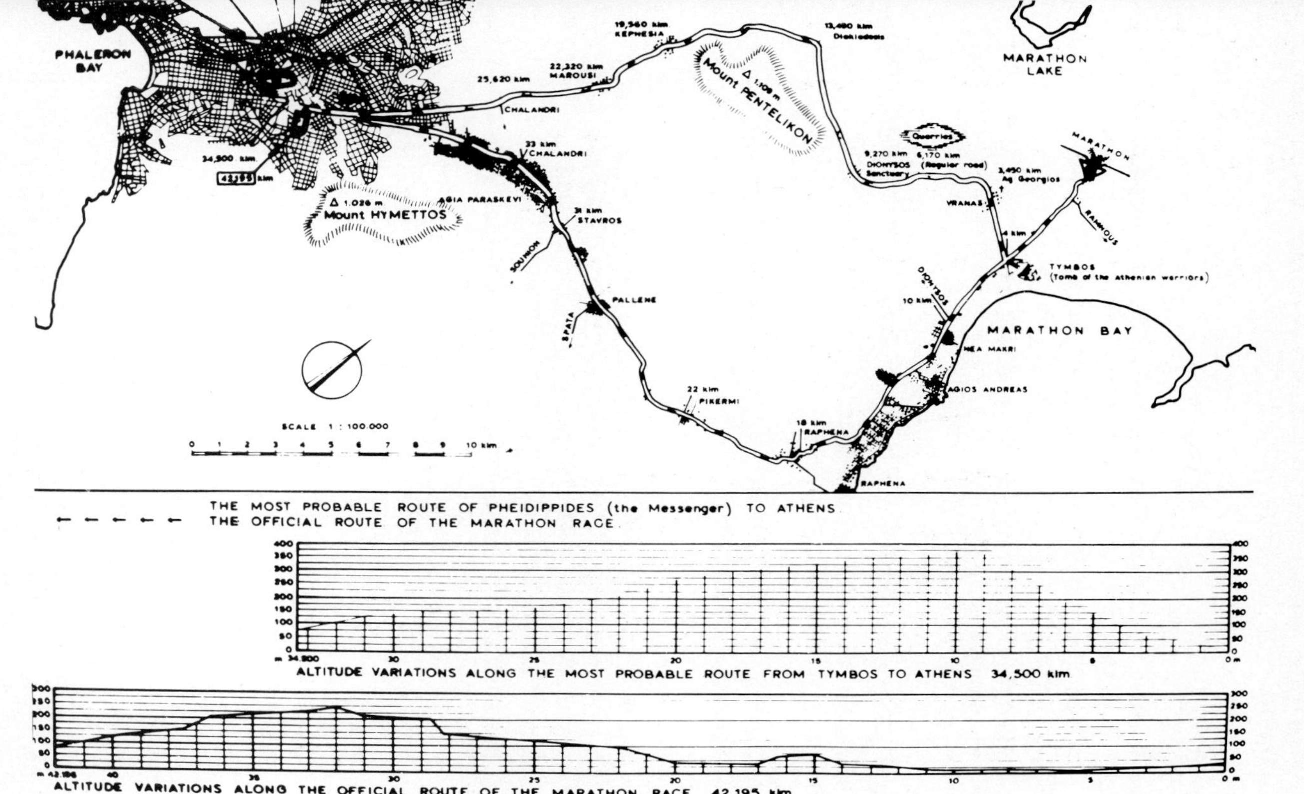

FIG. 1. Prof. Bréal of the Sorbonne, deeply imbued with the vision of the marathon, introduced the marathon race in the first Olympic Games in Athens. To be true to the spirit of this commemoration the start of the race should be at Tymbos, the actual ground of the battle, and the runners should follow the path through the Dionysos Sanctuary, the most probable route run by Pheidippides.

give a still greater significance to the marathon race and contribute to the promotion of the Olympic ideal.

References

1. Allinson, F.G.: The Original Marathon Runner. Clas. Weekly XXIV 152.
2. Bury, J.B.: A History of Greece. pp. 238, 239, 243, 244.
3. de Coubertin, P.: The Olympic Idea. 1966, pp. 116-117.
4. Diem, C.: Olympische Flamme. 2 (1942) 581.
5. Herod. VI, pp. 105-108, 112.
6. Ioannides, I.P.: Track and Field Q 75 (4):56-59, 1975.
7. Isokr. Panegyrikos. p. 86.
8. Loukianos: A Slip of the Tongue in Greeting. 3.
9. Ploutarchos: On the Fame of the Athenians. C 347.
10. Romaios, K.: The Marathon Runner of 490 BC. Gymnastiké Anagennesis, 4/5 (1962) 63-65.
11. Thoukydides: The Peloponnesian War, II 34, 5.

The Nemean Festival

Dale P. Hart

Introduction

Of the four ancient Greek Panhellenic game festivals (Olympic, Pythian, Isthmian and Nemean), the Olympic and Pythian Festivals have received the most attention by archeologists and historians. For the most part, the Isthmian and Nemean festivals have warranted only brief and sketchy comment, especially by sports historians. The most complete history and description of the Nemean Festival appeared in 1910.* The purpose of this paper is to provide a more accurate and complete history and description of the ancient Nemean athletic festival.†

Ancient Greece could never be classified as a nation since the Greek people were never politically united, except during the Roman era. Nevertheless, a number of common characteristics and shared experiences enabled the Greeks to view themselves as a unique race or group of people. Although the Greeks were widely dispersed and never politically united, they shared the following characteristics: a common descent, religious ideals, language and customs. One link which united neighboring city-states, especially during the early stages of Greek civilization, consisted of common worship and sacrifices at religious shrines.‡ In many cases, this common worship had the effect of politically uniting the participant city-states. The unification of Greece was also strengthened by the oracles, which

---

Dale P. Hart, Department of Physical Education, Brockport State College, Brockport, New York, U.S.A.

*The most complete history and description of the Nemean Festival appeared in Gardiner, N.E.: *Greek Athletic Sports and Festivals.* London: MacMillan and Co., Limited, 1910, pp. 66-67, 223-226.

†The continuation of a current large-scale excavation at ancient Nemea (under the auspices of the University of California at Berkeley) will most likely augment and perhaps alter the observations reported in this paper.

‡"Amphictyony" was the term given to the various religious-political Greek confederacies. Before the establishment of the first amphictyonies, there were no strong uniting ties among the Greek people. Each tribe worshipped in its own peculiar manner before its own altars. For a detailed discussion of the Greek Amphictyonies see Curtius, E.: *History of Greece*, Volume I. New York:Charles Scribner's Sons, 1867, pp. 123-131.

were most often under the supervision of an amphictyony.* The oracles served the purpose of moderating the problems among the Greek people. The Panhellenic Games or Festivals served as another binding force among the Greeks.

Origin of the Nemean Festival

Like the origin of many ancient Greek traditions and institutions, the origin of the Nemean Festival is shrouded in mythology. According to one myth, the origin of the Nemean Festival was directly related to the death of Opheltes, son of Lycurgus, who was king of Nemea. When the Seven against Thebes approached Opheltes' nurse to ask where they might find water, the nurse left her young charge in a grove of cypress trees while she accompanied the Seven to a spring, which was later called Adrastea. While the nurse was on this mission to find water, Opheltes was poisoned by a serpent bite and he died. The Nemean Games were supposedly founded in his honor. Another myth indicates the existence of a so-called Nemean lion who lived in a cave on Mount Tretus between Mycenae and Nemea. The lion had caused much destruction to the people of the countryside who wanted him killed. However, this lion could not be killed with any weapon of bronze, iron or stone. As the first of his labors for Eurytheus, Heracles was directed to kill this destructive animal. When Heracles arrived near Mount Tretus, he stopped at the hut of a peasant named Molorchus who had lost his son to the ravaging lion. Molorchus was preparing a sacrifice to Hera. Heracles told Molorchus that he intended to kill the lion and instructed the peasant to wait 30 days. If Heracles had not returned after 30 days, Molorchus was instructed to offer sacrifices to Heracles, the hero. If Heracles did return, the sacrifices would be made to Zeus. Heracles proceeded to the lion's cave and found the beast, but his arrows, sword and club had no effect on the animal, who retreated unharmed. Heracles then blocked one of the two entrances to the cave and strangled the beast

---

*An oracle can refer to an extremely holy location where a prophecy was given, the prophecy itself or the priestess located at the shrine who gave the prophecy. The priestess (oracle) was assumed to possess the ability to communicate with the gods. The patrons of the oracles were frequently given advice related to domestic and foreign affairs. For an in-depth discussion of oracles, see Holm, A.: *History of Greece*, Volume I. London:MacMillan and Company, 1894, pp. 225-231.

with his hands. He carried the lion to the peasant's house where the sacrifice was made to Zeus. The Nemean Festival was reorganized by Heracles in honor of Zeus [1, 3, 4].

From these two myths, one may conclude that the Nemean Games were originally funeral games, but they may have been altered at a later date to honor the god Zeus. There is some dispute as to whether the victor's crown at Nemea was made of parsley or of celery. If it was made of parsley, this would certainly support the idea that the games were originally funeral games, since parsley was sacred to the dead in ancient Greece [1]. On the other hand, if the crown had been made of celery, this too would seem a plausible connection with funeral rites, since the nurse laid the infant Opheltes on a bed of celery when she sought water. The umpires for the games always wore somber-colored garments to remind people that the games were connected with the death of Opheltes. The fact that the coins of ancient Argos, a city-state near Nemea, frequently represented the death of Opheltes further substantiates the myths surrounding the origin of the games [3]. The myth about Heracles slaying the Nemean lion is probably more contemporary than the Opheltes myth, since the Panhellenic Game Festivals had their origin prior to 1000 BC when athletics were frequently conducted as funeral rites. After the Mycenean period, many Greek athletic festivals began to assume a religious character; thus, the Nemean Festival was probably reorganized to honor the god Zeus [6, 7].

Control of the Nemean Festival

The first recorded Nemead occurred in 573 BC at Nemea. (Nemea is located on the Peloponnese about 13 miles southwest of Corinth.) Ancient Nemea was not known as a city but rather as a sanctuary of Zeus. Nemea was so small that it could not assert its independence, and even as a sanctuary, it was controlled by one of its neighbors [10]. Until about 460 BC the presidency of the games belonged to Kleonai, a small city to the east of Nemea. Some evidence accredits Corinth with the control of the Nemean Games during the decade of the 460s BC [2, 8, 9]. Another source indicates that Argos, a large city to the south of Nemea, got control of the games as early as 460 BC [5]. This seems plausible since Kleonai, when threatened by Corinth, aligned itself with Argos, thereby giving Argos the right to organize or share in the organization of the Nemean Games [10]. The games were actually transferred to the city of Argos in about the middle of the third century BC.* It is certain that the games were in Argos sometime before 235 BC, since Aratos held the games at Nemea in protest to those at Argos.† We are not sure whether they continued at Nemea beyond 235 BC, but they were definitely held at Argos by 225 BC.‡ Most sources suggest that the games were held in Argos during the late third and early second centuries BC.§ An inscription found at Nemea suggests that Mummius in 145 BC moved the games back to Nemea [2]. Recent discovery of archeological evidence at Nemea suggests a period of great activity during the middle of the second century BC, thus supporting the idea that the games were transferred to Nemea in 145 BC. We do not know just how long the games remained at Nemea; however, by the Imperial period the games were back at Argos [3]. Hadrian is accredited with reviving an interest in the games [3] and with starting winter games; however, it is uncertain during which years and where they were held. Recent excavations suggest that the stadium at Nemea was used until sometime during the second century AD; however, this does not imply that the games were held there. Most likely the games were held at Argos until Christianity abolished them due to their relationship to the worship of pagan gods [9].

The Importance of the Nemean Festival

The Nemean Games were especially athletic when compared to the Pythian and Isthmian Games. Only the Olympic Games were more important in terms of athleticism. Prior to the transference of the games to Argos, the games were almost totally athletic. The program of events could be compared to that at Olympia; however, the hoplite and hippios races seemed to be of special attraction at Nemea [4].

The importance of the Nemean Festival, in terms of Panhellenism, was less than the other three Panhellenic Game Festivals because the Nemean Festival was much more parochial. Records indicate that most of the competitors at Nemea came from the Peloponnese. Most likely this was because Nemea was located in a rather remote area

---

*Cf. Vollgraff, *Mnemosyne* 44, (1916), pp. 65-69, 221-232.

†Cf. Plutarch, *Aratos*, 28, 3-4.

‡Cf. Plutarch, *Cleomenes*, 17, 7.

§Cf. Plutarch, *Philaopoemen* 11, 1-2; *Flamininus*, 12, 2; *Polybros*, 2, 70, 4-5; *Livy*, 27, 30, 9; 34, 41, 1.

and Nemea had few attractions other than athletics [4]. This would seem especially attractive to the Peloponnesians, since they were purportedly more athletically minded than other Greek people.

Recent Excavations

Excavations at Nemea during the 20th century provide us with a somewhat more complete conception of the festival site. After the French School of Archeology ceded its rights to the American School of Classical Studies in Athens (1924), there have been several archeological campaigns at Nemea. Hill and Belgan (1924-1926) excavated structures they called the gymnasium and palaestra. In addition they discovered the water channel of the stadium. Inside the Temple of Zeus (a portion of which stands today), they discovered a unique crypt. It has been suggested that the crypt led down to the remains of a more ancient temple and that this crypt was in some way associated with their religious services. In front of the Temple of Zeus has been found an unusually long sacrificial altar (approximately 40 meters in length). The length of the altar attests to the importance of Nemea as a place of worship [8, 9].

The stadium at Nemea, which is about 450 meters from the Temple of Zeus, was created by leveling and extending out a race course (like a tongue) from a depression between two hills. Thus, the builders took advantage of the potential seating area between the two hills. Thus far the excavations provide evidence of an informal seating arrangement inside the stadium. Seats were carved out of the bedrock on the hillsides. It has also been found that the race course (if excavations confirm predictions) will be no longer than 180 meters, a rather short course when compared to other Greek stadia [8, 9].

Conclusion

The Nemean Festival has a history similar to the other Panhellenic Game Festivals. It had its origin during Mycenean times but was reorganized during the sixth century BC, much like the other Panhellenic Festivals. It did not achieve as much fame as the other Panhellenic Festivals because of its remote location and exceptionally strong Doric character. In addition, political instability over the control of the games most likely made them less popular among the Greeks. Continued excavations at Nemea should hopefully provide us with a more accurate account of the festival and games themselves.

References

1. Avery, C.B. (ed.): The New Classical Handbook. New York:Appleton-Century-Crofts, Inc., 1962, pp. 74, 341-342.
2. Brandeen, D.W.: Hesperia 35:326, 328, 1966.
3. Frazer, J.G. (trans.): Pausanias's Description of Greece. Volume III, by Pausanias. London:MacMillan and Company, 1898, pp. 92, 93, 307.
4. Gardiner, N.E.: Greek Athletic Sports and Festivals. London:MacMillan and Company, 1910, pp. 66, 225-226.
5. Grote, G.: History of Greece. London:John Murray, 1888, p. 290.
6. Harris, H.A.: Greek Athletes and Athletics. London:Hutchinson and Company, 1964, p. 35.
7. Holm, A.: History of Greece. London:MacMillan and Company, 1894, pp. 241-242.
8. Miller, S.G.: Excavations at Nemea 1975. Hesperia 45 (January-March 1976). (Page numbers cannot be given since author had access to manuscript before it appeared in *Hesperia.*)
9. Miller, S.G.: Excavations at Nemea 1973-1974. Hesperia 44:149, 171, 1975.
10. Tomlinson, R.A.: Argos and the Argolid. Ithaca New York:Cornell University Press, 1972, pp. 31, 136-137.

The Ancient Greek Pentathlon Jump: A Preliminary Reinterpretive Examination

Robert Knight Barney

Introduction

In the late eighth century BC post-Mycenean Greeks introduced the pentathlon event to the program of the oldest of the Crown Festivals — the Games at Olympia. The ancient pentathlon, comprised of five subevents (running, jumping, discus and javelin throwing and wrestling) remained a part of the Greek athletic festival scene until the virtual demise of organized sport in antiquity, some 400 years after the birth of Christ.

Of the five pentathlon subevents, the jump has aroused the most controversy and speculation in terms of scholarly efforts aimed at determining exactly how the exercise may have been carried out. To date, the theories advanced by investigators of the subject can be indexed into three distinct categories: (1) the espousals of the single jump hypothesists, (2) the theses of the double jump theorists and (3) the hypotheses of the multiple jump school of thought. Of the latter group two trends of possibility emerge: (1) the triple jump theory and (2) the quintuple jump thesis. However, each of the above hypotheses demonstrates weaknesses in interpretation of the primary literary and archeological evidence. Further, the scholarly juxtaposition of basic performance testing in jumping, coupled with intuitive logic, simply does not stand the test of critical inquiry. In his analysis of the known evidence on the pentathlon jump, in combination with performance tests on modern multiple jumpers, the writer advances the theory that the jumping exercise was a running quadruple leap. That particular type of jump is the best explanation pertinent to the evidence.

Robert Knight Barney, University of Western Ontario, London, Canada.

Some Common Consensus

Before considering in brief context the leading theories on how the jump was carried out, perhaps a short explanation might be helpful of those points that have achieved consensus among scholars. Particularly important are the following:

1. The collected evidence proves quite conclusively that the pentathlon jump was performed for linear distance rather than for height.

2. The pentathlon jumper always performed his competitive exercise while carrying hand weights called *halteres*. *Halteres*, while they quite conceivably could have been pressed into use in the gymnasium as ancient forms of dumbbell apparatus, were employed during the jumping exercise in the stadium to provide extra impetus for one's flight through the air, as well as to help the jumper come to a distinct landing in the *skamma* (landing pit). Philostratus tells us:

> The jumping weight is an invention of the pentathlete and was invented for use in jumping . . . and they gave him wings by means of this jumping weight; it is a sure guide for the hands and brings the feet firmly to the ground in good form. The rules show of what value this latter point is, for they do not permit the jump to be measured unless the footprints are just right (Philostratus, *Gymnastics*, as cited by Robinson [19]).

3. From repeated references in classic literature and a countless number of depictions on Greek pottery, we know also that the jumping exercise was accompanied by the music of the double flute or *diaulos*. Philostratus tells us of the value of the music to the jump:

> For the rules regard jumping as one of the most difficult exercises, and allow the jumper to be spurred on by the flute [19].

4. The point from which the jump originated and commenced to be measured was called the *bater*. It is thought by many that the *bater* in reference to the pentathlon jump may well have been one of the stone sills used also to mark the start (and in some stadia, the finish) of running races. In any event, the Greek term *bater* can have a broad connotation, meaning origin, point of departure, beginning, threshhold, treading point, etc.

Some Points of Contention

There are at least two major points of contention which have caused a great deal of controversy and speculation in trying to interpret the exact nature of the pentathlon jump. They concern (1) the distance that ancient pentathlon jumpers may have been able to leap and (2) the performance format of the jumping exercise itself, in terms of it being a single, double or some type of multiple jump.

The Distance

The literary record of Greek athletic achievement relative to distances that performers might have thrown the discus or javelin or leaped in the pentathlon jump is extremely limited. Left for modern man's contemplation, conjecture and interpretive logic, however, is the well-known epigram describing the leaping and discus throwing abilities (perhaps a lack of ability in the latter case) of one Phaÿllos of Croton, who triumphed twice in the pentathlon event at Pythian Festivals early in the fifth century BC. The epigram reports that Phaÿllos "jumped five over fifty feet and threw the discus five short of 100" [9]. The prodigious leap was reported to have carried Phaÿllos 5 feet beyond the *skamma*, at which point his impact on the hard ground resulted in his breaking a leg (Suidas, as cited by Harris [12]). Phaÿllos' performance thus surpassed a recorded 52-foot jump at Olympia by Chionis of Sparta in the middle of the seventh century BC (Julius Africanus, as cited by Gardiner [7]). Further, Ebert suggests [2] that an inscription recovered at Delos, interpreted by Werner Peek, alluded to the phrase: "Fifty feet jumped here . . ." The sum conclusion of the above is that jumps of over 50 feet seemed to have been possible under the format conditions for carrying out the pentathlon jump. Some scholars, however, have seen fit to cast aside the literary messages on length of jump, thus creating conflict with those investigators who have tended to accept the literature, at least as a starting point for interpretation. Of the disclaimers, Durant has remarked: "We must not believe all the Greeks have told us" [1]. Then, too, Gardiner has been particularly critical, attaching no credibility whatsoever to the recorded jumps of Phaÿllos and Chionis, passing them off as "alliterative jingle," classic examples of the farfetched sporting myth and "absolutely worthless, and such as no historian would think of recognizing" [9]. But historians must lean most on "that said" rather than on "that left unsaid." To do otherwise would be tantamount to committing scholarship's gravest felony — selection only of the evidence that lends credence to a point made, while ignoring that which tends to undermine a thesis. The fact remains that by far the greater number of investigators have accepted the literature on the Phaÿllos and Chionis jumps and have since labored long and tediously in interpretive effort aimed at seeking out the truth.

The Performance Format of the Jump: Single, Double or Multiple?

Of those who have made the most distinctive examinations of the pentathlon jump the most notable have been (1) a body of late 19th century German scholars in the fields of anthropology, archeology and classical history [3, 4, 15-17, 20], (2) the early 20th century English writer E. Norman Gardiner and (3) two somewhat more contemporary investigators, Joachim Ebert, the German, and Harold A. Harris, the distinguished classical scholar from Britain. Each has presented strong arguments for his particular stance on the subject.

1. *The single jump thesis:* Gardiner, the eminent British scholar of ancient Greek athletics, is perhaps the foremost exponent of the theory that the pentathlon jump was a single leap. Gardiner took strong exception to any 55-foot jump theory, pointing out that the earliest record of such a jump having been performed came from the writings of Zenobias, contemporary to Phaÿllos' time in history by six centuries. Further, Gardiner is of the stated opinion that the remarks of Julius Africanus, writing in the first century AD, in referring to Chionis' seventh century jump of 52 feet, made a simple coypist's error. Africanus' passage should have read 22 feet. Africanus' notation read vB′ (55 feet). Gardiner believes that the v (signifying 50) should have been a k (denoting 20). He points to the translation of Africanus in the Eusebian Chronicles (Armenian Latin) that reads: "duos et vigini cubitus" — 22 feet, according to Gardiner [9]. Gardiner, an unusually shrewd interpreter of the Greek athletic past, as literary and archeological recovery made since the time of his death have proven him to be, rejects the "more-than-one-jump" theory completely. "There is no evidence for the triple jump," he concludes. "The Greeks jumped very much as we do, that they took off from a hard *bater* and landed in the soft *skamma*" [9].

2. *The double jump thesis:* Harris, successor to Gardiner as the most penetrating scholar on the subject of ancient Greek athletics, is the major exponent of the prospect that the pentathlon jump was indeed a double leap. It is curious to note that prior to the 1968 Olympic Games in Mexico City, at which festival Robert Beamon of the United States astounded followers of track and field by long jumping in excess of 29 feet, Harris had at least posed the theory of a double jump: "The inescapable conclusion . . . would seem to be that the Greek long jump was a triple or more probably a double jump. If Greek jumpers gained some help from their weights, this makes

Phaÿllos' 55 feet and Chionis' 52 feet plausible as exceptional feats by oustanding performers at a double jump" [12]. Beamon's astonishing performance did much to substantiate Harris' feeling on the matter.

3. *The triple jump thesis:* The theory that the pentathlon jump was a triple jump became a popular conclusion of late 19th century German investigators of which Wassmansdorf was perhaps the first (Wassmansdorf, as cited by Jüthner [15]). Enlarging on Wassmansdorf's work, fellow countryman, Fedde [4] proposed a pentathlon jump of two preliminary skips followed by a long and assertive jump, all three segments taken in rapid succession. The "more-than-one-jump" proposition is admirably served by ancient literary comments which point to the fact that the pentathlon jump was an exercise more complex than that seen in the long jump of modern times. For instance:

a. In his commentary on Aristotle's *Physics*, Themistius cites the jump of the pentathlon as an example of motion which is not continuous [12]. Most investigators have interpreted Themistius' analogy in a way supporting the multiple jump theory. A single jump from takeoff to landing is certainly an example of continuous motion. A triple jump, or any multiple jump for that matter, is necessarily broken into distinct parts whereby linear motion is transferred to vertical motion and thence to linear motion once again — an excellent example of motion which is discontinuous.

b. In a lexicon of the 10th or 11th century AD encyclopedists present us with interesting definitions of the familiar term *bater.* Seleukos defines the term as "the edge of the jumping pit from which they make the first jump" [13]. Symmachos says that the *bater* is "the middle from which having jumped they jump again" [13]. Both definitions, by use of the words "first" and "again," point to the jump being more than one leap.

The modern triple jump record is currently a trifle over 58½ feet, thus prodding one to view an ancient Greek pentathlon triple jump of over 50 feet as entirely reasonable. But two questions are raised. What is really meant by Symmachos' statement concerning the "middle"? Did the term middle refer to the "middle jump" or the approximate geographical middle of the overall pentathlon leaping exercise? This writer is inclined to favor the latter, hence a discarding of the triple jump thesis in favor of a quadruple jump.

4. *The quintuple jump postulation:* Ebert [2] has treated in depth the prospect of the ancient pentathlon jump being an exercise in which the athlete, starting from an original point, executed five

successive standing long jumps. His argument is interesting in that such a jump would fit nicely into the mold of credibility built by the literary comments already noted (except Symmachos, using this writer's interpretation). Then, too, there would be little to argue about in terms of five standing broad jumps adding up to a distance in excess of 50 feet. The weakness of Ebert's argument is in its application to the archeology. The preponderance of vase painting and statuary evidence shows the jump to be an exercise encompassing running, stepping and jumping from one foot, rather than a performance in which the jumper takes off from a 2-feet parallel stance. Ebert clings to the belief that the ancient Greek starting posture for the running races was, in reality, not that at all but rather a standing long jump position, but this posture, where depicted on vases and reliefs, consistently portrays an athlete with no *halteres* in his hands, quite damaging to Ebert's theory. This writer remains highly skeptical of Ebert's thesis.

The Quadruple Jump Thesis

Any theory of the pentathlon jump must, out of necessity, be related to an acceptance, rejection or interpretive modification of the literary and archeological evidence. Thus, Gardiner's thesis can be seen to accept the archeology but is poorly served by the literature. Harris, on the other hand, accepts both the archeology and literature in the formulation of his hypothesis. However, his interpretation of Symmachos' definition of the *bater* presents definite questions for postulating that the jump was either a double or triple leap. Ebert's work, aside from the alarming quality of shunning the archeology entirely, is susceptible to the identical criticisms placed on Harris' interpretation of Symmachos. The only type of Greek pentathlon jump which can be explained by the body of original literature and which can bear the test of archeological application is a running, quadruple leap, the nature of which was not unlike our modern triple jump except that an extra "middle skip" was employed. An application of the evidence to support the theory renders the following:

Literary Evidence

1. An interpretation of the pentathlon jump as a multiple jumping exercise rests on a basic acceptance of the messages of Zenobias and Africanus on Phaÿllos and Chionis, respectively, together with Peek's interpretation of the Delos fragment. There being an absence of any other known record of jumping achievement

at this time, we must accept that which we have before us. The three references each allude to a jump of over 50 feet. Therefore, our jumping exercise must be the type of performance which could produce a leap that would measure in the vicinity of 50 feet.

2. Scholars have proposed several synonyms for the term *bater* but all refer to a point from which one starts, treads or leaves as a point of departure. Symmachos writing in the first century AD, a period when Greek athletics remained prominent, must have had some knowledge of the subject matter about which he wrote. Therefore, his definition of the *bater* as "the middle, from which having jumped, they jump again" can be taken as a valid description of a treading point in the approximate middle of the leaping exercise. There is little doubt that Symmachos' statement is the key point in the promulgation of the quadruple jump theory. The definition expressly implies that two jumps occurred from the midpoint of the exercise. Therefore, in order to achieve a relative geographical midpoint on the ground one had to necessarily execute an even number of jumps. The middle in a series of odd numbered jumps would be in the air during the middle jump. An odd number of jumps is not served by the literature.

3. Seleukos' definition of the *bater* as "the edge of the jumping pit, from which they make the first jump" causes some concern. Harris' first published interpretation of the Seleukos definition was made in 1960 [13]. In 1963 Harris reinterpreted the Seleukos statement to read "the edge, from which they make the first jump" [12]. This interpretation places the *skamma* at some distance from the *bater* with the performer carrying out all but the final leap on a hard packed surface and taking his last leap into the soft sand of the landing pit. Harris' original interpretation of Seleukos placed the initial takeoff point at the very edge of the *skamma* with the ensuing jump takeoffs being taken from points in the soft sand along the length of the *skamma*. This type of format (intermediate jumps from the soft sand) has been greeted with derisive scorn by most investigators. Ebert, however, felt that the sand in the *skamma* could have been solidly packed, rolled and watered to give the effect of a leaping exercise carried out on a surface much like the hard-packed sand near the water's edge on ocean beaches [2]. Ebert's idea has some merit in this regard but needs further study. The result of a running quadruple jump would be nearly the same, whether carried out on normal ground conditions with the last leap into a soft landing pit, or taken over a topographical plane on hardpacked, watered sand. If, however, the quadruple leap was started from the

bater at the edge of a long, soft landing pit and the intermediate treading places occurred within the pit, then a decrease in distance most likely occurred (Table I, Jumpers D and E).

Archeology

1. Any type of standing jump takeoff is ruled out by vase paintings, reliefs and statues. The jumper always performed with the *halteres* and to date we have no record of jumpers with *halteres* in hand assuming standing jump takeoff positions. What we do have for our analysis is a wealth of evidence supporting a short preliminary run (not more than 20 yards in most stadia), preliminary hops, skips or intermediate strides from an original *bater* and subsequent treading points, followed by an extended final leap with a 2-foot parallel landing position.

As a preliminary test in attempting to determine the validity of the quadruple jump, particularly in terms of the literature pointing to at least a 50-foot pentathlon jump, some performance tests were carried out using modern jumpers as subjects (Table I). Four experienced track and field long and triple jump performers were selected to demonstrate various jumping exercises. The four subjects were selected because of their particular expertise in previous jumping performance. Each had recorded long jumps of over 22 feet. Each had triple jumped over 46 feet. With very limited practice each performed a series of quadruple leaps using the hop-step-step-jump technique. The quadruple jumps, performed on a hard macadam surface, with the last landing in a soft sandy pit, produced distances

Table I. Jumpers Performing Various Types of Jumps Without Handweights (Best Mark of Three Attempts)

	1	*2*	*3*	*4*
Performers	*Long Jump*	*Triple Jump*	*Hop-Step-Step-Jump*	*Hop-Step-Step-Jump From Soft Sand in Landing Pit*
A	22′-6″	48′-5″	52′	
B	22′-2″	47′-1″	48′-6″	
C	22′-9″	47′-4″	47′-3″	
D	22′	46′-2″	47′-8″	42′-7″
E	24′-3″	47′-8″	52′-3″	48′-7″

Approach length = 60 feet (maximum)
Approach surface = rubberized asphalt
Takeoff board = wooden
Landing and striding pit surface = soft concrete sand

slightly in excess of 50 feet, thus fitting relatively well the Greek jumping distances left for our speculation. Two jumpers performed quadruple jump exercises with the intermediate steps and fourth jump being taken from the soft sand. Such exercises produced approximately a 4 to 5 foot decrease in distance leaped. With practice the decrease in distance from hard surface to soft surface performance may well be appreciably less.

Further tests are needed using larger samples of proven multiple jumpers. Further testing of jumping from soft sand must be done, since it is entirely possible that ancient Greek officials imposed *halteres* and surface conditions on athletes as hardships to be overcome rather than as aids in boosting performance.

Finally, the quadruple jump thesis suggests a pentathlon jump of the following description:

> With the accompaniment of flute music to help in timing his intermediate steps, the ancient Greek pentathlon jumper took a short running approach to a *bater*, striding from it and accomplishing a leap of greater distance than his next two "steps" but not as far as his last jump in the series of four. As he descends from his first leap, he lands on the same foot from which he took off, immediately takes two "as-long-as-possible" steps to gain as much further distance as possible but at the same time setting himself up for his last jump, from which he lands in the soft or hard-packed sand with feet in parallel fashion, *halteres* still in hand. Phaÿllos, unfortunately, achieved the Beamon-like performance of his era and soared well beyond the *skamma*, sustaining injury in the process. We are not told by the ancients what may have befallen Chionis, but he must have escaped serious injury or we should expect to learn all about it in the postmortems that invariably surround such athletic endeavor.

References

1. Durant, W.: The Life of Greece. New York:Simon Schuster Company, 1963, p. 214.
2. Ebert, J.: Zum Pentathlon der Antike. Berlin:Akademie-Verlag, 1963, pp. 43, 62.
3. Faber, M.: Philogus. 1891.
4. Fedde, F.: Der Fuenfkampf der Hellenen. 1888.
5. Gardiner, E.N.: Athletics of the Ancient World. Oxford:Clarendon Press, 1930.
6. Gardiner, E.N.: Olympia. Oxford:Clarendon Press, 1925.

7. Gardiner, E.N.: Greek Athletic Sports and Festivals. London:Macmillan and Company, Ltd., 1910, p. 309.
8. Gardiner, E.N.: Further notes on the Greek jump. J. Hellenic Studies. XXIV, 1904.
9. Gardiner, E.N.: Phaÿllos and his record jump. J. Hellenic Studies. XXIV, 1904, pp. 70, 76, 79, 80.
10. Harris, H.A.: Sport in Greece and Rome. London:Thames and Hudson, 1972.
11. Harris, H.A.: The method of deciding victory in the pentathlon. Greece and Rome. XIX(1), April 1972.
12. Harris, H.A.: Greek Athletes and Athletics. London:Hutchinson & Co., Ltd., 1964, pp. 81, 82.
13. Harris, H.A.: An Olympic epigram: The athletic feats of Phaÿllos. Greece and Rome. VII(1), March 1960, p. 5.
14. Hyde, W.W.: Olympic Victor Monuments and Greek Athletic Art. Washington:Carnegie Institution, 1921.
15. Jüthner, J.: Die Athletischen Leibestibungen der Griechen. (von Friedrich Breiu, ed.). Wien:H. Bohlau, 1965, p. 270.
16. Jüthner, J.: Uber Antike Turngeräthe. Wien, 1896.
17. Krause, J.H.: Die Gymnastik und Agonistik der Hellenen. 1841.
18. Peek, W.: Fünf Wundergeschichten aus den Asklepicion von Epidauros. 1963.
19. Robinson, R.S.: Sources for the History of Greek Athletics. Cincinnati, Ohio:R. S. Robinson, 1955, pp. 230, 231.
20. Wassmannsdorf, K.: Monatsschrift Für Das Turnwesson. 1885.

King Amenophis II: Analysis and Evaluation of His Athletic Ability

Zaki I. Habashi

The story of physical activity and human well-being in ancient Egypt is told in detail and with precision on walls of tombs and temples in such places as Sakkara, Luxor and Beni Hassan in Egypt and on reliefs and relics preserved in prominent world museums. Statues, reliefs, paintings and drawings accompanied with texts in hieroglyphs describe the ancient Egyptians' participation in sports and physical activities and of their interest in human well-being. These relics have been the topic of research by archeologists and Egyptologists from many lands for many years and the great majority seem to support the theory that sports, physical activities and games were an integral part of daily-life activities in ancient Egypt and a source of enjoyment and relaxation. Rich and poor, men and women, children and adults participated in various physical activities for pleasure. "Indeed, it has been stated as highly probable that the ancient Egyptians, like the modern, seized the occasion of any festival for athletic contests" [21].

Because of the ancient Egyptian belief in life after death, their tombs, especially those of the royal family and nobles, contained tools, furniture and articles used before death. Also, sporting equipment, found among the remains of the tombs, included hunting chariots, bows, arrows, harpoons, balls, fishing rods and hooks, slings, sticks and board games.

"Of the popularity of games among the Egyptians from the earliest times we have abundant evidence in the paintings of their tombs. The walls of Beni Hassan in particular present us with a truly marvelous display of games and sports" [15]. Egyptian youth were reared in a manner which was characterized by much physical activity. They were required to participate in exercises and activities

---

Zaki I. Habashi, California State College, Stanislaus, Turlock, California, U.S.A.

designed to make the body supple, strong and capable of great endurance and stamina. They also found great enjoyment in going on hunting and fishing expeditions [3].

The significance of researching physical activities in ancient Egypt was well expressed by Falkener [13] when he stated that many of our modern games have descended to us from ancient times, and some are depicted on the walls of Egyptian temples and tombs. It is important, then, to investigate physical activities in the ancient world and their role in the well-being of individuals in these ancient societies. Such research contributes to a better understanding of modern sporting activities and relates them to ancient sports. The ancient Olympic Games with their international sports competition, begun in 776 BC and revived through the efforts of Pierre de Coubertin in 1896, is an outstanding example of ancient traditions in sports and their effects upon modern times. International competition was, however, known to the Egyptians nearly 2000 years prior to the first ancient Olympic games, as explained in this study. It is interesting to note that these sporting activities stressed individual achievement and competition, a principle that has been emphasized in our modern Olympics [39].

It is with the theme of this international Congress — Physical Activity and Human Well-Being — that the writer investigated physical activities and sports in ancient Egypt. Research particularly carried out during the writer's 1972-1973 sabbatical in Europe and Egypt, as well as examination of relics and historical and Egyptological studies, supports the theory that the ancient Egyptians engaged in physical activities. Since sports is considered a socio-cultural force in every culture, it is essential to examine physical activities in ancient Egypt to determine whether they were sporting activities. It is the purpose of this study to investigate physical activities in ancient Egypt with emphasis on participation of King Amenophis II in sporting activities.

In order for a physical activity to be considered a sporting activity, certain characteristics and elements should be present. These elements and characteristics have been discussed by scholars and include "athletics" in Caillois' [4] classification of play under the category of Agon (competition), the element of "play for fun" as presented by Huizinga [24] who condemned modern sports for ignoring this essential factor, and "the effort to conquer an opponent, the self or an environment in play and only in play" by McIntosh [31]. Other elements and characteristics include the challenge that is provided, voluntariness, uncertainty of the outcome, unproductiveness, order, make-believe, physical prowess and physical skills.

Loy [2] describes "sports" as a specialized type of game, or any form of playful competition, whose outcome is determined by physical skill, strategy or chance employed singly or in combination. McIntosh [31] explains "sport" by stating that it should include the efforts to conquer and suggests the four categories of sports as skill, combat, conquest and eurthymics. Ibrahim (1975) categorizes "sport" into three categories — skill sport, combat sport and conquest sport. This writer, however, likes to classify sports into two different categories for the purpose of this study — combat sport and conquest sport — since skill is a common denominator in these two types.

In light of the studies of sports, its elements, conditions, definitions, theories and classifications as presented by Huizinga [24], Caillois [4], McIntosh [31], Loy [27], Ibrahim (1975), Brasch [1], DeVries [10], Lucas (1951) and others, the writer examined and evaluated King Amenophis II's participation in sporting activities.

Participation in a physical activity does not necessarily mean this activity is a sporting activity, neither does it automatically make the participant a sportsman or athletically inclined. Therefore, in order for a person to be considered an athlete or a sportsman, his participation in physical activities should satisfy specific conditions and meet certain criteria. The following criteria have been developed by this writer in light of the discussion and rationale of the above-mentioned scholars to serve as a measure to examine physical activities in ancient Egypt in general and the participation of Amenophis II in particular.

1. Participation in the physical activity is for pure enjoyment and diversion.

2. Participation in the physical activity requires skill and provides a challenge for the participant.

3. Participation entails equal opportunities and fairness for contestants.

Historically, participation in physical activity in ancient Egypt developed from an activity that did not require much competition or skill and evolved to a sport that was challenging and skillful. Hayes [21] states:

> In the New Kingdom, Egypt's most ancient sport, the hunting of wild game, transformed from a more or less static pastime, wherein the royal or noble huntsman stood

> on foot and fired into a group of animals penned up in an enclosure or driven toward him by his beaters, into a free-running, mounted horse across the deserts, wastelands, and velds of Africa and Western Asia. Thanks to the mobility of the chariot and the range and power of the composite bow the hunter was now able to run down and kill with relative ease the largest and most dangerous of beasts — the lion, the wild bulls, and the elephants and it was game of this type which became the quarry most avidly sought after by the sporting Pharaohs of the Eighteenth Dynasty.

Classic examples of physical activities in ancient Egypt were hunting lions, elephants, wild bulls, the hippopotamus, ostriches from a moving chariot, fowling with the throwstick from a papyrus boat, fishing with the hook, rowing, wrestling, stick fencing and horseback riding. These activities can be categorized as combat and/or conquest sporting activities that required skills and abilities as well as physical and mental qualities of endurance, thought, power, balance, dexterity, patience, courage, determination and the will to win in fair play. By the New Kingdom these qualities and skills had been developed and sharpened to a high level and advanced degree of proficiency.

Hippopotamus hunting, for example, was a dangerous and daring conquest sporting activity. Pharaohs, noblemen and attendants hunted the hippopotamus in ancient Egypt for sport and the common people hunted it for economic and professional purposes, since its valuable hide was used for helmets, javelins, shields and whips [38]. Men of all ranks liked to have representations of hippopotamus hunting in their tombs, since the thrill of danger made them proud of their success and the sport demanded exceptional skill, ability and courage [12].

Wrestling and stick fencing are examples of combat sporting activities and scenes of these activities are displayed on the walls of Medinet Habu, Beni Hassan and some tombs of the nobles. Wrestling was a favorite leisure activity among all classes [38]. It also was included in the athletic exercises in the military schools to develop agility, strength and suppleness [16]. "There can be little doubt that during the Eighteenth Dynasty, as later in the New Kingdom, competitive sports, such as wrestling and fencing with single sticks, were popular with the people of Egypt" [21]. These sports planted the seeds for international competition as we know it today, as some of the scenes on the walls in Medinet Habu present us with unquestionable evidence of international wrestling matches between Egyptians and Syrians and Egyptians and Libyans or Nubians with umpires judging and spectators including visitors from foreign lands. Both of these activities still are practiced by modern Egyptians.

Fowling with bow and arrow or the throwstick was another challenging conquest activity requiring exceptional athletic ability and skills; these activities also are depicted on the walls of numerous tombs and on relics. Judging the aiming angle and the time to release the bowstring and perceiving the exact spot where the arrow would meet the flying bird are skills that cannot be denied. Fowling with the throwstick in the marshes from a small floating papyrus boat unstable for the fowler required a sense of balance and coordination that made fowling more challenging. The throwstick was a simple but powerful weapon — a small thin piece of wood, bent in a peculiar way; when thrown it hit its mark with great strength, then returned in a graceful curve and fell at the feet of the marksman [12]. Erman's description of the throwstick would identify it as a boomerang. The terms "throwstick" and "boomerang" have been used interchangeably by various Egyptologists; however, this writer can differentiate between the two. The boomerang returns to the thrower while the throwstick does not. Carter [5], Hayes [22], Dieckman [11] and others referred to the two kinds; however, Steffen Wenig, Curator of the Bode Museum in East Berlin, Wolfgang Decker of Cologne University and other contemporary Egyptologists claim that the ancient Egyptians did not know the return kind. The currently accepted theory is that the Egyptians did not know the return kind [10, 23, 40].

Fishing, a conquest sport, was another amusement in which the ancient Egyptians particularly delighted. The favorite method of the sportsman was to use the slender two-pronged spear nearly 3 yards long; the most skillful fisherman speared two fish at once [12]. While the use of the spear was confined to the sportsman, the poorer classes employed the net and hook. Angling was another method enjoyed by the wealthy prior to the New Kingdom and required fast reaction time. During the New Kingdom, however, the adoption of the rod simplified the operation. The rod was short and apparently of one piece. Private ponds in house gardens of the wealthy provided excellent line fishing also [33]. An exceptional and rare method of fishing was with the bow and arrow. The only known scene is one found in King Tutankhamun's tomb depicting him on a stool and fishing in a pool of water utilizing this method [10, 37].

Hunting ostriches from a moving chariot was another activity where the skill and challenge involved could not be overemphasized since both the chariot and the ostriches were depicted as moving at an exceptional rate of speed. Scenes found in the tomb of Tutankhamun are classic examples of this conquest sport.

The above-described feats and many others are examples of commonly known physical activities in ancient Egypt in which people found a challenge to their physical abilities and a resort for their emotional well-being.

The climax of the physical activities movement and human well-being in ancient Egypt witnessed its golden age during the New Kingdom in general and the Eighteenth Dynasty in particular. Kings and nobles of the New Kingdom enjoyed sporting skills and qualities at a high degree of proficiency. Wilson [39] states:

> There is a minor but amusing aspect of the Empire, and that is the emphasis on sports and athletics which appeared in this period of extending and policing the conquered territory. Akin both to the traditional Egyptian love of games and to the spurt of physical energy that set up the empire, there was a brief period of glorifying the successful sportsman and athlete. It ran from Thut-mose III through Amen-hotep III, with a revival under Tut-ankh-Amon, and with the chief exponent of the outdoor life Amen-hotep II. The vigorous Thutmose III started the mode, telling us with relish how he hunted one hundred and twenty elephants in northern Syria, how "he killed seven lions by shooting in the completion of a moment and he captured a herd of twelve wild cattle within an hour, when breakfast time had taken place," . . .
>
> It was Amen-hotep II who left us the most engaging — and at the same time the most brutal — account of his muscular prowess. From his boyhood to his death he delighted in outdoor exercise and in his superiority over other competitors. In one of the Theban tombs the noble Min is shown with the young prince as he "gives the principles of lessons in archery. He says: 'Span your bows to your ears.' " The legend over the boy runs: "enjoying himself by learning about shooting in Pharaoh's Broad Hall of Thinis (by the Prince Amen-hotep)."

Among the 11 kings of the Eighteenth Dynasty, Amenophis II was referred to as "the athlete king." He assumed full responsibility of the throne and the well-spread Egyptian empire upon the death of his father, King Thutmose III in 1450 BC, when he was about 18 years of age. The empire extended from the Euphrates River to Nubia and the fourth cataract of the Nile River in the south. His reign as co-regent with his father for one year together with his training, education and preparation for both war and peace during his childhood and youth prepared him for his political as well as military successes. His military capability was soon proven when he successfully crushed a revolt that erupted in northern Palestine and spread throughout the Asian territories of the empire. His political insight also was expressed in his democratic rule [36]:

> It is not surprising that a prince with his background would possess an uncommonly democratic spirit toward his people. Amen-hotep II appears always to have retained intimate contact with the friends of his youth and to have surrounded himself with loyal officials selected from their ranks. If he appointed one of them to a distant post in his empire, he was not above reminding him on occasion by a personal letter of his continuing interest.

His preparation as a crown prince also included training in archery, hunting, aquatics and horsemanship. His daily activities included various sporting activities and his stela at Giza by the Sphinx gives a detailed account of his athletic achievements [36]:

> The enthusiasm for sports and contests of skill which was imparted to the royal pupil by his tutors, as well as the prince's great love for horses, has recently been revealed in one of the best characterizations which has survived from the ancient world. It consists of a series of episodes in the life of Prince Amen-hotep before his accession to the throne recorded on a stela discovered several years ago not far from the great sphinx at Giza.

Amenophis II was known as the "athlete king" who treated war as a sport with the challenge and the will to win and as the strongest man to draw a bow. He was not afraid to challenge his soldiers to contests in archery, running and rowing, confident of his own superiority. He was especially proud of his skill in shooting and had this depicted in the temples of Karnak and Medamud [37].

Amenophis II's talent and skill in archery was developed and promoted since he was a young boy. His lessons in drawing the bow are depicted in a scene found in the tomb of Min, Prince of Thinis, in West Thebes. The scene shows King Thutmose III giving lessons in shooting to the young prince [37]:

> (Min, Prince of Thinis) gives directions in shooting and says "span your bow up to your ear. Make strong your

> . . ." (The King's son Amenophis) disports himself in shooting lessons in the Court of the palace of Thinis).
>
> A favorite place for excursions was the point where the Great Sphinx stood just below the Pyramids at Giza; there was probably a rest-house of some kind there and the king and crown-prince honoured it with their presence when archery practices were held. The first to give us this information was Amenmose, a son of Tuthmosis I. Amenophis II, who loved to show off as a bowman of unequalled strength and accuracy, commemorated these shooting matches in great detail on a memorial stela [25].

Another scene examined by the writer displays Amenophis II's skill in archery on a rose granite relief found at Karnak. The king is shown target shooting from a war chariot at a copper disc used as a target. The end of the description reads that "His majesty performed his deed . . . before the eyes of the whole country" [34]. The above-mentioned stela relates [37]:

> He entered the northern foreground and found that they had set up for him four targets of Asian copper a hand's breadth thick, and the space between one stake and the next was twenty feet. His Majesty then appeared on his war chariot like Month in his strength. He spanned the bow and seized four arrows at once. Then he drove off and shot at them like Month in his trappings, and his arrows came out behind (the target) again. Then he attacked another stake. That was a deed that had never been done before and which man had never heard tell of; that an arrow was shot at a copper target, passed through and fell to earth . . .

According to Steindorff and Steele [36], the space between one stake and the next was about 35 feet.

The remains of a text from Medamud not far from Luxor describe a shooting contest in which King Amenophis II issued the challenge that special prizes would be offered to those who could equal him. "As all those who bore through the target as far as the arrow of his Majesty shall win these things! Then they shot at his target" [37].

Because of Amenophis II's interest in archery as a leisure activity, he frequently practiced shooting for enjoyment and diversion. Even while on a military campaign in Asia near Kadesh "the sport-loving king relaxed for a time for some target shooting and a hunt" [36].

His expertise in shooting qualified him to examine the workmanship of "three hundred strong bows, to compare the work of the men who made them and (distinguish) the skilled from the unskilled" [37]. On his stela it was recorded that "there was no one (in his army) who could span his bow" [37].

The discovery of his bow and furniture in his tomb shows his respect and love for the sport of archery. A bow decorated with inscriptions and inlay was found with Amenophis II in his tomb when it was discovered in 1898; it now is in the Egyptian Museum.

Horseback riding was known in ancient Egypt on a limited basis. Horses were introduced into Egypt by the Hyksos and their use in sporting activities quickly became evident. Pictures and relics showing horses pulling chariots in hunting are numerous. Horseback riding, however, has been an issue of controversy among scholars. One group believes that the ancient Egyptians used horses only to pull the chariot. Among this group is Desroches-Noblecourt [8]; she does refer to King Tutankhamun's lessons of horseback riding as exceptional. On the other hand, Schulman [35] gives several archeological evidences to support the theory that the ancient Egyptians rode the horse; his theory is supported by Hayes [21] and Wenig and Touny [37]. One of Schulman's evidences is a carved scene of horseback riding displayed on the west wall of the Luxor Temple; this scene was examined by the writer and shows a horseman riding with two legs on one side. The study of horseback riding by this writer seems to support the theory that horseback riding was known to the ancient Egyptians, although it was rare.

There are no known relics depicting Amenophis II on a horse. However, he is shown on a scarab feeding hay to his horses [8] and his above-mentioned stela relates that while still a youth he loved horses and took pleasure in them; he showed patience in getting to know their nature, learning about training them and breaking them in. As recorded on the stela, his father Thutmose III, pleased with his son's interest in horses, said [37]:

> Let him be given fine horses from the stalls of His Majesty which are in Memphis and say to him: "Look after them, break them in, train them and deal with them when they (resist?) you." Then they entrusted the King's son with the care of the horses in the King's stalls. And he did what he was asked of him. Reshef and Astarte rejoiced over him when he did all that his heart desired. He trained horses the like of which had not been seen before. They did not tire when he held the bridle and they did not sweat when

> they raced swiftly. He was accustomed to harness them with the curb-bit in Memphis . . .

Although rowing was not generally considered a sporting activity, it was an important aspect of daily life. The upper classes had attendants rowing them on the Nile or had lakes dug out solely for the purpose of rowing near their palaces [37]. Rowing in a light boat was a delight for the ancient Egyptians; from the boat they could pick lotus flowers, hunt birds, catch fish and even the hippopotamus [12]. There is only one known source relating a type of rowing contest. King Amenophis II tells on his stela near the Sphinx at Giza of his prowess in this activity [37]:

> Strong were his arms and he did not tire when he seized the oar and rowed at the stern of his boat as stroke for two hundred men. They stopped when they had only half a mile behind them. They were already exhausted and their limbs were tired and they were breathless. But His Majesty was strong with his twenty foot-long oar. He stopped and grounded his boat after he had rowed three miles without a pause. Faces beamed when they saw him doing this.

The study of King Amenophis II and relevant archeological evidence prove that his participation in archery, charioteering, rowing and hunting was for enjoyment and diversion. His success in these activities demonstrated mental and physical abilities of unusual strength, physical prowess, power, courage, patience, endurance, accuracy, will to conquer and the spirit of competition. These activities provided conditions and environments that were challenging to the king's ability and the principle of fair play was maintained throughout his participation. His interest in competition was evident, since his success in these activities depended upon his proven proficiency in these skills. "A hieroglyphic inscription lauds Pharaoh Amenophis II as a perfect athlete — 'strong of arm,' 'long of stride,' 'a skilled charioteer,' and efficient oarsman, and a powerful archer" [1]. Doctors who studied the mummy of Amenophis II felt that he must have been a man of unusual strength [32]. "Thutmose III's son and successor, Amenhotep II (1450-1425 BC), for example, has left a reputation for athletic prowess unsurpassed till the Roman Emperor Nero" [28]. "(He) is the epitome of the all-around athlete, equally proficient as oarsman, archer, and horseman" [32].

Summary and Conclusions

King Amenophis II, the fifth king in the Eighteenth Dynasty, participated in archery, charioteering, rowing and hunting which required superior physical and mental qualities. The analysis and evaluation of his participation in terms of the three criteria developed by this writer would lead to the conclusion that the king's physical activities could be classified as sporting activities of the conquest type and that his athletic ability reached a high degree of proficiency.

References

1. Brasch, R.: How Did Sports Begin? New York:David McCay Co., Inc., 1970.
2. Breasted, J.H.: A History of Egypt From the Earliest Times to the Persian Conquest, ed. 2. New York:Charles Scribner's Sons, 1937.
3. Bucher, C.A.: Foundations of Physical Education, ed. 7. St. Louis:The C. V. Mosby Company, 1975.
4. Caillois, R.: The structure and classification of games. *In* Loy, J.W., Jr. and Kenyon, G.S. (eds.): Sport, Culture, and Society. London:Collier-MacMillan, Ltd., 1969.
5. Carter, H.: The Tomb of Tutankhamen. London:Sphere Books, Ltd., 1972.
6. Centre of Documentations and Studies on Ancient Egypt. Hunting and Fishing in Ancient Egypt. Cairo:Darl El Hana Press, n.d.
7. Decker, W.: Die physische leistung pharaos. Köln: Historisches Institut der Deutschen Sporthochschule, 1971.
8. Desroches-Noblecourt, C.: Life and Death of a Pharaoh: Tutankhamen. London:George Rainbird Ltd., 1963.
9. Desroches-Noblecourt, C.: Un petit monument commomoratif du roi athlete. Cairo:Revue d'Egyptologie, 7, 1950.
10. DeVries, C.: Attitudes of the ancient Egyptians toward physical-recreative activities. Doctor of Philosophy Dissertation. Chicago:University of Chicago, 1960.
11. Dieckman, E.A.: Stone age guided missiles. Sports Afield 139:54-55, 121-123, 1958.
12. Erman, A.: Life in Ancient Egypt. Tirard, H.M. (trans.). London:MacMillan and Company, 1894.
13. Falkener, E.: Games Ancient and Oriental and How To Play Them. New York:Dover Publications, 1961.
14. Falls, C.B.: The First 3000 Years: Ancient Civilizations of the Tigris, Euphrates, and Nile River Valleys. New York:The Viking Press.
15. Gardiner, E.N.: Athletics of the Ancient World. Oxford:Clarendon Press, 1965.
16. Gosse, A.B.: The Civilization of the Ancient Egyptians. London:T. C. and E. C. Jack, Ltd., n.d.
17. Habashi, Z.I.: King Tutankhamun: Sportsman in antiquity. Research paper presented to the International Seminar of International Association for the History of Physical Education and Sports, Louvain, Belgium, March, 1975.
18. Habashi, Z.: King Tutankhamun: Sportsman in antiquity. Research paper presented to the California Association for Health, Physical Education, and Recreation, 1974.
19. Habashi, Z.I.: Historical and philosophical interpretation of relics depicting hunting in ancient Egypt. Research paper presented to the California Association for Health, Physical Education, and Recreation, 1971.

20. Habashi, Z.I.: Documentary photographs depicting physical activities in ancient Egypt. Research paper presented to the California Association for Health, Physical Education, and Recreation, 1970.
21. Hayes, W.C.: The sporting tradition. Cambridge Ancient History 2:333-38, 1962.
22. Hayes, W.C.: The Specter of Egypt Vol. II. Cambridge, Massachusetts: Harvard University Press, 1959.
23. Hess, F.: The aerodynamics of boomerangs. Sci. Am. 219:124-36, 1968.
24. Huizinga, J.: Homo Ludens. Boston:Beacon Press, 1950. Publishing Co., Inc., 1975.
25. Kees, H.: Ancient Egypt. James, T.G.H. (ed.). Chicago:University of Chicago Press, 1961.
26. Loy, J.W.: Socio-psychological attributes associated with the early adoption of a sport innovation. *In* Loy, J.W., Jr. and Kenyon, G.S. (eds.): Sport, Culture, and Society. Canada:Collier-MacMillan, Ltd., 1968.
27. Loy, J.W.: The nature of sport: A definitional effort. *In* Hart, M.M. (ed.): Sport in the Socio-cultural Process. Dubuque, Iowa:Wm. C. Brown Company Publishers, 1968.
28. MacKendrick, P. et al: Western Civilizations. New York:American Heritage Company, 1968.
29. Maspero, G.: Manual of Egyptian Archeology. London:Grevel and Company, 1895.
30. McIntosh, P.C.: An historical view of sport and social control. Int. Rev. Sport Sociol. 6:5, 1971.
31. McIntosh, P.C.: Sport in Society. London:C. A. Watts, 1963.
32. Montet, P.: Everyday Life in Egypt in the Days of Ramesses the Great. Maxwell-Hyslop, A.R. and Drower, M.S. (trans.). London:Edward Arnold Ltd., 1958.
33. Posener, G.: A Dictionary of Egyptian Civilization. London:Methuen and Company Ltd., 1962.
34. Schäfer, H.: König Amenophis II als meisterschutz. Orientalistische literaturzertung, Leipzig: 32:233-38, 1929.
35. Schulman, A.R.: Egyptian representation of horsemen and riding in the New Kingdom. Journal on Near East Studies. Chicago:The Oriental Institute of the University of Chicago 16:263-71, 1957.
36. Steindorff, G. and Steele, K.C.: When Egypt Ruled the East (revised by K. C. Steele). Chicago:The University of Chicago Press:Phoenix Books, 1963.
37. Wenig, S. and Touny, A.D.: Sports in Ancient Egypt. Leipzig:Iffrizin Anderson Nixö, 1969.
38. Wilkinson, J.G.: Manners and Customs of the Ancient Egyptians Vol. III. London:John Murray, 1837.
39. Wilson, J.A.: The Burden of Egypt. Chicago:The University of Chicago Press, 1967.
40. Wolf, W.: Das alte Agypten. Munchen:Deutscher Taschenbuchverlag, 1971.

Women in Sport in the Ancient Western World

Reet Howell

Time and space limitations restrict this analysis of the role of women in sports and games in the ancient western world, though this is nonetheless the most complete summary to this point in time. The ancient western world began with the advent of writing — cuneiform writing of the Sumerians and hieroglyphics of the Egyptians. This paper is not meant to infer that sports and games were not played prior to this time, that is, in the period of prehistory. Indeed, there is evidence of such activities, but it is beyond the scope of this paper. The subject of women in sports and games in the ancient western world has not been treated in its entirety, the closest attempt being the excellent thesis by Eisen [2]. This thorough, scholarly work unfortunately limited itself to the Egyptian, Minoan-Mycenean and Greek civilizations. This paper will concern itself with the total ancient western world and will include evidence of women in sport in the Sumerian, Hittite, Assyrian, Iranian, Egyptian, Minoan-Mycenean, Greek, Etruscan and Roman civilizations. Archeological and literary evidence was utilized, and visitations were made to the major museums and archeological sites in Egypt, Iraq, Greece, Crete and Italy.

The principal evidence of participation of women in the Sumerian civilization is in music, dancing and the use of game boards. The thesis by Meikle [11] evaluates this evidence. As he stated [11]:

> The division of labour and class distinction in Sumerian urban culture resulted in the formation of a professional class, or caste, of singers, dancers and musicians who, as members of the palace personnel, would have lived within the palace complex and relied on it for their living. It seems that they were called upon to entertain the king and nobility, perhaps after a successful harvest or a victory in battle.

Reet Howell, Department of Physical Education, San Diego State University, San Diego, California, U.S.A.

Various musical instruments have been discovered, and of course, where there is music there is dancing. The lyres discovered at Ur are perhaps the most famous instruments excavated, but in addition, the following instruments have been found: flute, lute, double pipes, harps, a type of oboe, percussion clubs, clappers, sistra, rattles, drums and silver pipes, and seal stones show the clapping of hands as well. One cylinder seal, for example [16], shows men feasting and drinking, and in the lower register we see a lyrist, a flutist and two other musicians and three dancers clapping their hands. One excellent terra-cotta figurine shows a woman playing double pipes [16], later utilized by the Greeks in certain athletic events; we see the great singer Ur-Ninna, who wears pantaloons and is probably also a dancer [15]; and a bronze pinhead, found at Telloh, shows two small dancing women [10].

Literary evidence also supports the dance [8], this being demonstrated in the delightful Sumerian poem, "Love Finds a Way":

> Last night as I the queen was shining bright,
> As I was shining bright, was dancing about
> As I was singing away while the bright light overcame the night.
>
> . . .
>
> My girl friend, she took me with her to the public square.
> There a player (?) entertained (?) us with dancing.

So dancing was not confined to the royal palace, as the public square is specifically noted. The importance of dance is noted by Sachs [18]:

> On no occasion in the life of primitive peoples should the dance be dispersed with. Birth, circumcision, and the consecration of maidens, marriage and death, planting and harvest, the celebration of chieftains, hunting, war, and feasts, the changes of the moon and sickness — for all of these the dance is needed.

Woolley found four gaming boards in the royal graves at Ur [24] and one has been found at Tell Halaf. Though we do not know for certain, it is a reasonable assumption that women utilized board games.

Similar conclusions about the participation of women in sports and games can be made for the Hittite civilization. Again, a considerable number of musical instruments have been unearthed. As Meikle stated [11]:

> They may be divided into three categories: idiophonic instruments which vibrated without any special tension and included concussion clubs, clappers, drums and cymbals; wind instruments such as pipes, horns and trumpets; and, stringed instruments such as the lute, lyre and harp.

One artifact in particular gives a fair representation of the range of instruments. Discovered at Karatepe, it is a banquet scene depicting King Asitawanda [22]. Musicians are seen playing the harp, lyre, clappers and cymbals. As for dancing, Meikle stated [11]:

> The representations of dancing are all connected to the religious rituals and ceremonial feasts. Gurney relates a ritual in which are mentioned "jesters" playing the arkammi, the huhupal and the galgalturi, three musical instruments, while other "jesters" hold up their hands and turn round in their places . . . The text captures the excitement of the moment as the "Master of Ceremonies" orders the singers and dancers to pick up their Ishtar-instruments and take up their positions.

This figure [5] is an excellent example of dancing, as is another [22] found at Carcemish, which as well as depicting the double pipes, clappers and lute, shows a dancer moving to the music. The dancer in this case is male, however.

One representation that should be noted is a scene involving King Aramas [22]. As he embraces his oldest son and successor, his younger children are depicted playing with dice, or knucklebones, and a top. Knucklebones were used as toys in Hittite communities [12]. Animal figurines, which it is felt were toys, have likewise been found. It is possible that these toys were utilized by girls as well as boys.

The thesis by Spier [20] is the best available source on the physical activities of the Assyrians (1814 BC-612 BC) and the Iranians (612 BC-642 AD), which included the Achemenian, Parthian and Sassanian dynasties, thus completing the main Mesopotamian civilizations. With respect to the Assyrian civilization, the use of music was extremely popular. The instruments excavated have been the harp, lyre, tamboura, tabor, psaltery, double pipes, horn, tambourine, cymbals, drums and rattle. Some of the musicians were female. Singing was likewise popular. There were female and male singers, trained from an early age. There is surprisingly little evidence of dance with the profusion of evidence of singing, music and feasts and banquets, and the representations that have been unearthed have men dancing. It would have to be assumed that women danced, particularly with the evidence of female singers and musicians. Likewise, there is evidence of dice and gaming boards, and it is possible these were used by girls and women.

There is a more extensive literature on physical activities among the Achemenians, perhaps because of their contact with the Greek world, in contrast to the Parthians and Sassanians, whose association with the Romans did not occasion a great cultural exchange. There is evidence of banquets and feasts, singing and music. The following instruments were used: drums, kettle drums and castanets, lyres, single and double flutes, an arghanum, similar to a bagpipe, trumpets, harps and mandolins. Dance was practiced by the Achemenians. Xenophon wrote [25] that when Cyrus returned to Persia he ". . . performed the customary sacrifice and led the Persians in their national dance and distributed presents among them all . . ." Moreover, stated Spier [20]:

> Several surviving objects of Parthian and Sassanian art depict dancing scenes. A silver cast cup of Sassanian origins, and dating to around the fourth century A.D., depicted female musicians surrounding a dancer who was holding castanets. A second silver gilt jug from approximately the same period showed four girls dancing among a bower of branches. Yet a further silver bowl from this same period is engraved with a banquet scene, in which one of the figures was a nude dancing girl who was throwing her veil into the air.

One other Parthian object, a small bone plaque, shows acrobats and dancers. It appears obvious that the Iranians, at future occasions, were entertained by musicians and dancers. There is evidence of a board game and toys, and it is possible that girls and women utilized them.

The thesis by Eisen [2] is the most complete work on the Egyptians from the point of view of women and sport (3100-30 BC). Perhaps the only criticism is that his analysis did not include all physical activities, neglecting, for example, women and dancing and board games.

It is essentially a question of definition and this occasions problems. One of the interesting points brought out by Eisen, neglected by sport historians in the main, is the relationship of the goddesses to physical activities. For example, the lion goddess Bast was associated with archery and the chase, and later to joy, music and dancing; Sekhet, with fowling, fishing and hunting, was known as "Mistress of Hunting," "Mistress of Sport"; Neith was likewise associated with hunting; Wadjet was known as "Goddess of Swimming," "Lady of Power"; Hathor was the patroness of music, joy, dancing and love, and in her honor women presented dances and acrobatics; the Syrian goddess Astarte was goddess of horses. There is evidence of women's participation in Egypt in music and dancing, board games, juggling, aquatic activities, acrobatics, hunting, fishing, chariot driving, mock-combat, foot races, and ball games.

The first evidence of women participating in ball games is in ancient Egypt. The tomb of Kheti shows three groups of women playing ball [14], and it is as if at least two team games are involved, a pick-a-back game where one person throws to another, and another activity where teams in a line throw to the women in another line. Similar representations in the tomb at Beni Hasan [2] depict juggling and the pick-a-back game. The dress and manner of doing the hair are generally stated as representative of a professional class of performer, but Eisen also puts forward the opinion that they could be women of high birth acting as priestesses.

Acrobatics and gymnastic exercises are seen in a great number of artifacts [2], as well as cultic dance. We see illustrations of tumbling, jumping exercises, partner gymnastics, the bridge and so on, again a first in the ancient western world. The performers appear to be highly trained. Eisen noted [2] that in Dendera, temple of the goddess Hathor, it is written:

> She is the lady of cheers, mistress of dance
> the lady of sistrum, the mistress of songs,
> the lady of dance, the mistress of wreath making
> the lady of beauty, the mistress of skipping.

Various cultic dances have been observed. One artifact at Karnak showed six different phases of the dance [2], with the gymnastic bridge being central.

A game requiring considerable skill is called "running in circle" by Eisen [2], but is more aptly called a swinging game. As Montet described it [13]:

> . . . two big girls stood back to back and stretched their arms out sideways. Four other little girls stood with their feet close to them and took their outstretched hands, holding themselves rigid as if they were hanging from them. When the word was given the whole group whirled around at least three times — unless they all fell down and brought the game to an end.

There are a number of bowls in the British Museum which show girls swimming. One poem emphasizes it as well [21]:

> I slip into the water to be with you, and for love of you I emerge with a red fish. It feels good in my fingers.

And a papyrus mentions girls rowing [2]: "The women went and came, and the heart of His Majesty was rejoicing to see them row." And the wife and daughter are shown in actual hunting scenes, but not actually participating — supporting the husband, showing loyalty, may be a better description. Fishing scenes may be similarly interpreted — rebaiting the hook, taking the fish off the hook and so on.

Women driving chariots are seen in the tomb of Pentu, as well as in the tomb of Mahu and Huy [2]. Eisen also mentions women participating in mock combat [2]. Hundreds of girls would attack one another with stones and clubs. And cultic foot races were also known, the chieftains, including Queen Hatshepsut, having to demonstrate their servitude or physical prowess. Dancing has likewise been mentioned, but there are many other representations, and Queen Hatshepsut is shown at a board game, and draughtsmen and these were found in her tomb, with knucklebones.

The physical activities of women in the Minoan-Mycenean civilizations have been extensively developed by Howell and Palmer [6], Putnam [17], and Eisen [2].

Eisen again developed the goddesses and their relationship to sports. The Mother Goddess is characterized as "Our Lady of Sports." As Eisen put it [2]:

> In Cretan belief she played an important role as the patroness of such sports as hunting, archery, and bull games. Artifacts such as seals, figurines, and frescoes depicted her as huntress, archer, toreador or a spectator of sport events.

We see the first evidence of spectators in the Minoan civilization, and women appear more prominently in such scenes than the men. The "Miniature Fresco of the Sacred Grove and Dance" depicts perhaps 500 spectators watching dancing [3]. The terra-cotta model found at Palaikastro [3] showed three female votaries dancing with outstretched arms, in a near semicircle, around a central female figure who is playing the lyre. Individual and group dances are seen in relative profusion.

The most unusual participation by women is in the bull-vaulting. There are many artifacts of women gripping the horns of the bull, but the "Toureador Fresco" [3] is the best example. Two female and one male acrobat are seen. Each wears a loin cloth and girdle; foot wear shows pointed shoes and short garters or stockings, and strips of leather are around the hands for a better grip. One female acrobat is depicted holding the horns, while the other appears to be assisting the landing of the vaulters. This is by far the most dangerous activity women are seen engaged in in the ancient western world.

Eisen believes [2] that there is the possibility of a female swimmer in a seal impression, but the evidence is not clear. The "Ring of Minos" also shows a woman rowing [2]. Hunting has already been mentioned, the Mother Goddess being depicted as a huntress — women are shown associated with the hunting of lions, deer, boar and are seen in chariots associated with the hunt. Women using the spear and the bow are in evidence in some of these artifacts. Fishing is also seen [2].

The discovery of numerous board games [6], particularly the Royal "Draught Board" from Knossos, and knucklebones and various toys leads one to the assumption that these activities may have been pursued by women and girls.

The extensive literature on the Greeks in comparison to the other civilizations and the limitation of space necessitate a brief summary. Greek women, according to Eisen, participated in the following physical activities [2]:

> Surviving literary sources, inscriptions, vase-paintings, and sculptures confirm the active participation of ancient Greek maidens in sports. According to these sources, women played ball-games, participated in gymnastics, swam, hunted, drove chariots, wrestled, throw [sic] the discus, and took part in foot races.

In addition to Eisen's list, dancing has to be added, plus board games and the use of toys and knucklebones.

Howell [7] has presented a paper on the participation of women in the Heraen games and their participation as owners of horses and chariots at Olympia. Moreover, Eisen again emphasizes the relationship of the Greek goddesses to sport.

The most complete analysis of the physical activity of the Etruscans is by Sawula [19]. The physical activities participated in by women are the following: dancing, which was extensively practiced, and again evidence of musical instruments is profuse, wrestling (Peleus against Atlanta), acrobatics, the game of kottabos, top spinning, perhaps game boards and even dice. Moreover, the Etruscan women are often depicted as spectators at athletic events.

The two most complete analyses of the Romans and their physical activities are by Lindsay [9] and Bishop [1]. They cite evidence of Roman women participating in the following activities: the use of hot baths, and presumably swimming, ball games, as spectators at the Colosseum and Circus Maximus, occasional gladiatorial combat ("dwarfs and women against each other" [9]) and women against women [9], running [9], swinging heavy weights [9] in the gymnasium, fencing [9], gymnastic contests [9], archery [9], hoop play [9], knucklebones [9], tops [9], dancing [1], exercising using dumbbells (or jumping using *halteres*) and throwing the discus [1]. Various children's games such as nut games and evidence of toys [1] including dolls and playing with pets as well as board games are additional activities done by girls and women.

This paper, then, involving both literary and archeological evidence, is a summary of the physical activities, rather than sport, in the ancient western world. As the evidence becomes more profuse, particularly with the Greeks and the Romans, more physical activities are seen. Those activities displaying commonality are music, dancing, board games and toys. Those particularly unique are the dangerous bull vaulting of the Minoans and the occasional gladiatorial combat among the Romans. The early civilizations, particularly in Mesopotamia, depict very few activities that women indulged in, which may have been a mirror of those cultures. However, it must always be kept in mind that our observations may be incorrect since they are, simply, a function of the available evidence. As Gottschalk put it [4]:

> . . . only a part of what was observed in the past was remembered by those who observed it; only a part of what was remembered was recorded; only a part of what was recorded has survived; only a part of what has survived has come to the historian's attention; only a part of what has come to their attention is credible; only a part of what is credible has been grasped; and only a part of what has been grasped can be expounded or narrated by the historian.

References

1. Bishop, W.H.: The Role of Physical Activities in Ancient Rome. M.A. Thesis, University of Alberta, Spring 1970, pp. 117, 155, 202-215.
2. Eisen, G.: Women in the Ancient World. M.A. Thesis, University of Massachusetts, pp. 46, 47, 56-67, 77, 94-100, 114, 115, 141, 142, 151.
3. Evans, A.: Palace of Minos, Vol III, Plate XVIII, pp. 67, 73-80, Fig. 144.
4. Gottschalk, L.: Understanding History. New York:Knopf, 1950.

5. Gurney, O.R.: The Hittites. Harmondsworth:Penguin Books, Ltd, 1966, Plate 29.
6. Howell, M.L. and Palmer, D.: Sports and Games in the Minoan Period.
7. Howell, R.: Women in the Ancient Greek Games. Paper presented at the Research Section, Western Society of College Physical Education Women, Asilomar, November 8, 1975 (to be published in the Proceedings).
8. Kramer, P.S.: The Sumerians. Chicago:University of Chicago Press, 1963, p. 25.
9. Lindsay, P.: Literary Evidence of Physical Education Among the Ancient Romans, M.A. Thesis, University of Alberta, August, 1967, pp. 83, 87, 112, 131, 149, 150, 175, 202, 217, 219.
10. Margueron, J.C.: Mesopotamia. Harrison, H.S.B. (trans.). London:Frederick Muller Ltd., 1965, Plate 9.
11. Meikle, D.F.: Recreational and Physical Acvivities of the Sumerian and Hittite Civilizations. M.A. Thesis, University of Alberta, Spring, 1971, pp. 16, 52, 163, 164.
12. Mellink, J.M.: A Hittite Cemetery at Gordion. Philadelphia:The University Museum, University of Pennsylvania, 1956, p. 42.
13. Montet, B.: Everyday Life in Egypt. London:Edward Arnold Macmillan, 1935, Vol. 4, p. 101.
14. Palmer, D.: Sport and Games in the Art of Early Civilizations, M.A. Thesis, University of Alberta, 1967, p. 49.
15. Parrot, A.: Sumer. Gilbert, S. and Emmons, J. (trans.). London:Thames and Hudson, 1960, Fig. 155, p. 126.
16. Pritchard, J.B.: The Ancient Near East in Pictures. Princeton:Princeton University Press, 1954, pp. 62, 220.
17. Putnam, J.: Concept of Sport in Minoan Art.
18. Sachs, C.: World History of the Dance. New York:W. W. Norton and Co., 1937, p. 4.
19. Sawula, L.W.: Physical Activities of the Etruscan Civilization. M.A. Thesis, University of Alberta, Spring, 1969, 194 pp.
20. Spier, D.L.: The Influences of Warfare on the Recreational Activities of the Ancient Assyrians and Iranians. M.A. Thesis University of Alberta, Spring, 1975, pp. 160, 161.
21. Touny: Sport in Ancient Egypt. p. 27.
22. Vieyra, M.: Hittite Art 2300-750 B.C. London:Alec Teranti, 1955, Plates 37, 53, 72.
23. Woolley, L.: Carcemish Report on the Excavations at Jerablus on Behalf of the British Museum, Part III, Trustees of the British Museum, London, 1952, p. 257.
24. Woolley, L.: Ur Excavations: The Royal Cemeteries, Vol. II. Oxford University Press, 1934, pp. 274-279.
25. Xenophon: Cyropaedia. Miller, W. (trans.). Loeb Classical Library, London: William Heinemann Ltd., 1914.

History of the Olympic Program and Perspectives for Its Future Development

Nadejda Lekarska

Introduction

A global revision of the Olympic Program is under way. It is the first of the kind. The purpose in view is to establish whether (a) the Olympic Program is fulfilling its primary goal to encourage the international development of sports, and vice versa, to reflect the level of popularity attained in the substance of the Olympic Games and (b) whether the Program is well proportioned, stable and capable of being kept under control, following the amendments of the standing rules.

Another important event which has the privilege of a first performance is the discussion on the Olympic Program at the 10th Olympic Congress in Varna in 1973. In addition to this the Commission on the Olympic Program is the first among the permanent IOC commissions to have prepared a study on the discussion at the Olympic Congress, which has been adopted by the IOC at Innsbruck this year as a basic document for the Olympic program. The questions at issue were both of present and historic interest. There is, however, a significant independent period when the enthusiasm of a few, inspired by the faith and energy of de Coubertin, was to be converted into a living reality. It is beyond doubt that the Olympic Games have given the initial impetus to an international development of sports despite the fact that the IOC has been at that time a lonely nucleus without subordinates. The success of the first Olympics was such that the IOC was compelled to keep the interest of the public alive, as well as to channel the powerful growth of the Games. The first move in that respect was to establish rules for Olympic competitions. In 1907 a commission was appointed to prepare the rules for four sports. At the same time the "legislation" and entire judging of the Olympic Games in London were placed in the hands of the

Nadejda Lekarska, Bulgarian Olympic Committee, Sofia, Bulgaria.

British Olympic Council which drew up the rules for 18 sports. The IOC did its best to build up the Olympic Program, but its members, though full of goodwill, were not specialists on technical matters. The majority of international sports federations came into being after World War I and in 1920 the technical organization of the Games was entrusted to the care of the International Federations. The substance of the Olympic Program, however, remained the privilege of the IOC. A world war interrupted the Games. Physical education and sports were steered into broader channels and the IOC was now concerned with a new problem — the rapid growth of the Olympic Games. It was worry about these new dimensions that gradually turned into potent fear. Reduction, believed to be the sole remedy, was a tendency stemming from uncertainty and a lack of knowhow on the management of the Program. Reduction having grown into an aim in itself has been more or less constantly included in the agenda of the IOC sessions. The same subject came up for discussion at the 10th Olympic Congress. It is against the background of these debates that I shall attempt to outline the historical development of the problems involved. On the basis of similarity and divergence in the substance of the discussions we have two groups of views.

Similar Views

Minimum and Maximum Number of Sports on the Olympic Program

This matter has a 26-year-old history. In 1957 a minimum of 15 sports was adopted and in 1962 a maximum of 18. The latter was a short-lived decision because of the risk of subjective appraisal involved. However, the minimum was maintained, although deprived to my mind, of an accurate meaning. No doubt it was a necessity at the time when the Olympic host cities were entitled to determine the substance of the Olympic Program (1954). The danger of staging anemic Olympic Games was then tangible. In 1964 the IOC decided to reestablish its former rights — to be the only judge of the Olympic Program. The possibility of organizing unsubstantial Games was thus, and still is, clearly avoided.

Continental Selection for Olympic Games

This problem has now been discussed for 50 years. In 1924 Jules Rimet, president of the International Football Association, suggested the establishment of pre-Olympic tryouts on the geographical principle for all team sports. It was in 1953 that a similar suggestion was adopted by the IOC. The delegates to the 10th Olympic Congress were, as a whole, against granting the Continental Games the right to be considered tryouts, particularly for the Olympic individual sports.

Criteria for the Admission of Sports to the Olympic Program

This is a new problem and was met with understanding and approbation by the Congress. It actually is a necessity in view of placing the Olympic Program on a solid basis of sound principles.

Divergent Views

Reduction of the Number of Entries

This matter was raised in 1952 though no decision was adopted. At the Congress the majority of IF representatives spoke against any reduction of the number of entries with reference to the established entry quota per sport and event. I believe this reduction to be of great importance in order to place as far as possible all Olympic sports on an equal footing.

Reduction of the Number of Events

It is to be noted that the Olympic Program has not increased by the number of sports but rather by the disorderly inflation of events within the individual sports. In 1896 there were ten sports and 42 events. In 1972 there were 22 sports and 191 events. While the number of sports has increased twice in the course of 80 years, the events have expanded five times during the same period. Some sports have reached the stage of stability, regarding their Olympic program, fairly early, while others mark extreme troughs and crests. If a certain debility may be considered normal at the beginning, when neither guidelines nor traditions existed, strong fluctuations at a later stage could hardly be justified. The Olympic Games have obviously served as an experimental field for the introduction of a deletion of events. At the 10th Olympic Congress the tendency for the reduction of events was met negatively on behalf of the IFs, though positively by a large number of representatives mainly of the NOCs.

Centralization and Decentralization of the Olympic Games

Centralization referring to the Games implies the respect of the principle for unity of time and place, that is, the staging of the

Games in one place within an established period. This very important principle is now countered by a number of sports officials. The problem has a rich past. The first move to split the Games was made in 1907. The idea then was to stage the Olympics in two distinct cycles — indoor sports in April and outdoor sports in June. In 1952 a suggestion was advanced to transfer some sports from the Olympics to the Olympic Winter Games. The nine consulted IFs have all refused such transfer. Winter sports have their specific snow and ice landscape. Any other indoor sport would be considered an outsider. The ideas of decentralization have in the meantime increased. Suggestions advocate three cycles — winter, spring and summer, or: winter, athletics and swimming separately and all other indoor and outdoor sports in a third cycle; the awarding of the Games to a country and not to a city; a joint organization of the Games by two or more neighboring countries. All extreme suggestions, however, found no response at the Congress. To decentralize the Games completely would inevitably lead to the loss of their specific character as a forum not only of top performance but also as a gathering of world youth united under the aegis of peace.

Team Sports

The dispute over team sports has honorably celebrated its 50th birthday. One of the arguments against team sports was that the Games are supposed to be contests between individuals and not between nations. This concept has now been, for a long time past, outdated. At the time when the Olympic Games were founded team sports were by far not popular. At present the world of sports would be poor without them. No voice was heard against team sports at the 10th Olympic Congress. They have by now honorably defended their right to be on the Olympic Program.

New Tendencies

In 1968 an ad hoc Program Commission, composed of an equal number of IOC and NOC members, was set up under the presidency of Dr. A. Csanadi of Hungary. It started its activity with a total revision of the Olympic Program. The study revealed the lagging behind of the Olympic women's program, a lack of balance between various sports and an unjustified increase of events within the individual sports. It was also noted that the rules governing the Olympic Program were outdated; that the reduction of the Olympic Program had become an aim in itself; that the Program had no global concept to lean on. The Commission approached all these problems carefully and most of the suggestions advanced to the Executive Board and the IOC were adopted. New rules were drafted, measures were taken to overcome the shortcomings of the women's program, a reduction of entries was accomplished following a well-established system so as to avoid any disparity between them and some events were deleted with the consent of the respective IFs. The Commission which has obtained a permanent IOC status prepared criteria for the admission of sports to the Program and is at present preparing guidelines on the Olympic status of events, as well as such on the recognition of sports which are not included in the Olympic Program. The Commission works diligently without overtones nor wishful thinking.

A few words on the development of the women's program: It indicates a very poor increase in the number of sports from two in 1900 to ten in 1972. Between 1900 and 1920 there were four sports. From 1920 to 1936 this number remained unchanged. The sports differed, however. Between 1948 and 1972 there were ten sports, and between 1972 and 1976 four new sports were added. They are 14 now, three of which are a joint participation with men. At present the women's program reflects an encouraging development of women's sports on the international level.

Perspectives for Future Development of the Olympic Program

The future may be near and distant. I think that the near future as a historic concept might be extended to the end of this century. As for the distant one, any forecast would be a daring pretension. I presume that the number of athletes from different countries will be increasing. The development of sports on the continental level indicates that two of them — Africa and Asia — which include the largest number of developing countries, are actually on the up and up. Considering the number of affiliated national federations, affiliated to the respective international federations, we find that Africa is ahead of Europe and the Americas in track and field, basketball, boxing and football, level with the Americas in volleyball and slightly behind Europe. Asia is ahead of the Americas in football and field hockey, but ahead of both Europe and the Americas in volleyball, etc. Participation coming from an increased number of countries is an enjoyable perspective. Should peace prevail in the world, which we ardently hope and believe, there would be no doubt that the financial and technical means of the Olympic host cities will increase. If in addition the admission of new sports and events is kept under control according to the established standards and criteria, we might expect the maintenance of the principle of unity of time and space though in a more flexible form. This would imply awarding the Games to a country and not to a town. Should this be adopted then a space limit around the central city will probably be established, taking into consideration the difference in size between countries and the danger of turning the Olympic Games into a string of separate world championships. One organization center where the opening and closing ceremonies shall be held shall probably be maintained in the future, too!

It is most probable that the Program shall be cleared of all that is superfluous. Circumstances indicate a new and far more constructive attitude toward the problems of the Olympic Program. In comparison with the past, when its development was rather incidental, the view at present is ripe in favor of a well-balanced and coherent Program. Never before had the leadership of the IOC attached such marked attention to the updating of the Olympic Program. A favorable wind is blowing!

The Olympic Movement Restored: The 1908 Games

Maxwell L. Howell and Reet Howell

The Modern Olympic Games began in 1896, and a mere 12 or 13 nations were represented [6, 7]. It would be incorrect to say those nations sent athletes, since national selections of teams and indeed national teams, competing in the official uniform of the country, simply had not emerged. Robert Garrett, the wealthy Princeton undergraduate, reportedly not only paid his own way but that of the other Princeton undergraduates. The lone Australian entry, E. H. Flack, was residing in London and competing for a track club there. The Greek government went bankrupt and a private citizen, George Averoff, built the Olympic stadium. The stadium was built on ancient lines which occasioned considerable problems for the athletes, particularly in the throwing events and rounding the curves in the running events.

The 1896 Games were poorly attended, low-key and basically for the athlete who had enough money to pay his own way. There were many farcical aspects, particularly in the swimming events held in Piraeus harbor, where the swimmers were dropped in the water and tread water until the starter fired his gun. The simple fact, however, was that the 1896 Games were an unmitigated success. They were handled intelligently with warmth and sincerity, and the national pride of the Greeks was felt by all. The Royal Family even acted as judges — the whole nation was involved. It was an excellent start for the Olympic movement and a credit to Greek organization and the persistence of the man who conceived of the overall plan, Baron Pierre de Coubertin. It appeared that a new social movement had been successfully launched, and all looked ahead to the 1900 Games to be held in Paris in conjunction with the World Exposition.

But the French showed apathy toward the Games, and de Coubertin was shunted aside, Daniel Mèrillon being appointed in his stead [5]. It was felt that the Olympic Games might detract from the World Fair, and so it was deemphasized [1]. The organization was

---

Maxwell L. Howell and Reet Howell, San Diego State University, San Diego, California, U.S.A.

poor, the Hungarians, British, Danes and Swedes complaining that they could get no replies from Paris following letters. And de Coubertin's plans incorporated the traditional activities of the Olympics, but he projected motor car racing, fireman's drill and ballooning [4] and even announced that there would "be special competitions for professionals" [4]. The Olympics was not even mentioned in the advertising, it being named Concour Internationaux d'Exercises Physiques et du Sport.

The teams were placed all over Paris, the U.S. representatives usually being quartered according to the university they came from. The track and field was held at the Bois de Boulogne, but the Racing Club de France, which owned the property, refused to cut the trees and hence in the throwing events the equipment often landed in the trees. The track was bumpy and sloped, the take-off jump was loose, and so on. Swimming was held a considerable distance from Paris, and the fencing events began on May 14 and ended June 24.

The French insisted on holding events on a Sunday, and many Americans withdrew — the universities of Chicago, Michigan, Syracuse, Princeton and Yale withdrew.

The Olympic movement received a considerable setback in Paris in 1900 and a worse one in 1904. Originally established for Chicago, the Olympic Games were given to St. Louis because of the World Exposition commemorating the purchase of the Louisiana Territory. The U.S. authorities, aware of criticism in selecting a U.S. city, stated that a ship would be sent to pick up European athletes. No ship arrived. England and France did not send a competitor to St. Louis, and Baron Pierre de Coubertin did not attend. Many American universities refused to participate — Harvard, Yale, Pennsylvania, Columbia, Dartmouth, Georgetown, Amherst, Michigan, Wisconsin, Minnesota and the Western minor colleges. The countries that participated were Germany, Greece, Hungary, Canada, Australia, Zululand, the Transvaal and Cuba.

The management of the Fair advertised all local sports events as "Olympics," and there were consequently some 390 "Olympic Champions," though officially there were only 88 [1]. As for the Kaffir and Transvaal representatives, they were working concessions at the fair and decided to compete.

The facilities were better than Paris, though the swimming facilities were poor. Valuable trophies were given to the winners, and A. G. Spalding even gave a team championship trophy, won on a dispute by the New York Athletic Club. Of 23 track and field events, the U.S. scored 22 firsts, 22 seconds and 20 thirds. The 1904 Olympics was scarcely more than a U.S. Olympics.

The marathon turned into a disgrace from the first to the finish. Fred Lorz was later found to have ridden a number of miles in an automobile. It is a wonder the winner Thomas J. Hicks ever made it, since he was given brandy, strychnine and raw eggs during the race.

But the ultimate in farce occurred in the handicap events, where even high school boys competed against Olympic champions. Etienne Desmarteau, for example, the Olympic 56-pound Canadian champion, actually threw the weight farther than when he won the Gold Medal and took fourth place. And the "Anthropology Days" continued the farce, as Pygmies and Kaffirs and Ainus and Patagonians and so on competed against one another. What, indeed, had happened to the Olympic movement? It had become a mere sideshow for World Fairs.

The 1906 Games in Athens aided in the restoration of respectability, but it is not officially recognized. However, its stabilizing influence was considerable.

The Olympics, it has to be conceded, had not captured the imagination of the world, and was not the social movement that the Baron believed it would be. The Baron, the French and the English did not even appear at St. Louis. A great responsibility, therefore, shifted to the organizers of the 1908 Games in London.

Actually, the 1908 Games were scheduled for Rome, but the 1906 Vesuvius eruption occasioned financial difficulties, and the organizers asked to be relieved of the responsibility. Great Britain offered its services, and the Games were awarded to London, though it had not been planned there until at least 1920. Again, the Games were held in conjunction with a worldwide exposition, the Franco-British exhibition.

After the experience of the 1900 and 1904 Olympics, when running Games in conjunction with expositions of world importance was proven to be a failure, predictably the 1908 Games was doomed. However, the organizers of the Franco-British exhibition were enthusiastic and agreed to build the stadium and other facilities at their own expense. Indeed, one quarter of the gross receipts would go to the British Olympic Committee. The stadium, which was built at Shepherd's Bush in London, had a seating capacity of 7,000, and had the unique features that the swimming pool and diving tower were actually in the stadium as well as a cycling track. Because of the heavy financial involvement of the organizers of the exhibition, they wanted the Games to be a success and did all they could in its promotion.

Because it was a Franco-British exhibition, the French and British wished to do well, and the French government gave 50,000 francs to allow the various sporting associations to compete in the London Olympics (London *Times*, June 1, 1908). The English philosophy was quite clear (London *Times*, July 11, 1908):

> It is commonly said, and, indeed, is put forward as a conclusive argument in favor of the modern Olympic movement, that international athletics encourage international amity. This is only the case if they are organized in so orderly and impartial a manner that every competitor, whether he has won or lost, goes away satisfied and feeling that every opportunity has been given and every courtesy shown to him. That this will be the case at the Olympic Games of London no Briton and, we feel sure, none of our foreign visitors can doubt, and, if that be so, the Games cannot fail to be an immense value both to those who take part in them and to the nations to which they belong.

American attitudes, alas, were different, and the headlines of the *New York Times* (July 12, 1908) were perhaps indicative of the problems that were to emerge: "American Athletes Sure of Success; Trainer Murphy and Manager Halpin Confident that Premier Honors Will Be Won By U.S."; "Britishers Fear Yankee Athletes"; "We Will Knock The Spots Off the Britishers." The American philosophy of competition, at least as openly expressed, was certainly different to the British.

The Games were well organized, with none of the haphazard scheduling and difficulty of finding out about events that scarred the 1900 and 1904 Olympics. Indeed, the only criticism was that the officiating was solely in the hands of the English (London *Times*, July 11, 1908):

> The management of each branch of the games is exclusively in the hands of the associations governing that sport in this country. They provide all officials, and are responsible for the proper conduct of the competitions. The representation of foreign countries will take no part in the management . . . but each nation or country competing has the right to appoint three members of a Comite d'Honneur through which any protests or objections may be conveyed to the proper authority.

The actual Olympic Games were divided into four phases: (a) the first part of the summer games, including polo, tennis and golf; (b) the stadium events, which were mainly track and field and swimming; (c) the rowing and yachting events; and (d) the winter games, which included skating, association football and rugby. The four divisions extended from April until the end of October.

There were problems, as there were problems in previous Olympics, and as there have been problems in every subsequent Olympics. The Finnish athletes marched flagless, refusing to carry the Russian flag, and Irish athletes were upset because they competed for Great Britain [8]. Particularly upsetting was the fact that the flags of Sweden and the United States were surprisingly missing from those flying at the stadium, which perturbed those nations concerned (*New York Times*, July 14, 1908).

The main discordant note was the continual friction between the English and the United States officials and competitors. Reading the *New York Times* and the London *Times* daily it was as if two different Games were in progress. The London *Times* generally reported matters in a scholarly manner; the *New York Times* (July 13, 1908) was concerned with highlighting incidents that were occurring and claiming discrimination against the United States. For example, the pole vault:

> As was to be expected, some little friction has developed over the rules concerning some of the contests. The Americans have put in a claim that they ought to be permitted to dig a hole for the pole in the vaulting competition. This has been decided against.

This was not even reported in the London *Times*. Again, the Americans were incensed, on the fourth day, by the point scoring system used by the English (*New York Times*, July 17, 1908): "Athletes Aroused Over Point Scoring: English System of Marking Olympic Victories Would Make England Sure Winners." Again, this controversy, insofar as the United States was concerned, was not even reported in the London *Times*, and James E. Sullivan, the President of the American Olympic Committee, announced to the American press an American scoring system.

On the fifth day a controversy erupted about the tug-of-war, the United States complaining about the heavy boots the British wore. The headline of the *New York Times* (July 18, 1908) told the story: "English Unfair in Olympic Games"; "U.S. Protests Against Method of Holding the Tug-Of-War Complaint is Dismissed"; "Liverpool Team Wears Monstrous Shoes That Arouse Ire of Americans Who Kick in Vain."

The London *Times* (July 18, 1908) reported in a matter-of-fact manner:

> A serious controversy has arisen between the American athletes and the BOC. America's chief cause of complaint is the arbitrary manner in which their protest against the flagrantly unfair method of conducting the tug-of-war was dismissed.

The basis of the ruling was that they were the same shoes worn by the Liverpool policemen in their ordinary work.

On the sixth day of competition the United States lodged a protest re the draw in the 800-meter run and it was, therefore, a relief when the next day there was no competition, being Sunday. The relief was short-lived, and the greatest controversy of all erupted in the 400-meter run. The London *Times* (July 24, 1908) described it in this manner:

> Two Americans were leading with the Englishman Halswelle third. Halswelle closed until about even when the American who was next to him began to run wide, with the result that soon after Halswelle turned the bend he was forced very nearly onto the bicycle track. The interference with Halswelle appeared to the judges so palpable that they broke the tape while the race was still in progress before the runners reached the winning-posts. It certainly seemed as if the Americans had run the race on a definite and carefully thought out plan. It was not as if Carpenter, the one who forced Halswelle to run wide and elbowed him severely as he tried to pass him, had himself taken a wide curve at the bend and then run straight on. He appeared rather to run diagonally crossing in front of the Englishman so that he was obliged to lose several yards. That is a fair and impartial account of what happened as far as it could be judged from the stand,

The *New York Times* (July 24, 1908) reported: "Carpenter of Cornell Easily Beats England Crack, But Is Disqualified for Foul. Officials Claim Bump Race to be Re-Run, English Crowds Boo American Performers for No Reason Whatsoever."

The race was declared void and a re-run was ordered. The American runners refused to run, and in an Olympic rarity Halswelle won in a walkover.

On the last day of competition, the United States lodged another protest, this time against Tom Longboat, the Indian marathon runner with the Canadian team, on the grounds of his professionalism. Longboat was given permission to compete, though he was not a factor in the race.

But the marathon turned out to be the most dramatic event of the Games and again resulted in the American protest which, however, was upheld.

The London *Times* (July 25, 1908) reported it in this manner:

> And at last he comes. A tired man, dazed, bewildered, hardly conscious, in red shorts and white vest, his hair white with dust, staggers on to the track. It is Dorando, the Italian. He looks about him, hardly knowing where he is. Just the knowledge that somehow, by some desperate resolve of determination, he must get round the 200 yards to the tape of the finish keeps him on his feet. Fifty yards, and it cannot even be that. He falls on the track, gets up, staggers on a few yards, and falls again, and yet again, and then he reaches the last turn. The goal is in sight, though his closed eyes cannot see it. He is surrounded by officials almost, if not quite, supporting him, urging, and cheering him on. If they were not there he would fall. He cannot run straight and yet 50 yards from the end he suddenly bursts into a pathetic, almost a horrible, parody of a sprint, drops again ten yards from the tape, rises, staggers forward over those last terrible few yards, and has reached his goal.

But Dorando was disqualified because of the physical assistance he received in the most dramatic event of the Games. Johnny Hayes of the United States was awarded the victory following the American protest. Feelings were assuaged when Queen Alexandra made a special award in Dorando's honor.

The protests have been highlighted in this paper, but they were essentially from the United States with the exception of a French protest in cycling. The U.S. team and officials were win-oriented, perhaps overeager, and certainly were far ahead in athletic ability and training techniques. Things taken for granted in the United States, for example a hole for the pole vault, could not be taken for granted elsewhere in the world.

Other countries disagreed with the U.S. about the conduct of the Games. The Swedish team had this to say (London *Times*, September 28, 1908):

> Thanks for the great hospitality and kindness shown to the Swedish Olympic competitors and to state at the same time how greatly they appreciated the good will and fair play which governed the spirit in which the games were conducted.

There were lessons to be learned, to be sure. The officiating obviously could no longer be the sole responsibility of the host country, and a better method of handling protests had to be achieved. Incidentally, the official 1908 report stated that each appeal had to be accompanied by a deposit of 1£, which would be lost if the original decision were correct. One might reflect that the U.S. Olympic budget was considerably depleted during the Games. American summaries of the 1908 Games have generally been prejudiced, whereas in retrospect it is felt by the authors that the Olympic movement was saved, that it "turned the corner," so to speak. The 1908 Games achieved wide acceptance, it was not an appendage to a world exhibition. Eighteen nations and 981 individuals participated in the march past, a considerable change from the other three Olympics [2]. There were 109 events participated in. The organization and administration of the Games were effective, and the problems that did appear were obvious and were remedied in future Games. Ugly scenes resulting from excess nationalism were evident even after the Games. As Cook wrote [3]:

> Their official representatives celebrated their return to the United States by a disgraceful campaign of slander and misrepresentation.

The moderate view of the London *Times* appeared to sum up the majority opinion (London *Times*, July 27, 1908):

> The games have not been all plain-sailing. The perfect harmony which every one wished for has been marred by certain regrettable disputes and protests, and objections to the judge's rulings . . . But, at all events, the main object . . . has been the promotion of international courtesy and friendly feeling, as well as the interests of true sport . . . Let it be granted then . . . that there could have been mistakes on all sides. What else could we expect and what, after all, does it matter, as long as we part friends? That, fortunately, we may and will do. We have seen each other, all we of the 20 nations who have competed in the games, face to face, and learnt, as we did not know before, what manner of men we all are. We have seen wonderful feats of athletic skill accomplished, many of them greater than any that have been recorded in the history of the world.

Overall, it can be adjudged that the 1908 London Games restored the Olympic movement, after the farces of 1900 and 1904.

Acknowledgment

Appreciation is expressed to George R. Mathews for his research in the (London) *Times* and the *New York Times*.

References

1. Barcs, S.: The Modern Olympic Story. Hungary:Corvina Press, 1964, pp. 25, 26, 32.
2. British Olympic Council, Cook, T.A. (ed.): The Official Report of the Olympic Games of 1908. London: The British Olympic Association, 1909.
3. Cook, T.A.: International Sport. London: Constance and Co., Ltd., 1910, pp. 228.
4. de Coubertin, P.: The Mutiny of the Olympic Games. North Am. Rev. June 1900, pp. 804, 808-889.
5. Howell, R. and Howell, M.L.: The 1900 and 1904 Olympic Games: The Farcical Games. Paper presented to the VI International HISPA Seminar, Trois-Rivieres, Quebec, July, 1976.
6. Howell, M.L. and Nurmberg (Howell), R.: The Value and Future of the Olympic Games. JAMA 221:982, 1972.
7. Howell, M.L.: The Ancient Olympic Games and the 1896 Games: Differences and Future Prospects. Address Given to the International Olympic Academy, Olympia, Greece, July 1971. (Published in the Proceedings of the International Olympic Academy.)
8. Kieran, J.: The Story of the Olympic Games. New York:Stokes Co., 1937, pp. 85-100.

L'idée olympique de Pierre de Coubertin et Carl Diem et son aboutissement dans l'académie internationale olympique

Norbert Müller

Les expressions 'Olympie' et 'Jeux Olympiques' sont aujourd'hui, d'un usage courant. Cependant, la seule importance d'Olympie dans l'Antiquité, n'a pas suffi à faire revivre Olympie et les Jeux Olympiques au 20ème siècle. Le mérite en revient au français Pierre de Coubertin, dont le but était initialement le renouveau corporel et moral de la jeunesse, et l'idéal celui du pédagogue anglais Thomas Arnold [15-17].

A partir de 1892, les efforts de Coubertin portêrent surtout sur l'internationalisation des sports à l'aide des Jeux Olympiques rétablis [6]. Il fut particulièrement motivé dans son action, par la redécouverte archéologique d'Olympie de 1875 à 1881 [8].

Pour Coubertin cependant, les Jeux Olympiques n'étaient que le cadre institutionalisé de la réalisation de ses conceptions anthroposophiques, qu'il nommait au début l'Idée Olympique, puis après 1912, l'Olympisme. Cette idée devait surtout réunir le plus de gens possible dans un Mouvement Olympique.

L'Idée Olympique a un sens profond et des possibilités éducatrices multiples qui vont bien au delà des Jeux Olympiques. Pour le montrer, Coubertin eut recours à un grand nombre d'initiatives. Parallèlement à une imposante production littéraire, qui s'étale sur plus de 60.000 pages imprimées, il convoqua entre 1897 et 1925, sept Congrès Olympiques* [19], et ajouta en 1912, un concours artistique au programme olympique. Puis, il apporta son concours à l'établissement de centres sportifs communaux, tel que l'Institut Olympique de Lausanne en 1917, et incita même à la création

Norbert Müller, Département d'éducation physique, Université de Mainz, République fédérale d'Allemagne.

*Le Havre, 1897; Bruxelles, 1905; Paris, 1906; Lausanne, 1913; Paris, 1914; Lausanne, 1921; Prague, 1925; Berlin, 1930.

d'universités populaires en 1920 [5]. 'Il faut toucher les masses' [7], aimait à répéter Coubertin. Ces mots retracent mieux qu'aucuns autres, son programme après 1918. Mais, trente ans après leur rétablissement, bien que les Jeux Olympiques eussent pris une importance insoupçonnée, le but initial de Coubertin, qui était le perfectionnement moral de l'humanité sur les bases d'une éducation olympique utilisant à la fois le corps et l'esprit, n'avait pu être atteint. Seule cette constatation, permet de comprendre pourquoi, après son renoncement à la présidence du CIO en 1925 à Prague, il fonda l'Union Pédagogique Universelle et en 1926, le Bureau International de Pédagogie Sportive. Son but était 'la création d'une pédagogie productive, claire d'idées et sereine de critique' [3].

Cependant, même à travers ces institutions, Coubertin ne réussit pas à implanter ses conceptions pédagogiques universelles, dans les différents systèmes éducatifs des pays représentés. Il dut reconnaître, que ses buts qui dépassaient le simple cadre des Jeux Olympiques, n'étaient pas réalisables. Mais, comment eut-il pu désavouer l'oeuvre qui était le but même de sa vie?

Les idées de Coubertin furent reprises par l'allemand Carl Diem, une génération plus jeune que lui, et qui mieux qu'aucun autre avait compris sa façon de voir. Son expérience personnelle des Jeux Olympiques intermédiaires de 1906 à Athènes, son premier contact avec l'Antiquité grecque, et les idées défendues par Coubertin avaient enthousiasmé Diem. Ce qui réunissait Diem et Coubertin, c'était leur conviction pédagogique, l'amour des arts, et leurs idées réformatrices pour un humanisme moderne. Pour ces deux hommes, le sport était, par la variété de ses exercices physiques et par son esprit de compétition, le renouveau dont l'humanité moderne avait besoin. Seul, le sport était susceptible d'ammener chacun de nous à une humanité profonde et accomplie. Tout comme Coubertin, Diem avait une énergie infatigable, qui s'exprimait surtout dans son activité littéraire et son action organisatrice [9].

Aux Jeux Olympiques de 1936, Diem essaya en sa qualité de secrétaire général, de façonner les Jeux d'après les conceptions de Coubertin, et pour faire comprendre, au delà de la compétition, le rôle pédagogique de l'Idée Olympique. Encore sous l'impression première du succès des Jeux Olympiques de 1936, Coubertin proposa au gouvernement allemand au début de 1937, la création d'un 'Centre d'études olympiques' qui assurerait la 'protection et le développement de son oeuvre' [4]. Après la mort de Coubertin en septembre 1937, c'est à Diem seul qu'il incomba de poursuivre l'oeuvre pédagogique de Coubertin. Diem 'l'héritier moral' de

Coubertin, fut nommé en 1938, directeur de l'institut International Olympique de Berlin. En mars 1938, Diem suggéra au Comité Olympique Héllenique, la création d'une Académie Olympique, qui en qualité 'd'Ecole supérieure de l'Olympisme,' aurait pour mission de faire comprendre l'Idée Olympique à la jeunesse internationale [12, 13]. Malheureusement, la deuxième guerre mondiale vint interrompre le travail olympique et comme en 1914, dévia même l'olympisme de son idéal humanitaire. Après 1945, Diem proposa une nouvelle fois, la création d'une AIO [11]. Cependant, ce n'est qu'après bien des difficultés de tous ordres que, avec l'aide d'un membre grec du CIO Jean Ketseas et le soutien du Comité Olympique Héllenique, qu'enfin en 1961, elle fut réalisée [18].

Après la mort de Diem en décembre 1962, c'est l'AIO qui a pris l'héritage olympique en main. De 1961 à nos jours, près de deux milles étudiants et deux cents professeurs de 70 nations, se rencontrent chaque année au congrès annuel d'Olympie. Tout au début, l'AIO eut à faire face à de nombreuses difficultés d'ordre technique; mais depuis 1966, l'Académie est dotée d'un bâtiment moderne.

A chacune des Sessions, des savants de renom et des membres du CIO prennent la parole. Environ 250 exposés sont présentés, se répartissant à l'intérieur de neuf domaines:

1. Histoire des Jeux Olympiques et du sport;
2. L'Olympisme;
3. Les Jeux Olympiques et le Mouvement Olympique;
4. Les questions de pédagogie sportive;
5. Science de l'entrainement et du mouvement;
6. Philosophie du sport;
7. Médecine du sport;
8. Psychologie du sport;
9. L'informatique sportive.

En dehors des cours donnés, les participants discutent autour de problèmes actuels tels que le Mouvement Olympique, la question de l'amateurisme, l'avenir des Jeux, et la question de l'amélioration des performances sportives. Chaque fois, les conclusions de ces discussions sont acheminées au CIO, qui peut les utiliser lors de réglements de cas épineux [20].

Quatre enquêtes empiriques, réalisées par l'auteur entre 1968 et 1973, auprès des participants de sessions, permettent d'apprécier les réalisations de l'AIO [18].

Quel est le succès de l'AIO?

La réponse à cette question, ne peut être que multiple. Bien que certains exposés n'auraient pas eu besoin du cadre de l'AIO, la participation de nombreux savants renommés, qu'on ne retrouve habituellement qu'aux congrès scientifiques à l'occasion des Jeux Olympiques, ont mis l'AIO bien au-dessus de tous les congrès spécialisés habituels. Vraiment, il n'y a aucune institution comparable à l'AIO et à la forme de ses sessions. Dans aucune école supérieure de sport, dans aucun congrès d'académie, le lieu et le temps du déroulement des rencontres n'y sont plus heureux. Nulle part ailleurs, les problèmes du sport moderne, ne peuvent se discuter dans un cadre plus stimulant, que le paysage de ce stade mis à jour depuis 1961. Ces facteurs, liés à un engagement multilatéral, dans une recherche active de solutions aux problèmes du Mouvement Olympique, donnent l'impression, qu'une poursuite des conceptions de Coubertin et de Diem, est encore actuellement possible. Toutefois on ne peut savoir, si les deux milles participants, qui à ce jour, ont visité l'AIO, se sont comportés par la suite, dans leurs pays respectifs, en multiplicateurs de l'Idée Olympique'.

Cependant, les enquêtes faites montrent que la plupart quittent l'AIO, avec la ferme intention de collaborer à l'Idée Olympique. Du point de vue publicateur, c'est surtout dans les pays d'expression allemande, qu'une manifestation de l'idée olympique semble la plus marquée, mais c'est peut-être dû au grand nombre de participants allemands et autrichiens.

Les échanges sur le plan humain autant que les travaux spécialisés, ont fait de l'AIO un organisme de grande valeur. Dans aucune autre manifestation sportive, même aux Jeux, les participants, organisateurs et conférenciers n'ont jamais offert l'image d'une communauté plus pleine d'harmonie. Les rencontres et la compréhension internationales, qui représentent une part essentielle de l'Idée Olympique, trouvent à l'AIO une réalisation absolue. Vivre simplement, ainsi que le demandait Coubertin aux participants d'Olympie, est plus pleinement réalisable à Olympie, que dans un village olympique; de plus, à l'AIO, tous les participants se connaissent, ce qui n'est pas le cas à l'intérieur d'un village olympique où l'on retrouve plus de 10.000 personnes. La pratique des exercices sportifs, revêt une grande importance, selon la conception de Diem, et l'un des caractères essentiels de l'AIO est de montrer, qu'on peut réaliser dans la pratique, l'harmonie entre le corps et l'esprit. D'après les enquêtes effectuées, 85% des participants veulent participer une nouvelle fois à une session de l'AIO. Ce pourcentage reflète bien le succès de son enseignement. Même si la paix qui règne dans cette communauté annuelle, est "une paix à temps" [21], l'AIO contribue ainsi pour une part importante à l'entente internationale, et satisfait aux exigences de Coubertin:

> Demander aux peuples de s'aimer les uns les autres n'est qu'une manière d'enfantillage. Leur demander de se respecter n'est point une utopie, mais pour se respecter, il faut d'abord se connaître [2].

A l'avenir, grâce à plusieurs sessions annuelles, l'AIO devrait permettre la participation d'un plus grand nombre de jeunes, et non seulement d'étudiants, afin d'étendre son emprise éducatrice. Le programme de ces sessions devrait initier aux questions olympiques fondamentales. Diem attendait aussi de l'AIO, l'établissement 'scientifique du fondement de l'Olympisme' [10]. L'exposé de ces notions, devrait couvrir plusieurs cours d'été, d'une durée de plusieurs mois. Par les cours qu'il fit en 1961, Diem voulait donner le coup d'envoi et en faire l'essai. Cependant, une chose est certaine, si l'AIO veut devenir 'l'université d'été de l'Olympisme' et si les sessions annuelles veulent prodiguer une "studium generale" de l'Olympisme, alors il est nécessaire, qu'elle revêt une plus grande extension, dans le temps, la méthode et le contenu.

Si, selon les conceptions de Coubertin, l'AIO se veut 'un centre d'études olympiques' destiné 'à sauver et à faire progresser son oeuvre' [4], alors il faut qu'elle abrite continuellement un centre de recherche olympique, ainsi qu'on a commencé de le faire à l'Institut Olympique de Berlin. Parallèlement à la rédaction des Textes de Coubertin et autres grands représentants de l'Olympisme, la mission d'un tel centre devrait être aussi, le rassemblement à un même endroit de toute la littérature olympique. Un groupe d'experts devrait être formé, afin que dans l'esprit de solidarité olympique désiré, le contenu spirituel de l'Idée Olympique puisse être transmis, et pour que des stages d'organisation sportive soient réalisés. D'après les conceptions de Diem, des années 1938, l'AIO devrait être 'la réalisation scientifique commune de tous les pays' [14]. Le but proposé est toujours valable, mais il exige que l'AIO soit supportée par le CIO, les Comités nationaux olympiques et la Grèce, tous ensemble. Pour la 'sauvegarde et le progrès'[1] de l'oeuvre olympique de Coubertin, son ami Carl Diem dont il disait il est "génial et enthousiaste" [1], fonda l'Institut Olympique de Berlin. A la suite de ce testament spirituel, peu de temps après, l'AIO vit le jour.

L'oeuvre de rénovation des Jeux Olympiques et de 'réconciliation entre la force corporelle et la force intellectuelle' entreprise par

Coubertin, survécut à deux guerres mondiales, pendant lesquelles, l'Idée productrice de paix, cependant, ne put pas arriver à s'imposer. Diem continua l'oeuvre entreprise et mit ses espoirs dans l'AIO, qui avec le temps devrait donner à l'Idée Olympique, la crédibilité nécessaire.

Références

1. Coubertin, P. de: Discours du Baron de Coubertin pour la Clôture des Jeux olympiques de Berlin. *dans* Coubertin, P. de, L'Idée olympique, discours et essais. Stuttgart, 1966, p. 135.
2. Coubertin, P. de: Les assises philosophiques de l'Olympisme moderne. Message radiodiffusé, Berlin, 4 août 1935. *dans* Coubertin, P. de, L'Idée olympique, discours et essais. Stuttgart, 1966, p. 133.
3. Coubertin, P. de: Discours d'ouverture du Congrès olympique de Prague. *dans* Coubertin, P. de, L'Idée olympique, discours et essais. Stuttgart, 1966, p. 93.
4. Coubertin, P. de: Lettre au Reichsportfuhrer en date du 16 mars 1937. Revue olympique, 1:1938, p. 3.
5. Coubertin, P. de: Appel pour la création d'un enseignement universitaire ouvrier. Anthologie. Aix-en-Provence, 1933.
6. Coubertin, P. de: Une campagne de vingt-et-un ans. Paris, 1909. *dans* Mémoires olympiques. Aix-en-Provence, 1931.
7. Coubertin, P. de: XXV° Anniversaire des Jeux olympiques. Lausanne, 1919.
8. Curtius, E. *dans* Adler, F. (ed) Die Ergebnisse der von dem Deutschen Reich verstalteten Ausgrabung. Berlin, 1890-97, Vol. I à Vol. VI.
9. Diem, C.: Ein Leben für den Sport. Erinnerungen aus dem Nachlass. Dusseldorf, 1975.
10. Diem, C.: Elis per Neuzeit. *In* Olympische Akademie. Bericht über die vom NOK für Deutschland und dem griechischen Olympischen Komitee gemeinsam veranstalteten ersten Session der Olympischen Akademie. Dortmund, 1962, p. 20.
11. Diem, C.: Lettre à A. Brundage. Berlin, 18 décembre 1945.
12. Diem, C.: Coubertins Herz im ewigen Olympia. Reichsportblatt. Berlin, 12 April 1938.
13. Diem, C.: Lettre au Comité olympique hellénique. Berlin, 6 septembre 1938
14. Diem, C.: Der Tag vom Olympia. Revue olympique. Berlin, 2: 1938.
15. Findlay, J.: Arnold of Rugby. His School-Life and Contribution to Education. Cambridge, 1897.
16. Heintz, C.: Thomas Arnold aus seinen Briefen. Nach dem Englischen von A. P. Stanley. Potsdam, 1897.
17. McIntosh, P.: Physical Education in England Since 1800. London, 1952, p. 31.
18. Müller, N.: Die Olympische Idee Pierre de Coubertins und Carl Diems in ihrer Auswirkung auf die IOA. Thèse de doctorat, Gratz, 1975, pp. 112-142.
19. Réglements des Congrès olympiques de 1894 à 1930. Comité olympique bulgare. Sofia, 1973.
20. Reports of the Summer Sessions of the International Olympic Academy. Hellenic Olympic Committee (ed). Athens, 1962-1976.
21. Schelsky, H.: Friede auf Zeit. Osnabrück, 1973.

Les sports face à la politique

Louis Burgener

Recherches

Dans les documents publiés lors des Séminaires et Congrès de l'HISPA (Association internationale d'histoire de l'éducation physique et du sport) dont les membres proviennent de quelque cinquante pays de tous les continents, des centaines de communications ont été publiées, parmi lesquelles un bon nombre examine les sports face à la politique. L'HISPA possède plusieurs groupes internationaux de travail, dont celui de "Sport et politique" suscite des recherches intensives. En outre, quelques-uns de ses membres ont préparé une bibliographie choisie "Sport et politique," limitée à environ huit cents titres allemenands, anglais ou français, qui sera un instrument utile aux chercheurs, notamment aux politicologues et aux historiens. Enfin, une partie de mes travaux personnels examine les rapports entre les sports et les collectivités publiques à divers échelons. Partout, les méthodes utilisées ont été celles de l'histoire, de la sociologie et de la science politique, appliquées aux situations diverses.

Forte des recherches antérieures sur l'emprise de l'état totalitaire, qu'il soit historique ou contemporain, l'opinion répandue par les milieux intéressés veut que les sports et leurs dirigeants aient été les victimes toutes désignées de la politique et de l'Etat.

Pour le contrôle de cette thèse, nous allons nous limiter aux dernières décennies durant lesquelles les mass-media, la démocratisation et la commercialisation des sports et loisirs, la centralisation politique et administrative, enfin le nationalisme suscité par les competitions ont profondément marqué les relations entre les sports et la politique.

Les secteurs local et régional

Les sports, en particulier les activités physiques liées à des compétitions, sont politiques en ce sens qu'ils concernent des personnes (athlètes ou spectateurs) dans un milieu organisé poli-

---

Louis Burgener, Berne, Suisse.

tiquement pour l'ensemble de la vie humaine. En général, ils nécessitent l'appui des collectivités publiques pour l'entraînement, les constructions (stades, salles, piscines, etc), les loisirs et les compétitions (police des routes, ordre public). Grâce à leurs adhérents nombreux, tous électeurs, et répartis dans plusieurs partis politiques, les sports bénéficient, au niveau local, d'appuis parfois supérieurs à ceux des autres loisirs, tels que la musique, le théâtre, la lecture et le cinéma culturel.

Dans les régions, les dirigeants et les entraîneurs entretiennent avec les autorités des relations plus officielles, en "groupes de pression" permanents qui disposent du soutien des députés. A cet échelon, l'aide matérielle, fournie par l'économie concernée, dépasse déjà largement les prestations financières des athlètes et de leurs associations. Cells-ci dépendent ainsi des bailleurs de fonds, individuels ou collectifs, qu'il faut satisfaire à tout prix. Mais lorsque les spectateurs enthousiastes doivent voter des dépenses publiques aux compétitions, payées par leurs propres impôts, ils sont assez réticents. En Suisse, les citoyens de l'Etat de Berne et de la Ville de Zurich refusèrent, en 1969, un crédit pour organiser les Jeux olympiques d'hiver de 1976, tandis que ceux du Valais et de Grisons acceptaient ces dépenses promettant des recettes touristiques à la région. En vain, puisque Denver (Colorado, USA) fut choisi par la suite. Cependant, les électeurs de cette région refusèrent les crédits, de sorte que ces Jeux furent organisés par Innsbruck, sans consulter les citoyens autrichiens.

Au niveau national

Doté de la souveraineté, l'Etat possède les moyens indispensables aux sports de niveau international. Ceux-ci constituent un instrument de prestige diplomatique, d'expansion économique et surtout de propagande idéologique. Suscité par les mass-media et par ceux qui en tirent profit, le nationalisme est entretenu par une émulation effrénée qui prend parfois l'allure d'une véritable "guerre." A ce niveau, les fédérations sportives sont bien établies, les associations internationales étant faibles par rapport aux organisations nationales qui disposent de solides appuis au Parlement, au Gouvernement et dans l'Administration.*

D'autre part, les féderátions multi-sports, rattachées à un ensemble culturel ou politique comme les organisations socialistes,

*En Suisse, un groupement ad hoc de parlementaires de tous les partis soutient les demandes des fédérations et de l'administration centrale des sports; dans bien des pays, un Ministère spécial s'occupe de la Jeunesse et des Sports.

catholiques, etc., sont influentes par leurs très nombreux membres de tous âges, actifs ou passifs.* Réticentes à l'égard des hautes compétitions et de ceux qui en vivent,† elles restent fermement attachées au sport amateur, source de santé et de joie, moyen de garder le contact avec d'autres loisirs (chant, randonnées, beaux-arts, littérature) et avec des partenaires de même opinion politique, religieuse ou philosophique.‡

En face se situent les fédérations engagées dans les compétitions internationales, Jeux olympiques et championnats mondiaux. Le succès à tout prix§ dicte la marche à suivre, fût-elle au détriment de la santé publique et des sports populaires. La responsabilité en revient en premier lieu aux managers et bien moins aux athlètes payés.‖ Quant aux compétitions mondiales comme les Jeux olympiques, elles mobilisent chez l'organisateur des efforts et des sommes publiques énormes qu'aucun gouvernement ne pourrait dépenser s'il avait à demander l'avis par un référendum populaire, comme c'est la coutume dans les démocraties directes dont les citoyens décident des grandes dépenses et des impôts. Aiguillonnées par le prestige, des nations participantes consacrent des moyens démesurés à leurs athlètes, sans égard pour les autres besoins nationaux. L'examen objectif des sports devenus instrument politique a été fait sans ménagement en ce qui concerne le national-socialisme d'Allemagne (1933-1945), mais les chercheurs s'attachent de plus en plus à d'autres régimes, bien que dans plusieurs Etats, l'administration centrale des sports et les fédérations bénéficiares ne montrent aucun enthousiasme pour des enquêtes pareilles.

---

*En Suisse (6 millions d'habitants), la Société fédérale de gymnastique/SFG compte plus de 300.000 membres, dont un nombre appréciable occupe des situations importantes en politique locale, régionale et fédérale.

†Lors de la fête centrale de la SATUS (fédération ouvrière du sport), le 26 octobre 1974, à Zurich, le Conseiller fédéral (Ministre) suisse W. Ritschard, socialiste, a prononcé un discours dans lequel il a violemment attaqué le sport de haute compétition et ses tenants; la presque totalité des journalistes "sportifs" ont passé ce discours sous silence.

‡Le parti socialiste suisse dispose d'un ensemble d'organisations qui touchent divers domaines de la culture populaire; il en va de même du côté catholique.

§Le professeur G. Schönholzer de Berne, bien connu en médecine des sports, qualifie le sport de "Erfolgssport" lorsque tout est subordonné au succès et au prestige.

‖Plusieurs études ont déjà été consacrées à la puissance des managers et de leurs organisations. Nul doute que les juristes vont examiner le statut "syndical" des athlètes que réclament les mêmes droits (liberté de l'emploi, etc.) que les autres travailleurs.

Excitée par les mass-media qui ne péchent jamais par la modestie, la nation veut des médailles et des prix. Lorsque ceux-ci sont obtenus, un délire passager s'empare de certains journalistes*; les fédérations en profitent pour obtenir de nouveaux moyens auprès des autorités. En cas d'échec, les mass-media et les managers arrachent au Pouvoir des efforts supplémentaires, parfois même des changements dans les structures scolaires où le sport éducatif doit céder la place au sport spécialisé, prometteur de performance. Jamais un ministre n'a osé résister à des pressions pareilles, car le sport de haute compétition ne saurait être critiqué et soumis aux besoins généraux de l'Etat.† Ce dernier va jusqu'à la limite permise par les lois, et il n'hésite pas à accorder parfois des avantages supplémentaires, moins visibles dans les comptes publics. Bien des pays ont créé des Instituts scientifiques des sports dont les recherches fondamentales ou appliquées (médecine, biologie, psychologie, sociologie) sont au bénéfice presque exclusif des compétitions internationales. D'autres domaines de recherche, par exemple l'histoire et la science politique appliquées aux sports, sont délaissés et démunis de crédits (participation à des réunions scientifiques; publications), à moins qu'ils ne servent, eux aussi, l'Etat et ses managers des sports.‡

Les sports dans différents régimes politiques

Parmi les Etats totalitaires, l'Allemagne hitlérienne (1933-1945) a été l'objet d'analyses multiples et pénétrantes, encore que souvent partiales. La mise au pas des fédérations diverses s'y est faite

---

*Cf. l'enthousiasme éphémère suscité par les journalistes après les succès suisses aux Jeux olympiques d'hiver de 1972, à Sapporo.

†Cf. le Dr. H. Winzenried, député de Berne/Suisse: "Ich bin von versechied ensten Seiten recht massiv ersucht worden, dem verlangten (Olympia) Kredit keine Opposition zu machen . . . Noch selten ist es vorgekommen, dass eine so unvollständige Botschaft dem Grossen Rat (= Parlement régional) unterbreitet wurde, weil die Verfasser annehmen durften, dass wohl niemand es wagen würde, einen Kredit, der dem heute so überwerteten Spitzensport zugute kommt, anzuzweifeln." (Débats du Grand Conseil, Berne, 2 Sept. 1969).

‡Citons deux exemples choisis dans les démocraties (et non pas dans un pays totalitaire): — un institut gouvernemental des sports, astreint par la loi à subventionner les recherches et publications, a refusé tout crédit d'impression à une grande "thèse d'Etat," parce qu'un chapitre de cette thèse ne convenait pas à la politique d'expansion de cet institut; mais celui-ci dépensait alors des sommes considérables pour des publications favorables à sa mise en vedette dans l'opinion publique.

— une administration centrale des sports, organe du gouvernement, a cherché à nuire à un universitaire, parce que celui-ci avait publié trois articles critiques sur la politique des sports dans des revues spécialisées.

facilement, car bien des managers se sont offerts et soumis au Pouvoir, parfois dans des circonstances avilissantes, tandis que les sportifs socialistes et communistes, voués à la persécution, se sont retirés autant que possible dans la clandestinité, pour s'offrir plus tard à leur régime politique avec une promptitude égale. Seules les organisations religieuses ont su résister quelque peu à l'Etat totalitaire.

Dans les pays centralisés ou à régime présidentiel, les sports, pour obtenir des fonds, doivent aussi se placer dans le cadre national, mais l'Etat ne réclame, en général, aucun engagement idéologique en sa faveur, soutenant même les sports des partis d'opposition. Les chocs d'idées y sont parfois violents, et de cette contestation peut sortir un compromis bénéfique à tous.

Les "démocraties populaires" à parti unique et dirigeant ont supprimé le secteur privé de l'économie et circonscrit toutes les libertés individuelles selon les besoins de l'Etat. Tous y relève de la politique — l'éducation, les loisirs, les sports, les sciences — car le Pouvoir et ses organes contrôlent tous ces secteurs.

Tel n'est pas le cas dans les "démocraties référendaires" où le peuple et les partis décident des lois et des grandes dépenses. Une fois de plus, les sports s'adaptent à la situation, trouvant des supporters parmi les députés de différents partis, tous sensibles au mieux-être de la population et à la sympathie des électeurs.

Pour les "pays en voie de développement," les sports constituent un excellent moyen d'éducation et d'enrôlement de la jeunesse, mais aussi un domaine dans lequel il est relativement aisé de concourir avec les nations industrialisées, surtout lorsque celles-ci prêtent des entraîneurs et prennent certains frais à leur charge.

La centralisation administrative des sports

Presque partout, les sports se sont donné une forte centralisation pour augmenter leur pression permanente sur les pouvoirs publics. Dotée de quelques avantages, cette centralisation entraîne toujours des dépenses accrues, un nombre grandissant de fonctionnaires sans améliorer, en proportion, les services sur le "front," au niveau des usagers et du peuple. Car cette concentration n'échappe pas aux lois de Parkinson, ni aux tendances expansives propres aux monopoles. Alors que les trusts et les cartels de l'économie restent sous le contrôle vigilant de l'Etat et de l'opinion publique, les grandes administrations des sports agissent parfois à l'abri d'investigations indiscrètes et de surveillance des autorités. Cette centralisation des sports prête à critique lorsque des politiciens et des administrateurs essaient de diriger les recherches scientifiques, de faire sentir leur "nuisance value" à des chercheurs indépendants par le retrait d'enseignement, le refus de subsides, etc. Elle devient odieuse quand elle prétend régler toutes les initiatives concernant les sports dans un Etat à économie privée et aux libertés individuelles garanties par la constitution. Si cette centralisation s'allie avec les organes du Pouvoir, les sports de ce pays sont presque étatisés.

Conclusion

Faute de place, il a été impossible de citer de nombreux livres excellents et de signaler des controverses aussi rudes qu'utiles, ce dont je m'excuse auprès des auteurs.

En général, les sports et leurs dirigeants se sont vite intégrés au régime politique en place, tout heureux d'obtenir ainsi un appui officiel et de contrôler une part importante des loisirs et de l'éducation. On dira que cette intégration est indispensable à la survie des sports et de leurs managers dans les régimes centralisés ou totalitaires. Ailleurs, les impératifs des compétitions internationales, prônées par les mass-media, semblent dicter une concentration administrative dont les bénéficiaires des sports de prestige veulent étendre l'influence aux autres domaines, par exemple l'éducation, les loisirs, etc., puis à l'ensemble de la nation, sans en respecter parfois les besoins majeurs. La mobilisation devient totale lorsqu'elle embrigade toute la jeunesse dans une compétition générale et les adultes de tous âges dans un système de loisirs plus ou moins imposés, surveillés par l'Etat. Alors les fonctionnaires des sports, indispensables au gouvernement, éclipsent tous les autres, puisqu'ils attachent les jeunes et les adultes au régime, contribuent à la santé publique, préparant les gens à mieux travailler et les entraînent au service militaire. Alors les sports et leurs dirigeants s'élèvent au rang d'un service national, omniprésent de l'enfance jusqu'à la vieillesse. A mesure qu'il grandit et s'implante, ce service devient un des meilleurs agents de l'Etat, si ce n'est le service privilégié. L'avenir nous dira à qui cette évolution générale profitera.

De toute évidence, les relations entre les sports et la politique augmentent de jour en jour, à tous les niveaux. Leur examen objectif apportera des lumières sur les mobiles des responsables et les résultats effectifs. Il aidera sans doute les managers à placer les sports et leurs personnes dans un cadre plus général, respectueux de tous les besoins essentiels de la communauté dans laquelle s'exerce leur action.

The History of Yabusame (Shooting Arrows From Horseback)

Kohsuke Sasajima

Introduction

The government changed from the hands of nobles to the warrior class at the end of the 12th century, and this period known as the feudal age continued for nearly 700 years to the middle of the 19th century.

The feudal age can be divided into two terms, namely, the first and the later feudal age. The first feudal age was from 1192 to 1568, and the later feudal age was from 1573 to 1868. During the feudal age the administration was conducted by the Kamakura, Muromachi and Tokugawa Shognate.

Civilization in the first feudal age was developed with Buddhism as a background, while civilization in the later feudal age was cultivated with Confucianism.

During the first feudal age battles were fought chiefly with bows and arrows; however, since guns were introduced by the Portuguese in 1543 and rapidly diffused across the country, they replaced bows and arrows as major weapons on the battlefield. However, arrow-shooting was still practiced eagerly during the first feudal age as a necessary accomplishment and a method of culture for the warrior class. The warrior class in the Kamakura Era mostly respected arrow-shooting and to be a skilled shooter was an honor to them. Thus, arrow-shooting which had been regarded as a ceremonial function during the Heian Era (794-1192) changed into a military art.

The warrior class in the Kamakura Era trained themselves in both arrow-shooting while walking and from horseback. The representatives of arrow-shooting from horseback were the Kasakake (arrow-shooting at a target from a galloping horse), Inuoimono (arrow-shooting at dogs from horseback) and Yabusame (arrow-shooting at three targets from a trotting horse) which were called Mitsumono —

Kohsuke Sasajima, Keio University, Japan.

three essential techniques. However, these three techniques were not created in the Kamakura Era. They were demonstrated in the Court as Court functions during the Heian Era, previous to the Kamakura Era; and these techniques came to be demonstrated as functions of the warrior class during the Kamakura Era.

However, these functions were forgotten during the years from the end of the reign of the Murimachi Shognate to the end of the disturbance of the age of civil wars. They were revived in 1725 by Yoshimune, the eighth Shogun of the Tokugawa Shognate government in the Edo Period, who adopted them as methods of training for the warrior class.

The horses used at that time were smaller in stature than those of the present age. They are said to have been 140 cm in height and 280 to 300 kg in weight.

My paper will deal with the history of Yabusame.

Yabusame

According to the available records, Yabusame was first performed in Kyoto in April 1096. "Azuma Kagami" (record book in the Kamakura Era, written at the end of the 13th century) tells us that Yabusame was performed for the first time at Kamakura on August 15, 1187, and it became popular thereafter. Yabusame was last performed on August 16, 1265, according to records. However, it is said Yabusame was performed until about 1328 when the Kamakura Shognate was overthrown. According to records, Yabusame was performed for the last time in Kyoto on November 27, 1484.

Since Yabusame had divine and ritual factors more significant than Kasakake and Inuoimono, it was performed mainly at shrines and temples: in Kyoto at Iwashimizu Hachiman Shrine, Jonanji Temple, Imahie Shrine, Kamo Shrine, etc., while in Kamakura and its nearby areas at Tsurugaoka Hachiman Shrine, Mishima Shrine, and others. Yabusame which had been abandoned was revived by Yoshimune, the eighth Shogun of the Tokugawa Shognate, on October 17, 1725, 240 years after its last performance. This arrow-shooting technique is demonstrated by the Ogasawara and Takeda schools as a ritual service at festivals even today at Kamakura Hachiman Shrine, Meiji Shrine, Tosho-gu at Nikko and at other shrines.

The length of a riding ground and the intervals between targets vary among different schools. In the case of the Ogasawara School, the length is 218 meters and the interval is 72.7 meters, and the distance between the riding strip and target is 7 meters. In the Takeda School, the length is 327 meters, and the two distances are 109 meters and 11 meters, respectively. The sizes of targets are about 55 cm square in both schools, and the targets are 1 cm thick, respectively. These targets are tied onto the tips of poles about 1 meter long. As to the number of shooters, there is no definite rule; however, in general, 8, 10, 12 or 16 shooters participate in this game. The distances are indicated in the books handed down by means of the length of a bow; therefore, some of them cannot be indicated exactly by the metric system.

Thanks to the efforts made for the improvement of horses since the Meiji Era through introduction of Arabian and thoroughbred horses, they now are about 160 cm in height and about 430 kg in weight. Horses thus improved are used in Yabusame. However, the length of the riding strip and the distance between targets are left unchanged from the time when horses whose heights were from 135 cm to 140 cm and whose weights ranged from 280 kg to 300 kg were used. Therefore, in view of the speed of the horse at the present time, to perform Yabusame is technically more difficult now in comparison with former years.

Yabusame had a strong characteristic as a function dedicated to God. This arrow-shooting technique was interrupted during the age of civil wars and revived in 1725 with an aim to train shooters. However, even in those days, Yabusame was still performed universally as a divine function. In Japan where the civilization has been introduced from Europe and America since Meiji Restoration, other arrow-shootings have been completely forgotten, while Yabusame is still being performed at the present time. The reason is that Yabusame has long been performed as a dedication to God.

Bibliography

Imamura, Y.: The History of Physical Education in Japan. Tokyo:Fumai Do Book Store, 1970.

Imamura, Y.: Complete Collection — Military Arts, Vol. 3 — Arrow-Shooting from Horseback. Tokyo·Jinbitsu Orai Sha, 1965.

Kotaka, K.: Games and Sports of Japan. Tokyo:Haneda Book Store, 1943.

Outline of Japanese Classic Literature. Azuma Kagami (Record in Kamakura Era). Tokyo:Iwanami Book Store, 1954.

Sakai, K.: History of Games and Sports in Japan. Tokyo:Kensetsu Sha, 1932.

The Life of an Early Sportswoman, Eleonora Sears

Joanna Davenport

In today's open and tolerant society it is certainly not startling when one sees or reads about girls and women engaging in all sorts of athletic activities from skydiving to karate. As females have broken down the barriers that prohibited them from heretofore men's sports, it has ceased to be even that sensational when hearing that another woman has become the first of her sex to accomplish some new feat.

When you really think about it, however, what has happened has been incredible. In the course of the last few years we now have girls as Little League ball players, girls racing in the soapbox derby and women competing successfully as jockeys, race drivers and football players. Even outside the realm of sport it is no longer surprising when we see people referred to as lady "firemen" and lady "policemen."

It is interesting to speculate whether there were women many years ago who would have loved to have pursued the very same activities and occupations that are available to their sex today. However, we know that due to tradition, convention and the strict custom of the day it was necessary for these women to curb their real desires. In the sports area the proper feminine role was to be the demure spectator as the men participated in strenuous and vigorous sport. But at the beginning of this century there was such a woman who did not cater to convention, tradition or social mores and entered into sports with the same vigor and enthusiasm usually displayed by men. This early pioneer sportswoman was Eleonora Sears who, according to Frank Menke, editor of *The Encyclopedia of Sports*, "blazed a pathway for women which never had been taken before" [10]. Today, women take the freedom they have for granted. But it took a courageous and fascinating individual like Eleonora Sears to break through conservative customs and bring sports for women into the limelight.

Joanna Davenport, University of Illinois, Urbana, Ill., U.S.A.

Eleonora Randolph Sears was born of a prominent, affluent Boston Brahmin family on September 28, 1881. Her heritage included being the great-great-granddaughter of Thomas Jefferson and the niece of the first U.S. tennis champion, Richard Sears. Eleo, as she was called, grew up to be an extremely attractive, poised young lady who delighted in doing the unusual and pursued her activities with all the determination and dedication more common to the woman of today. Even though she was one of the most popular bachelor girls in the society centers of Newport, Rhode Island, and Bar Harbor, Maine, and acclaimed as the "Belle of Boston," it was in the area of sports that she devoted her enthusiastic energies. Unlike the majority of her female counterparts who, if they did any activity at all, gently tapped a croquet ball or went "swimming" by standing in the water, she was constantly excited by the thought of trying and doing activities whether or not they be men's sports. It is reported that she had such natural ability that often she watched men play a game, practiced the skill for a short time and subsequently challenged a man in the same event and distinguished herself by beating him [10].

Combining her wealth with her interests she participated in all sorts of athletics that ranged from tennis, squash, riding, sailing, golf and swimming to polo, trapshooting and walking. The following testimonial to her versatility was written by Victor Jones, the late Boston Globe veteran sports reporter, five days after she died in 1968.

> Eleo Sears . . . was probably the most versatile performer that sports has ever produced — not just the most versatile female performer, but the most versatile, period . . . she could handle more sports completely than anyone who has yet come along. . . . Her range was really quite unbelievable [8].

It is impossible within the time limits of this paper to describe in detail the varied pursuits of this early sportswoman, since she was athletically active for most of her life. It seems appropriate, then, to point out some of her many accomplishments and to highlight her most popular activities.

One of the first interests in her varied sporting career was tennis. As early as 1903 she was acclaimed as the tennis queen of Newport due to her victories in club tournaments. Even in matches where she was not the winner it was usually reported that the most spectacular competition was the contest involving Eleonora Sears. Her aggressive style of play and overwhelming desire to win were always exciting aspects for the spectators to view. Her tennis exploits were not just confined to championships at the exclusive country clubs. She was four times National Womens Doubles Chmpaion — twice as a partner of Hazel Wightman in 1911 and 1915 and twice with Molla Bjurstadt in 1916 and 1917. She was also National Singles Runner Up in 1912 and National Mixed Doubles Winner with Willis Davis in 1916 [12].

Before moving on to her other sports it is important to mention one more aspect of Eleo's achievements on the court. In the early years of tennis in America, it was a leisurely game as played by women. Due to their bulky dress of a long skirt over a tight fitting corset with a long-sleeved, high necked blouse it was customary for females to stand near the baseline and without much effort or movement chop the ball over the net. The only stroke in their tennis repertoire, other than the chop, was the underhand serve. As can be imagined, the slow pace of the early game plus the restricting outfit did not suit Eleo with all her energy and talent. She very early developed a volley and seems always to have competed with an overhead serve. Her dress, though proper, was more conducive to active play. She and May Sutton Bundy, also a champion tennis player, are credited with rolling up their shirt sleeves, thus starting the style of a comfortable costume for activity [3].

Her nonadherence to conventional dress was not just confined to tennis. She followed the same pattern in riding and caused such a sensation by her new outfit that the reaction was publicized nationwide. It was the custom in the early 1900s for all female riders not only to wear long skirts while on horseback but to ride the horse in a contraption known as a side saddle. Eleo was not only an excellent rider but a skillful daring hunter and, additionally, the first female polo player in her country [2]. Riding authorities claim that this side saddle was appropriate and safe for riders who went at a leisurely pace and took jumps with careful deliberation. But to an aggressive competitive rider like Eleo the saddle was inefficient and cumbersome, with one leg locked behind the other. Consequently, she dressed in what were then called trousers and now are called breeches or a habit and rode the most sensible way just like the men — with one leg on each side of the animal. By this change in custom she is acknowledged as being one of the first women to ride a horse astride [9]. Many females were shocked at this masculine dress and a club in California even issued a resolution asking Eleonora Sears to "restrict herself in the future to the normal feminine attire" [9]. The opinions of others did not faze her and it appeared that the resolution spurred her on to wear her trousers even when she was not riding. In 1963, still spry at 82 years of age, she commented on this event when she was interviewed by Amory. "Trousers, trousers, trousers! They were always talking about my trousers. They weren't trousers, at all — they were perfectly good riding breeches" [2].

Her next sporting milestone occurred in the game of squash. She is recognized as the first woman squash player in the United States. She began playing around 1918 before women were allowed to even enter men's clubs, let alone play squash on the courts. There are many stories that she, again, defied the traditional pattern and demanded that she be allowed to use the facilities at these exclusive male retreats.

There is certainly no denial that her position as an affluent Boston society woman gave her the license to do such a thing. But it is important to keep in perspective in all these revolutionary activities that even though Eleo is considered by many as the prime liberator for women in sports, she was not in any way what we term today a feminist or a "woman's libber." It was more a case that if Eleo Sears wished to do something, she did it without the concomitant motive that other women would benefit by her actions. Competition was the spice of her life and many of these so-called traditional barriers seemed to have spurred her on to challenge and conquer. As Rice, the renowned sports writer once said, Eleonora Sears lived the once popular song "Anything You Can Do I Can Do Better" [13].

As squash became recognized as an acceptable sport for women, there soon developed enough interest to have national championships, of which the first was held in 1928. Not surprisingly, Eleo was the winner and continued in tournament play until the age of 70. Often referred to as "The Mother of Squash" she was at one time President of the National Women's Squash Association and captain of its international team.

Any review of the life of Eleonora Sears would not be complete without including some mention of her famous walks. As indicated previously, she gained a great deal of publicity by her athletic exploits. But to many historians her greatest reputation and sensational accomplishments occurred in walking. A customary walker who often went from her home in Boston to her summer place — a distance of 20 miles — she amazed the public by her spectacular achievements in long distance walks. In her early thirties she covered the 108 miles between Burlingame and Delmonte, California, in 19 hours and 50 minutes [1]. Her favorite contest was between Boston and Providence, Rhode Island, which is a distance of 47 miles. Her best time was in 1916 when she finished in 9 hours and 53 minutes [14]. Garbed in her usual hiking costume of a short coat and skirt, socks rolled down to her heavy hiking boots and her familiar felt hat she was always followed by her chauffeur in the car. Even in France she caused a sensation when she traveled 100 miles in 39 hours and 42½ miles in 8 hours and 35 minutes [5].

In 1960 at 79 years of age, she competed against one of her grooms in a 10 mile walk at her horse farm in North Carolina. It is not surprising that she considered it a rather humorous standard when the late President John F. Kennedy stated that the United States Marines should be able to hike 50 miles in 20 hours [11].

It is a tribute to this phenomenal woman that in many sports today there are trophies bearing her name that are symbolic of a champion. Each year there are sailing races to determine the winner of the Sears Cup, tennis players play for the Sears bowl and riders compete at the National Horse Show to win the Sears Challenge Trophy for the best confirmation hunter. This first lady of American sports won 240 cups herself during her lifelong athletic career [4]. Always colorful in whatever she did her character is best illustrated by a remark she made to a reporter after one of her famous walks in Paris. It seems that he had implied in a previous article that she was past her prime in tennis and was like an ordinary player. He greeted her after the walk with a cheerful "How do you do." She replied, "I do very well and see here, young man, I'm not ordinary at anything" [7]. No statement could have been truer than that one. A living legend ceased when Eleonora Sears died on March 26, 1968, at the age of 87. Her years had indeed been exciting ones and she richly deserved the title given to her by the *New York Times*, "Pioneer of Women's Sports" [6].

References

1. A Horseless Lady Rider. The Literary Digest. January 16, 1926, p. 60.
2. Amory, C.: Bostonian Unique-Miss Sears. Vogue, February 15, 1963, p. 82.
3. Durant, J. and Bettmann, O.: Pictorial History of American Sports. New Jersey:A. S. Barnes and Company, 1973, p. 148.
4. Eleonora Sears Dies at 87. Boston Traveler, March 27, 1968, p. 14.
5. Eleonora Sears in Long Hike. Boston Herald, June 11, 1934, p. 5.
6. Eleanora (sic) Sears, Pioneer in Women's Sports, Dies. New York Times, March 27, 1968, p. 37.
7. Izenberg, J.: Superwoman. The Newark Star Ledger, December 25, 1962, p. 14.
8. Jones, V.O.: Eleonora Sears Most Versatile Ever. Boston Globe, March 31, 1968, p. 44.

9. Laney, A.: Name the Sport . . . She's Competed. New York Herald Tribune, October 25, 1962, p. 29.
10. Menke, F.G.: The Encyclopedia of Sports. New York:A. S. Barnes and Company, 1969, p. 1065.
11. Miss Sears Would Have Left Marines in Dust. Boston Herald, February 6, 1963, p. 31.
12. The Official United States Tennis Association Yearbook and Tennis Guide with the Official Rules 1976. Massachusetts:H. O. Zimman, Inc., 1976, pp. 285-288.
13. Rice, G.: The Tumult and the Shouting. New York:A. S. Barnes and Company, 1954, p. 238.
14. 2 Pacemakers Worn Down by Stride. Boston Herald, June 12, 1933, p. 2.

Thomas Kirk Cureton, Jr.: A Historical Sketch of His Professional Life and Contributions to Physical Activity and Human Well-Being

Walter Cryer

Introduction

In 1948, as a student at the University of Illinois, the writer first became acquainted with Dr. Thomas Kirk Cureton, Jr., who was becoming known throughout the world as an expert on physical fitness. Not only was he gaining recognition for his scientific approach to anthropometry, kinesiology, physiology, tests and measurements, and sports (especially aquatics), but he also exhibited a personal application of his fitness program. Those who have seen Dr. Cureton perform in a demonstration-lecture situation are impressed with his amazing physical strength and stamina. Here is a physical educator who puts into practice what he professes.

Youth and Schooling

As a young boy Curteon was intensely interested in physical activities — sports, games, swimming — and was proficient in athletic skills. At one time he had an opportunity to follow in his father's footsteps in the banking business. He decided this was not for him and pursued electrical engineering. Even though he graduated from Yale University with a degree in electrical engineering, his life-long interest developed in physical activities.

While attending Yale he became interested in body building gymnastics and was fascinated with a Dr. Henderson's physiological work done with oxygen intake on the Yale rowing crew which had won the 1924 Olympic Gold Medal. This was the first time he had seen oxygen intake work done, and it so intrigued him that he wanted to become involved with that type of research.

Walter Cryer, Brigham Young University, Provo, Utah, U.S.A.

Cureton probably would never have entered physical education work had he not encountered Robert J. H. Kiphuth, the director of the Yale Gymnasium and swimming coach. Kiphuth had just returned from Europe and the Scandinavian countries, excited with the new ideas concerning calisthenics and body building exercises. Kiphuth's ideas concerning training and conditioning of men and his great enthusiasm impressed him. Cureton participated in the evolution of the various land drills and hard training, became a student leader and succeeded in earning two varsity letters in swimming under Kiphuth's coaching. Incidentally, Cureton also ran on the cross-country team and usually ran the 5- to 6-mile distances, averaging less than six minutes per mile.

Work at Suffield Academy

Cureton's first professional work was at Suffield Academy (1925-1929) in the position of director of physical education and athletics. While there he incorporated the formal military gymnastics and the therapeutic and conditioning aspects of physical education from abroad. He also included the newer and more socially important aspects of physical education programs such as sport and games.

While organizing a new program in health and physical education, teaching classes and coaching, Cureton found himself making great use of his engineering background and his developed ability to organize effectively. The facilities were in a bad state of repair and the equipment he needed for conducting his program was virtually nonexistent. Students and faculty were recruited to help carry out the plans for a fairly extensive remodeling of existing facilities and building additions to the athletic plant. Funds were limited. Cureton wrote:

> . . . Some of the freshmen were surprised to find that they were expected to become carpenters, gardeners, concrete mixers, and laborers of almost any type as a regular part of their athletic training. . . . The whole campus buzzed with activity every afternoon after school was out.

Cureton had a variety of coaching experiences at Suffield which included among others the girls' basketball team, the hockey team, fall track and cross country and spring track.

Work at Springfield College

Some of Cureton's finest professional contributions were made when he was on the Springfield College faculty from 1929 to 1941. He was instructor in mathematics and chemistry. He was also responsible for supervision of graduate work, a course in research methods, corrective physical education and the thesis seminar. Cureton's position as freshmen swimming coach led to his being named to Varsity Coach of Swimming in 1931. Thereafter he directed all aquatic courses at Springfield, which included swimming, life saving, canoeing, methods of teaching and aquatic administration.

Because Springfield College was a YMCA institution, it was both logical and natural for Cureton to get involved in the YMCA programs while he was there. His early exposure to the YMCA as a youth continued to develop into a lifetime interest which projected him into international eminence as a YMCA aquatic authority and physical fitness expert.

Camp aquatics played an important role in providing practical experience for Cureton early in his career. He instigated a series of medical examinations, physical tests and measurements; individualized prescriptions of exercises and types of programs; kept a detailed record of the progress of each camper; taught a daily lesson in body mechanics, with follow-up corrective work for those needing it; and planned a program of character education.

A gifted person with a great capacity for work, Cureton not only carried out his teaching, coaching and administrative responsibilities, but also pursued advanced studies in his profession contributing a great number of writings to physical education literature. From 1929 to 1941 his work included about 50 papers on swimming, applied physics and body mechanics, and kinesiology. Some of these writings which may well be considered a pioneering effort exemplified his interest in testing and measuring the body in a variety of ways, his ingenuity in developing and improving several measuring devices and his use of various statistical analyses in correlating measurement data.

As Cureton became better educated he desired to develop programs at the doctorate level and conduct more definitive research. He knew he needed better facilities provided by a university. He also realized that he would need to collaborate with experts in various other sciences who would be available in a university setting. He decided to accept the offer of the University of Illinois and open a new kind of laboratory called the Physical Fitness Research Laboratory.

Work at the University of Illinois

Cureton spent 28 productive years (1941 to 1969) at the University of Illinois as a professor and director of the Physical Fitness Research Laboratory. He was involved in a variety of scientific studies in the laboratory, but he was especially interested in projects that involved cardiovascular fitness. He probably has one of the best collections in the world of studies that objectively evaluate the meaning of cardiovascular tests.

To better understand how Cureton accomplished so much work, as reflected in the voluminous publications he produced, a cursory inspection of the organization of the Physical Fitness Research Laboratory and its programs may be helpful. Through the years Cureton achieved several objectives for his laboratory. He obtained information concerning the work productivity of the human body through physical fitness tests for endurance, flexibility, agility, strength, power and balance. These tests with their normative standards are among the many he developed and critically evaluated. Following a diagnosis of physical condition based on the tests, conditioning exercises were prescribed and leadership provided for youth and adults. Most of the tests and norms he used have been outlined in certain of his books.

Another important objective of Cureton's laboratory was to provide learning experiences and opportunities for graduate students to develop their scientific research projects. He firmly believed that physical education, in order to rank with other professions such as medicine, dentistry and engineering, demanded well-trained experts with a strong scientific basis for the theories expressed. The quality of the work of 107 doctorate students Cureton assisted may be judged from a perusal of the numerous books and articles published based on the work done there.

The laboratory also became a center for contract research work in the area of physical fitness. Contracts were received for research concerning the relationship of dietary aids to physical performance. Various companies wanted to have their equipment tested and standards developed for their own use.

As the work accomplished by Cureton and his assistants in the laboratory became well known, it stimulated great interest. Professional and amateur athletes, coaches, governmental officials from several countries, scientists, heads of corporations and other visitors to the laboratory all wanted to find answers to their questions about physical fitness. He received calls from people who wanted to be tested and invitations to conduct physical fitness clinics. Cureton found himself continually answering correspondence which requested the services of the physical fitness research staff and laboratory. Frequently, requests were made for results of his experiments, for tests of physical fitness and for copies of his articles and books concerning the three main programs of the laboratory involving youth, athletes and adults.

Youth

Cureton's original idea of extending the resources of the Physical Fitness Research Laboratory into a youth unit with a definite administration, budget and research procedure evolved into a comprehensive program of research with young boys, ages 8 to 14. This summer youth program proved to be an excellent source of material for research which resulted in articles published in several prestigious journals and a monograph.

Athletes

One of Cureton's major contributions to physical activity was made in the field of athletics. He tested hundreds of athletes and compared the results with test results of hundreds of other individuals. Professional athletes, Olympians, world-record holders and national champions were among those tested. His battery of tests containing over 100 test items helped the scientists, coaches and athletes themselves understand the physiological characteristics and psychological traits which were unique in a champion. He also showed how these unique characteristics and traits could be further developed or could be acquired through a certain specialized program of exercise.

A primary example of the tests conducted and the caliber of athletes tested is in Cureton's book, *Physical Fitness of Champion Athletes.* This text related the results of extensive testing done of 76 Olympians and national champions in seven sports. When Cureton made his tour around Europe in 1952 he was often questioned about the book by medical doctors and others. At the time Cureton was probably recognized as one of the highest authorities on physical fitness testing of athletes in this country and possibly the world. This work was continued during his 1960 world tour.

Adults

Besides testing and training adults in the lab, Cureton conducted hundreds of physical fitness clinics around the world. In general, Cureton did four things at his physical fitness clinics: (1) lectured on the principle of adult fitness work and showed movies of his Physical Fitness Research Laboratory at the University of Illinois and of work completed with both men and women; (2) administered a battery of tests at eight stations and gave group interpretations of these tests; (3) demonstrated the type of progressive (low-, middle-, high-gear) calisthenics programs which he believed was the best pattern for adults in middle age and had the people attending the clinic join him in the gym and in the swimming pool; and (4) conducted personal interviews based on test records and made suggestions for improvements.

Dr. Cureton summarized approximately 25 years of his work with the middle-aged adult in his book *The Physiological Effects of Exercise Programs on Adults.* This book has a comprehensive bibliography and a collation of theses with Cureton's interpolation of meanings. It is an excellent reference to the technical aspects of his work with middle-aged adults. This area of his many contributions to physical activity and human well-being has probably had the greatest impact in the world.

Summary

In view of his remarkable physical ability, his great capacity for work and his insatiable desire to learn, it is not surprising that Thomas Kirk Cureton, Jr. chose to direct his energies toward research in the discipline of physical fitness. He attributed his own vigor and stamina not only to natural endowment but also to training and programmed exercise. As a proponent of physical fitness, he was a living example of the value of the principles he has learned and taught. A very able, voluble speaker and articulate debater, Cureton encouraged and inspired people as he related personal experiences, shared his knowledge and presented physical fitness demonstrations throughout his career around the world.

He championed new ideas which originally caused controversy in the profession, such as his ideas concerning swimming skills and tests, artificial respiration, exercise for cardiac patients, wheat germ oil and aerobic oxygen intake. Even though some of Cureton's works have been criticized by colleagues, discounted by medical doctors and taken to court by a federal agency, he did not become discouraged and quit. Rather, he stood firm in his beliefs and continued to progress in his chosen profession. His major assertions have not been disproved; they stand as a testimony of his diligence and perseverance, his exactness in research, his intelligence in problem solving and his enthusiasm for physical fitness.

Whether Cureton's vigor, determination and productivity will definitely earn him a place as a champion of physical fitness in the profession of physical education remains to be seen. He certainly merits the distinction of being one of the most if not the most significant physical fitness educators in the world to date, and he is deserving of the title, "Father of Physical Fitness in the World." His works may well become classics in physical education and other professions.

The "Edmonton Grads": The Team and Its Social Significance From 1915 to 1940

John Dewar

Women's basketball becomes an official event of the Olympic Games on July 1976 in Montreal. It is fitting that this historical event take place in the homeland of the outstanding women's basketball team of all time, the Edmonton Grads. The Edmonton Commercial Graduate Club, most often referred to as the Edmonton Grads, was founded and coached by J. Percy Page for 25 years. They established a record and an image in the period from 1915 to 1940 that is unparalleled in basketball.

In the *Toronto Globe and Mail* (April 5, 1975, p. 48) Dick Beddoes, one of Canada's most controversial and widely read columnists, wrote:

> Basketball, as everybody knows, is a game played in Jockey shorts, scored by adding machine, invented by Dr. James Naismith of Almonte for the YMCA, and occasionally turned into profit by the Mafia.
>
> It is a game in which you try to thrust a ball 30 inches in circumference into a basket 24 inches in diameter, the tightest squeeze in sports. It is a game which depends more upon altitude than attitude. Using both, the Bruins representing University of California at Los Angeles this week won their 10th U.S. college title in 12 years.
>
> When UCLA coach John Wooden announced his retirement a few days ago, he and his UCLA teams were hailed for the "greatest record" in basketball history. This still small voice murmurs "Oh?"
>
> What about the Edmonton Grads? The world's playpen has never been dominated, it says here, by another such all-conquering team.

John Dewar, Laurentian University, Sudbury, Ontario, Canada.

> The Grads, from 1915 until they disbanded in 1940, played 522 games. They won 502 and lost 20, for a winning percentage of 96.2. They had winning streaks of 147 and 78 games. In four Olympic Games — in Paris in 1924, Amsterdam in 1928, Los Angeles in 1932, Berlin in 1936 — they played 27 games and won 27.
>
> The Grads first won the Canadian title in 1922 and never relinquished it until their dispersal in 1940. Naismith, the game's inventor, would say of them in 1936: "The Grads have the greatest team that ever stepped on a basketball floor."
>
> Wooden? UCLA? Let 'em go earn a similar accolade. No?

Mr. Beddoes certainly supports the Canada first policy and like many young boys growing up in Western Canada before and during the Depression he had learned of the famous Edmonton Grads.

An article in *The Canadian Magazine* (March 8, 1975, p. 9), a national weekly distributed by 13 newspapers and having Canada's largest circulation, noted the Grads in this way:

> The Grads were not merely the best female basketball players in Edmonton, but in Alberta, in Canada, in the world — and maintained that dominance, incredibly, for the quarter of a century between 1915 and 1940.

Are these quotes nationalistic nostalgia being conjured up out of the past by a prejudiced press or were these young women from a pioneer urban community of Western Canada truly a sports phenomenon?

Dr. James Naismith, the friendly father of basketball, stated on at least three occasions that the Grads and their founder and coach, Mr. J. Percy Page, were well above the ordinary. In Guthrie, Oklahoma, on July 6, 1926, Naismith watched the Grads retain their "international championship" by defeating the hometown Redbirds in a two game total point series. During halftime of the second game the originator of the game addressed the crowd of 5,000:

> It is doubtful if any girls' game has ever equalled that of tonight in all round strategy, brilliance of play and doggedness, both in attack and defence.*

*Special to *Edmonton Journal* from Guthrie, Oklahoma, July 6, 1923.

This was true praise from the conservative doctor. Again on October 28, 1929, while visiting Canada to see the Edmonton team play he noted:

> The Grads have the greatest team that ever stepped out on a basketball floor.*

Earlier in 1925 he had written:

> It was a distinct pleasure for me to see your team play in Guthrie against the Redbirds. On looking over your girls' record in Canada, the United States and in Europe, I was prepared to see a superior brand of play, but I never expected to see such skill as they demonstrated upon this occasion.
>
> In 1892, at the request of a group of teachers, I organized two girls' basketball teams playing the boys' game, and I found that, due to their lack of experience in athletic contests, the reaction of the girls to the game was vastly different from that of the boys. I was particularly anxious, therefore, to see how the boys' style of game affected the social attributes and the general health of your players, and I can assure you that it was with no little pleasure that I found these young ladies exhibiting as much grace and poise at an afternoon tea as vigorous ability on the basketball court. I can only conclude that this is due very largely to the fine womanly influence of Mrs. Page, supporting your own high standards of sportsmanship and coaching ability.†

Further credence to the credibility of the Grads credentials was given by Dr. Forest "Phog" Allen, the father of basketball coaching. This now legendary official and coach refereed the Guthrie Grad games of 1925 and declared that the Grads' superb condition and style of play were the best in the history of the game. This famous Kansas leader, who was to coach the United States to their first basketball Olympic Gold Medal in Berlin, wrote as follows:

---

*Sitting on Top of the World." *Grad Publication*, 1940, p. 29.

†Excerpt from a letter to Mr. J. P. Page, Edmonton, Canada, from James Naismith, July 8, 1925.

> Without a doubt your splendid aggregation is the most consistent, the best conditioned team of girls that I have ever seen in action. The basket shooting was, at times, uncanny.
>
> I have seen college teams composed of men that would have to hustle to take their measure.
>
> Gentility in their play and manners both on and off the field made this super-Canadian team an outstanding conviction for the highest type of womanly strength and charm. "The game is the thing," and let me add that the game is very much worth while so long as we stress clean living and high deportment in the striving for success.
>
> "God make us wise to know,
> How strong the stalk must grow,
> That rears so fair a flower."*

The people of Edmonton, Alberta, in the 1920s and 1930s certainly concurred with the learned Doctors Allen and Naismith of Lawrence, Kansas.

In an interview with the author in Edmonton, Alberta (May 25, 1976) Mr. Claire Hollingsworth, an important part of the Commercial Graduate Basketball Club, stated: "I don't think any team representing Edmonton has ever captured the imagination and support of the citizens like the Grads did."

The Grads became the center of the Edmonton sports scene in 1923. This fame was slow to come for the black- and gold-clad team of high school graduates.

The new McDougall Commercial High School basketball team under the direction of their principal coach J. P. Page won the city and provincial championship in 1915. The graduates of the team convinced Mr. Page to form the "Grads" that same year. Eight years' domination of Alberta basketball followed and were culminated in 1922 with the Club challenging for their first Canadian championship. The trip to London, Ontario, to play the Eastern champion "Shamrocks" of that city was financed by the Grad players and private donations. Six players made the trip and returned to Edmonton with that pioneer city's first "Dominion" championship.

---

*Excerpt from a letter to Mr. J. Percy Page, Edmonton, Alberta from Forest Allen, Director of Athletics and Basketball Coach, University of Kansas, July 8, 1925.

The local press noted these exploits, but their efforts and victories of 1922 were almost unnoticed by the general public.

> The Commercial Graduates' Club of Edmonton took a strangle hold on the ladies' dominion basketball championship here last night when they defeated the London Shamrocks, eastern Canadian titleholders, by a score of 41-8. In view of the fact that the local girls have held the Ontario title two years in succession, during which period they have not lost a game, the westerners were not considered very seriously but no sooner had the game commenced than the Edmonton girls brought the thousand spectators up with a start by staging a brand of basketball that was actually dazzling.*

It would be left to sports promoter "Deacon" White, local businessmen, and some short-shorted girls from Cleveland, Ohio, to change the public image of the Grads. Mr. White and Coach Page saw the possibility of international and interregional play on a new hardwood floor in the Edmonton Arena. The potential gate from thousands rather than a few hundred supporters was first to be realized in a series against the Cleveland Favorite-Knits, self-declared world champions. This series also inaugurated challenge competition for the Underwood Trophy. Charles Defieux, a writer for the *Edmonton Journal* (June 15, 1923, p. 20), reported:

> World's Champions!
>
> Only two words it's true, but believe you me, Mr. Populace, they're the choicest duo to be found under the cover of the well-known Webster's dictionaries kept in Edmonton households this day. Local citizens, every one, are today walking around with stately carriage as fittingly behooves one who resides in a community that is fortunate enough to possess such a treasure as a world's championship.
>
> The Commercial Grads brought fame to Edmonton, Alberta, and Canada last night when in the final fixture of the two-game world's ladies' basketball series with the Favorite-Knits of Cleveland they again defeated the U.S. champions and carried off the laurels by a margin of twenty points. Last night's score was 19 to 13 and the

*Special to the *Edmonton Journal* from London, Ontario, May 17, 1922.

official figures for the series read Commercial Grads 53, Favorite-Knits 33.

Mary Dunn Dixon, the starting left guard for the Grads, on May 20, 1976 recalled her reaction to the series to this author:

> Very exciting, thrilling game, played on a fine hardwood floor built in sections. Thousands of fans were there and the Cleveland Favorite-Knits had little shorts with World Champions down the side. So after we defeated them we decided we were the world champions.

The two games with Cleveland and subsequent 1923 challenges from Toronto, Chicago and Warren, Ohio, drew an average of 5,000 spectators. When the Chicago team came within three points in the first of two games the high attendance for the season of 6,500 was attained. The people came to see if the Grads were invincible. This essentially became the attendance pattern for the Underwood Trophy and other challenge games, the greater the likelihood of a possible Grad defeat, the larger the crowd. However, for 17 years, from 1923 to 1940, the basketball followers of North America never saw the Grads relinquish the trophy. They won every series, playing 120 games and losing only six of them. On their 25th anniversary the team was presented with the Underwood Trophy as a permanent possession.

The gate receipts from the 1923 and similar 1924 challenge contests filled the coffers of the Grads and enabled them to move into a widening international field for further competition. The July Olympics of 1924 in Paris saw the first of four Olympic exhibition series from which the Edmonton team was to emerge undefeated in 27 games and to establish for themselves a permanent place in the hearts of Albertans.

Additional triumphs in Amsterdam (1928), Los Angeles (1932) and Berlin (1936) created a living basketball legend in the prairie west of Canada.

The reporting of their return from Paris in 1924 is exemplary of the people's reaction (*Edmonton Journal*, August 30, 1924):

> Cheering thousands will be on hand at the Canadian National railway depot and city market square shortly after 10:50 o'clock tonight when the world champion Commercial Graduates girls' basketball team arrives home. Excitement is being shown all over the city and it seems

likely that the crowds will be nearly as large as when the Prince of Wales visited Edmonton.

In the years of the great Depression, the people of this still very British city would come to hold the Grads as a greater part of their tradition than the dashing Prince of England.

The Edmonton Grads were a socially significant factor in Edmonton, Alberta, Canada. In 1921 Edmonton was a city with only one resident in four with a local commitment based on tradition or birth.

The accomplishments of their Grads was to help create the regional unity evident in the Alberta Capital prior to World War II.

Mr. John Percy Page, coach, teacher, parliamentarian, Lieutenant-Governor of Alberta from 1959 to 1965, died on March 5, 1973. His life — conservative, honest and unspectacular — had provided the steady influence necessary for the building of this sports phenomenon. The bond that was established between his players' lives on in regular reunions and in the minds of all those people who were fortunate enough to have their lives touched by the Edmonton Grads.

These women from Western Canada showed that there was no dichotomy between strength and beauty. They gave a new, true and lasting dimension to the game of women's basketball.

The Edmonton Commercial Graduate Basketball Club have rightfully become for Alberta and Canada a 20th century sports legend.

Bibliography

Collections

The Edmonton Commercial Graduate Club Collection. The Alberta Provincial Museum and Archives. Edmonton, Alberta.

Books

Clark, S.D.: Urbanism and the Changing Canadian Society. Toronto:University of Toronto Press, 1961.

Simmons, J.: Urban Canada. Toronto:The Copp Clark Publishing Co., 1969.

Wise, S.F. and Fisher, D.: Canada's Sporting Heroes. Don Mills, Ontario:General Publishing Co., 1974.

Edmonton Grads. The Royal Bank of Canada, Montreal, 1975.

Periodicals

Cruikshank, H.: These girls fight to win. Liberty, Dec. 29, 1936.

They Win! Colliers, May 16, 1929.

Newspapers

The Calgary Herald, 1915-1940.
The Edmonton Bulletin, 1915-1940.
The Toronto Star Weekly, 1926.

Personal Interviews (Taped)

Mrs. Gladys (Fry) Douglas, May 20, 1976, Edmonton, Alberta.
Miss Daisy Johnson, Edmonton, Alberta, May 23, 1976.
Mrs. J. P. (Maude) Page, Edmonton, Alberta, May 23, 1976.

Author Index / Auteurs

Aguilera, R.R., ix
Aitken, B.W.W., 143

Barney, R.K., 279
Bélanger, L., ix
Bélanger, Y., ix
Bernett, H., 49
Blackstock, C.R., 237
Borotra, J., ix
Bouet, M.A., 13
Boutin, M., 179
Burgener, L., 333

Cagigal, J.M., 59
Carlisle, R., 111
Cryer, W., 349
Cumming, G.R., ix

Davenport, J., 343
Davidson, S.A., 255
Davydov, V.V., 119
de Mulder, H., 131
Dewar, J., 357

Erbach, G., ix

Falize, J., ix

Godbout, P., ix

Habashi, Z.I., 289
Hart, D.P., 273
Holbrook, L., ix
Houde, G., ix
Howell, M.L., 317
Howell, R., 301, 317

Ioannides, I.P., 267

Kanaar, A.C., 199
Kenyon, G., ix
Kozar, A.J., 245
Kulinkovich, K.A., 211

Landry, F., ix
Lieper, J.M., 229
Lekarska, N., 311
Loiselle, J., ix
Lotz, F., ix

MacAloon, J.J., 161
Martucci, J., 187
McKelvey, G., ix
Meshizuka, T., ix
Michaud, G., ix
Miller, D.L., 153
Müller, N., 327

Noel-Baker, P., ix

Orban, W.A.R., ix

Petit, J.-C., 171

Roditchenko, V.S., ix, 25
Ross, S., 97

Sasajima, K., 339
Sheedy, A., ix
Shephard, R.J., ix
Souelem, N.M., ix
Sprynar, Z., 125
Stoljarov, V.I., 87

Ueberhorst, H., 217

VanderZwaag, H.J., 35

Woodstock, P.S., ix

Zeigler, E.F., 3

Subject Index 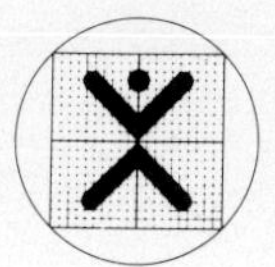 Sujets

AIESEP, 60
Amateurism, 35-47, 69-72, 230, 234
  considerations in sports, 36-40
  meaning of, 35, 36
Amenophis II, 289-300
Anthropology, 171-178
Anthropometry, 238, 257
Anti-Semitism, 51
Arnold, Ernest Herman, 257
"Aryan Paragraph," 50

Basketball, women's, 357-364
Behavior modification, 200, 201
Bonuses, 73

"Cage complex," 199
CIEPS-ICSPE, 60
Collectivities, structure of, 6
Commercial fees, 73
"Communitas," 167
Competition, 36, 37
Competitive time, significance of, 179-186
Contracts, 73
Coubertin, Baron Pierre de, 211, 317-319, 327-332
Cureton, Thomas Kirk Jr., 349-355

Diem, Carl, 327-332

Edmonton Grads, 357-364
Educational slogans, 66
Effective time, aspects of, 179-186
Egypt, athletics in ancient, 289-300
Elite sport, 64, 66, 71, 76
Epistemology, 106
Equipment and facilities, 39-41
Esthetic values, 7, 8
Ethics, 4-11
  naturalistic, 5
  moral law, 5, 70
Existence, concept of, 171-178

Fatalism, 199
Festivals
  meaning of, 187-197
  origins of, 187-197

FIEP, 60
From Athens to Melbourne, 213

General Systems Theory, 106
Germanophobia, 50
German "Play movement," 51
Gulick, Luther, 257

Habilitation and rehabilitation, 200, 205
Halteres, 280, 287
Handicapped
  fear, 202
  habilitation and rehabilitation, 200, 205
  pain, 201, 202
  self-image of, 199, 200
  sport for, 204, 205
Heidegger, thoughts of, 171-178
Hellenism, 162, 163
History of the Olympic Games, 212
Hitchcock, Edward, 238, 257, 258
Homo
  faber, 143-148, 150
  tempestivus, 147-151
Human movement as a field of study, 111-118

IAPESGW, 60
ICHPER, 60
Ideology
  criterion of exclusivity, 50
  national and racial superiority, 50
Israel, festivals in ancient, 187-197

Jahn, gymnastics of, 50

Kahanamoku, Duke, 246

Man, concept of, 171-178
Marathon, 267-272
McKenzie, R. Tait, 237-266
Military training and sports, 51-53
Mill of Kintail, 237
Modern Olympic Games, 213
Monotheism, 153
Moral law, 5

SUBJECT INDEX /SUJETS

Motor-organic skills, 120, 121
Movement and time, aspects of, 179-186

Naismith, James, 238, 256-258
National identity, 13-24
Nationalism and chauvinism, 50
Nemean festival, 273-278
  control, 275, 276
  importance, 276, 277
  origin, 274, 275

Olympia, Athens, Rome, 213
Olympic experience, 3-11
Olympic Games, 13-24, 71
  as cult of humanity, 165-168
  religious themes and structures in, 161-169
Olympic Memories, 219
Olympic movement, 13-24, 211
  religious themes and structures in, 161-169
Olympic Program, history of, 311-316
Olympic Trumpets, 213
Olympism
  concept of, 25
  in North America, 229-235
  political-philosophic aspects of, 25-33
  in socialist countries, 211-215
  in Western Europe, 217-228

Participants, 67, 68
Pentathlon jump, 279-288
Physical education, 97-109
Play, theologies of, 154, 155
Polytheism, 153
Professionals, 69-72
Propaganda activities, 66
Pythian festival, 273, 281

Records, 37-39
Religio athletae, 161
Religious
  terminology, 161
  themes and structures, 161-169
Role, structure of, 6

Sacred symbols, 165, 166
School sport, 64
Sears, Eleonora, 343-348
Sixty Years of the Olympic Games, 212
Snowy Olympics, 213
Social values, 3-11
  esthetic, 7, 8
  instrumental, 4
  intrinsic, 4
"Sokol," 50
Spectators, 67, 68
Sport
  bourgeois ideology of, 28, 55
  ceremonies and events, 13-24
  degradation of, 51-53
  diagnosis, 59-85
  economic dependency of, 53-55
  external determination and instrumentation of, 49-58
  humanistic value of, 87-95
  as individual praxis, 72-77
  as liberating or alienating force, 131-141, 153-159
  and military training, 51-53
  as political propaganda, 66
  program, 13-24
  as spectacle, 72-77
  theory of, 119-123
  as weapon of class struggle, 55
  women in, 301-309, 357-364
  for working class, 55
"Sport for all," 64, 66, 71

Theologies of play, 154, 155
Time
  concepts of, 179-186
  effective, 179-186
  and movement, aspects of, 179-186
Training, 41, 42

Underwood Trophy, 361

Women
  basketball, 357-364
  in sports, 301-309

Yabusame, 339-341

A listing of the COMPLETE SERIES from the International Congress of Physical Activity Sciences Meeting

SERIE COMPLETE des ouvrages du Congrès international des sciences de l'activité physique

694 BOOKS 1 and 2
PHYSICAL ACTIVITY AND HUMAN WELL-BEING

694A BOOK 3
BIOCHEMISTRY OF EXERCISE: Regulatory Mechanisms in Metabolism During Exercise

694B BOOK 4
EXERCISE PHYSIOLOGY: Fitness and Performance Capacity Studies

694C BOOK 5
SPORTS MEDICINE: Electrocardiography, Hypertension and Other Aspects of Exercise

694D BOOK 6
BIOMECHANICS OF SPORTS AND KINANTHROPOMETRY

694E BOOK 7
MOTOR LEARNING, SPORT PSYCHOLOGY, PEDAGOGY AND DIDACTICS OF PHYSICAL ACTIVITY

694F BOOK 8
PHILOSOPHY, THEOLOGY AND HISTORY OF SPORT AND OF PHYSICAL ACTIVITY

694G BOOK 9
SOCIOLOGY OF SPORT: Sociological Studies and Administrative, Economic and Legal Aspects of Sports and Leisure

694H BOOK 10
ICE HOCKEY: Research, Development and New Concepts

694 VOLUMES 1 et 2
L'ACTIVITE PHYSIQUE ET LE BIEN-ETRE DE L'HOMME

694A VOLUME 3
BIOCHIMIE DE L'EFFORT: Le métabolisme au cours de l'effort physique : les mécanismes de contrôle

694B VOLUME 4
PHYSIOLOGIE DE L'EFFORT: Etudes physiologiques de la condition physique et de l'aptitude à la performance

694C VOLUME 5
MEDECINE DU SPORT: Electrocardiographie, hypertension artérielle et autres aspects de l'exercice physique

694D VOLUME 6
BIOMECANIQUE DU SPORT ET KINANTHROPOMETRIE

694E VOLUME 7
APPRENTISSAGE MOTEUR, PSYCHOLOGIE DU SPORT ET ASPECTS PEDAGOGIQUES DE L'ACTIVITE PHYSIQUE

694F VOLUME 8
ETUDES PHILOSOPHIQUES, THEOLOGIQUES ET HISTORIQUES DU SPORT ET DE L'ACTIVITE PHYSIQUE

694G VOLUME 9
SOCIOLOGIE DU SPORT: Etudes sociologiques et aspects administratifs, économiques et juridiques du sport et du loisir

694H VOLUME 10
LE HOCKEY SUR GLACE: Incidences de la recherche et nouveaux concepts

NOTICE

By decision of the Scientific Commission, *French* and *English* were adopted as the two official languages of the International Congress of Physical Activity Sciences – 1976.

In these Proceedings, the communications appear *in the language in which they were presented* for French and English and *in English* as concerns the papers which were delivered in either German, Russian or Spanish. Abstracts in the two official languages accompany each paper included in Books 1 and 2 and the seminar presentations in the other books of the series.

AVERTISSEMENT

Les langues *anglaise* et *française* furent adoptées par la Commission scientifique comme langues officielles du Congrès international des sciences de l'activité physique – 1976. De ce fait, les communications apparaissent au présent rapport officiel *dans la langue où elles ont été présentées* pour ce qui est de l'anglais et du français, et dans la langue *anglaise* pour ce qui est des communications qui furent faites dans les langues allemande, russe et espagnole.

Des résumés dans chacune des deux langues officielles accompagnent chacune des communications qui paraissent aux Volumes 1 et 2 ainsi que les présentations faites par les conférenciers invités dans les autres volumes de la série.